This precious thing was brought to us by Lynne Wilson, (wife of one of "our" Geneva missionaries) and is a testament to our Savior's love for women of faith.

With our love,

Joan and Jim

December 2017

Christ's
EMANCIPATION OF
Women

IN THE NEW TESTAMENT

LYNNE HILTON WILSON

To my Daughters:
Jane, Mariah, Hannah and Rebekah

(and someday theirs)

Library of Congress Control Number: 2015940082 (hardcover)
ISBN-13, 978-1-935743-07-1 (hardcover)

Library of Congress Control Number: 2015939761 (softcover)
ISBN-13, 978-1-935743-06-4 (softcover)

For information please address Good Sound Publishing, Palo Alto CA 94306.
Visit us at www.GoodSoundPublishing.com

Christ's
Emancipation of Women
In the New Testament

TABLE OF CONTENTS

TABLE OF BIBLE ABBREVIATIONS

- ASV=America Standard Version
- ABT=Anchor Bible Translation
- CEB=Common English Bible
- ESV=English Standard Version
- DBT=Darby Bible Translation
- HCS=Holman Christian Standard
- ISV=International Standard Version
- JB=Jerusalem Bible
- JST=Joseph Smith Translation
- KJV=King James Version
- NASB=New American Standard
- NAB=New American Bible
- NEB=New English Bible
- NET—New English Translation
- NIV=New International Version
- NJB=New Jerusalem Bible
- NKJV=New King James Version
- NRSV=New Revised Standard
- RSV=Revised Standard Version
- TEB=Transparent English Bible
- TNIV=Today's New International
- WEB=World English Bible
- WNT=Weymouth New Testament
- WYC=Wycliffe Bible
- YLT=Young's Literal Translation

Introduction

During His ministry, Jesus Christ restored sight to the blind and mobility to the lame. He restored the higher law of love and forgiveness. He restored Melchizedek Priesthood authority to act in God's name. Yet one of the most important things He restored is rarely discussed: He restored the sacred nature of the family and marriage by re-establishing a noble image of women and children.[1]

In order to appreciate the dramatic change that Jesus made to the role of women and their relationships, we need to place His teachings in the context of His day. How did Jewish, Greek, and Roman men treat women and children? Combing through their volumes of documents, letters, poems, plays, histories, and holy books leaves the impression that in many cases their family relations went awry.[2] We find startling differences when we compare their pages of misunderstandings, oppression, and dysfunctional relationships, to the New Testament stories of Jesus' tender interactions with women and children.

Christ made abrupt and radical changes that restored women to a place of value with eternal potential. This book opens a window into family life during the time of the New

---

[1] Many scholars have looked at family life in the ancient world. See the bibliography for studies used in this study.

[2] For example, from the Apocrypha: Joshua ben Sira in, *Ecclesiasticus* (also known as *Wisdom of Sirach* or *Sirach,* 180 BC)*, Esdras* (c.90 BC- AD 96), and *Fourth Maccabee* (63 BC). There are many writings from contemporaries of New Testament figures such as Philo Judaeus of Alexandria (20 BC to AD 50), Titus Flavius Josephus, the Jewish-Roman historian (AD 37-101), *Apocalypse of Moses, Assumption of Moses* (AD 7-29), *Apocalypse of Baruch* (c. AD 50-100), *First Book of Enoch* (c. 167 BC-AD 14), *Second Enoch* (c. AD 1-50), *The Psalms of Solomon* (c. 69-40 BC), etc. To gather context, even though the *Mishnah* was not redacted until AD 220, it claims to record rabbis from the Pharisaic tradition who lived during the late Second Temple era.

1

Testament in order to better appreciate Jesus' transformative teachings about women—teachings that are still influencing families today.[3]

The introduction first provides a short historical background; it next offers twelve definitions for historical words, events, dates, people; and it finishes with helpful questions to use as tools to approach challenging scriptural passages.

I. Historical Background

The Jewish world was patriarchal (as were Roman, Egyptian, and Mesopotamian societies).[4] This hierarchal system directly impacted interpersonal relationships. Generally speaking, at the time of the New Testament, women and children were kept at home as much as possible so as not to be exposed to things of the world. The public domain was man's territory. Only a husband could deal with land and financial matters. Many did not treat men and women equally and considered women inferior "in all things."[5] In one case, women were blamed for all evil.[6] Women were only "sanctified through

---

[3] The impact of the Lord's teachings continues to bless the world. Bruce C. Hafen, "*Covenant Hearts: Why Marriage Matters and How to Make it Last*," (Salt Lake City, UT: Deseret Book, 2005). Shortly before he presented the "Proclamation to the World," President Gordon B. Hinckley said, "In my judgment, the greatest challenge facing this nation is the problem of the family, brought on by misguided parents and resulting in misguided children." Lisa Ann Jackson, "Strong Families Key to Future, President Hinckley tells Colorado Forum," *Ensign* (July, 2003).

[4] Paula S. Fass, *The Routledge History of Childhood in the Western World* (New York City, NY: Routledge, 2013). For more see appendix 2.

[5] Flavius Josephus, trans. William Whiston, *Josephus Complete Works: Against Apion* (Grand Rapids, MI: Kregel Publications, 1978), II. 25.

[6] Ben Sira, *Ecclesiasticus*, 25:17; "The wickedness of a woman is all evil," and 25:19, "All wickedness is but little to the wickedness of a woman: let the portion of a sinner fall upon her." *Ecclesiasticus* was preserved in the Apocrypha (which was included in the Latin Vulgate and some King James Versions, KJV), as well as in the Greek collection of Jewish sacred writings

2

the deeds of men . . . the anomaly of women is worked out . . . by assigning her to a man's domain."[7]

Most often, Jewish records spanning two centuries before and after the New Testament express little evidence that their authors understood the benefits of a mutually supportive, sensitive, affection-based companionship with one's spouse— let alone the relationship's eternal importance. Eve and her daughters were seen as the cause of most troubles in life: "Of the woman came the beginning of sin, and through her we all die."[8] Many shared this view and felt that women should be "punished for bringing death into the world," hence they must suffer to bring forth life.[9] At least some of the men of the time, blamed Eve and her daughters for perpetuating evil on earth.

Unlike the scriptural account of Genesis 3:20 that records Adam naming Eve, or "Life" in Hebrew, "because she was the mother of all living," we find an interpretation giving the earth the title of "the mother of all things," not Eve. The same teacher went so far as to blame women for men's sins, "For from garments cometh a moth, and from a woman the iniquity of a man."[10] In a "historical romance" from the late Second Temple era about the earth's first couple, we get a feel for the prevailing attitudes about spousal relationships. Eve should tremble in the

---

known as the Greek Septuagint (LXX) and portions found in the Dead Sea Scrolls, Masada, and Cairo Geniza.

[7] Jacob Neusner, ed., *Dictionary of Judaism in the Biblical Period* (Peabody, MA: Hendrickson, 1999), 676. Furthermore, the "biblical society was defined in terms of its male members as indicated by the census in Exodus 20, and in Numbers 1 and 26, which counted adult males but no women or children" 673. That said, a census was often taken to know the military potential or tax base, which corresponds only to males being counted.

[8] Ben Sira, *Ecclesiasticus*, 25:24.

[9] Fred Skolnik and Michael Berenbaum, eds., *Encyclopedia Judaica, 2nd ed.* 22 vols. (Detroit, NYC, San Francisco: Thomson Gale, 2007), 21:161.

[10] Ben Sira, *Ecclesiasticus*, 42:13-14. These misogynist statements continued as Philo, a contemporary of the apostle Paul, wrote, "Why then do you prevent and misapply the name of good-will which is a most excellent and humane one, and conceal the truth, exhibiting as a veil an effeminate and womanly disposition? For are not those persons womanly in whose minds reason is overcome by compassion?" Philo, *Special Laws,* 29.3.156.

presence of her husband as a sign of her humble servitude: "The Lord said: . . . thy wife shall tremble when she looketh upon thee." And an angel instructed Adam, "Thus saith the Lord; I did not create thy wife to command thee, but to obey."[11] This became a breeding ground for pride: "Give not the power of thy soul to a woman, lest she enter upon thy strength, and thou be confounded."[12] As we shall see, this type of baggage damaged the image of women and family relationships.[13]

But it was not all bad.[14] Jewish thought at the time covered a spectrum of attitudes toward women and children.[15] Positive sentiments such as this one were recorded: "Children, and the building of a city shall establish a name, but a blameless

---

[11] Robert H. Charles, ed., *The Apocrypha and Pseudepigrapha of the Old Testament* (Oxford, England: Clarendon Press, 1913), 2.134. The Jewish Pseudepigrapha written by professional Jewish scribes sometime between 200 BC and 100 AD.

[12] Ben Sira, *Ecclesiasticus*, 9:2. The quote was proceeded by, "Be not jealous over the wife of thy bosom, lest she shew in thy regard the malice of a wicked lesson" (9:1).

[13] Dallin H. Oaks, "The Great Plan of Happiness," *Ensign* (Nov 1993), 73. "Some Christians condemn Eve for her act, concluding that she and her daughters are somehow flawed by it. Not the Latter-day Saints! Informed by revelation, we celebrate Eve's act and honor her wisdom and courage in the great episode called the Fall."

[14] As a sampling, I examined Ben Sira's *Ecclesiasticus* for each use of "wife / woman / women" throughout the entire text. I found 41 negative references to women and 18 positive examples.

[15] C.D. Yonge, trans, *The Works of Philo: Complete and Unabridged* (Peabody, MA: Hendrickson Publishers, Reprint 2004), 817One of those positive find. s is from Philo's teachings. He described Abraham and Sarah's relationship in glowing terms: "but Abraham, marveling more and more at the love of his wife for her husband thus continually being renewed and gaining fresh strength, . . . and also of the honour in which he held his wife." The quote actually discusses Abraham's taking Hagar to wife. The ellipsis portion continues, "and also at her spirit of forecast so desirous to provide for the future, takes to himself the handmaid who had been approved by her to the extent of having a son by her; though as those who give the most clear and probably account say he cohabited with her only till she became pregnant; and when she conceived, which she did after no long interval, he then desisted from all connection with her, by reason of his natural continence."

wife shall be counted above them both."[16] More frequently, though, the positive feelings were a bit reserved: "If she [a wife] have a tongue that can cure, and likewise mitigate and shew mercy: her husband is not like other men."[17]

This cultural stereotype infiltrated the many aspects of family life and inhibited relationships for generations. According to the rabbinic law, those who served belonged to the inferior class of women, children, and slaves.[18] By the time of the New Testament, respect, cooperation, and love between spouses were not necessarily the aim of marriage. Righting these wrongs was one of the powerful legacies of Jesus' ministry. By placing the cultural background adjacent to Jesus' teachings, one can see the emancipation he offered. The truths He taught transformed the cultural worth of women.

II. Twelve Historical Definitions: Names, Events, Dates, Peoples

1. Apostolic Church

The church organization between the death of the Lord and the death of the apostles (approximately AD 100) is referred to as the Apostolic Church. The four Gospels and the

---

[16] Ben Sira, *Ecclesiasticus,* 40:19.
[17] Ben Sira, *Ecclesiasticus*, 36:25. Also, "The beauty of a woman cheereth the countenance of her husband, and a man desireth nothing more" (36:24).
[18] Jacob Neusner, *The Economics of the Mishnah* (Chicago, IL: University of Chicago Press, 1990), 27. "One should train for the job all those who are employed on the estate, whether slaves or children or women." David Sedley, *Oxford Studies in Ancient Philosophy, XXV* (Oxford, England: Oxford University, Winter *2003)*, 213. Josephus, *Against Apion.* 2.25. Philo, *A Volume of Questions and Solutions to Questions which arise in Genesis,* I.29. Joachim Jeremias, *Jerusalem in the Time of Jesus* (Philadelphia: Fortress Press, 1969), 367.

Epistles are our firsthand source for information on Christian family life during this era.[19]

2. Babylonian Captivity

Political animosity arose between Babylon and Judea in the late seventh century BC. Some Israelites left Judea just prior to the final and most destructive Babylonian invasions, including Lehi and his family in 600 BC. Most Israelites were deported to Babylon in waves. The first wave took many educated and wealthy people, such as the prophet Daniel. Another large group included King Zachariah in approximately 587 BC. Their exile ended under King Cyrus in 538 BC (2 Chronicles 36:23).

Yet the majority of the Jews did not return to Palestine. By counting the number of exiled priesthood holders, we find that one sixth who were taken captive returned to Judea.[20] Many had become Hellenized and chose to stay in Babylon or moved to lands across the Mediterranean. Those who did return found their land populated in part with Gentiles; they were no longer a completely separate people.

3. Intertestamental Period (400 BC-4BC)

The time between the New and Old Testaments is known as the intertestamental period. Christians refer to the era from Malachi (c. 420 BC) to John the Baptist as "400 years of silence," because it was the time without the voice of a prophet.

---

[19] When fourth-century church leaders closed the canon and systematized the Christian scripture, they placed the Epistles or letters in order by their length. Luke organized the book of Acts chronologically, but the Epistles are organized by size, starting with Paul who wrote the most.
[20] Raymond Brown, *The Birth of the Messiah* (New York: Doubleday, 1979 and 1999), 258 (pages taken from 1979 edition). "18,000 priests and Levites in Palestine in Jesus' time."

A brief overview of what happened in the Jewish world during those centuries is described in appendix 1 of this book.[21]

4. Jewish Pilgrimage Feasts: Passover, Pentecost, and Tabernacles

Deuteronomy announced the pilgrimage feasts: "Three times in a year shall all thy males appear before the LORD thy God" (Deuteronomy 16:16). Jewish pilgrims from around the Roman Empire traveled to their holy city, Jerusalem, for special feast weeks. [22] During pilgrimages, Jerusalem's population swelled from ten to possibly one hundred times its normal size of twenty-five to fifty-five thousand.[23] The three major pilgrimage feasts spanned the warmer half of the year: Passover fell in the early spring, Pentecost fifty days later, and Feast of Tabernacles in the autumn (Exodus 23:16-17).[24]

---

[21] The Apocrypha can be found in some Bibles and includes: *1 and 2 Esdras, 1 and 2 Maccabees, Tobias, Judith, Ecclesiasticus or Wisdom of Sirach, Baruch.*

[22] The Jewish population (which included peoples from various tribes of Israel) were scattered throughout the Empire, but tended to cluster together in communities. . The five major Jewish city centers in the Roman Empire were: Jerusalem, Antioch, Alexandria, Jericho, and Rome Even though the New Testament writers use of "Jews" as a generalization for all Israelites, they also specify that Paul was a Benjaminite, Zacharias and Elisabeth from the tribe of Levi, and Anna from the tribe of Asher.

[23] Jeremias, *Jerusalem*, 83. Bruce, *New Testament History,* 38. Historians looking at the whole country estimate the population of all Palestine between 500,000 and 600,000. Although Josephus' numbers sound very exaggerated, he claimed that over two million pilgrims celebrated a Passover. Josephus, *Antiquities,* XVII.217; *Jewish Wars,* 2.12.

[24] Judith Baskin and Kenneth Seeskin, *The Cambridge Guide to Jewish History, Religion, and Culture* (New York, NY: Cambridge University, 2010), 300. A more complete list of all the Jewish holy days span the whole year: *spring*—Passover, Leg B'Omer, Shauvot; *summer*—Tishb'av; *fall*—Rosh Hashanah, Yom Kippur, Sukkot, Shemini, Atzeret, Simchat Torah, Hanukkah; *winter*—tu B'Shevat, Purim.

a. **Passover or Feast of Unleavened Bread** remembers the flight of the children of Israel out of Egypt on the night when God slew the first-born Egyptians. Hebrews sacrificed a lamb and spread the blood over their doors so that the destroying angel would pass over them. They left in haste without the required time for their bread to rise; hence, it is also known as the feast of unleavened bread (Exodus 12:17).

b. **Pentecost, Feast of Weeks,** or **First Fruits,** celebrates the first barley harvest, and remembers the time when Moses led the fleeing children of Israel to Mount Sinai, and presented the people to the Lord (Exodus 23:16).

c.   **Tabernacles, Booths, or Sukkot** marks the "ingathering" of the final harvest (Deuteronomy 16:3; Leviticus 23:34). The feast renews the covenant between God and Israel—which at one time included reading the Torah every seventh year. The booths recalled the days when Israel wandered in the desert and the Lord illuminated the camp by night with a pillar of fire and by day with a cloud.

Although the feasts were initially for all, by the time of Herod's Temple, some rabbis stipulated that women, children, and those incapable of the journey did not have to attend.

> All are subject to the command to appear excepting a deaf-mute, an imbecile, a child, one of doubtful sex, one of double sex, women, slaves that have not been freed, a man that is lame or blind or sick or aged, and one that cannot go up on his feet. . . . Who is deemed a child? Any that cannot ride on his father's shoulders and go up from Jerusalem to the temple mount.[25]

This optional list did not keep women, children, or disabled

---

[25] *Mishnah, Moed: Hagigah.* 1.1. Rabbinic debate continued to ask, who is a child: "And the School of Hillel say: Any that cannot hold his father's hand and go up." Hillel, the father of Rabbinism, led a school for those who desired a strict interpretation of the Mosaic and oral laws.

from attending though. It is clear that many females joined in other religious celebrations too.[26]

5. Four Major Jewish Sects[27]

a. **Pharisees or "separatists":** The most popular and lasting group during the late Second Temple period. According to Josephus, they were "the most accurate interpreters of the laws."[28] Their Scripture included: The Law, Prophets, Writings, and oral laws. They emphasized purity from following the rites of the oral laws, tithes of money and food, and strict Sabbath observance.[29] They also believed in the resurrection.

b. **Sadducees:** Sadducees focused their belief in the Torah and the temple.[30] As a result, when the temple was

---

[26] *Mishnah*, *Taanith*, 4:8. Rabbi Gamaliel reported: "There were no happier days for Israel than . . . [when] the daughters of Jerusalem used to go forth in white raiment; and these were borrowed, that none should be abashed which had them not. . . . And the daughters of Jerusalem went forth to dance in the vineyards. And what did they say? 'Young man, lift up thine eyes and see what thou wouldest choose for thyself: set not thine eyes on beauty, but set thine eyes on family; for Favor is deceitful and beauty is vain, but a woman that feareth the Lord she shall be praised."

[27] In addition to these major groups, there were Hasidim, Sicarii, and others. See appendix 1.

[28] Josephus, *Antiquities of the Jews,* XIII. 297-298. He claims there were 6,000 Pharisees.

[29] Paul J. Achtemeier, *Harper Collins' Bible Dictionary* (San Francisco, CA: HarperCollins, 1996), 842.

[30] David Noel Freedman, ed., *Anchor Bible Dictionary*, (New York: Doubleday, 1992), 5.892. This opinion is not held by all biblical scholars. Jerome and other early church Fathers connected the name Sadducee with "righteous / *saddiq,*" possibly connecting the Sadducees to the ancient high priest family name of King David's high priest, Zadok. By the end of the Second Temple, the positions allocated for chief priests were often given to those Sadducees willing to play political roles as liaisons between the Jewish people and Roman leaders. Jealous vying for political appointments fostered ulterior motives between some of the priesthood leadership of the era. The four Gospels credit the chief priests and scribes for condemning Jesus to

destroyed, few of their sect and writings survived. One Sadducean author's writings were preserved in the Apocrypha as: *Ecclesiasticus* or *Sirach*. The Sadducee party filled most of the chief priests' seats at the time of the New Testament. They did not believe in life after death, instead they believed that "one is survived by one's good reputation and by one's children."[31]

c. **Essenes**: The strictest observers of The Law, the Essenes believed that the Jews had apostatized and that the office of high priest been corrupted. Retreating from society, they believed they were a remnant to save apostatized Israel. Their "teacher of Righteousness" taught celibacy, predestination, and strove to develop priesthood purity.[32] They lived in communal groups where they shared owner-ship and supported themselves through manual labor. They purified themselves through daily cold mikveh baths and wore white linen as the priests did. They ate their meals together, the evening meal in silence.[33]

d. **Zealots:** The zealots were Jewish nationalists who resisted Roman occupation of Israel. Judas the Galilean, the most famous of the Zealots, led a revolt against paying taxes to the Emperor in AD 6. Their final attempt at freedom in AD 66 led to the Jewish war and the fall of Jerusalem in AD 70 and Masada in AD 74.[34]

---

death: "But with loud shouts they insistently demanded that he be crucified, and their shouts prevailed" (Luke 23:23, NIV; see also: Mark 14:43; 55; Matthew 27:20, 41, 62, John 11:57; 18:3, 35).

[31] Judith R. Baskin and Kenneth Seeskin, *The Cambridge Guide to Jewish History, Religion, and Culture* (New York City, NY: Cambridge University Press, 2010), 45. "Passages from the Wisdom of Ben Sira express ideas that were also central to Sadduceeism (14:16-19)."

[32] Baskin and Seeskin, *The Cambridge Guide to Jewish History*, 46.

[33] Skolnik, *Encyclopaedia Judaica,* 6.511. Philo claims there were 4,000 Essenes (6.510).

[34] Scott Hahn ed., *Catholic Bible Dictionary* (New York City, NY: Random House, 2009), 970.

6. Mishnah and Talmud

After the destruction of the Second Temple, Jewish rabbis compiled the teachings of their greatest rabbis from the Second Temple era into the *Mishnah*. It roughly covers thoughts from the third century BC to the third century AD (edited and compiled between AD 180 and 220).[35] The word *Mishnah* means to repeat or a retelling of the story. An elaboration of the *Mishnah* in the form of rabbinic debate was published in the *Gemara* (or interpretation). In the fifth century AD, both the *Mishnah* and *Gemara* were combined into the *Talmud* (which translates from Hebrew as "Learning" or "Instruction").

7. Numbers with Biblical Symbolism

In the Bible, numbers often had symbolic meaning and were used figuratively as well as literally. Here are two of the most common uses:

• 7—Whole, complete, perfect—stemming from God's creation of the earth in seven periods (Genesis 1:1-24); Noah's experience with seven (Genesis 7:10; 8:10, 12); and every seventh day of the week being sanctified (Exodus 20:8-11). We find the number seven used regularly in the temple ritual (i.e., "And the priest shall ... sprinkle of the blood seven times before the LORD" Leviticus 4:6, 16; 16:14, 19; etc.), and in the traditional feasts such as Pentecost: "Seven weeks shalt thou number unto thee: begin to number the seven weeks . . ." (Deuteronomy 16:9). We find Sabbatical years every seven years (Deuteronomy 15:1; 31:10), and Jubilee every seven time seven years (Leviticus 25:8). Jacob's term of service for his wives and herds in Genesis 29 was seven years each. Pharaoh

---

[35] Anat Feinberg, "*Mishnah*," Skolnik, *Encyclopedia Judaica,* 14. 319-330. Rabbis Hillel and Shammai from the time of Herod's Temple made up most of the "Law by the Scribes / Soferim." Jewish scribes divided the Talmud into six sections called "Orders / Sedarim." They comprise 63 Tractates / Massektoth," with 36½ having a commentary or Gemara.

had a dream of seven cows foretelling the seven years of plenty and famine in Genesis 41. Solomon completed the temple in seven years in 1 Kings 6:38. Elisha prophesied a seven-year famine in 2 Kings 8:1. These are just a few examples of the biblical use of numbers to add meaning to its message.

• **40**—Purification—stemming from a woman's forty- day purification period after the birth of a male, and forty times two for a female (Leviticus 12:2-8).[36] It rained for forty days and nights on Noah's ark (Genesis 7:4); the flood remained on the earth forty more days (Genesis 8:6); Moses prayed and fasted on Sinai for forty days and nights (for possibly two occasions, Deuteronomy 9:18); and the children of Israel wandered in the wilderness for forty years (Numbers 14:33; 32:13).

8. Oral Laws and Commandments

Rabbis carefully counted each law written in the Torah and found 613 separate commandments.[37] They debated over the best way to implement and protect these Mosaic commandments and decided to "raise up many disciples, and make a fence around The Law."[38] They figuratively fenced in their beloved Law of Moses with ten thousand commandments that became known as the "*oral laws*" or oral Torah. These extra rules systematized the law of Moses and governed a pious Jewish life. The oral laws functioned as a buffer zone around the Torah to avoid any chance of breaking one of the laws of Moses. For example, from the commandment to keep the Sabbath day holy came thirty-nine definitions of work, which

---

[36] See footnote 158.

[37] Macy Nulman, *Encyclopedia of Jewish Prayer* (Lanham, MD: Rowman and Littlefield, 1996), 220. By the Middle Ages, prayer shawls incorporated 613 threads for the commandments; "According to the Talmud, wearing *tzitzit* is equal in merit with observing the entire Torah. The numerical value of the word *tzitzit* equals 613, the number of precepts in the Torah."

[38] *Mishnah, Avoth,* 1:1.

then developed into hundreds of oral laws detailing forbidden work on the Sabbath.[39]

9. Scripture—Septuagint—Torah

The oldest known manuscripts or portions of the Old Testament date from c.250 BC. Written in Greek, they are taken from the translation known as the **Septuagint** (LXX). According to legend, the translation was made by seventy-two Hellenistic Jews from Alexandria in seventy-two days.[40] The "Scriptures" include, the "Law," or the first five books of Moses (or the "Torah" in Hebrew). No one felt the need to close the Jewish canon, so sacred texts known as the "Writings" and "Prophets" remained an open canon until AD 90. The Jews closed their canon, following the Christian precedent to canonize their Scripture. The **Torah**, also known as The Law or Pentateuch, included the first five books of Moses (Genesis, Exodus, Leviticus, Numbers, and Deuteronomy). Most Israelites across the Roman Empire, including the Essenes, Pharisees, Sadducees, and even their distant relatives, the Samaritans, held the Torah as their holiest writings.[41]

The "Law" was canonized by Ezra in 444 BC. The collection of scripture known as "The Writings" was not canonized until over a century after the Second Temple period.[42] Different translations of the Bible include different lists of books. In the King James Version (KJV) "The Writings" include Judges, Ruth, Esther, Chronicles, Ezra, Nehemiah, Ester, Job, Psalms, Proverbs, Ecclesiastes, the Song of

---

[39] *Mishnah, Moed: Shabbath,* 7:4; 8:3, 8.5, 10.5, 6. See footnote 609 of this book for examples.

[40] Stephen M. Wylen, *The Jews in the Time of Jesus: An Introduction* (New York: Paulist Press, 1996)*,* 47.

[41] Bernhard W. Anderson, *Understanding the Old Testament, 2nd Ed.* (New Jersey: Prentice-Hall, 1957) 554-555. The Jews had an open canon until AD 90, at the "Council of Jamnia," a rabbinic academy sought to add more Scripture (i.e., Ben Sira, *Ecclesiasticus, Ezra 4*).

[42] Brown, *Birth,* 208.

Solomon, and Lamentations. The collection of Scripture known as "The Prophets" was divided by length into Major and Minor Prophets and extended from Joshua to Malachi. The books quoted most often in the Dead Sea Scrolls were Deuteronomy, Isaiah, and Psalms. The latter two are the most quoted in the New Testament outside of The Law.[43]

10. Second Temple (538 BC to 70)

The Babylonians destroyed Solomon's Temple in 586 BC. Approximately fifty years later, a portion of the Jews returned to their homeland. Shortly thereafter, the Jewish Governor Zerubbabel began the plans to rebuild their temple (Ezra 3:2; 4:2; 5:2; Ezekiel 1, 7; 2 Chronicles 3:1). The Second Temple, or Zerubbabel's Temple, was finished in 516 BC. Other additions and updates were made over the next four centuries.

In 20 BC, the eccentric builder "King Herod the Great" began an extensive reconstruction of the temple. Technically speaking, Herod's Temple (20 BC-70 AD) was still part of the Second Temple. With careful engineering and land-fill, Herod's crews flattened and expanded the size of Mount Moriah's natural peak to include a thirty-five-acre expanse.[44] The

---

[43] Brown, *Birth*, 48. The New Testament authors recited many known Scriptures from the prophets. For example, in the Gospel of Matthew the author structured the book around fourteen Old Testament prophecies of the Messiah—each in conjunction with a phrase similar to this: "all this was done, that the scriptures of the prophets might be fulfilled" (Matthew 26:56). Matthew's fourteen fulfillment citations can be found in: Matthew 1:22; 2:5b, 15, 17; 23; 3:3; 4:14; 8:17a; 12:17; 13:14a, 35; 21:4; 26:56; 27:9a. The number fourteen was significant in Hebrew orthography because it represented David.

[44] David Noel Freedman, ed., *Eerdmans' Dictionary of the Bible* (Grand Rapids, MI: Eerdmans Publishing, 2000), 1283. The temple expanse covered 144,000 square meters, or a little over 35 acres. Josephus, *Against Apion*, I. 22. Josephus described the lot: "There is about the middle of the city a wall of stone, whose length is five hundred feet, and the breadth a hundred cubits, with double cloisters; wherein there is a square altar, not made of hewn stone, but composed of white stones gathered together, having each side twenty cubits long, and its altitude ten cubits. Hard by it is a large edifice,

extension incorporated remains from Solomon's royal palace and stables.[45] Ten thousand skilled craftsmen finished Herod's designs eighty-three years later. A Jewish proverb exclaimed, "He that has not seen the temple of Herod has never known what beauty is."[46] Josephus described more of its details:

> Now the outward face of the temple in its front . . . was covered all over with plates of gold of great weight. Thus, at the first rising of the sun, it reflected back a very fiery splendor, causing those who forced themselves to look upon it to turn their eyes away, just as they would have done at the sun's own (blinding) rays.[47]

Only seven years after its completion, in AD 70, the Romans destroyed the temple.[48] Therefore references to

wherein there is an altar and a candlestick, both of gold, and in weight two talents: upon these there is a light that is never extinguished, either by night or by day. There is no image, nor any thing, nor any donations therein; nothing at all is there planted, neither grove, nor anything of that sort. The priests abide therein both nights and days, performing certain purifications, and drinking not the least drop of wine while they are in the temple."

[45] History remembers King Herod the Great for his jealousy-motivated murders of thousands, and for his grandiose building programs. The latter included eight major fortresses (Masada, Machaerus, Herodium in Perea, Alexandria, Cypros, Hurcania, and the Herodium southeast of Bethlehem), two elaborate Hellenistic cities (Augustus and Caesarea Maritima), and his crowning jewel, the temple of Jerusalem.

[46] Babylonian Talmud, *Baba Bathra*. 4a.

[47] Josephus, *War*, 5.222-23. The quote continues, "But this temple appeared to strangers, when they were at a distance, like a mountain covered with snow. For as to those parts of it that were not gilt, they were exceedingly white. On its top it had spikes with sharp points to prevent any pollution of it by birds sitting upon it." Josephus also described two bronze pillars overlaid with gold, ten gold lampstands, seventy golden lamps, cedar and cypress gates covered with silver and gold, porticos made up of forty-eight bronze pillars, twelve metal legs of the laver, an altar, and four hundred bronze bells. Charlesworth, *Jesus and Temple,* 6-7.

[48] Alec Garrard, *The Splendor of the Temple* (Grand Rapids, MI: Kregel, 2001), 12. Different historians claim different dates, for the start and finish of Herod's Temple—but always within a year or two. For religious purity, only priests were allowed to work on the construction of the Sanctuary. King Herod trained ten thousand skilled artisans, one thousand of whom

the Second Temple era mean the time from when Zerubbabel initiated construction on the temple in 538 BC until the Romans destroyed Herod's expanded temple in 70 AD. This overlaps with portions of the Old Testament, the intertestamental era, and New Testament.

11. Synagogue

During the Second Temple period, the word synagogue referred to either a religious service or a building.[49] Often small neighborhoods of Jews gathered in larger homes for their worship. If a community had a large enough Jewish population and adequate funding, it might have a designated building of worship or synagogue.[50] Synagogues were used for Scripture study, prayer, community meetings, storage of archives and Sabbath worship. They were also used as judgment halls, schoolhouses, treasuries, hostels, council halls, and banquet halls. In first century Palestine, the Sabbath worship service began early Saturday morning and lasted until noon. They sang

---

were priests, as stonemasons or carpenters to oversee the other nine thousand builders and one thousand machines. Supposedly, temple worshipers never missed a day of offering sacrifices throughout the decades of reconstruction. See Charlesworth, *Jesus and Temple,* 5; appendix 1.

[49] Howard Clark Kee and Lynn H. Cohick, *Evolution of the Synagogue* (Harrisburg, PA: Trinity Press, 1999), 91. "The basic meaning of the Greek *synagogue* is 'a gathering, a collection,' and can be used either of people or of things . . . Jews in antiquity coined the word *proseuche* to designate a place (usually a building) of prayer." See also 12, 14, 17, 20. Scripture scrolls were found in the synagogue in Masada. First century Jews referred to places of worship as *synagogue* and *proseuche* (Josephus, *Against Apion,* 14.216; 16.164; *Vit.* 277ff; 290; 295; *BJ* 2.289-92; Matthew 9:35; Mark 13:9; Luke 4:16-30; Acts 9:20; 13:15; 18:4, 17).

[50] From the time of Herod's Temple archaeologists have uncovered synagogues in Jerusalem, Masada, the Herodium, and Capernaum, and dating to 246-21 BC, near Alexandria. Before the destruction of Jerusalem, other buildings identified as synagogues appear in Magdala, Chorazin, Shuafat, Kiryat Sefer, and Jericho, and outside of Palestine in Delos, Ostaia, and Gamla. Michael Avi-Yonah, "Synagogue Historical Roots," Skolnik, *Encyclopedia Judaica,* 19. 364-366.

psalms, recited the *shema* (a special group of Scriptures found in Deuteronomy 6:4-9; 11:13-21; and Numbers 15:37-41) and eighteen benedictions.[51] Men read a section from the Torah, and the Prophets (i.e., Isaiah, Jonah, etc.) and expounded on it.[52] Their service closed with the priestly blessing from Numbers 6:24-26.[53] Synagogue worship differed for men and women.[54] Women did not read the Torah, give their opinion, or verbally pray during the service.[55]

12. Important Historical Authors

a.   **Ben Sira** (born c. 170 BC[56]): The author of the longest book in the Apocrypha, *Ecclesiasticus* (also known as

---

[51] Skolnik, *Encyclopedia Judaica,* 1.73-34. From the time of the Second Temple, Jews offered a set "eighteen benedictions," which began by referring to God: 1. of the patriarchs, 2. nature, and 3. sanctification. The prayer then petitioned God for: 4. understanding, 5. repentance, 6. forgiveness, 7. redemption, 8. healing, 9. food, 10. gathering of exiles, 11. restore His righteous reign; 12. against heretics, 13. mercy for the righteous, 14. Jerusalem, 15. the messianic king, 16. hear our prayers, 17. return God's presence to the temple, and 18. thanks to God for all his mercies. The prayer had slight variations for certain Sabbath services or holy days.

[52] Craig S. Keener, *The IVP Bible Background Commentary* (Downers Grove, IL: InterVarsity Press, 1993), 56. A Jewish man stood to read the assigned Scripture passage of the day and then sat down to discuss it. This signified the higher place of God's word over man's interpretation (see Luke 4:16, 20-21).

[53] Joseph A. Fitzmyer, *The Anchor Bible: The Gospel According to Luke I-IX* (New York: Doubleday, 1981), 531.

[54] *Mishnah, Kiddushin,* 4:13. The *Mishnah* forbade women from teaching in the synagogue. Gender separation and silencing in religious meetings led to prejudices about the religious nature of women. If participating in the public worship taught one to be more holy, then women missed out.

[55] Dan W. Clanton, *The Good, the Bold, and the Beautiful: The Story of Susanna and its Renaissance Interpretation—The Library of Hebrew Bible/Old Testament Studies* (Bloomsbury T&T Clark Intern., 2006), 23.

[56] Baskin and Seeskin, *The Cambridge Guide to Jewish History,* 45. This text claims Ben Sira wrote approximately 200–175 BC, while scholars move the dates a decade later or so. The citations from *Ecclesiasticus* in this book are from various Bible editions that include the Apocrypha (e.g., KJV,

Sirach, or the *Wisdom of Sirach,* or *The Book of the All-Virtuous Wisdom of Joshua ben Sira*). His writings harmonize with Sadducees' thought. His writings are not included among the hundreds of scriptural citations in the New Testament, but they are referenced in the Talmud. He worked in Jerusalem as a scribe and associated with the intellectual aristocracy. His conservative voice called for obedience to God's laws and had a lasting influence on Jewish society.

b. **Philo of Alexandria** (20 BC-AD50): An educated devout Jewish writer from the Hellenistic world of Alexandria, Egypt. He studied Greek as well as Jewish thought. He admired Plato and envisioned himself a Jewish philosopher. He tried to reconcile biblical teachings to Greek philosophy. His ideas heavily influenced Jewish and Christian thought.

c. **Josephus** (AD 37-100): A Jewish priest, Pharisee, military commander, and scholar. As an eyewitness of Herod's Temple, he is arguably our best source for temple information.[57] After leading a rebellion in Galilee, he surrendered to the Romans. Titus took him to Rome to write the history of the Jews for his captors. Scholars often question Josephus' numbers as exaggerated.

III. Guiding Questions

When we look at the entire body of the Christian Scripture about women's roles in early Christian worship, a few glaring verses stick out as conflicting with the Lord and His apostles' other statements and examples about women. Readers of the

---

RSV), and Charles, ed., *The Apocrypha and Pseudepigrapha of the Old Testament.* For more on Ben Sira, See page 285, in appendix 1.

[57] James H. Charlesworth, ed., *Jesus and Temple—Textual and Archaeological Explorations* (Minneapolis, MN: Fortress Press, 2014), 2.

Bible have the challenge of working with edited, translated texts. In the case of the Epistles, the reader has the additional challenge of having access to only half (or less than half) of the original correspondences. Textual historians and priests preserved hundreds of different Greek manuscripts and thousands of fragments for each Epistle in the New Testament, none of which is exactly the same.[58]

The textual changes are only part of the problem in understanding the Epistles; doctrinal and cultural challenges also interfere with our modern perception of the Epistles. The reader often has to speculate on what behavioral problem precipitated the apostle's advice, or what question triggered an answer. When I come to an unclear passage, I ask myself:

- Was the author referring to a specific problem?
- Is this consistent with what the author wrote elsewhere?
- Did the author mean this?
- What do other English or Greek translations have to say about this?
- Did Joseph Smith address this verse anywhere?
- What question drew out the answer or discussion?[59]
- Is this doctrine or practice in harmony with the restored gospel and modern Scripture?

These questions will help us later on when we tackle some of the difficult passages about women.

---

[58] Fifty-five hundred ancient Greek copies or portions of the New Testament survive. The oldest 116 papyri date from the second to eighth century, 300 parchments in capital letters (or uncials) date from the third century, and 1,800 in lower case letters (or minuscule) from the ninth century. Richard Holzapfel, Eric Huntsman, Thomas Wayment, *Jesus Christ and the World of the New Testament* (Salt Lake City, UT: Deseret Book, 2006), 7.

[59] Joseph Smith Jr., *History of the Church of Jesus Christ of Latter-day Saints* (1844; reprint Salt Lake City, UT: Deseret Book, 1980), 5.261.The Prophet Joseph Smith taught, "I have a key by which I understand the scriptures. I enquire, what was the question which drew out the answer?"

Chapter 1
Women Released from their Cultural Baggage

Jesus entered a society with many deeply instilled barriers to His teachings. He shocked his audiences with declarations of His Messiahship (i.e., Luke 4:21-28). Equally as shocking, He appreciated and validated women and children (Mark 14:4-6; Luke 7:39; 10:40; etc.). As decisively as He cleansed the temple, Jesus attacked the cultural falsehoods that surrounded Jewish family life. He tore down false practices and notions regarding women, children, and family relationships. He denounced centuries of harmful traditions that destroyed marital partnerships and led to misogyny.

The four Gospels describe Jesus refusing to follow the traditional social barricades that impeded relationships between men and women. As we read, the Lord speaks to women (John 4:7-27), incites their education (Luke 10:39-42), heals them (Mark 7:25-29), asks them to speak out as witnesses (Matthew 28:5-10), touches them (Mark 5:30-34; Matthew 28:9), and teaches the eternal nature of their marriage relationships (Matthew 5:3-11; John 17:21; Ephesians 5:25, 31). This was considered scandalous.

In order to demonstrate how dramatically Jesus changed family relationships, one must understand what Jewish family life was like and how it contrasted with what Jesus taught. By placing the Lord's teachings and doctrine within their social context, His teachings become overpowering in their significance and beauty. This chapter highlights five cultural customs that affected women and then contrasts them with Christ's empowering changes.

I. Segregation

Cultural Background and Baggage

Jewish pharisaic traditions kept men and women physically segregated.[60] Men and women "should not mingle."[61] This physical segregation led to emotional segregation, which developed into misunderstandings. Women were seen as a cause of temptation, so they were veiled, silenced, and kept away from men as much as possible.[62] Especially in the city, Jewish women were discouraged from going outside in order to avoid being seen by men. This protocol existed in Jerusalem and extended to other large cities where Jews lived. For example, in Alexandria, the third largest

---

[60] John H. Elliott, *Anchor Bible: 1 Peter* (New York City, NY: Random House-Doubleday, 1964), 568. "As roles and status were gender-specific and clearly demarcated, so was the social space that was proper to males (public) and females (domestic, private)." Then he quoted Xenophon (c.430-353 BC), an Athenian soldier: "God from the first adapted the woman's nature, I think, to the indoor and man's to the outdoor tasks and cares. For he made the man's body and mind more capable of enduring cold and heat, and journeys and campaigns; and therefore imposed on him the outdoor tasks. To the woman, God assigned the indoor tasks" (ibid., 569).
[61] *Mishnah, Middot* 2.5; also see Charlesworth, *Jesus and Temple,* 15.
[62] Geoffrey W. Bromiley, *International Standard Bible Encyclopedia*, B.L. Bandstra and A.D. Verhey, "Sex," 4. 431. To "avoid tempting another to immorality; thus they were veiled in public and segregated as much as possible from men. At the synagogues and Herod's Temple they were excluded from the court of the men."

city in the Greco-Roman world, the Jewish philosopher Philo (20 BC to AD 50), described his view of the ideal separation of men and women in public.

> Marketplaces and council-halls, law-courts and gatherings, and meetings where a large number of people are assembled, and open-air life with full scope for discussion and action – all these are suitable to men both in war and peace. The women are best suited to the indoor life which never strays from the house . . . A woman then, should not be a busybody, meddling with matters outside her household concerns, but should seek a life of seclusion.[63]

This view of segregated women was accepted for centuries as the social norm at the time of the New Testament. A more relaxed attitude about gender separation existed outside of the cities and Palestine. Although most Jewish girls and women remained at home, they, as one historian described it, were "confined at home as in a prison."[64]

The segregation continued inside wealthy Pharisee and Sadducee homes with separate quarters exclusive to members of their gender.[65] Shortly before and during the time of the New Testament, when these traditions were heavily entrenched in Jerusalem and beyond, contemporaries described segregated living spaces where women "were always kept in seclusion and did not even appear at the house-door, and their unmarried daughters, who were limited to the women's quarter, women who for modesty's sake shunned the eyes of men, even their closest relatives, now became exposed to people who were not

---

[63] Judaeus Philo, *Special Laws III.,* 7 vols. (London: William Heinemann, Ltd., 1967), 3.169, 171.
[64] Skolnik, *Encyclopedia Judaica,* 21:161.
[65] Philo, *Philo's Flaccus*, 70.

22

just unfamiliar men."[66] Even in the home, though, if a male guest came for a meal, the women and girls were not to eat at the same table, but could silently interact with the company as a servant.[67] Pious Jerusalem families limited their interaction by gender except on rare occasions.

Synagogue worship was also segregated.[68] Men were commanded to attend their Sabbath worship services, but women were not. If a woman chose to attend a synagogue service, she sat separately. Within a few decades after the time of the New Testament, rabbis added separate entrances for men and women and lattice barriers to keep the women unseen and unheard.[69] Women did not read the Scriptures, give their opinion, teach, or pray verbally during the service, but they

---

[66] Philo of Alexandria, Pieter Willem van der Horst, trans., *Philo's Flaccus: The First Pogrom* (Boston, MA: Brill, 2003), 70. Scholars refer to this time as the Hasmonean (140 BC to 37 BC) and Herodian (37 BC to AD 68).

[67] Leonard J. Swidler, *Jesus was a Feminist: What the Gospels Reveal about His Revolutionary Perspective* (Landham, MD: Rowman & Littlefield, 2007), 76. John Baggett, *Seeing Through the Eyes of Jesus: His Revolutionary View of Reality and His Transcendent Significance for Faith* (Grand Rapids, MI: Eerdmans, 2008), 128.

[68] Michael Avi-Yonah, "Synagogue Historical Roots," Skolnik, *Encyclopedia Judaica,* 19. 364-366; also 354-355. In the diaspora there is evidence of "women [acting] as donors to the synagogues and participants within manumission ceremonies. In general, the climate within the diaspora seems to have been more conducive for allowing women to assume more active roles within the synagogue." The New Testament mentions specific synagogues in Capernaum (Mark 1:21), Nazareth (Luke 4:16), Damascus (Acts 9:2), Antioch in Pisidia (Acts 13:14), Iconium (Acts 14:1), Thessalonica (Acts 17:1), Berea (Acts 17:10), Corinth (Acts 18:8), and Ephesus (Acts 18:19). In addition there were synagogues in Jerusalem for specific immigrants such as the synagogue of the Libertines, Cyrenians, and Alexandrians (Acts 6:9).

[69] Jeremias, *Jerusalem in the Time of Jesus,* 374. Archeologists found a lattice separation for gender in a Mesopotamian synagogue from AD 245. Between the third and seventh century, galleries were built to keep the women on separate floors from the men in addition to their separate entrance. Michael Avi-Yonah, "Synagogue Historical Roots," Skolnik, *Encyclopedia Judaica,* 19. 364-366.

were allowed to listen in silence.[70] Gender separation and silencing in religious meetings led to prejudices about the religious nature of women.[71] If participating in the synagogue worship taught one to be more holy, then women missed out.

Inside one's home, women participated in religious worship, especially in maintaining the kosher food laws, Sabbath observance, lighting the candles, offering table blessings, and reciting the *shema* (Deuteronomy 6:4-9; 11:13-21; and Numbers 15:37-41).[72] Much of the Jewish worship was communal and occurred outside the home, and in that sphere, women's worship was restricted compared to men's. Men felt it an honor to have 613 commandments and pitied women who were only required to live six commandments.[73]

---

[70] *Mishnah, Kiddushin*, 4:13. Dan W. Clanton, *The Good, the Bold, and the Beautiful* (New York, NY: T & T Clark International, 2006), 23; "There is no firm evidence for women functionaries" in leadership roles. Most women were illiterate, but even those who could read were discouraged from reading the Law or Torah (Genesis, Exodus, Leviticus, Numbers, Deuteronomy).

[71] As an example of the evolution of limitations placed on woman's religious opportunities, we read in Deuteronomy 11:18-19, "Lay up these my words in your heart and in your soul. . . . And ye shall teach them your children." But sometime before 132 BCE when the Greek Septuagint (LXX) translated this passage, they interpreted it as "you shall teach them to your sons." Later still, after the destruction of the temple and the rabbinic schools took over Judaism, we read a commentary on these verses in *Sifre Deuteronomy 46*, ". . . your sons and not your daughters." Different schools of thought debated how much religious law a father should teach his daughter as we will discuss in chapter 7, but all sons had the religious duty to learn the Torah.

[72] Clanton, *The Good, the Bold, and the Beautiful*, 24; "From kosher laws to the recitation of the *shema*, from private prayer to Sabbath practices, not only would women have been present, they would have been active participants due to their dominance in the private, domestic sphere."

[73] *Mishnah, Berakhoth* 3:3, outlines the six commandments for women: 1) Light the Sabbath lamp or candles in their homes, 2) Offer table blessings over the food (also required for children and minors), 3) Prepare the dough offering, 4) Say eighteen benedictions (see footnote 51) which was also required for slaves and minors, 5) Maintain the *mezuzah* on the door of their homes, 6) Observe the laws of niddah that dealt with menstruation.

24

An element of protection underscored these rules: girls were segregated in hopes of keeping them chaste. From the Apocrypha, the Jewish leader Ben Sira counseled fathers to keep an eye on their unmarried daughters, even inside their homes, to avoid all risks of their being defiled, "lest she make thee a laughingstock to thine enemies, and a byword in the city, and a reproach among the people, and make thee ashamed before the multitude."[74] The Jewish code of law, or *Mishnah*, recorded an example of "a young maid [who] once went out to draw water from the spring and she was forced."[75]

Yet for the most part, these confining regulations oppressed and demeaned women.[76] They created a culture of fear and mistrust between the sexes.[77] This gave rise to a lack of appreciation and reinforced negative gender stereotypes of women as dangerous temptresses.[78] Segregation often inhibited a woman's ability to contribute within her community, to serve outside of her home, to join in public worship, and to access education.[79]

Changes by Jesus

Jesus did not live by these segregating restrictions for women. He refused to isolate women and treated them as valued individuals. He allowed women and children to join the

---

[74] Ben Sira, *Ecclesiasticus*, 42:11.

[75] *Mishnah, Ketuboth* 1:10.

[76] Ben Witherington III, *Grace in Galacia* (London and NY: T&T Clark International, 2004), 271, credited to Rabbi Judah b. Elai (c. AD 150) in *Berakoth* 7:18 and *Jer Berakoth* 13b; and to Rabbi Meier (c. AD 150) in *Bab Menahoth* 43b. Jewish rabbis from the second century after Christ supposedly began their morning prayers by saying, "Blessed be He that He did not make me a Gentile; blessed be He that He did not make me a slave; blessed be He that He did not make me a woman."

[77] Charles, **The Apocrypha and Pseudepigrapha,** 2.134. See page 4 in this book, and Evelyn and Frank Stagg, *Woman in the World of Jesus* (Philadelphia, PA: Westminster Press, 1978), 34.

[78] Skolnik, *Encyclopedia Judaica,* 21:161

[79] Ben Sira, *Ecclesiasticus*, 26:14-15.

group of five thousand and later the group of four thousand who gathered to hear Him teach in Galilee (Matthew 14:21; 15:38).[80] He refuted those who wanted to send the women and children away (Mark 10:13-14; Matthew 15:23). He welcomed women to stay in the same room as men (Luke 7:38-40). He did not segregate the unclean, whether they were sick or sinful or social outcasts.

All three synoptic Gospels recorded Jesus' remarkable interaction with an unclean woman on a crowded street in

| Woman with an Issue Of Blood |

Galilee (Matthew 9:19-22; Mark 5:24-34; Luke 8:43-48). The story begins with a throng of people accompanying Jesus across town to the home of Jairus, a ruler of the synagogue, to heal Jairus' daughter. En route, an "unclean" woman tries to touch Jesus to receive His healing virtue. This woman was labeled "unclean" because, for over a decade, she had an "issue of a blood," possibly a hemorrhaging uterus.[81]

More specifically, for the past twelve years, the Mosaic law forbade her from going out in public, touching anyone, worshipping in the synagogue or temple, or sharing her husband's bed (Leviticus 15:19-28). As a result of her condition, her husband had probably divorced her (Deuteronomy 24:1).[82] Since physical disabilities were seen as the consequence of sin, and a woman's menses made her "unclean" (Ezekiel 36:17-18), we assume that at least some of her neighbors and family had probably accused her of

---

[80] Interestingly the Scripture records there were "five thousand men, beside women and children," meaning that the women and children were allowed to be there by the Lord, but not counted by whoever recorded the event (Matthew 14:21; 15:38). This gives us a feel for the cultural practices that did not include women in their tallies.

[81] Julie Smith, "A Redemptive Reading of Mark 5:25-34," *Interpreter* (2015). Smith skillfully argues that "the story of the woman with the hemorrhage of blood redeems the story of the fall of Eve by paralleling and then inverting that text."

[82] *Mishnah Gittin,* 9.10; *Yebamoth,* 14.1.

wickedness and rejected her.[83] The Gospel of Mark also included that she was destitute because she spent all her money on medical help (Mark 5:26).

Yet this faith-filled and determined woman sought healing from the Lord: "If I may touch but his clothes, I shall be whole" (Matthew 9:21; Mark 5:28). To do so, she broke the segregation protocol that had banished her to a life of seclusion—she went outside into a crowded street and tried to hide herself in the pack following Jesus. When she touched His outer garment, or the hem of His tunic, Jesus immediately felt that "virtue has gone out of me," or more literally, "power has gone forth from me" (Luke 8:46 KJV and RSV). Jesus gave part of Himself in order to heal the woman physically. This in turn led to her healing socially and emotionally as well. It took amazing bravery for the woman to answer Jesus' direct question, "Who touched me?" (Mark 5:31).

In that throng of townspeople hurrying through the village to Jairus' home, she showed her faith, courage, and humility; "When the woman saw that she was not hid, she came trembling, and falling down before him, she declared unto him before all the people for what cause she had touched him, and how she was healed immediately" (Luke 8:47). Jesus offered no reproach for her breaching social propriety—instead he praised the depth of her faith: "Your faith has brought you salvation" (Luke 8:47, ABT). And then Jesus offered a departing blessing, "Go in peace" (Luke 8:48).[84] In this poignant story, Jesus defied the cultural norms that marginalized women. By acknowledging, touching and healing this woman, He set a new standard for the way women should be treated.

---

[83] Their culture assumed that God sent death, illness, or deformities, because of sin (Job 20:11; Exodus 20:5; John 9:2; etc.). The opposite also held, that the righteous are spared pain. See footnotes 591, 592, 593 in this book.

[84] 1 Samuel 1:17 also repeats this same promise given to another woman of great faith, Hannah. The high priest Eli prophesied of a forthcoming son as she prayed in the Tabernacle and then said, "Go in peace." We can find many parallels between Luke's birth narratives and Hannah's account. Brown, *Birth,* 335, 357.

II. Communication

Cultural Background and Baggage

An obvious extension of the fact that men and women were segregated was that they did not directly communicate with each other. Simply stated, Jewish men were instructed not to speak very much with women. The *Mishnah* directed, "Talk not much with womankind," followed by the appalling phrase, "they said this of a man's own wife: how much more of his fellow's wife!"[85] Along the same vein, Ben Sira recorded, "A silent wife is a gift from the Lord; her restraint is more than money can buy."[86] Equally extreme, a renowned Rabbi Joshua claimed that any girl or woman found speaking to a man in the street was guilty of breaking the law of chastity unless there was evidence to the contrary.[87] With or without that extreme inference, speaking with the opposite gender was avoided for fear it might result in something scandalous: "Do not speak excessively with a woman lest this ultimately lead you to adultery!"[88]

Another Jerusalem rabbi taught that men who talked to women demonstrated misplaced priorities that would end in damnation: "He that talks much with womankind brings evil

---

[85] *Mishnah, Avoth* 1:5. In 1963 Philip Blackman translated the same passage "engage not in much gossip with womankind." The text of the *Mishnah* varies significantly with different translators.

[86] Ben Sira, *Ecclesiasticus*, 26:14-15. Ben Sira's request for silence may be literal, but just as likely, it may refer to a wife who did not speak against her husband, but honored his will.

[87] *Mishnah, Ketuboth* 1:8. "If they saw her speaking with some man in the street and said to her, 'What manner of man is this?' [and she answered], 'His name is NN and he is a priest,'... R. Joshua says: We must not rely on her word, but she must be presumed to have suffered intercourse . . . unless she can bring proof for her words."

[88] *Babylonian Talmud, Nedarim. 20a.* The Talmud postdates the New Testament but is occasionally cited as an example of the ripple effect that earlier thinking had on Judaism over time. It gives evidence of how the prohibitions of communication spread to extreme conclusions.

28

upon himself, neglects the study of The Law and at the last will inherit Gehenna [hell]."[89] Another rabbi misused the Scriptures to defend the lack of communication with women: "We have not found that the Almighty spoke to a woman except Sarah."[90] In his view, because the Holy Book did not record God speaking to women, neither should men.

This cultural background sheds light on why it seems that

| Joseph and Mary |

the young Mary and her betrothed Joseph barely communicated with each other. During Mary's espousal to Joseph, he discovered her pregnancy, "before they came together" (Matthew 1:18). As an upright law-abiding Jew, Joseph felt bound to obey The Law and divorce Mary. At that point he did not understand the miraculous nature of Mary's conception.

One has to wonder if Mary had tried to explain angel Gabriel's visit to Joseph. Had she told Joseph why she left Nazareth? Had she tried to resolve the misunderstanding? Luke later tells us that Mary "kept all these things, and pondered them in her heart" (Luke 2:19). Perhaps she was culturally not allowed to speak privately with Joseph. Fortunately, God found another way to transmit information to Joseph, sending an angel to share the good news of the miraculous conception. In response to the angel's call, Joseph immediately finalized the marriage (Matthew 1:23-24). By the time the couple journeyed south to Bethlehem, they had been married several months, though the narrative attests that Joseph "knew her not till she had brought forth her firstborn son" (Matthew 1:25).

Changes by Jesus

Jesus did not silence women, but spoke with them respectfully. In Bethany, he spoke directly with both Mary and Martha (Luke 10:42). In Samaria, He conversed with the woman at the well (John 4:7-27). In Galilee, He called to a

---

[89] *Mishnah, Avoth* 1:5.
[90] *Jerusalem Talmud, Sotah.* 7.1, 21b.

29

crippled woman, bent over perhaps from osteoporosis, and spoke the healing words to her, "Woman, thou art loosed from thine infirmity" (Luke 13:12). In Jericho, He conversed with Salome, the mother of James and John, politely asking her, "What do you wish?" (Matthew 20:21, NASB). She felt safe to make her request as well as to receive His answer, even though it included a gentle reproach: "Ye know not what ye ask . . . to sit on my right hand, and on my left, is not mine to give, but . . . my Father['s]" (Matthew 20:22-23). In Jerusalem, on the road to Golgotha, He sensitively observed the women crying and comforted them, "Daughters of Jerusalem, weep not for me" (Luke 23:28). Over and over again, Jesus' example cut through layers of segregation and silence to offer dignity and deference to women.

The longest recorded conversation that Jesus had with a woman is His encounter in Samaria with the

| Samaritan Woman |

woman at the well (John 4:7-28). Only John's Gospel records this dialogue that took place thirty miles north of Jerusalem in the Samaritan capital city of Sychar.[91] By the time of the New Testament, sharp animosity had existed for over a thousand years between Judea and Samaria. The mutual disrespect, blasphemy, retaliation, and impertinence on both sides grew from generation to generation.[92] When traveling between Jerusalem to Galilee

---

[91] The New Testament refers to Samaritans throughout its first five books as both enemies and neighbors of Judea and Galilee. In addition to this account in John 4, the New Testament mentions Samaritans in the following examples: Jesus is called a Samaritan (John 8:48), in the parable of the Good Samaritan (Luke 10:33), and finally the healing of the Samaritan leper (Luke 17:16). Some scholars suggest that Stephen was a Samaritan as he quotes the Samaritan Bible in Acts 7, not the Septuagint. Darrell L. Bock, *Acts: Baker Exegetical Commentary on the New Testament* (Grand Rapids, MI: Baker Academic Publishing, 2007), 284.

[92] F. F. Bruce, *New Testament History,* 342. In AD 51, a pilgrimage of Galileans opted to take the shorter route through Samaria, but they were "roughly handled" by the Samaritans, resulting in at least one dead. In retribution, a group of Jewish Zealots massacred the Samaritan district indiscriminately.

most Jews chose to avoid Samaria by taking a longer route around it. Jesus did not.[93]

On one such trip, the Lord and His disciples arrived at Sychar around the time of their midday meal.[94] He rested near Jacob's well and sent His disciples into the city to buy bread for their noon meal (John 4:8). As He rested, "a Samaritan woman came to draw water, [and] Jesus said to her, 'Will you give me a drink?'" (John 4:7, NIV). This was an unusual request because a religious Jew would never eat anything touched by someone ritually "unclean," especially a Samaritan. The whole trip would have been repulsive to a devout Jew from Jerusalem: walking on a Samaritan road, going into a Samaritan town, eating Samaritan food, and drinking Samaritan water.[95]

Yet, when Jesus asked the Samaritan woman for a drink of water from her pot, He had higher motives in mind than simply quenching His thirst. John explained that this Samaritan woman chose to walk further out of town to get her water from Jacob's well (John 4:12). As the chore of hefting water was physically taxing, and carrying it difficult, one wonders why she chose the "sixth hour" or

Woman at the Well

---

[93] Josephus, *Antiquities,* XVII.10.9; XX. 6.1; *Wars*, IV. 8.1; *Life,* 52. Three major routes led from Judea to Galilee during the period of Herod's Temple. The shortest route went directly through Samaria. Josephus reports that Roman troops chose the shortest route through Samaria, and a few Galilean Jews chanced it. But rarely would a Judean Jew contaminate himself by traveling through that "impure" country. Instead, Jews from Jerusalem chose the safest routes by avoiding Samaria entirely, even if it added an extra day to their journey.

[94] Raymond E. Brown, *An Introduction to the New Testament* (New York: Doubleday, 1997), 343. Archeologists have found two ancient cities near Jacob's well that may be ancient Sychar. Shechem was two miles from Jacobs well and Askar, about one mile north of Jacob's well.

[95] The imagery of water is also poignant because water was a most critical issue in Palestine—politically, socially, and physically. The availability of water governed many of life's decisions. In this story, it appears that there was plenty of water in the well and Eastern hospitality ensured service, even by a woman in Samaria.

noon—the hottest time of day.[96] This was not a common hour to go to the well; most people went in the cool of the early morning. Also, archeologists speak of a copious spring on the other side of town that would have been closer and easier to draw her water.[97] Both of these details suggest that the woman unnecessarily added more hardship to her task.

However, when we learn about the details of her life–her past divorces and current sins–we imagine that she may have tried to avoid the social gathering place—filled with the daily gossip or scorn of her neighbors—by walking alone further out of town. The extra work involved in the unusual time and location may have been worth the isolation.

John's record includes the woman's astonishment at Jesus' breach of social rules.[98] The woman correctly asked Him, "How is it that thou, being a Jew, askest drink of me, which am a *woman* of Samaria?" (John 4:9). Jesus' behavior slashed through strongholds of Judaic social norms: He spoke to a

---

[96] Day lasted from 6:00 a.m. to 6:00 p.m. and night was divided into three or four watches (depending on whether the watch was Jewish or Roman). In the Jewish world, the new day began with night just as in the creation it was dark before light.

[97] Clinton E. Arnold, ed., *Zondervan Illustrated Bible Backgrounds Commentary: John, Acts* (Grand Rapids, MI: Zondervan, 2002), 2877.

[98] Tensions arose between northern and southern Israel dating back to King Solomon's death and split of the kingdom. Problems flared up worse than ever after the Babylonian captivity. Ezra 4:1-4 and Nehemiah 2:19-20 explain that the Jews returning from their Babylonian captivity refused the Samaritans' help to rebuild the temple. Zerubbabel's team turned away the Samaritans who had no proper genealogical evidence of Levitical descent. In retribution, the Samaritans conspired with the foreign overlords to prevent the Jews from rebuilding the walls of Jerusalem, reconstructing the city, and rebuilding the temple. Samaritans retaliated by claiming the Jews apostatized and built their own temple on Mount Gerizim (2,890 feet) near their capital city, Shechem, in the fourth century BC (around the time of Alexander the Great). In 128 BC, any hope of healing their rift was shattered by the Jewish retribution. Under orders from the high priest, John Hyrcanus, Jewish activists destroyed the Samaritan Temple on Mount Gerizim and captured the city of Shechem. The demolition of the temple on Mount Gerizim could not have been more offensive. For more information on the return from Babylon, see appendix 1.

woman, He spoke to a Samaritan, and He asked to drink water from an unclean pot. His actions reinforced His message that God is no respecter of persons (2 Chronicles 19:7; Acts 10:34).[99]

Yet, the Lord's conversation pulled His listener in a different direction than she anticipated. The woman questioned the social and religious propriety of His request, so Jesus proposed that she ask Him for living water—reversing their roles. "If thou knewest the gift of God, and who it is that saith to thee, Give me to drink; thou wouldest have asked of him, and he would have given thee living water" (John 4:10).

| Living Water |

In the New Testament, the doctrines of Christ become *living water* for disciples. The Old Testament uses "living water" to describe a spring or running water, in contrast to "dead" or stagnant water stored in a cistern.[100] Living water was a rich prize.[101] Christ redefined "living water" as something even more valuable: the doctrines, the truths, and the revelation that flow from Him.

However, the Samaritan woman was initially deaf to this higher symbolism. Ironically, she responded, "Art thou greater

---

[99] This raises the interesting question of whether or not Jesus considered the Samaritans part of the tribe of Israel. He told the gentile Syrophoenician woman that His mission was to preach only to Israelites (Matthew 15:26-27; Mark 7:26-28; Luke 16:20-22), yet John 4:42 says that the Lord's first community of followers were Samaritans.

[100] The Scriptures often associate living water with the temple and eternal life (Jeremiah 2:13; Isaiah 8:6; 1 Nephi 11:25). The Book of Mormon affiliates "living waters" with the tree of life, the love of God, and salvation (1 Nephi 11:25).

[101] In the *Babylonian Talmud*, "Torah" was used as a symbol of water: "Oh ye who are thirsty, come to the water." Talmud, *Abodah Zarah*, 5.7. "What is meant by 'water' is Torah." Similarly, in apocryphal 2 Esdras 14:37 (also known as 4 Ezra 9:26): "'Ezra, open your mouth and drink what I give you.' So I opened my mouth, and was handed a cup full of what seemed like water, except that its colour was the colour of fire. I took it and drank, and soon as I had done so my mind began to pour forth a flood of understanding." The Eastern Orthodox Church canonized Ezra, which dates to sometime between 165 BC and 50 BC.

than our father Jacob, which gave us the well?" (John 4:12).[102] To which Jesus answered, "Whosoever drinketh of this water shall thirst again: But whosoever drinketh of the water that I shall give him shall never thirst; but the water that I shall give him shall be in him a well of water springing up into everlasting life" (John 4:13-14). Only aware of her literal need for sustaining water, the woman thought on a physical plane: "Sir, give me this water, that I thirst not, neither come hither to draw" (John 4:15).

The challenges of getting water from a well, in addition to the social stigmas of her life, would have made the prospect of never again thirsting a welcome offer—but that was not the Lord's message. He patiently taught her to look beyond her sphere of understanding, and explained that He was not referring to sustaining her physically, but eternally (John 4:14). Jesus wanted to emancipate her from her spiritual bondage, so He opened the doorway for her repentance by revealing His divine mantle and omniscience.

After Jesus divulged His knowledge of her five divorces in her tainted past and the fact that she currently was living in

---

[102] Note that the woman mentioned Jacob—one of the patriarchs. This is in keeping with Samaritan belief that accepted the patriarchs (Abraham, Isaac, and Jacob), but not many of the Old Testament prophets. The Samaritans' core beliefs came from the Pentateuch (Genesis, Exodus, Leviticus, Numbers, Deuteronomy) and were handed down orally:
  1. Belief in one God.
  2. Moses as the greatest and final, or "seal," of the prophets
  3. The Torah as the word of God, and rejection of all else as Scripture
  4. Mt Gerizim as the chosen place for God's Temple.
  5. Expectations of a final day of rewards for the righteous and punishment for the wicked.
Bruce W. Hall, *Samaritan religion from John Hyrcanus to Baba Rabba: A Critical Examination of the Relevant Material in Contemporary Christian literature, the writings of Josephus, and the Mishnah* (Sydney, Australia: Mandelbaum Trust, University of Sydney, 1987), 270. Other scholars add a sixth tenet that includes appearance at the end of time of a "Restorer" who would appear to usher in a new dispensation, teach the law, and restore the proper modes of worship. Kent Jackson, and Robert Millet, *Studies in Scriptures: The Gospels* (Salt Lake City, UT: Deseret Book, 1986), 5.205.

sin, she humbly acknowledged, "I perceive that thou art a prophet" (John 4:19). Her response after such a humiliating and embarrassing disclosure from a complete stranger spoke of the open and humble condition of her heart. Rather than feeling defensive, running away, or retreating in self-pity, the woman acknowledged Jesus as a prophet and then moved to the next logical step of asking for His prophetic insight into a standard doctrinal question that often surfaced between the Jews and Samaritans. In fact, the woman's question gave evidence to her faith in Jesus as a prophet (John 4:19-20). She asked Him, "Where is the correct place to worship?" Mount Gerizim in Samaria (as the Samaritans believed) or Mount Moriah in Jerusalem (as the Jews believed).

To the Samaritans, Mount Gerizim was the most holy place on earth. In addition to the location of their late temple, they believed Mount Gerizim was sacred because it existed before the creation; that it was the first land to appear after the waters were gathered together; that it was as a twin of the Garden of Eden; and that it was the only land not covered by the flood.[103] Although the Jews had destroyed their temple, they believed the sacred site would someday house the true temple, and that it would be the only place to survive at the end of the world.[104]

> Samaritan Beliefs

The woman asked again for earthly evidence while Jesus' answer stretched her upward to heavenly principles. He explained that the location was not the key issue in worship; it was *who, why,* and *how* one worshiped. True worship comes from the condition of one's heart, "true worshippers shall

---

[103] Jeremias, *Jerusalem in the Time of Jesus*, 352-358. They taught that Mount Gerizim was the place where Noah disembarked from the ark, the place where Abraham brought Isaac to be sacrificed, the burial site of Joseph their patriarch, and the location of the final judgment. Alan David Crown, Reinhard Pummer, Abraham Tal, eds., *A Companion to Samaritan Studies* (Tübingen, Germany: Mohr Siebeck, 1993), 100.

[104] In 128 BC as part of Jewish revolt to cleanse their land of foreigners, a group of Jewish activists, working under the direction of the high priest, demolished the Samaritan Temple on Mount Gerizim. See footnote 98, on page 32, and appendix 1.

worship the Father in spirit and in truth" (John 4:23). This dramatic conversation broke through walls of ethnic bigotry.

This became the earliest Johannine scriptural reference of Jesus' announcing His Messiahship. "The woman saith unto him, I know that Messias cometh, which is called Christ: when he is come, he will tell us all things. Jesus saith unto her, I that speak unto thee am He" (John 4:25-26). This bold declaration stands in contrast to the many times in the Gospels when the Lord limited what He divulged due to the skepticism of His audience (Mark 13:4; Luke 20:2-8; 22:67; John 3:10-12; 3 Nephi 17:2; etc.). But here He forthrightly communicated with a woman (in particular, a sinning Samaritan woman), honoring her with great insight.

John's description of what happened next offers profound symbolism: she left her water pot. Her pot can be seen as emblematic of the cares of the world, her old life, and her old source of sustenance. She left it all behind for her new life that led her to share the living water or good news—the gospel—of Jesus the Messiah with her community, who may have become the first branch of believers.

> She left her water pot

The story ends with two other social shocks. Unlike their Jerusalem neighbors, the Samaritan community listened to and acted on a message from a woman—and not just any woman, but a sinning adulteress. Second, the author chose to mention that Jesus and His disciples stayed with the Samaritans preaching the gospel for two days and that many believed, "for we have heard him ourselves, and know that this is indeed the Christ, the Saviour of the world" (John 4:42).

Commentaries on this story often illustrate Jesus' rejection of racial prejudices, yet just as profound, we see that Jesus speaks to and teaches *a woman* with remarkable openness. He broke down enormous social barriers and trusted her to witness the truth of His Messiahship. He trusted her with the mysteries, and He trusted her to change. In this manner, Jesus empowered her and those of us who also have water pots to leave behind.

III. Dress

Cultural Background and Baggage

In the Jewish world, dress was an important symbol of one's station and values. Strict modesty was necessary in order to communicate one's chastity.[105] Even though the Old Testament did not forbid it, the Jewish society of the late Second Temple era (20 BC to AD 70) required a married Jewess to be completely covered outside her home.[106] If she did not entirely drape herself,[107] her husband could divorce her and not have to pay for the marriage contract fee. The public protocol required a woman to cover her hair, face, and body.[108] If a Jewess uncovered her head in public, it was interpreted as a sign of rejecting God: "You have departed from the way of the daughters of Israel, whose habit it is to have their heads covered, and you have walked in the ways of idolatrous women who walk about with their heads uncovered."[109] The biblical scholar Joachim Jeremias described their custom of veiling their faces with a complex arrangement of "two head veils, a head-band on the forehead with bands to the chin, and a hairnet with

---

[105] Judith Lynn Sebesta, Larissa Bonfante, *The World of Roman Costume* (Madison, WI: University Press, 2001), 8. "Dress serves to distinguish friend and foe in war and in peace; divine and imperial figures, wife, prostitute, and defeated barbarian mother with child."

[106] Skolnik, *Encyclopedia Judaica,* 21.161.

[107] Judith Lynn Sebesta, Larissa Bonfante, *The World of Roman Costume* (Madison, WI: University Press, 2001), 155, 186. Also see chapter 6 of this book on "Divorce."

[108] *Philo,* Yonge, trans., 817. Philo described the head covering as a "symbol of modesty, which all those women are accustomed to wear who are completely blameless." This quote is in Philo's discussion of Numbers 5:18, dealing with a woman accused of adultery. Nearly two centuries before the time of the Lord, Ben Sira surmised that he could determine if a woman had broken the law of chastity by the only part of the body unexposed: "The fornication of a woman shall be known by the haughtiness of her eyes, and by her eyelids" (*Ecclesiasticus*, 26:12, Douay-Rheims Bible).

[109] Sebesta and Bonfante, *The World of Roman Costume,* 186.

ribbons and knots, so that her features could not be recognized."[110]

The veiling was so extensive that on one occasion, a chief priest in Jerusalem did not even recognize his own mother as the person in front of him being tried for adultery.[111] Several generations after the New Testament, as rabbinic Judaism expanded their definition of modesty to include covering a woman's ankles. The Talmud warned against "voyeurism" because it may lead to adultery: "He who looks at a woman's heels . . . is as if he had intercourse with her."[112]

Outside of the city, the dress code differed slightly.[113] This is one reason why Jews in the city looked down upon their less pious kinsmen in the country.[114] It was not practical for women in the country to wear such extensive wrappings because many farmers needed their wives' and children's help in the fields, and it would have severely impeded their productivity. Over the centuries, artists who depict New Testament scenes rarely portray women in public with their face

---

[110] Jeremias, *Jerusalem,* 359. We get a feel for how much of a woman was veiled in a story of a pious woman named Qimhit, who claimed to keep her head covered even in the house as a sign of her uprightness: "May it (this and that) befall me if the beams of my house have ever seen the hair of my head." Ibid., 360.

[111] Jeremias, *Jerusalem,* 359. "It was said that once, for example, a chief priest in Jerusalem did not recognize his own mother when he had to carry out against her the prescribed process for a woman suspected of adultery."

[112] *Babylonian Talmud, Nedarim,* 2.4, 58c. "R. Josiah said: He who gazes at a woman eventually comes to sin, and he who looks even at a woman's heel will beget degenerate children." Another translation reads, "He that looks upon a woman's heel is guilty of an act of lewdness." This led to the counsel for men never to walk behind a woman—even if she were his wife—in case he might "see her heels." Talmud, *Berakot,* 61a.

[113] Sebesta and Bonfante, *The World of Roman Costume,* 186, "Women of Arabia may go out veiled, and women of Medea with their cloaks looped over their shoulders."

[114] Jeremias, *Jerusalem,* 362; "there is no indication that the custom of wrapping up the head was observed as strictly in the country as in the town."

and bodies completely draped, yet the writings from observant Jews from the time suggest that it was so.[115]

Changes by Jesus

The rigor of the Jewish dress code provides an interesting backdrop for the story in Luke about the woman who washed Jesus' feet with her hair.[116] Given that women were to be covered in public settings, one can better understand the shock of Jesus' host when an uninvited woman approached Jesus and unbound her hair (Luke 7:36-50). Instead of condemning the woman, Jesus acknowledged her thoughtfulness, humility, love, and faith as she wiped His feet with her hair. More astonishing, when the Pharisaic host questioned Jesus' morals for allowing an uncovered woman to touch Him (which was interpreted as evidence that she was "morally uncovered"[117]), Jesus condemned the host (Luke 7:44-46).

> A Woman Washes Jesus' Feet

I entered into thine house, thou gavest me no water for my feet: but she hath washed my feet with tears, and wiped them with the hairs of her head. Thou gavest me no kiss: but this woman since the time I came in hath not ceased to kiss my feet. My head with oil thou didst not anoint: but this woman hath anointed my feet with ointment. According to Luke's record, Jesus pointed out that the host had neglected to offer his traveling guests the opportunity to wash upon arrival.

---

[115] *Mishnah, Nashim: Sotah,* 3. 8. "How does a man differ from a woman? He may go with his hair unbound and with garments rent, but she may not go with hair unbound and with garments rent."

[116] Luke is the only Gospel to tell this story, although shortly before Jesus' death the other three Gospels tell of Mary anointing Jesus in Bethany with pure nard, and wiping His feet with her hair (see John 12:1-8; Matthew 26:6-13; Mark 14:3-9).

[117] Craig Keener, *1–2 Corinthians* (New York: Cambridge University Press, 2005), 92.

Walking in sandals on dusty stones or unpaved roads left one's feet callused, cut, and encrusted with dirt. Decorum dictated that a host provide the means for guests to wash before entering a house. At the very least, hosts provided basins of water for their guests; in more polite settings, the host assigned a servant or child to do the menial task of washing the guests' feet. Foot care was such a filthy job that it was often delegated to slaves.[118] In their homes, children often had the assignment to wash their fathers' feet each day.[119]

In washing Jesus' feet with her own hair, this woman entered into the role of "servant" or "child" of Christ. This act of submission to Jesus was a demonstration of her repentant heart, and Christ freely forgave her: "Her sins, which are many, are forgiven; for she loved much" (Luke 7:47). She seems to exemplify that discipleship of Christ requires submission to Him as servant to master, child to father. She also became yet another example of Jesus' acceptance of social outcasts and of His rejecting restrictive social norms for women.

In this account, we have no evidence that Jesus verbally condemned the woman for breaching the rules of dress by uncovering her hair. Rather, by allowing her to continue, He communicated an acceptance. When He needed to speak out or to educate about one's clothing, He did. But rather than condemning uncovered hair, He condemned those who dressed and acted for social aggrandizement: "Beware of the scribes, which desire to walk in long robes, and love greetings in the markets, and the highest seats in the synagogues, and the chief rooms at feasts" (Luke 20:46). He denounced dress as a form of pride. The Lord maintained a higher perspective around physical dress standards that fostered pure love rather than unhealthy rigid social standards.

---

[118] In Greek, "servant" is the same word as "*doulos* / slave, bondman, man of servile condition," and similarly a female servant or handmaid, was a "*doule* / female slave, bondmaid" (see John 15:15; Luke 1:38). See chapter 8.
[119] See chapter 7.

After Jesus' death, the Lord's apostles counseled women and men to cover themselves with a different type of clothing—the armor of God:

> Put on the whole armour of God, that ye may be able to stand against the wiles of the devil…. Wherefore take unto you the whole armour of God, that ye may be able to withstand in the evil day, and having done all, to stand. Stand therefore, having your loins girt about with truth, and having on the breastplate of righteousness; And your feet shod with the preparation of the gospel of peace; Above all, taking the shield of faith, wherewith ye shall be able to quench all the fiery darts of the wicked. And take the helmet of salvation, and the sword of the Spirit, which is the word of God (Ephesians 6:12-17; 1 Thessalonians 5:8).

The Armor of God

In Christianity, clothing took on an important figurative meaning.[120] More important than concerning oneself with outer adornments, the apostles asked followers of Christ to put off the natural man in order to put on the armor of God. Christians dress in God's armor as they live God's commandments and apply "the enabling power of His atonement."[121] With its protection, one becomes more holy and less worldly.

---

[120] Clothing also took on emblematic meaning for the afterlife as John the Revelator described "white robes" given to those who died as martyrs of truth (Revelation 6:11; 7:9, 13-14). The white robe represented their purity by "wash[ing] their robes, and made them white in the blood of the Lamb" (Revelation 9:14). And Isaiah described, "[God] hath clothed me with the garments of salvation, he hath covered me with the robe of righteousness, as a bridegroom decketh himself with ornaments, and as a bride adorneth herself with her jewels" (Isaiah 61:10). These clothes empower one with immortality.

[121] David A. Bednar, "The Atonement and the Journey of Mortality" *Ensign* (April 2012).

IV. Women's Responsibilities

Cultural Background and Baggage

The most important duty of Jewish women at the time of Christ was to bear and raise children. Bearing children was so crucial that if a wife were barren for ten years, her husband had a religious obligation to divorce her.[122] Some rabbis diminished women's contributions in this sacred role: "All we [men] can expect from them [women] is that they bring up our children and keep us from sin."[123] Clearly, this statement does not recognize the nobility in motherhood. Raising children was often seen as a menial task on par with other household tasks.

Spousal Responsibilities

A Jewess' household responsibilities are enumerated in the *Mishnah* as the "duties which a wife must perform for her husband" and included "grinding flour and baking bread, washing clothes and cooking food, nursing her child, making his bed and working in wool. If she brings one servant with her, she need not grind."[124] These duties would be increased or decreased depending on how many other women, children, or servants could help. Without slaves or children it fell to a wife to wash her husband's face, hands and feet, and "prepare his cup."[125] Often multiple generations lived in the same home or close to one another and shared in the work.[126]

A chaste wife was an utmost requirement in honoring her husband.[127] In Philo's list of wifely virtues, sexual commitment

---

[122] See chapter 6 of this book under "Divorce."

[123] Bromiley, *International Standard Bible Encyclopedia*, "Sex," 4.431.

[124] *Mishnah, Ketuboth, 5:5.*

[125] Ibid.

[126] Ken Campbell, ed., *Marriage and Family in the Biblical World* (Downers Grove, IL: Inter-Varsity Press, 2003), 232.

[127] *Philo*, Yonge, trans., 138. Philo recounted the patriarch Judah's reverie on a virtuous woman: "Perhaps then, according to my prayer, she is truly a

to her husband received a triple emphasis through modesty, chastity, and cleaving. Rabbis often debated their views on social concerns that involved women and her virtue.[128] In one such dispute, a twist of suspicion is found in a rabbi's description of a woman's work: she must always keep busy or her "idleness leads to unchastity." Another rabbi refuted with this general observation: "Idleness leads to lowness of spirit."[129]

Next, a wife must be subservient to her husband.[130] Philo explained that a husband, "delighting in his master-like authority, is to be respected for his pride: but the woman, being in the rank of a servant, is praised for assenting to a life of communion."[131] Most Jews referred to a wife as her husband's property: "He that possesseth a good wife, beginneth a

---

virtuous mind, a citizen wife, excelling in modesty, and chastity, and all other virtues, cleaving to one husband alone, being content with the administration of one household, and rejoicing in the authority of one husband." Ironically, Philo has these words coming out of Judah's mouth in reference to Tamar, after Judah mistook her for a harlot and slept with her, making nearly every statement incongruous. The story screams of a double standard for men and women.

[128] Seven of the *Mishnah* tractates deal with women and family life. Five of them deal with transition periods of marriage, divorce, and widowhood (Kiddishin, Detubot, Gittin, Sotah, and Yebamot). One volume or "tractate" specifically deals with women's menstruation, *niddah.*

[129] *Mishnah, Ketuboth,* 5:5.

[130] Ben Sira, *Ecclesiasticus,* 44-50. A discriminatory attitude grew stronger throughout the period of the Second Temple. Throughout the entire apocryphal book of *Ecclesiasticus* we find praises for male Old Testament heroes without mentioning the noble women in their past. Yet in the Old Testament we find many positive relationships between men and women— like *Job* giving his three daughters gifts of inheritance (Job 42:15; also see Numbers 27:7). But that changed as we draw closer to the time that surrounded the New Testament. M. Jack Suggs, Katharine Doob Sakenfeld, James R. Mueller, eds., *The Oxford Study Bible: Revised English Bible with the Apocrypha, 2nd Ed.* (New York: Oxford University Press, 1992).

[131] Philo, *A Volume of Questions and Solutions to Questions which arise in Genesis,* I.29. In the same volume, Philo describes the creation of Adam and Eve: "God, when first of all he made the intellect, called it Adam, after that he created the outward sense, to which he gave the name of Life [Eve]" (I.53). He felt man was the intellect and woman the senses.

possession."[132] As her husband's subservient property, a respectable wife was to honor her husband: "a wife who honors her husband is accounted wise by all."[133]

Wives were to take counsel from their husbands, not to give it. Josephus explained why Adam was cursed in the Garden of Eden: "Because he weakly submitted to the counsel of his wife."[134] This attitude potentially fostered a sense of superiority and self-importance in the man that could inhibit the development of cooperation, unity, and selflessness between companions.[135] We see a lack of mutual respect in such statements: "Better is the iniquity of a man, than a woman doing a good turn, and a woman bringing shame and reproach."[136]

It appears that male dominion became skewed.[137] The Jewish historian Josephus (AD 37-101) justified a man's feeling superior to a woman by saying, "for says the Scripture, 'A woman is inferior to her husband in all things.'"[138] The "Scripture" that Josephus claimed is unknown, but his views on women are similar to those of other writers from the same era.[139] Josephus further added that women were only "sanctified

---

[132] Ben Sira, *Ecclesiasticus*, 36:26.

[133] Ibid., 26.26.

[134] Josephus, *Antiquities of the Jews*, I.1.4.

[135] Ben Sira, *Ecclesiasticus*, 33:20, 23; "Give not to son or wife, brother or friend, power over thee while thou livest; . . . In all thy works keep the pre-eminence."

[136] Ibid., 42:14. Also statements like, "As long as thou livest, and hast breath in thee, let no man change thee." Yet on the other hand, we also find in the same text, statements that praise humility, "The greater thou art, the more humble thyself, and thou shalt find favour before the Lord" (3:18, 21).

[137] Ibid., 26.25; "A headstrong wife is regarded as a dog." Submission was often tied with remaining silent—see page 28.

[138] Josephus, *Against Apion*, II. 25. Neusner, ed., *Judaism in the Biblical Period*, 676. Furthermore, the "biblical society was defined in terms of its male members as indicated by the census in Exodus 20, and in Numbers 1 and 26, which counted adult males but no women or children" (673). Censuses were often taken to know the military potential or tax base.

[139] Peder Borgen, *Philo of Alexandria: An Exegete for His Time* (Netherlands: Brill, 1997), 58. A biblical scholar, Carras, observed ten points

through the deeds of men . . . the anomaly of women is worked out . . . by assigning her to a man's domain."[140]

Financial Responsibilities

In cities, Jewish women worked outside of their homes only if abject poverty required it. In cases of widowhood, divorce, or other experiences that caused extreme poverty, a woman was allowed to work as a cook, baker, spinner, weaver, laundress, inn-keeper, female hairdresser, midwife, or mourner.[141] However, a negative social stigma still fell on any woman who worked in these jobs, and any pay earned by the wife or daughter was paid directly to (and kept by) the man of the house.[142] Husbands or fathers bore the sole responsibility for breadwinning.

In the country, economic necessity allowed some women to work outside of their homes to help with the harvest or other farm needs. Archeologists estimate that "90-95 percent of the population of ancient Palestine would have been rural peasants," living off the land or sea.[143] Though frowned upon in the city, in agrarian communities some "maidens" went to the well for water and women assisted their fathers or husbands in the fields as needed.[144] Even though few records survived from

---

about which both Philo and Josephus wrote. The second point was, "Women are to have a subservient role to their husbands."

[140] Josephus, *Against Apion*, II. 25.

[141] *Mishnah, Ketuboth,* 4.4, A "mourner" was a woman paid to cry and scream and throw dirt in the air in a demonstration of sorrow. This became a required part of mourning. See chapter 6, quotations found in "Women and Mourning."

[142] Ben Witherington III, *Women and the Genesis of Christianity* (Cambridge, England, NYC: Cambridge Press, 1990), 4.

[143] Reta H. Finger, *Of Widows and Meals: Communal Meals in the Book of Acts* (Grand Rapids, MI: Eerdmans, 2007), 100. Also see, Daniel Sperber, *Roman Palestine 200-400, the Land: Crisis and Change in Agrarian Society as Reflected in Rabbinic Sources* (Tel Aviv, Israel: Bar-Ilan University, 1978).

[144] Jeremias, *Jerusalem,* 362. "Ordinary families could not adhere strictly to the totally retired life of the *woman* of rank, who was surrounded by her

the rural segment of the population, we do find some texts that describe women working in the fields: "a woman that returned from the harvest . . . or from olive-picking or from the vintage."[145] This female contribution to the family coffers offered women more value in the country than in the city.

Changes by Jesus

Christian women had many similar responsibilities to those of their Jewish peers: bearing children, serving one's family, loving one's husband, and serving those in need (1 Timothy 5:14; Titus 2:4). But the Lord made abrupt and fundamental changes to the priorities placed upon women. He never referred to women as possessions, nor did He dominant or try to control them (Matthew 9:22; 15:28; Mark 14:6; Luke 13:12; John 4:4-21; 8:10; etc.). The Lord's restored church likewise denounces such treatment.[146]

---

household of servants; and the main reasons for this were economic ones. For example, a *wife* had to help her husband in his profession, perhaps by selling his wares (M. Ket. ix.4). We may also see this relaxation of custom among ordinary people in the description of the popular feasts which took place in the Court of Women, during the *nights of the feast of Tabernacles*; the crowds were so exuberant that finally it became necessary to construct galleries for the women, to separate them from the men (T. Sukk.iv.I, 198.6). Moreover, in the country there were further relaxations. Here, the *maidens went to the well* (M. Ket. i.1o; Gen. R. 49 on 18.20, Son. 49.6, 425); the married women engaged in agricultural work together with her husband and children."

[145] *Mishnah, Yebamoth,* 15.2.

[146] Elder Richard G. Scott, "Honor the Priesthood and Use it Well," *Ensign* (Nov 2008), 46: "In some cultures, tradition places a man in a role to dominate, control, and regulate all family affairs. That is not the way of the Lord. In some places the wife is almost owned by her husband, as if she were another of his personal possessions. That is a cruel, mistaken vision of marriage encouraged by Lucifer that every priesthood holder must reject. It is founded on the false premise that a man is somehow superior to a woman. Nothing could be farther from the truth."

The Gospel of John tells us that Jesus "loved Martha, and her

| Mary and Martha |

sister, and Lazarus" (11:5). When He went to their home in Bethany for a special dinner party, He noticed that Martha was frustrated with her sister's lack of help. Even if the hostess had servants (which she probably did), Martha's workload was huge.

From the perspective of most law-abiding Jews, Martha's sister Mary was out of line to sit at Jesus' feet to learn from Him. Not only did Mary neglect her responsibilities, but she was also speaking to a male guest, and it appears that she delved into areas of learning The Law, both of which were forbidden to women. Some rabbis taught that if a woman spoke with a man other than her husband, it was cause for a divorce.[147]

On the other hand, Martha acted as an upright Jewess preparing the meal and home for her honored guest, Jesus. She asked the male leader to correct her errant sister: "Lord, dost thou not care that my sister hath left me to serve alone? bid her therefore that she help me" (Luke 10:40). Jesus certainly did not mean that serving others is not important (as we discuss in chapter 8). His response to Martha sounds like a reminder of priorities to the modern reader.

Yet to that ancient society, His response would have been utterly shocking: "Martha, Martha, thou art careful and troubled about many things: But one thing is needful: and Mary hath chosen that good part" (Luke 10:41-42). Jesus' support of Mary's behavior was a revolutionary endorsement of female spiritual engagement, learning and communication.

The last phrase in Luke 10:42 is also interesting, "which shall not be taken away from her." We need to examine that phrase in the world of the Second Temple. At that time everything a girl or woman earned or found legally belonged to her male guardian.[148] A female had no claim on anything tangible—including her children, who were the property of

---

[147] *Mishnah*, *Ketuboth* 1:8. See chapter 6.
[148] Witherington, *Women and the Genesis of Christianity*, 4.

their father (and in the case of divorce, the father had full custody).[149] A female did not even have ownership of her own life: her father or husband could sell her into slavery.[150] As a slave, a girl's freedom and chastity could be taken away, as could her earnings, property or food.

With this as background, we find even more meaning in the Lord's promise that her relationship with Him—and her knowledge could not be taken away. Not only would Mary be able to learn and live a richer life from her experience, but also she would own her knowledge beyond this life. The Lord's words apply to the eternal spectrum as we read in D&C 130:18, "whatever principle of intelligence we attain unto in this life, it will rise with us in the resurrection."

In addition to the benefits of educating women, this story validated male and female interaction. Jesus' example indicated that it was acceptable for women to participate in the world of the mind and of the spirit, and not exclusively in the traditional domestic tasks.

Like their Master, the apostles also encouraged women to participate, sanctioned their study, and authorized them to take an active role in building the kingdom of God, even in public settings. A shining example of a woman from the Greco-Roman world who embraced these opportunities is Lydia of Thyatira, a Christian convert living in Philippi. She led her

| Lydia |

household in her spiritual pursuits. The Bible does not tell us anything about her marital status, but speaks of her noble accomplishments. Lydia "worshipped God," accepted the missionaries' message, had an open heart, and followed the counsel of the apostle Paul (Acts 16:14). She had such a strong positive influence, that when she was baptized, her entire household, including servants, followed her example. We also learn that she sold a rare and expensive purple dye, and she had a home large enough to host the apostle Paul and his fellow missionaries (Acts 16:15). She was a disciple of Christ and a

---

[149] Beryl Rawson, ed., *The Family in Ancient Rome: New Perspectives* (Ithica, NY: Cornell University Press, 1987), 36. See chapter 6 of this book.
[150] *Mishnah, Ketuboth,* 3.8.

48

spiritual leader, who was able to provide for herself and for others both temporally and spiritually.

There are many other examples of women in the New Testament who took proactive roles in their worship and in building the kingdom. These include women like the prophetess Anna (Luke 2:36-38), Mary and Elisabeth (Luke 1:39-56), Dorcas or Tabitha (Acts 9: 36-42), Damaris (Acts 17:22-34), Philip's four prophetic daughters (Acts 21:8-14), Phebe (Romans 16:1-2), Prisca (Acts 18:13, 18-19, 24-28), Lois and Eunice (2 Timothy 1:5), all of whom receive tribute throughout this book. They each followed the Lord's counsel to put His teachings first in their lives, above their cultural traditions, and in some cases, other loved ones if necessary: "If anyone comes to me and does not hate his own father and mother and wife and children and brothers and sisters, yes, and even his own life, he cannot be my disciple" (Luke 14:26, ESV).

The Gospels of Matthew and Mark also included the need for disciples to forgo society's influences that take them away from the Lord's work (Matthew 19:29; Mark 10:29). If being subservient to a husband or father kept one of them from following God, then the Lord summoned His disciples to forsake them and "come after me" (Luke 14:27).

The Lord also added another responsibility for women, "Come unto me, all ye that labour and are heavy laden, and I will give you rest. Take my yoke upon you, and learn of me" (Matthew 11:28-29). Women became students of the Savior and referred to Him as "teacher." For example, Mary Magdalene addressed the risen Lord, "'Rabboni!' (which means Teacher)" (John 20:16; NIV); and Martha "called her sister Mary aside. 'The Teacher is here'" (John 20:16, NIV). He empowered those who listened to learn. Even though these are standard titles, they had extra meaning in the context of women learning from Jesus. He wanted His hearers to think on their own, and He gave assignments, such as this: "Go ye and learn what that meaneth, I will have mercy, and not sacrifice for I am not come to call the righteous, but sinners to repentance" (Matthew 9:13).

Jesus began certain parables with the injunction, "Now *learn* a parable of . . ." (Mark 13:28; emphasis added, also see Matthew 24:32). The Master Teacher educated on the Galilean hills, by the sea, in the synagogue, in houses, and in the temple to men, women, and children of all classes. Learning from Him provides spiritual, emotional, and social emancipation.

V. Witnesses

Cultural Background and Baggage

Jewish magistrates did not allow women to act as legal or official witnesses in a court of law.[151] Jewish law formally silenced a woman's legal testimony because men did not think that women could be trusted. One source claimed that the custom stemmed from rabbinic interpretation of Genesis 18:15, "Sarah denied, saying, I laughed not." From Sarah's response, the rabbis extrapolated that all women were liars and unworthy of acting as witnesses.[152] Josephus rationalized women's disqualification as witnesses because of the "levity and boldness of their sex."[153]

---

[151] Josephus, *Antiquities,* IV.8:15. *Encyclopedia Judaica,* 21.161. However, there are exceptions to this standard. "For example, rabbinic literature excludes women altogether as witnesses in a court of law. . . . In the Second Temple period, however, women apparently did serve in such a capacity. For example, one Dead Sea Sect text suggests that wives were encouraged to give evidence against their husbands in the Sect's tribunal (*1Qsa* 1 10-11)." *Jewish Women A Comprehensive Historical Encyclopedia,* Tal Ilan, "Post-Biblical and Rabbinic Women," *jwa.org/encyclopedia.*

[152] *Mishnah*, *Shebuoth,* 4:1, interpreted Leviticus 5:1 as "[The law about] 'an oath of testimony' applies to men but not to women."

[153] Josephus, *Antiquities,* IV.8:15. The full quote reads: "But let not a single witness be credited, but three, or two at the least, and those such whose testimony is confirmed by their good lives. But let not the testimony of women be admitted, on account of the levity and boldness of their sex. Nor let servants be admitted to give testimony, on account of the ignobility of their soul; since it is probable that they may not speak truth, either out of hope of gain, or fear of punishment."

The subject of female witnesses came up later in a rabbinic dialogue in Deuteronomy 19:15, ". . . at the mouth of two or three witnesses, shall the matter be established." One rabbi asked, "Is a woman also qualified to give testimony?" Another answered with a scriptural example from Deuteronomy 19:17. The Scripture explains that when someone presents a false story about another, "then both the men, between whom the controversy is, shall stand before the LORD, before the priests and the judges." Later rabbinic writings concluded that because the Scripture mentioned only two men, then women were excluded.[154] With these and other rationalizations, Jewish leaders kept women from speaking as a witness in legal matters.

Even outside of a court of law, some rabbis would not trust a woman's word without additional proof. On a maiden's wedding night, she had to produce various "tokens of virginity" because "we may not rely on her word, but she must be presumed to have been trampled of man unless she can bring proof for her words."[155] These accounts sound as if a girl or woman were guilty until proven innocent.

Changes by Jesus

Fortunately, Jesus validated a woman's judgment by trusting her word as witness and by treating her as capable of speaking the truth. Over and over again Jesus called and accepted women among His witnesses. Beginning with the birth narratives, we see God authorizing women as witnesses: the priestess Elisabeth, the mother Mary, and the prophetess Anna (Luke 1:41-45; 1:46-55; 2:36-38). But would people at the time of Christ's birth have believed their witnesses?

---

[154] Tal Ilan, *Jewish women in Greco-Roman Palestine* (Peabody, MA: Hendrickson, 1996), 163; "the meaning of the 'two' in the other instance is men and not women." This rabbinical debate dates to the Talmud.
[155] *Mishnah, Ketuboth* 1.7 also 1.6. This example was not recorded until after the time of the New Testament.

The fact that Luke chose to include them in his Gospel

| Zacharias |
| Elisabeth |

gave their words credence in the early church. Luke followed the Lord's example and allowed women to speak as witnesses. Beginning in the temple when the angel Gabriel struck the priest Zacharias dumb, the likely candidate for a witness could not offer a verbal testimony of his vision (though perhaps his nonverbal witness spoke louder).[156] For nine months, his wife, the priestess Elisabeth, witnessed of their miraculous birth. When it was time to name their son, the local leaders wanted to name him after his father, Zacharias. Only Elisabeth was able to give voice, and she corrected the authorities: "Not so; but he shall be called John" (Luke 1:60). Her unsolicited interruption may have offended the local Jewish authorities, but Luke included her voice as part of the prophetic story of her son.

Luke also included the humble testimony of Mary's acceptance of her calling from the angel Gabriel: "Behold the handmaid of the Lord; be it unto me according to thy word" (Luke 1:38).[157] Other prophets testified of Mary as "a precious

---

[156] The New Testament chronologically begins and ends at the temple as recorded in Luke's Gospel, with several temple encounters between (Luke 1:5, 9, "A certain priest named Zacharias . . . his lot was to burn incense when he went into the temple of the Lord;" Luke 24:53, "And were continually in the temple, praising and blessing God. Amen"). After introducing a temple priest and priestess, Luke announced an angel in the temple sanctuary (Luke 1:8-21). We meet at the temple again with the forty-day-old Christ child and his parents (Luke 2:24-25). In the next story, twelve years later, they are back once more at the temple (Luke 2:46). Next Jesus cleansed the temple (John 2:15), followed by His teaching there (Matthew 21:23, 26:55; Mark 14:19; Luke 21:37; John 7:14, 28). The Lord stood outside of the temple and prophesied of its destruction (Matthew 24:2). His death caused the rending of the temple veil (Mark 15:38), yet his apostles continue to preach at the temple daily, praising God and being filled with the Spirit (Acts 2:46-47). Paul received a vision of the Lord in the temple (Acts 22:17). Unmistakably, the temple is central to New Testament events, theology, and empowerment. The temple stands as a witness of the Savior.
[157] "Handmaiden" is the word for female slave (see chapter 8 of this book). This is in part a fulfillment of Joel 2:28-29, "I will pour out my spirit upon all flesh; and your sons and your daughters shall prophesy, your old men

and chosen vessel" (Alma 7:10), and that "she was exceedingly fair and white…most beautiful and fair above all other virgins" (1 Nephi 11:13, 15). By her honored role, she is known as the greatest woman to have lived.

Shortly after Gabriel's visitation to Mary, she eloquently testified to Elisabeth, "My soul doth magnify the Lord, and my spirit hath rejoiced in God my Saviour" (Luke 1:46-47). Mary's witness became a shining example to all generations that followed. Her words seem to have universal application for all women, young and old, who have felt the Spirit of the Lord calling them:

Virgin Mary

> For He has regarded the lowly state of His maidservant; For He who is mighty has done great things for me, and holy is His name. And His mercy is on those who fear Him from generation to generation. He has shown strength with His arm; He has scattered the proud in the imagination of their hearts. He has put down the mighty from their thrones, and exalted the lowly. He has filled the hungry with good things, and the rich He has sent away empty. He has helped His servant Israel, in remembrance of His mercy, as He spoke to our fathers, to Abraham and to his seed forever (Luke 1:48-55, NKJV).

Mary is the role model for all other women who seek to be handmaidens of the Lord and witnesses of Christ.

Forty days following the birth of the Lord, Joseph and Mary and the infant Jesus went to the temple to fulfill the Mosaic law for a woman's purification offering following childbirth (Leviticus 12).[158]

Anna the Prophetess

---

shall dream dreams, your young men shall see visions: And also upon the servants and upon the handmaids in those days will I pour out my spirit."
[158] Leviticus 12:2-4 describes a woman's purification period after childbirth—forty days for a boy and eighty for a girl, to "make an atonement for her, and she shall be cleansed" (Leviticus 12:7). The Mosaic law required two offerings, "the one for the burnt offering, and the other for a sin offering" (Leviticus 12:8). This is part of the reason the number forty

There we meet the third female witness of the Savior, a widow. One of the most devout temple worshipers in the New Testament: the valiant prophetess Anna.[159] She is the only woman in the New Testament given the title prophetess.[160] The widow "departed not from the temple, but served God with fasting and prayers night and day" (Luke 2:37).

Anna's diligence at age eighty-four (or 103 depending on how Luke counted) was rewarded one day when she spiritually recognized the forty-day-old infant Jesus as the promised Messiah: "She coming in that instant gave thanks likewise unto the Lord, and spake of Him to all them that looked for redemption in Jerusalem" (Luke 2:38). Anna raised her voice to all those who hoped for the Messiah. The Greek text is in the imperfect tense, meaning "she kept speaking" or spread abroad her witness of the child.[161] Her role as a prophetess continued as her testimony of the Christ child came from "the Spirit of Prophecy."[162]

---

became synonymous with purification or a purification period in the Bible. An explanation from Second Temple period describes why the purification was different for a male and female. Philo "alludes to this when he says that 'man's formation being more perfect than woman's . . . only required half the time, that is forty days; but woman's nature being less than perfect, took twice as many days—eighty" (Malan, *Adam and Eve*, 210). The Second Temple pseudepigraphic book of *Jubilees* looked to the creation to explain the doubling of time; as Eve was created second, it follows that the birth of daughters should take twice as long for purification (Jubilees 3:14). James VanderKam, *Book of Jubilees* (Sheffield England, Sheffield Academic Press, 2001), 31. We see the same doubling before postpartum bathing: "in the eighth night after the birth of a boy and the sixteenth night after the birth of a girl." Steinberg, *Encyclopedia of Jewish Medical Ethics*, 184.

[159] Anna is the Greek form Hannah, meaning "favor" (1 Samuel 1-2). As Anna joins Simeon in the temple she becomes a second witness. This is Luke's pattern of having two witnesses offer a double proclamation of Jesus' greatness. Luke's Gospel is filled with parallelisms in his examples.

[160] Luke 2:36. See appendix 4. In the Old Testament the title "prophetess" is given to five women: Miriam, Deborah, Huldah, Noadiah and Isaiah's wife (Exodus 15:20; Judges 4:4; 2 Kings 22:14; Nehemiah 6:14; Isa 8:3).

[161] Fitzmyer, *Anchor Bible: Luke I-IX*, 431.

[162] The "Spirit of prophecy" was described by Joseph Smith: "No man is a minister of Jesus Christ, without being a Prophet. No man can be the

Perhaps the clearest witness of Jesus' divinity during His ministry came from a woman. He asked a close friend, Martha,

| Martha As Witness |

if she believed that He had power over death. John recorded her inspired answer of the Lord's divine nature: "Yea, Lord I believe that thou art the Christ [or in Hebrew, the *Messiah*], the Son of God, which should come into the world" (John 11:27). Her vibrant testimony shines as a second witness beside Peter's in Caesarea Philippi, voicing almost the same words.

TABLE 1

Martha (John 11:27)	**Peter** (Matthew 16:16)
She saith unto him, Yea, Lord I believe that Thou art the Christ, the Son of God, which should come into the world.	Simon Peter answered and said, Thou art the Christ, the Son of the living God

The Lord endorsed and fostered Martha's testimony, "I am the resurrection, and the life: he that believeth in me, though he were dead, yet shall he live: And whosoever liveth and believeth in me shall never die. Believest thou this?" (John 11:25-26). Her resounding testimony is one of the few—and possibly one of the most powerful—testimonies of Christ that John included in his Gospel text.

Each of the Gospel writers documented that devout women remained beside Jesus at His cross and at the tomb (Matthew 27:55-56, 61; 28:1; Mark 15:40-41; 16:1; Luke 23:55-56; 24:1-10; John 19:25; 20:1). They also emphasized that these women were the first witnesses of the resurrection.

---

minister of Jesus Christ, except he has the testimony of Jesus & this is the Spirit of Prophecy." Andrew F. Ehat and Lyndon W. Cook, ed., *The Words of Joseph Smith: The Contemporary Accounts of the Nauvoo Discourses of the Prophet Joseph* (Provo, UT: Religious Studies, BYU, 1980), 10-11. Joseph intended this statement to refer to all humanity, not only one gender.

Unfortunately, the social prejudice against women as reliable witnesses also affected the apostles. Initially they did not believe the women who ran from the empty tomb with the angel's message that Jesus had risen (Matthew 28:5-6).

By the time the Gospels were recorded, the Christian authors had learned more of the Lord's expansive teachings, and all four authors honored the women who were at the tomb enough to mention several of them by name as table 2 shows:

TABLE 2

Matt 27:56	Mk 15:40; 16:1	Luke 24:10	John 19:25
Mary Magdalene	Mary Magdalene	Mary Magdalene	Mary Magdalene
Mary mother of James and Joses	Mary mother of James and Joses	Mary mother of James	Mary wife of Cleophas
		Joanna wife of Chuza	
			Jesus' mother
Mother of Zebedee's Children	Salome	Other women	Jesus' mother's sister

At first, trapped in their culture and fears, the apostles did not believe the women's witness: "their words seemed to them as idle tales, and they believed them not" (Luke 24:11). In Mark's Gospel, the women "neither said . . . any thing to any man" (Mark 16:8). Either the story was remembered that way, or they could not trust their witness.[163] Even Jesus' closest companions were originally entrenched in this cultural baggage.

John's Gospel explains that the women's account piqued Peter's and John's curiosity enough that they wanted to see for themselves. After the two men saw the empty tomb they returned to "their own home" (John 20:10). But Mary

| Mary Magdalene Witnesses |

Magdalene could not leave yet; she stood next to the tomb weeping when the resurrected Lord appeared to her. How beautiful and empowering—especially with the cultural view of women—that Jesus chose a woman as His first witness of the miraculous resurrection! This moment is perhaps the most powerful example we have of the Lord tearing down the anti-female societal values of the time.

The Gospel of John honors Mary Magdalene as the first eyewitness of the resurrected Lord. According to John's account, Jesus entrusted her with relaying His message, "go to my brethren, and say unto them, I ascend unto my Father, and your Father; and to my God, and your God" (John 20:17).

This act alone demonstrates Jesus' veneration of women, raising them to a place of legal standing and giving them a voice in His religious order. Combined with the other female witnesses of Jesus' birth, ministry, death, and resurrection, we see the Lord championing women with opportunities and power. This legacy carried into the young apostolic church.

---

[163] David Noel Freedman, ed., *Eerdman's Dictionary of the Bible* (Grand Rapids, MI: Eerdman's Publishing, 2000), 859. A second century Bishop, Papias, claimed that Mark was "Peter's interpreter," according to the Roman Church historian Eusebius (AD 263 -340). For centuries, Christian tradition taught that the Gospel of Mark was actually Peter's message recorded by Mark while he was with Peter imprisoned in Rome. Biblical scholars debate this theory now.

Chapter 2
Women Teach and Serve in Christianity

Of the many ways in which Christ radically altered women's opportunities and roles in the pages in the New Testament, His influence on women's worship is one of the most obvious. In contrast to the limited worship opportunities that existed for women in Judeo-Greco-Roman cultures, Christianity invited women to participate more fully in religious worship. Christian women prayed, prophesied, served, and administered in the church. The New Testament includes numerous expressions of gratitude for women's service, suggesting that their ministry was not only appreciated but also exemplary.[164] This chapter looks at some of these exemplary women in the apostolic church—both named and unnamed. It also addresses some unclear statements in the New Testament —attributed to Paul—that seem to demean women and curb their worship opportunities.

---

[164] Acts 1:14; 9:36; 16:1, 36; 17:4, 12, 34; Romans 1:8; Philippians 4:3; and many more. Often the KJV uses the word "man" or "all" or "brethren," but in the Greek it is not gender specific and originally meant "humanity" or all saints.

I. Women in the Apostolic Church

The New Testament includes the names of forty-five females, at least thirty of whom are described as devoted followers of Christ (the complete list, with scriptural references is in appendix 4). The apostle Paul spotlights many women who worked closely with him in the apostolic church. He variously described these women as co-worker, witness, disciple, servant of the church, sister, mother, wife, yokefellow, deaconess, and one "prominent among the apostles" (Romans 16:7, ISV). We will look closely at faithful women who served in the apostolic church—nine named and three unnamed examples.[165]

Leaders of House-Churches

The term "house-church" is frequently used in New Testament literature to describe early Christian branches of the church that met in the saints' homes.[166] Paul refers to these "house-churches" in his closing remarks to the saints in Corinth when he says, "Aquila and Priscilla salute you much in the Lord, with the church that is in their house" (1 Corinthians 16:19). The saints worshiped and partook of the sacrament in house-churches. The book of Acts includes both house-churches and the temple as places for early Christians to worship: "And they, continuing daily with one accord in the

---

[165] There is not enough scriptural information about the other four women to warrant their placement here, but they are listed in appendix 4.

[166] Everett Ferguson, ed. *Encyclopedia of Early Christianity, 2nd Ed* (Abingdon, England: Routledge, 2013), 546. "None of the earliest house-church meeting places can be positively identified archeologically, as the house-church organization implies that no specific changes were made in the building itself. The earliest evidence of a house converted architecturally into a place of Christian worship is from Dura-Europos, dated c. 241-256. It is a typical house with rooms grouped around a central court." This is located in modern eastern Syria, along the Euphrates River. For more references on house-churches see Colossians 4:15; Philemon 1:2; Romans 16:5, 10-16, 23.

temple, and breaking bread from house to house" (Acts 2:46; also see 1:13-14; 20:7-12, 20).

The New Testament includes four exemplary women who led house-churches. Their stories provide a glimpse into the significant contributions to early Christian worship made by females. Men were usually the heads of households, but if for some reason the men of the house were not able to lead, a woman may have taken charge. Records throughout the Roman Empire attest that several women acted as a head of their household.[167]

1. Mary, the Mother of John Mark (Acts 12:12)

The first house-church mentioned in the apostolic church belonged to a wealthy Jerusalem disciple named Mary (the sixth of seven women mentioned with the same name—see appendix 4). We may safely assume that her husband was dead because she appears to have led her own household. She became a prominent woman in the church and the mother of the evangelist John Mark.[168] Luke recounts that after the Apostle Peter's miraculous release from prison by an angel, "he came to the house of Mary the mother of John, whose surname was Mark; where many were gathered together praying" (Acts 12:12). The rest of the book of Acts suggests that the Jerusalem

---

[167] Carol Meyers, Toni Craven, Ross Shepard Kraemer, ed. *Women in Scripture: A Dictionary of Named and Unnamed Women in the Hebrew Bible, the Apocryphal/Deuterocanonical Books, and the New Testament* (Grand Rapids, MI: Eerdmans, 2001), 63.

[168] David Noel Freedman, ed., *Eerdmans Dictionary of the Bible* (Grand Rapids, MI: Eerdmans Publishing, 2000), 859-861. John Mark is first mentioned in Acts 12:25; 15:37. We know him from the New Testament as the companion of both Paul and Barnabas, and nephew to Barnabas. The early Christian leaders, Papias (c. 120), Irenaeus (c. 180), Clement of Alexandria (c. 195), and Eusebius (c. 315) refer to Mark as Peter's scribe in writing the Gospel of Mark. However, modern critical biblical scholars doubt this second to fourth century claim. David W. Bercot, ed., *A Dictionary of Early Christian Beliefs* (Peabody, MA: Hendrickson Publishers, 1998), 422-433.

saints often gathered there, and that her home became a Christian center for refuge and hospitality.

2. *Lydia (Acts 16:14, 40)*

One of the women who opened her home for church meetings and who "labored with [Paul] in the gospel" was Lydia (Acts 16:14-30, 40), a wealthy land owner and business-woman and "a seller of purple." She housed Paul as well as his companions (Silas, Luke and Timothy) on his second gentile mission when they arrived in the city of Philippi. [169] Lydia was originally from Thyatira, a city in Asia Minor (modern-day Turkey) in the province of Lydia, which is possibly the source of her name (Acts 16:14). The Lydians were famous for dying textiles, which may explain why Lydia sold the expensive dye known as "purple."[170] As a seller of the purple she would have walked in wealthy circles and possibly held prominence in society.

The Book of Acts describes Lydia as a gentile who "worshiped God." This title was used to identify investigators or those who embraced monotheism with Jehovah as their God, but not necessarily all the tenets of Judaism at that time (Acts 16:14). These gentile proselytes who accepted monotheism and upheld the laws of Moses were still welcome to worship with the Jews even without being constrained to live all 613 of the

---

[169] The Roman capital city of Philippi was founded by Philip, the father of Alexander the Great, as a frontier fortress. The nearby gold mines helped make him rich. It became a Roman colony when Octavius (who became Augustus Caesar) and Antony conquered Brutus and Cassius (who committed suicide there). Philippi was a walled city with a military and agricultural center. Not many Jews lived there.

[170] In the ancient world, "purple" was a rich dye associated with royal or expensive fabrics. The valuable substance was extracted from crustaceans that grew along their Mediterranean coastline. For most of biblical history the Phoenicians or Syrians controlled the indigenous harvest of this dye, ensuring a monopoly (see Exodus 25:4; 2 Chronicles 2:7, 14; 3:14; Proverbs 31:22; Song of Solomon. 3:10; Mark 15:17-20; John 19:2-5; Revelation 17:4; 18:12, 16).

Mosaic laws. This was especially significant for men, as this meant they did not need to undergo the often-fatal adult circumcision.[171]

Lydia met Paul during a Jewish worship service. When the four missionaries arrived in Philippi, they "went out of the city by a river side," on the Sabbath, because "prayer was wont to be made" (Acts 16:13). Paul and his companions "sat down, and spake unto the women which resorted thither" (Acts 16:13).[172] The "Lord opened" Lydia's heart and "she attended unto the things which were spoken of Paul" (Acts 16:14). She was not only baptized, but also influenced all of her household to convert to Christianity.[173]

Her generosity and love for the Lord's servants led her to invite Paul and his companions to stay in her home: "If ye have judged me to be faithful to the Lord, come into my house, and

---

[171] Alan F. Segal, *Paul the Convert: The Apostolate and Apostasy of Saul the Pharisee* (New Haven, CT: Yale University, 1990), 105. W. D. Davies, *Paul and Rabbinic Judaism* (Philadelphia, PA: Fortress Press, 1980), 121, explains the steps for Jewish conversion: "Now the process by which a man was made a proselyte was threefold: it consisted of circumcision, immersion in water (i.e., baptism), and the presentation of an offering in the temple. Of these rites baptism assumed a growing importance."

[172] Acts 16:1-4, describes Timothy joining Paul and Silas on their second gentile mission. The text also suggests that Luke joined Paul's missionary force. In the book of Acts, when the narrative includes "we" passages, it is assumed that the author, Luke, joined Paul. By studying the "we" passages, bible scholars assume that Luke stayed in Philippi—or at least did not rejoin Paul for seven years (approximately AD 51-58) until Paul came back to Philippi. (It is in Acts 20:6 that the "we" pronoun joins the story line again.) The complete "we" passages are: Acts 16:10, 12, 17 (second mission between Troas and Philippi); 20:5-15; 21:1-18 (end of third mission from Philippi to Jerusalem); 27:1-28:16 (Paul as a prisoner from Caesarea to Rome). Also, it appears that Luke was with Paul during his first (Colossians 4:14; Philippians 24) and second Roman imprisonments (1 Timothy 4:11).

[173] We do not know if the Christian conversion of "households" were conscripted or individual choices. Knowing the importance of agency in Christ's church, I would be surprised if the apostles baptized any against their will. That said, I presume in some cases, a servant may have felt like an eight-year-old Mormon child who eagerly accepts baptism to belong to the same organization as the rest of the family.

abide there" (Acts 16:15). The four missionaries moved in and remained there until forced to leave due to persecution (Acts 16:40). Luke recorded that Paul was whipped and then imprisoned, but, after a miraculous release (the walls of the prison collapsed in an earthquake, culminating in the conversion of the jailer), Paul and his companions returned briefly to Lydia's house: "and when they had seen the brethren, they comforted them, and departed" (Acts 14:40).[174]

In addition to her home being a refuge for the apostle and missionaries, Lydia's home also became the "house-church" or location for Christian converts in Philippi to worship for years (Philippians 1:3-7; 4:1).

3. *Chloe (1 Corinthians 1:11)*

The apostle Paul began his scolding letter to the saints in Corinth with a report from those "which are of the house of Chloe" (1 Corinthians 1:11). Paul must have known that her house had a good reputation and was trusted among the saints, because he acknowledged the "house of Chloe" as the source of his information (which was especially delicate, considering that the feedback was negative). Paul probably developed his respect of Chloe and her household during his eighteen-month-long stay in Corinth on his second mission, and he renewed that friendship when he returned to Corinth at the end of his third mission.

Between Paul's first two visits to Corinth, Chloe's people reported to the apostle that the Corinthian saints had "contentions among [themselves] . . . every one of you saith, I am of Paul; and I of Apollos; and I of Cephas; and I of Christ"

---

[174] Paul wrote to the Philippian saints over a decade after Lydia's conversion. In the Epistle, he mentions two other women by name, Euodias and Syntyche. As he exhorts the saints to unity, he calls on the two ladies to "be of the same mind in the Lord" (Philippians 4:2).

(1 Corinthians 1:12).[175] These divisions may have been within or between multiple house-churches in Corinth. After Paul's eighteen months there, he sent Timothy and other missionaries to serve in Corinth: "I have planted, Apollos watered; but God gave the increase" (1 Corinthians 3:6). With a large population and strong missionary force, the saints most likely had multiple house-churches with various leaders, but only Chloe is singled out in 1 Corinthians as one who led a house esteemed by Paul to be a reputable source.

4. Priscilla / Prisca[176] (Acts 18:2-3, 18-19, 26; Romans 16:3-5; 1 Corinthians 16:19; 2 Timothy 4:19)

Paul first met Priscilla and her husband Aquila when he arrived in Corinth on his second apostolic mission. Priscilla and Aquila were Jewish refugees who had fled Rome when rioting between the two groups prompted Claudius Caesar (reigned AD 41-54) to expel all Jews and Christians from the capital city (Acts 18:2-3).[177] However, due to the vast number of Jews in Rome, the task of enforcing the edict became too daunting. Priscilla and Aquila had already fled to Greece (Acts 18:2) by the time Claudius had modified his edict to forbid Jews and their splinter groups, including Christians, from holding meetings.[178]

---

[175] Paul heard several other problems among the Corinthian saints: "It is reported commonly. . ." which may have come from the same trusted source of Chloe or her people (1 Corinthians 5:1).

[176] Paul consistently refers to her in his letters as Prisca, while Luke writes out Priscilla.

[177] Thirty years earlier (c. AD 19), Tiberius Caesar had also expelled the Jews from Rome for a time. See appendix 2. Claudius Caesar's reaction against the Jews and their splinter groups may also have been tied up in the Jewish problems in Palestine that accompanied Agrippa I's death; a resurgence of Zealots developed from AD 48-52.

[178] F. F. Bruce, *New Testament History*, 295-304. Regardless of Claudius' attempts to suppress Jewish / Christian arguments, Christianity grew during his reign, thanks in part to the efforts of missionaries like Priscilla and her husband.

The couple generously welcomed Paul into their new home in Corinth as a fellow Christian and "because he was a tentmaker" (Acts 18:3, NIV). Priscilla and Aquila converted from Judaism to Christianity before Paul moved in with them.[179] Paul presumably worked with Aquila making canvas or leather tents to support himself (Acts 20:34; 1 Corinthians 4:12; 9:12; 1 Thessalonians 2:9; 2 Thessalonians 3:8).[180] He stayed with them for a year and a half, after which his hosts joined him as missionaries and sailed with him to Ephesus (Acts 18:18).

It appears that our heroic couple may have worked as missionaries for almost a decade. We know that they were back in Rome by approximately AD 57 because Paul included a personalized note to them in his Epistle to the Romans (Romans 16:3). He refers to them as "my helpers in Christ Jesus: Who have for my life laid down their own necks: unto whom not only I give thanks, but also all the churches of the Gentiles" (Romans 16:3-4). They must have also hosted a house-church in Rome, because Paul then greets "the church that is in their house" (Romans 16:5). Priscilla and Aquila became Paul's lifelong friends (1 Corinthians 16:19), and they stand as ideal examples of a Christian couple unified in the Lord's work.

Women honored for Faith and Good Works

5. Tabitha [in Greek, Dorcas] (Acts 9:36-42)

The virtuous disciple Tabitha came from the Judean coastal community of Joppa and holds the distinction of being the only woman in the New Testament referred to by the feminine form of the Greek word "disciple / *mathetria.*" (However, the Greek of Acts 9:36 suggests that there were

---

[179] Ronald Brownrigg, *Who's Who in the New Testament* (NYC, NY: Routledge, 2002), 16.

[180] Richard Lloyd Anderson, *Understanding Paul* (Salt Lake City, UT: Deseret Book, 1983)*,* 335–336. Robert J. Matthews, *Selected Writings of Robert J. Matthews: Gospel Scholars Series*, 287–288.

others.)[181] As a Christian disciple, she broke the pharisaic restrictions against women and became a female pupil of the gospel and a public figure among the needy. The Christian community knew Tabitha for her contributions of time and service: "she was always doing good and helping the poor," which included making for others "shirts and coats" (Acts 9:37, NIV, 9:39, ISV).

Bible readers know her best as the woman whom Peter raised from the dead, as recorded in the book of Acts. Luke, the author, begins Tabitha's story as she becomes ill. Two men run to the neighboring town to ask the apostle Peter to help them. Acts 9:39-40 reads:

> When he was come, they brought him into the upper chamber: and all the widows stood by him weeping, and shewing the coats and garments which Dorcas made, while she was with them. But Peter put them all forth, and kneeled down, and prayed; and turning him to the body said, Tabitha, arise. And she opened her eyes: and when she saw Peter, she sat up.

Her healing had a great impact "throughout all Joppa; and many believed in the Lord" (Acts 9:42). Tabitha's healing allowed others to develop faith, thus opening the way for their spiritual healing.

In Luke's two volumes of Scripture (the Gospel and Acts), he recorded three similar miracles that were performed first by Jesus, then by Peter, and finally by Paul. Luke introduced Tabitha as his example of Peter raising the dead (Acts 9:40), which paralleled Jesus raising Jairus' daughter (Luke 8:52-54), and Paul raising Eutychus (Acts 20:9-10). Luke organized the structure of his two books using parallel comparisons between the Lord and His apostles. Luke's Gospel tells of these three people—two females and one male—who were brought back from the dead to stand as witnesses that

---

[181] Meyers, Craven, Kraemer, ed., *Women in Scripture*, 159.

God's power, whether the healing is given by Jesus or His servants, "is the same" (D&C 1:38). Mark also adds that miracles "follow them that believe" (Mark 16:17).[182] Tabitha's restored life acts as a powerful female witness.

6 & 7. Eunice and Lois (Acts 16:1-3; 2 Timothy 1:5)

In his Epistle to Timothy, Paul praises Timothy's faithful mother and grandmother by name: Eunice and Lois. He commends these two faithful women for teaching their son and grandson, respectively, about Christ. Timothy's father was a Gentile, so the women had taken it upon themselves to teach him. Timothy learned so well what Paul said: "I am reminded of your sincere faith, which first lived in your grandmother Lois and in your mother Eunice and, I am persuaded, now lives in you also . . . how from infancy you have known the Holy Scriptures" (2 Timothy 1:5; 3:15; NIV). Eunice and Lois instilled their faith into Timothy, by fostering a love of the holy word from his "infancy" (2 Timothy 3:15, NIV). Whether these two women were literate or simply had many Scriptures memorized we are not told, though they provided Timothy with opportunities to study, inspiring him by the example of their faith. The enthusiasm for the Scriptures exemplified by this mother and grandmother was contagious, such that their posterity developed a deep love for God's words.

We do not know when Lois and Eunice converted to Christianity. Perhaps it took place during Paul's first apostolic mission to their home town Lystra. Yet we do know that by Paul's second and third apostolic missions, Timothy had joined him in the missionary force (Acts 16:1-2; 18:5; 19:22; 20:4). Through their work together, Timothy became like family to Paul: "Timothy, my own son in the faith" (1Timothy 1:2, 18; 2 Timothy 1:1-2; 1 Corinthians 4:17).[183] Rather than emphasizing

---

[182] Outside of Luke's writings, John includes the story of Lazarus raised from dead (John 11:43).

[183] Timothy is mentioned in seven of the New Testament Epistles, but his gentile birth father is left unnamed. It appears that Luke felt Timothy's

his own role in developing Timothy's spirituality, Paul credits those two most influential women in Timothy's early life—Lois and Eunice—for teaching and preparing him. These women demonstrated the crucial principle that our most efficacious missionary work is often within our own families. One of the greatest gifts a parent can give a child is an inheritance of faith, as Eunice and Lois modeled.[184] These two women lived the truths of Christianity to the fullest, blessing their posterity with faith even in a divided-faith home.

8. Phebe (Romans 16:1-2)

We assume Phebe was a gentile convert to Christianity because her name comes from Greek mythology.[185] Paul recommends her to the Roman saints as a stalwart member and laborer in the kingdom: "I commend unto you Phebe our sister, which is a servant of the church which is at Cenchrea: That ye receive her in the Lord, as becometh saints, and that ye assist her in whatsoever business she hath need of you: for she hath been a succourer of many, and of myself also" (Romans 16:1). He also expresses appreciation for her generous service. He called her "sister," just as he called his beloved Timothy "brother" (1 Thessalonians 3:2 and 2 Corinthians 1:1). His familial words suggest a kindred partnership.

An analysis of two of the Greek words used to describe Phebe sheds even more light on her role among the Corinthian saints. First she is described as "servant / *diakonos*" (Romans 16:1). The New Testament uses the word "*diakonos*" thirty times, which is translated in the KJV as either "minister" (twenty times), "servant" (seven times), or "deacon" (three times). Paul's choice of words implies that Phebe had a church

---

mother and grandmother were more important to Christianity than his father, so he includes their names—Lois and Eunice.

[184] Anderson, *Understanding Paul,* 362; also see appendix 2.

[185] Meyers, Craven, Kraemer, *Women in Scripture,* 135-136. *Phoibe* is a female name, but it was used "in the masculine form, [as] an epithet of the Greek god Apollo."

assignment and was acting under the authority of her church office.

Another definition for *diakonos* is the "discharge[r] of certain obligations in the community, . . . the servant of a spiritual power." [186] It describes one who cares for the poor, assists with missionary work, or has an office as a servant of God. Thus, a few English Bibles translate her title more literally as, "deaconess" or "deacon" (e.g., RSV, NJB, NRSV, and NIV).

Romans 16:1-2

NIV	YLT	ISV
I commend to you our sister Phoebe, a deacon of the church in Cenchreae. I ask you to receive her in the Lord in a way worthy of his people and to give her any help she may need from you, for she has been the benefactor of many people, including me.	And I commend you to Phebe our sister—being a ministrant of the assembly that is in Cenchrea—that ye may receive her in the Lord, as doth become saints, and may assist her in whatever matter she may have need of you— for she also became a leader of many, and of myself.	Now I commend to you our sister Phoebe, a deaconess in the church at Cenchrea. Welco me her in the Lord as is appropriate for saints, and provide her with anything she may need from you, for she has assisted many people, including me.

Whatever the translation, Paul communicates that Phebe received a call of responsibility to minister in the early church. She then acted in conjunction with her church position and used

---

[186] G. Kittel, ed., Geoffrey W. Bromiley, translator, *Theological Dictionary of the New Testament* (Grand Rapids MI: Eerdmans Publishing, 1965), ii. 87-89.

her means and influence to build the church. Christianity opened the way for her to expand her service and exert her influence into her church community.

The second word used to describe Phebe, "succourer / *prostatis,*" is used only once in the KJV New Testament (Romans 16:2). It designates a woman who is a "protectress, patroness, helper."[187] Other English translations use "sponsor" (CEB), "helper" (ASV, NAS, NKJV, RSV, WEB), "patron" (ESV), and "benefactor" (NRSV, HCS, NIV). The noun can also "denote a position as a leader, president or presiding officer."[188] Although no English translation reads "Relief Society President," I think her responsibilities may have been similar.

She may also have consecrated her wealth for the benefit of the church, as she is called a benefactor or patron in behalf of Paul and others (Romans 16:2, NIV, ESV). Certainly, he respected her and opened the door for her to receive the same esteem from the church leaders in Rome. Phebe traveled on official church business as a missionary or church worker under the apostle's direction, and it appears that she personally transported Paul's Epistle to the Roman saints.[189] Her story offers the modern reader a glance at the leadership opportunities held by women in early Christianity.

9. Junia (Romans 16:7)

The book of Romans introduces another outstanding woman named Junia (a Latin name commonly given to Roman girls) who labored with Paul.[190] In the closing chapter of the

---

[187] Walter Bauer, revised by F. Wilbur Gingrich, Frederick W. Danker, *A Greek–English Lexicon of the New Testament and Other Early Christina Literature, 2nd ed.* (Chicago, IL: University of Chicago Press, 1979), 718.
[188] Meyers, Craven, Kraemer, *Women in Scripture,* 135.
[189] Ibid. This conclusion comes from examining other mail carriers for Paul, like Epaphroditus in Philippians 2:25-30 and Tychicus in Colossians 4:7-9.
[190] Ibid., 107. Scholars who have looked for the name Junia, found that it "occurs over 250 times among inscriptions from ancient Rome alone," but it is always used as a female's name, never a male.

Epistle to the Romans, Paul asks the Roman saints to "Greet Andronicus and Junia, my kinsmen and my fellow prisoners." The Greek word for "kinsman" had a broad definition, so Andronicus and Junia could have been close family members or distant relatives connected through the tribes of Israel or Benjamin.

Paul mentions Andronicus and Junia together, as if they were married or siblings. The two of them became Christians before Paul's own conversion, "who also were in Christ before me" (Romans 16:7). This information about their long-standing discipleship explains why they were "well known to the apostles" (Romans 16:7, ESV). The Greek text of this verse also suggests that Junia was even "prominent among the apostles" (CEB, RSV, NRSV). Other translators interpret the phrase to mean that Andronicus and Junia were actual apostles, "outstanding among the apostles" (Romans 16:7, NIV), or "leaders among the apostles" (NIRV). The Greek can be read either way.[191] The word "*apostolos*" means "ambassador of the Gospel; officially a commissioner of Christ . . . [a] messenger, he that is sent."[192] We do not know what church assignments Junia and Andronicus filled. What we do know is that Junia was a noble woman of great faith, a long term member—despite persecution and imprisonment—and a great witness of Christ.

---

[191] Of the eighty-one times we find *apostolos* in the New Testament, the KJV translated it seventy-eight times as "apostle," twice as "messenger," and once as "one sent." Of the four Gospels, only the book of Luke uses "*apostolos*" regularly, with Mathew and Mark using it once each and John not at all. Luke uses it to identify Jesus' closest companions or the Quorum of the Twelve apostles (Luke 6:13). Yet as the church grew, the rest of the biblical writers seemed to differentiate between members of the "Twelve" and other "apostles" or "those sent." In addition to the original Twelve apostles of the Lord, the New Testament refers to "*apostolos*" as Matthias (Acts 1:26), James the Lord's brother (Galatians 1:19), Paul (Romans1:1; Galatians 1:1, 17, etc.), Barnabas (Acts 14:14), Apollo (1 Corinthians 4:6, 9; 3:4-6, 22), Timothy and Silvanus (1Thessalonians 1:1 with 2:6), and possibly, Junia and Andronicus (Romans16:7).

[192] James Strong, *The New Strong's New Exhaustive Concordance of the Bible* (Nashville, Atlanta, London, Vancouver, TN: Thomas Nelson Publishers, 1995), 12; Greek dictionary for "*apostolos*."

Unnamed Women

The New Testament contains over twice the number of references to unnamed women as it does to named women. From fictitious women in Jesus' parables to women as real as His own sisters, the New Testament records the stories of 111 anonymous women.[193] In Scripture, unnamed does not mean unnoticed or unimportant. Appendix 4 includes all 180 women referenced in the New Testament. In addition to some of the best known unnamed women mentioned previously (i.e., the Samaritan woman at the well and the woman with a twelve-year hemorrhage), two groups of unnamed women deserve specific attention, as they stand out as energized disciples in the apostolic church: Philip's four prophetess daughters and the sisters from Philippi, including Paul's "yokefellow" (Philippians 4:3).

1. Four Prophetesses

Luke records that Philip the evangelist from Caesarea had four prophetic daughters: "four daughters, virgins, which did prophesy" (Acts 21:8-9).[194] With only six words preserved about them, we learn that the girls acted as instruments in God's work, were morally pure, possessed the Spirit of the Lord, and actively used the gift of prophecy to bless others. Because "the testimony of Jesus is the spirit of prophecy," we can surmise that the girls had testimonies of Jesus the Christ as their Savior

---

[193] Appendix 4 lists 45 named women, 94 unnamed actual women, 14 unnamed fictional women, and 27 general references to women. Although the mother of the Lord is named in the synoptic Gospels, John does not name her, but refers to her as "mother of the Lord," so she receives two references in the appendix, but I do not count her twice.

[194] Phillip is one of the men chosen to serve the widows in Acts 6:3, "Look ye out among you seven men of honest report, full of the Holy Ghost and wisdom, whom we may appoint," which list also includes Stephen.

and Redeemer (Revelation 19:10).[195] About the same time, Paul admonishes all the saints in Corinth to seek the gift of prophecy (1 Corinthians 12:10, 31). Regardless of whether the sisters recognized this apostolic endorsement, they were inspired to use this gift of the Spirit (Acts 21:9). In this signal verse, we learn a great deal about Philip's four daughters and honor each of them as a saint and prophetess of God.[196]

2. The Sisters from Philippi

On Paul's second apostolic mission, he felt a special call to Philippi, a chief city of Macedonia (Acts 16:12-40).[197] A dozen years later when Paul was imprisoned (possibly in Rome), the Philippian saints sent someone to help him. Paul wrote to thank the saints for their thoughtfulness and faithfulness.[198] In the last phrase of Philippians 4:3, Paul

---

[195] Joseph Smith confirmed John the Revelator's message in a sermon, when he spoke, "John the Revelator says that the testimony of Jesus is the Spirit of prophicy [sic]. Now if any man has the testimony of Jesus has he not the spirit of prophecy and if he has the spirit of prophicy [sic]. I ask is he not a prophet and if a prophet will[,] he can receive revalation [sic]" (Ehat and Cook, Words of Joseph Smith, 230).

[196] The word "prophetess" is used eight times in the Bible to describe several women (Luke 2:36-38; Revelation 2:20; Exodus 15:20, Judges 4:4; 2 Kings 22:14; Nehemiah 6:14; and Isaiah 8:3); although the word is not defined. Most refer to women who prophesied, though in Isaiah, "the prophetess" meant she was the wife of the prophet. Philip's daughters are not included in that number, although perhaps they should be, as Acts 21:9 reads "virgins, which did prophesy."

[197] Paul went to Philippi following his vision that called him to northern Greece (Macedonia): "there stood a man of Macedonia, and prayed him, saying, Come over into Macedonia, and help us" (Acts 16:9). Paul, Timothy, and Silas immediately left Troas in Asia and entered Europe via northern Greece (c. AD 50-52). Philippi was located at the foot of Mount Pagaeus on the highway Via Egnatia that links the east and west across the Roman Empire. The city, ten miles inland, was the "chief city" in the north-eastern region of Greece (Acts 16:12).

[198] The Philippians sent Epaphroditus, a companion and co-worker to help Paul in prison. At the time the letter was written, Epaphroditus was recovering from an illness and returning home (Philippians 4:18; 2:25-26).

specifically thanks the "women which labored with me in the gospel," establishing the church in Philippi (Philippians 4:3). From an ancient perspective, Paul's acknowledgment of those women shows a major innovation to Judeo-Greco-Roman worship. It suggests that women had the opportunity to serve in a religious setting, and that they were most likely testifying and witnessing in public—all of which Paul's Pharisaic upbringing prohibited. His expression of gratitude speaks not only of his appreciation for the women, but also of his willingness to broadcast the women's example to other Christians. He empowers women with opportunities to serve and trusts them to help build the Kingdom of God.

3. Yokefellow

In the same Epistle to the Philippians, Paul asks his "yokefellow" for special help: "I intreat thee also, true yokefellow, help those women which labored with me in the gospel" (Philippians 4:3). This verse tells us not only that Paul valued the women who served with him, but also that another woman worked side by side with the missionaries and apostles. This term "yokefellow" expresses a close relationship and is evidence of women's new roles in the nascent Christian church. By giving instructions to *"help"* the women in the ministry, we see his sensitivity to the needs of women in Philippi.

Paul's personal note to his "true yokefellow" in this verse has piqued the interest of biblical students for centuries (Philippians 4:3). To whom did Paul refer when he used the tender title of yokefellow / *suzugos*? The Greek word means "co-yoked . . . *colleague*," and comes from the root *suzeugnumi*, "to yoke together . . . in marriage."[199] In today's parlance the terms "soul mate," "loyal companion," "colleague," or "spouse" might be used. These definitions share similarities to that of the word "help meet / *'ezer*"—"an authority corresponding to

---

[199] Strong, *Exhaustive Concordance of the Bible,* 85. Greek dictionary of "yokefellow / *suzugos.*"

him"—which described the relationship between Adam and Eve (Genesis 2:18, KJV, ISV).[200] While we do not know with certainty the gender of Paul's *yokefellow*, the context of verse 3 (an exhortation to, "help those women") allows us to assume that she was indeed a female.[201] Clement of Alexandria (who was writing c. AD 200 and worked from earlier sources) identifies the "yokefellow" from Philippians 4:2 as Paul's wife.[202] If that were the case, it implies that she, too, experienced a change of heart, converting to Christianity, and was similarly devoted and hard-working in the cause of Christ.

Paul's Marriage. Whoever the yokefellow was, as a strict Pharisee (Acts 26:5) Paul would have most certainly married when he was a young man. He had to comply with Jewish protocol, which pressed all boys to marry close to age eighteen.[203] Significant commandments given to every young man included marriage;[204] at one point Paul boasts, "touching the righteousness which is in the law, [I am] blameless" (Philippians 3:6). We also find scriptural evidence of Paul's marriage in 1 Corinthians 9:5, wherein he claimed to have "power to lead about a sister, a wife, as well as other apostles,

---

[200] The forthcoming biblical translation *Transparent English Bible* is more allegiant to the literal text. It honors the words over accepted interpretation, modern grammar, or dogma. It translates "help meet" as "his one before."

[201] Other scholars suggest the "'yokefellow' was a bishop or overseer." James Dunn, John Rogerson, *Eerdmans Commentary of the Bible* (Grand Rapids, MI: Eerdmans, 2003), 1401.

[202] Clement of Alexandria, *Stromata* ("Miscellanies") 3.6.74-76, also cited in Eusebius, *Ecclesiastical History* 3:30.

[203] *Mishnah*, *Avoth*, 5:21. Also as a "young man / *neanias*," Saul acts as a witness for the Sanhedrin in Acts 7:58, which would have required compliance with this very important Jewish protocol. Unlike the modern English usage, "young man / *neanias*" in New Testament Greek covered a broad span of years between ages twenty-four and forty. William F. Arndt et al., *Greek-English Lexicon of the New Testament, 2nd ed*. (Chicago: University of Chicago Press, 1979).

[204] *Mishnah*, *Avoth* 5:21 lists the ideal man's life including, "[eighteen] to the bride chamber." See chapter 4 under "Marriage," and chapter 7 under "Children's education."

and as the brethren of the Lord, and Cephas [Peter]." Paul denounces those who preached celibacy in his list of wickedness: "The Spirit speaketh expressly, that in the latter times some shall depart from the faith, giving heed to seducing spirits, and doctrines of devils . . . Forbidding to marry . . . which God hath created to be received with thanksgiving of them which believe and know the truth" (1 Timothy 4:1-3). Regardless of who Paul's wife—or his yokefellow—was, Philippians 4:3 speaks of men and women working in harmony to build the church.

II. A Puzzling Passage in 1 Timothy 2:9-15

The Epistles attributed to Paul speak positively in at least twelve examples of women teaching or preaching in the church.[205] Unlike these positive illustrations, a passage in 1 Timothy, which reduces woman's opportunity for participation in church services, seems inconsistent and sticks out like a sore thumb. Either 1 Timothy 2:9-15 is incongruous with the other dozen examples, or we have misunderstood the author's intent regarding Timothy. This paradoxical passage deserves to be addressed, if only to show that it clashes with the teachings of Christ and the majority of the apostles.

In nearly every chapter of 1 Timothy, the author warns against the problem of false and inappropriate teachers (e.g., 1

---

[205] Looking at whole Pauline sphere, references that show support of women teaching include: Romans 12:7; 16:1-2; 1 Corinthians 12:28-29; Galatians 6:5-6, "*hekastos* / everyone;" Ephesians 4:8, "*anthropos* / male or female," 4:11, 29; Philippians 4:3, 2 Timothy 2:2; Titus 2:3-4; also see Acts 18:26). Modern critical biblical scholars question the Pauline authorship of the pastoral letters and others. Only seven Epistles are generally accepted as pure Pauline (Romans, 1 & 2 Corinthians, Galatians, Philippians, 1 Thessalonians and Philemon). However, in this book, I refer to the author as Paul of the entire traditional corpus (Romans through Hebrews), even though that is debated at present by scholars.

Timothy 1:3; 2:12; 3:2; 4:11; 6:2, 3).[206] It is as if a misty fog of apostasy were already seeping into the new church.[207] Paul (the traditional author) writes as the older and more experienced apostle guiding his beloved younger leader, Timothy, as the latter supervised the region of Ephesus (1 Timothy 1:3).[208] Paul also knew that area of the church, as he had lived with the saints in Ephesus for three years during an earlier mission (Acts 19:1, 20:31). Tradition holds that the apostle John also lived and presided there at one time.[209] With these two apostles living, teaching, and supervising the region of Ephesus, we can imagine that the saints in Ephesus had been well taught.

In this letter, the author counsels men on how to pray appropriately and respectfully (1 Timothy 2:8).[210] His next words act as a linking phrase, "In like manner also . . .," as he advises women. We might assume that Paul will continue his discussion on appropriate prayer, but he does not, perhaps because praying in anger or with doubts was not a problem for them. Instead, he counsels women to "adorn themselves in modest apparel, with shamefacedness and sobriety; not with broided hair, or gold, or pearls, or costly array; but (which becometh women professing godliness) with good works" (1 Timothy 2:9-10).

---

[206] William Farmer, ed., *The International Bible Commentary* (Collegeville, MN: Liturgical Press, 1998), 1733. "First Timothy could be entitled, 'The Gospel of Paul in Conflict with False Teaching.'"

[207] Anderson, *Understanding Paul*, 317, 344, 371-373.

[208] Ibid., 314-17. Richard Lloyd Anderson supports the traditional dates of the writing of 1 Timothy to fall sometime between AD 63 and 66 after Paul's first Roman imprisonment, during another Pauline Mediterranean ministry. It appears that Paul taught Timothy on his first Gentile mission in Lystra, after which Timothy joined Paul on his second apostolic mission, and became a beloved companion ever after (Acts 16:2).

[209] Bromiley, *The International Standard Bible Encyclopedia,* 1.171, ". . . however, in harmony with the well-founded tradition that Ephesus was the scene of John's later activity."

[210] Paul singles out "men / male / *aner*" in verse and gives them specific instruction on how to pray "lifting up holy hands, without wrath and doubting" (1 Timothy 2:8).

Some of the words in the KJV are archaic and can lead to misunderstandings throughout this difficult passage, but it is evident that the author wants Christian women to replace worldliness and self-promotion with selfless service.[211] Starting with the KJV phrase "shamefacedness and sobriety," a few twentieth century translations can help clarify 1 Timothy 2:9.

1 Timothy 2:9

KJV	JB	NAS	RSV	Welch-Hall[212]
Shame-facedness and sobriety	Quietly and modestly	Modestly and discreetly	Modestly, and sensibly	In good taste, in a manner that brings honorable respect

The author sees a specific problem with some women's materialistic desires and prideful attitudes. Four times in the same letter, he cautions those who tried to impress others by their appearance (1 Timothy 5:6, 13; 6:9, 17). He contrasts eternal and superficial priorities.

It appears that Paul's concern with women's worldliness was only a tangent to the larger problem of misplaced values and false teaching infiltrating the church community (1 Timothy 6:3-5). His specific concern with women's hair (verse 9) may stem from the fact that for generations, Jewish culture required

---

[211] The churches under Timothy's care in Ephesus were not the only ones with this problem. In the book of Revelation, John describes the great harlot and mother of abomination with similar ornaments: "the woman was arrayed in purple and scarlet colour and decked with gold and precious stones and pearls" (Revelation 17:4). Peter, too, disapproved of women who prioritized their worldly adornments over inner goodness: "Your beauty should reside, not in outward adornment—the braiding of the hair or jewelry, or dress—but in the inmost centre of your being, with its imperishable ornament, a gentle quiet spirit which is of high value in the sight of God" (1 Peter 3:3-4, NEB).
[212] John W. Welch and John Hall, *Charting the New Testament* (Provo, UT: FARMS, 2002), 15-14.

moral women to hide or cover their hair. (The Talmud also lists several rules for men's hair.[213]) As we discussed in chapter 1, Pharisaic Jews insisted that a woman veil herself head to toe when she left her home.[214] If that same woman converted to Christianity, she then had the freedom of going out with her hair uncovered. Some women may have over reacted with their new freedom and concentrated more time and money on their hair adornments than on more worthwhile or charitable activities. Or perhaps part of the problem may be that male Jewish-Christian leaders (possibly even the converted Pharisee Paul) found the women's new freedom in dress and uncovered hair too startling.

With this as context, let us now take a close look at the first puzzling verse: "Let the woman learn in silence with all subjection" (1 Timothy 2:11).[215] First of all, any encouragement for women to learn the gospel should be seen as great progress and as a positive cultural breakthrough. For many previous generations women were kept from studying their Scriptures at all, and now that prohibition is clearly lifted. Secondly, Paul's pharisaic background taught that women should remain quiet around men.[216] A woman joining in religious worship was rare, but her offering opinions or questions on religious topics must have been a drastic change to which many men were not accustomed.

---

[213] Steinberg, *Encyclopedia of Jewish Medical Ethics*, 954. "A groom during his seven days of wedding feasts is allowed to cut his hair. . . . A *Priest (Kohen)* may not let his hair grow wild but is obligated to cut it every thirty days, . . . A *High Priest* cuts his hair every Friday. A *king* cuts his hair every day. The men of the watch in the temple cut their hair on Thursdays in honor of the Sabbath."

[214] Although Greco-Roman women did not have to keep their heads and bodies covered, and as many of the converts were gentiles previously, this was not an issue for them. Nevertheless, for their leaders who were often converts from Judaism, like Paul, it may have been an issue.

[215] This verse sounds similar to 1 Corinthians 14:34-35, discussed in chapter 3 in this book. In that discussion we argue that words were added by a later editor.

[216] See chapter 1, "Communication."

Third, considering alternate translations can help to elucidate Paul's meaning. Many twentieth century English translations (NEB, NAS, NIV, etc.) change the word "subjection" to a form of the word "submit." It is true that anyone—male or female, young or old—learns best when he or she has a humble or submissive attitude as a learner. None of these translations uses the KJV word "silence."

1 Timothy 2:11

KJV	NEB	JB	Welch-Hall[217]
Let the woman learn in silence with all subjection	A woman must be a learner listening quietly and with due submission	During instruction a woman should be quiet and respectful	Let women learn in serenity, with deference in peace of soul

The recurrence of words like "quiet," or "peace," and "silent" implies that irreverence may have been a problem in some church services (also see 1 Corinthians 14:26-33 and chapter 3 in this book). Allowing women to bring their children to worship services would have added to the problem of irreverence (or at least made sounds that the men were unaccustomed to hearing in that setting, and may have found distracting). However, Paul does not single out women for this problem. An earlier letter reads: "We beseech you, brethren . . . study to be quiet, and to do your own business, and to work with your own hands, as we commanded you" (1 Thessalonians 4:10, 11). Paul's counsel to reverently listen and learn is similar to latter-day revelation which teaches: "Learn of me, and listen to my words; walk in the meekness of my Spirit, and you shall

---

[217] Welch and Hall, *Charting the New Testament*, 15-14.

have peace in me" (D&C 19:23).[218] The Spirit directs learning when one submits reverently to God.

The next verse continues in a condemnatory manner: "But I suffer not a woman to teach, nor to usurp authority over the man, but to be in silence" (1 Timothy 2:12). This verse echoes rabbinic statements from the late Second Temple era and beyond when women were not allowed to teach or speak in public, but sat separated from men in the synagogue, with no authority to testify.[219] Recall how the Lord and His apostles called Christian women to witness and testify of Jesus as the Son of God. Just a few chapters later, the author attacks all false teachers, not just the gender of the instructor: "If any man ["*ei tis* / whoever, anyone," male or female] teach otherwise, and consent not to wholesome words, even the words of our Lord Jesus Christ, and to the doctrine which is according to godliness . . . from such withdraw thyself" (1 Timothy 6:3, 5).

Did Paul add these verses in chapter 6 to clarify 1 Timothy 2:12? Also 2 Timothy 2:2 invites all upright church members to teach, preach, and witness: "The things that thou hast heard of me among many witnesses, the same commit thou to faithful men [*anthropos* / human, female or male], who shall be able to teach others also." The Greek and later translations call for both men and women to become committed teachers.

By looking at the entire canonized corpus attributed to Paul, we find Paul inviting all to participate and teach, because "there is neither Jew nor Greek . . . male nor female: for ye are all one in Christ Jesus" (Galatians 3:28). Yet the Jewish tradition perpetuated Rabbi Eliezer's teachings, "[Women] may not teach young children."[220]

In contrast, Paul teaches that older women should teach younger women to be wise (Titus 2:4).[221] This was a vote of

---

[218] Also see D&C 32:1; 90:15; 97:1; 107:99-100; 136:32.

[219] Josephus, *Antiquities,* IV.8:15; *Mishnah, Shebuoth,* 4:1, only certain men could act as legal witnesses, "but not . . . women."

[220] *Mishnah, Kiddushin* 4.13.

[221] Welch and Hall, *Charting the New Testament,* 15-14; summary of Titus 2:2-5. The only word for "aged" in the New Testament *Textus Receptus* is

confidence that mature women had wisdom and were capable of teaching with the Spirit of God. By juxtaposing these examples of women teaching with his complaint of inappropriate teaching, it appears that Paul worried about falsehoods, not gender.[222] We must again ask, what problem was the author trying to address? His main concern was to stop those who would usurp the priesthood authority and foster falsehoods (1 Timothy 1:6-8; 4:12; 5:17).[223]

The author concludes his argument by referencing the creation story from Genesis: "For it was Adam who was first created, and then Eve. And it was not Adam who was deceived, but the woman being deceived, fell into transgression" (1 Timothy 2:13-14, NASB). This verse retells the Genesis garden account with a punch at Eve's transgression (Genesis 3:1-13). Unlike most Christians, Latter-day Saints honor Adam and Eve as a prophet and prophetess, among the noblest of all mortals. Modern apostles have called the fall of Adam and Eve one of the "pillars of eternity."[224] Yet, in the late Second Temple era

---

found here and in Philemon 1:9 when Paul refers to himself as aged (ten years or so before his death). Welch and Hall chose to translate verse twelve as: "the *wife* should not teach or usurp authority over her *husband*" giving the verse a family setting. A home setting does not fit into the framework of the letter though, and it seems out of place in a section tackling false teachers who impinged on the worship services.

[222] Anderson, *Understanding Paul*, 317-319, 330-331.This confusing verse may hearken back to Paul's urgent call for Timothy to denounce false teachers who were usurping proper priesthood authority, "you may command certain people not to teach different doctrines" (1 Timothy 1:3, Richard Anderson's literal translation; also see 1 Timothy 1:4, 7; 2 Peter 2:1; etc.).

[223] Ibid., 317. Anderson sees this letter "from the opening warning about rebuking false teachers to the closing language . . . [as a] sober warning against those reforming the revealed gospel." A lack of respect for authority was a regular problem in other New Testament churches too—see1 Corinthians 9:1-5; 16:11; Titus 2:15.

[224] Bruce R. McConkie, *Sermons and Writings of Bruce R. McConkie* (Salt Lake City, UT: Bookcraft, 1989), 190. Elder McConkie gave this talk at a BYU Devotional on February 17, 1981 and referred to the three pillars as the creation, the fall, and the atonement.

we find several derogatory statements about Eve.[225] Instead of honoring Eve as the one who brought life, they emphasized: "through her we all die."[226]

Still, these verses in 1 Timothy 2:13-14 do not seem to honor our first parents either.[227] The text seems to force a cause and effect relationship between Eve partaking of the fruit and women not teaching or acting with authority.[228] We find this type of scriptural interpretation in the *Mishnah*, which condemns women in general as liars, because Sarah lied (Genesis 18:5).[229] This verse seems out of harmony with Paul's other statements and those from our living prophets.[230] These facts make me wonder if the verse, as it stands, was written or even intended by Paul.

The text continues in the same way: "Notwithstanding she shall be saved in childbearing, if they continue in faith and

---

[225] Ben Sira, *Ecclesiasticus,* 26:1. See introduction.

[226] Ibid., 26:12-17.

[227] Standing against this interpretation, the New Testament describes Adam and Eve as important pieces in the puzzle of earth life. Paul writes: "For as in Adam all die, even so in Christ shall all be made alive" (1 Corinthians 15:22). Luke traced Jesus' genealogy through his adopted father Joseph's lineage back to Adam (seventy-seven names). In that genealogy, he honors the first parents not only as the lineage that brought the Savior, but also gave Adam the noble title "the son of God," the only other person besides Jesus to share that name in the New Testament (Luke 3:38).

[228] As discussed in the introduction and chapter 1, some Jewish writers from this era blamed Eve for the fall, death, and all of life's trials (i.e., Ecclesiastics 25:24). 2 Esdras blamed Adam, "For the first Adam, burdened with an evil heart, transgressed and was overcome, as were also all who were descended from him. Thus the disease became permanent; the law was in the hearts of the people along with the evil root; but what was good departed, and the evil remained. (4 Ezra 3:20-21). Others blamed Satan (Wisdom of Solomon 2:24-25). Ben Sira blamed all women for Eve's choice, thus rationalizing the need for men to control their wives and daughters as much as possible in order to keep sin under control (Ben Sira, *Ecclesiasticus*, 26:12-17).

[229] *Mishnah, Shebuoth,* 4:1; see chapter 1, "Witnesses."

[230] D&C 25: 3, 7; "thou art an elect lady, whom I have called . . . to expound scriptures, and to exhort the church, according as it shall be given thee by my Spirit."

charity and holiness with sobriety." Parents have the responsibility to obey all of God's commandments, which include bringing children into the world, but this does not mean that one without children cannot be saved. Moreover, bearing a child does not bring salvation; as Paul drills, only Christ Jesus "hath saved us" (2 Timothy 1:9).

Joseph Smith made a significant clarification to 1 Timothy 2:15 by changing "she" to "they," which gave to both parents the responsibility and blessing of childbearing.

1 Timothy 2:15 (emphasis added)

KJV	JST
Nothwithstanding *she* shall be saved in childbearing, if they continue in faith and charity and holiness with sobriety.	Notwithstanding, *they* shall be saved in childbearing, if they continue in faith and charity and holiness with sobriety.

God designed Adam and Eve in a way to create offspring, and to raise them in a family unit, "in faith and charity" (1 Tim 2:15).[231]

Akin to Joseph Smith's emphasis on having both parents join in God's work of redemption through childbearing, Elder M. Russell Ballard of the Quorum of The Twelve restates the mutual relationship of both childbearing and priesthood power:

---

[231] I find it interesting that in chapter 2, the Prophet Joseph Smith only adds the plural "they," not feeling the need to change any other verses (other than the spelling of braided and to change "but" to "for" in verse 12. We do not know exactly when he made these changes—he may have done so during his initial editing in 1830-31 or when he returned to the text afterwards. However, by the time Joseph asked the Church to publish his translation of the Bible, he had already called women to preside in the Relief Society, had empowered women to offer healing blessings, had called women to teach in worship services, and had ordained women with a washing and anointing to the Abrahamic priesthood.

Men and women have different but equally valued roles. Just as a woman cannot conceive a child without a man, so a man cannot fully exercise the power of the priesthood to establish an eternal family without a woman. In other words, in the eternal perspective, *both the procreative power and the priesthood power are shared by husband and wife.* And as husband and wife, a man and a woman should strive to follow our Heavenly Father. The Christian virtues of love, humility, and patience should be their focus as they seek the blessings of the priesthood in their lives and for their family.[232] (Emphasis added.)

Elder Ballard confirms the unified work of spouses in Christ's restored Church: the power of God is seen in both procreation and priesthood powers (1 Corinthians 4:20).

Paul's message in 1 Timothy 2:15 also speaks of women's special role in God's plan as co-creators.[233] In this role, English translators emphasize two very different interpretations for the offspring. Either God prepared a way for Adam and Eve and their posterity to be saved through "the Child" (ISV, referring to Son of God); or, in the context of verse 13, bearing children is part of God's plan for humanity (NASB).[234]

---

[232] Elder M. Russell Ballard, *Ensign* (May 2012): 19.

[233] For more on this verse, see chapter 5 of this book.

[234] Focusing on another word in 1Timothy 2:15 also helps our understanding of this verse. Adam and Eve must join in the process of salvation, in being "saved / *sozo* / *rescued,*" by populating the earth and developing "faith . . . charity and holiness" (1 Timothy 2:15, KJV). The New Testament uses "saved / *sozo*" to teach humanity what they must contribute to their salvation by building on their belief with faith, prayer, baptism, hope, example, works, and obedience as found in other verses that use "saved / *sozo*" as shown below.1) "Believe on the Lord Jesus Christ, and thou shalt be saved" (Acts 16:31; Romans 10:9; 1 Corinthians 1:21)

2) "Call on the Lord [to] be saved" (Acts 2:21; Romans 10:13)

3) "Baptism doth also now save us" (1 Peter 3:21; also Acts 2:40-41)

4) "We are saved by hope" (Romans 8:24)

5) "For what knowest thou, O wife, whether thou shalt save thy husband? or how knowest thou, O man, whether thou shalt save thy wife?" (1 Corinthians 7:16)

WYC	NASB	NAS
But she shall be saved by generation of children, if she dwell perfectly in faith, and love, and holiness, with soberness.	But women will preserved through the bearing of children if they continue in faith and love and sanctity with self-restraint.	Even though she will be saved through the birth of the Child, if they continue in faith, love, and holiness along with good judgment.

Paul's counsel on the need for childbearing (either generally, or specifically to produce the Son of God) may be interpreted as gender-specific to Eve and her daughters, but as we see throughout his Epistles, Paul promotes the joint efforts of both husband and wives in creating and raising children unto the Lord.[235]

The tenor of 1 Timothy 2:13-15 appears less respectful to women and is thus inconsistent with the Lord's example, other statements from the New Testament Epistles, and modern

---

6) "For by grace are ye saved through faith" (Ephesians 2:8)

7) "Received . . . the love of the truth, that they might be saved" (2 Thessalonians 2:10)

8) "Take heed unto thyself, and unto the doctrine; continue in them: for in doing this thou shalt both save thyself, and them that hear thee" (1 Timothy 4:16).

9) "To save him . . . shew thee my faith by my works" (James 2:14-18; also Matthew 9:22; 14:30; 19:25; 27:42, 49; Mark 5:23, 28; 6:56; Luke 8:36; 13:23; 23:39; John 11:12).

10) "He which converteth the sinner from the error of his way shall save a soul from death, and shall hide a multitude of sins" (James 5:20).

[235] For example, Ephesians 6:4 reads, "fathers, provoke not your children to wrath: but bring them up in the nurture and admonition of the Lord," and 1 Thessalonians 2:11: "As ye know how we exhorted and comforted and charged every one of you, as a father doth his children." Also see Colossians 3:21; Ephesians 5:31; 1 Timothy 5:1; Hebrews 12:7, 9, etc.

apostles. These few verses seem to contain lingering ideas from the culture of the time, and need to benefit from the Lord's liberating ideas. This inconsistency may be the possible result of a different author, editorial changes, a misunderstanding, or even the author's mood on a given day. Rather than accepting them blindly, students of the Scriptures are responsible to seek the spirit of revelation and to confirm truth through one's own mind and heart (D&C 8:2-3).

The emancipating changes that Jesus set in motion took time and resolve for people to absorb and incorporate. The cultural baggage that fettered the perception of women was not easily removed. After centuries of wallowing in unhealthy thought patterns, practices, and relationships, early Christians had the daunting task of changing their thinking and behavior. Most of the New Testament writings speak of women who valiantly served the Lord and dynamically helped build His church. Those sister saints were emancipated and empowered by the truth that set them free (John 8:32).

Chapter 3
Christian Women Prophesied and Veiled
for Special Prayer

The majority of the New Testament encourages women to pray, serve, teach and witness.[236] As highlighted in the previous chapter, the Lord authorized early Christian women to teach and to serve in the church. This chapter focuses on how Christianity empowered women to pray and prophesy in the church at Corinth. The first example from 1 Corinthians 11:2-13 shows that women were empowered to pray and prophesy with a veil over their heads. In early Christianity women wore a veil in certain prayers as a symbol of their authority to act in ordinances and of their humility before God. The second example reviews sections in the same book which encourage

---

[236] Matthew 5:3-11; 9:19-22; 14:21, 15:23; 38; 28:5-10; Mark 7:25-29; 14:4-6; Luke 7:39; 10:4, 39-42; 13:12; John 4:7-27; 8:10; 17:21; Acts 1:14; 9:36; 16:1, 36; 17:4, 12, 34; Romans 1:8; Philippians 4:3; and Ephesians 5:25, 31; etc.). Often the KJV uses the word "man" or "brethren" which in the Greek, is not gender specific and originally could refer to both. After carefully counting each piece of advice to women and men in the New Testament (and by Paul specifically), I found more positive statements than negative ones.

women to prophesy, followed by a confusing section in 1
Corinthians 14:31-35, that contradicts earlier guidelines. We
will carefully examine that perplexing passage in its context.

I. 1 Corinthians 11:2-13

Cultural Background for Veiling Women

The Christian practice of women veiling to pray differed
from the cultural use of the day. By way of background, for "a
Roman woman, 'to get married' and 'to veil oneself' were
exactly the same word. . . . The veil was the flag of female
virtue, status, and security."[237] Avant-garde Roman women of
the first century were "more keen on showing off [their]
elaborate hair-style than on constantly wearing an old-fashioned
veil."[238] Ancient coins of aristocracy feature royal women
wearing head coverings for a social or fashion statement.[239]

Wife of Hadrian, after 136   Faustina I, Wife of Ant. Pius, 138-140

---

[237] Sarah Ruden, *Paul Among the People: The Apostle Reinterpreted and
Reimagined in His Own Time* (New York: Pantheon Books, 2010), 85. "The
veil held great symbolism: it reminded everyone that all freeborn women,
women with families to protect them, were supposed to enter adulthood
already married and that they were supposed to stay chastely married or else
that they were chastely widowed until the end of their lives." Ruden
elaborated, "the ancients believed that it was female hair's nature to inflame
men, almost like breasts or genitals: men experienced women's hair as
powerfully inescapably erotic" (88). She then quotes pages of Roman poetry
as evidence.
[238] Ibid., 86.
[239] Permission, to use photo from http://www.beastcoins.com received
September 4, 2014.

In other circles, a pharisaic Jewish woman veiled herself head to foot whenever she left her home as a symbol of modesty and female subservience.[240] In Middle Assyrian law, a wife claimed the right to wear a veil in public to differentiate her standing from a concubine or slave.[241] Her veil was a sign of prominence and authorized her actions and inheritance as a legal wife.[242]

Paul Among the Corinthians

In 1 Corinthians, Paul wrote to a culturally mixed audience of Christian converts in an attempt to redirect their understanding about women praying and prophesying while veiled.[243] He first encountered the Corinthians on his second

---

[240] Judith Lynn Sebesta, Larissa Bonfante, *The World of Roman Costume* (Madison, WI: University Press, 2001), 8, 155, 186. Fred Skolnik and Michael Berenbaum, eds., *Encyclopedia Judaica, 2nd ed.* 22 vols. (Detroit, New York, San Francisco: Thomson Gale, 2007), 21.161. Philo, Yonge, trans, *Philo*, 817; Jeremias, *Jerusalem in the Time of Jesus,* 359, 362. From a later date, Mishnah, *Nashim: Sotah,* 3. 8; *Babylonian Talmud, Nedarim,* 2.4, 58c; *Berakot,* 61a.

[241] Hennie J. Marsman, *Women in Ugarit and Israel: Their Social and Religious Position in the Context of the Ancient Near East* (Boston, MA: Brill Academic Publishers, 2003), 123. During the Middle Assyrian period (covering the second half of the second millennium BCE), each will had to record the right of inheritance for a legal wife. The Babylonian Laws of Hammu-rabi (1700 BCE) declare that a wife's inheritance was given as a marital gift or as an heir's share of her husband's inheritance. See Sophie Lamare-Defont, "Inheritance Law of and through Women in the Middle Assyrian Period," in *Women and Property in Ancient Near Eastern and Mediterranean Societies*, ed. Deborah Lyons and Raymond Westbrook (Boston, MA: Center for Hellenistic Studies, Harvard University, 2005), 1.

[242] Ruden, *Paul Among the People*, 88. Ruden sees Paul's request for Christian women to wear a veil as "Paul was being protective rather than chauvinistic." The lack of a veil may have been distracting to men "and stigmatizing to women."

[243] Jerome Murphy-O'Connor, "1 Corinthians 11:2-16 Once Again," *CBQ* 50/2 (1988): 267. The veil also had religious significance for those who worshiped the Egyptian goddess, Isis. The cult instructed women to anoint and cover their heads with a light piece of linen fabric while praying.

apostolic mission (Acts 18:1-11).[244] During his eighteen months there he established a branch of Christianity. Yet, after his departure, Paul's correspondence speaks of the infant church's challenges in maintaining pure doctrine (1 Corinthians 1:11; 5:9; 7:1; and 16:10-11).[245] The content of the letter insinuates that they struggled with their conflicting religious backgrounds and suffered from inexperienced membership and leadership.[246] This is not surprising in light of the fact that Corinth had a reputation for wealth, worldliness, and immorality.[247] The city's unique geography allowed it to control the neck of land between mainland Greece and the Peloponnesus, which made it a double port city. As a double port city, it seemed to have a double portion of promiscuity.[248] Paul's letters contended with these

---

[244] Geoffrey W. Bromiley, *International Standard Bible Encyclopedia*, 1.7724. Twentieth century archeologists working in Corinth found a broken lintel stone that announced the "Synagogue of the Hebrews" and other artifacts mentioned in the New Testament.

[245] Richard Lloyd Anderson, *Understanding Paul* (Salt Lake City, UT: Deseret Book, 1983), 131. Two canonized letters remain from Paul's correspondence to the Corinthian saints, which make up approximately one fourth of the Pauline Scripture. Seven traces of letters have been detected. Anderson deduces "first" Corinthians was written during Paul's third mission just before he left Ephesus (between c. AD 55 and 57). The letter suggests that most of the saints in Corinth were poor, some slaves, and all affected by their society.

[246] Evidence of the diversity among the saints is that half of the names mentioned in 1 Corinthians are Greek and the other half are Latin.

[247] In the tenth century BC, the Dorian Greeks first built an ancient city on an isthmus at the base of a 1,886-foot rocky summit (the "Acrocorinth"). On top of the mountain they built a temple to Aphrodite. Between 625 and 585 BC, they cut a five-foot-wide track through the rock peninsula connecting the ports on the Aegean and Adriatic Seas to create a more direct sailing route around southern Greece. It saved travel time as merchants could pull or wheel their ships across the four-mile isthmus. The city was also well known for the Isthmian games, wich their citizens hosted every two years.

[248] Robert L. Millet, *Studies in Scripture: Acts to Revelation* (Salt Lake City, UT: Deseret Book, 1987), 6.178, 81, 91. Over time the verb to *korinthiazein* or "to live like a Corinthian" came to mean "to live a dissolute life." The phrase "to play the Corinthian" meant to visit a house of prostitution. To *korinthiazomai*, meant "to practice fornication." A "Corinthian girl," became another name for a prostitute. Bromiley, *International Standard Bible*

deceptive traditions.

Commentary on 1 Corinthians 11:2-13

In 1 Corinthians, Paul boldly corrects the saints on many issues, including the need for women to veil during certain ordinances that dealt with prayer (1 Corinthians 11:2-13).[249] He teaches the Corinthian women that they could participate in the sacred experience of speaking by divine inspiration, with their veils signifying their authority to do so. Many biblical scholars find these verses about hairstyles or equality[250] "a jumbled mess."[251] With this as a disclaimer (and as a challenge!), I also draw on restored doctrine to help decipher the early saints' practice of covering a woman's head during certain prayers.[252]

Encyclopedia, 1.773. Raymond E. Brown, *An Introduction to the New Testament* (New York: Doubleday, 1997), 513. Leadership Ministries Worldwide, *1 & 2 Corinthians: The Preacher's Outline and Sermon Bible* (Chattanooga, TN: Alpha-Omega, 2003), 1. The word Corinth was also used as a metaphor for fertility. Under Roman rule, Corinth's temple to the Roman goddess Venus housed one thousand priestesses who served as prostitutes in behalf of the goddess of love.

[249] Brown, *Introduction to the New Testament,* 522. Brown sees chapters 10 and 11 as Paul's discussion of problems affecting community worship. He concludes that Paul "resorts to the authority of his own custom and those of the churches." Craig S. Keener from Eastern Seminary sees Paul addressing a "clash of social values: . . . uncovered hair to many connoted seduction and immodesty." *1–2 Corinthians* (New York: Cambridge University Press, 2005), 92.

[250] William Orr and James Arthur Walther, *Anchor Yale Bible Commentaries: 1 Corinthians* (New York City, NY: Random House-Doubleday, 1976), vii; "it is perilous to try to modernize Paul." Sarah Ruden speaks of this whole passage in parentheses with "grounds for considering these verses not genuine . . . rough . . . clunky repetition." A few pages later she bemoans, "the passage doesn't flow, . . . it sputters with emotion, gets incoherent, changes tactics, and ends almost with a snarl." *Paul Among the People,* 85, 88.

[251] M. Catherine Thomas, personal correspondence with the author.

[252] As a disclaimer, my thoughts on 1 Corinthians 11:2-13 do not purport to be a culminating study on the scholarship available on this difficult passage. My observations come through my LDS lens. I understand that many real

As I study these verses one by one, I find that the symbolism of the prayer veil points to the exalted role of woman.

11:2 Now I praise you, brethren, that ye remember me in all things, and keep the ordinances, as I delivered them to you.

Paul opens the subject by commending the Corinthian saints for keeping the ordinances he taught them. The word "ordinances" carries significant meaning for Latter-day Saints, but the Greek word "*paradosis* / ordinance" has a broader definition that includes "*handing over, delivery,* hence *teaching committed to a pupil . . . transmission, handing down,* hence *that which is received.*"[253] Modern English translations use "directions" (DBT), "traditions" (RSV, ESV, NASV), or "teachings" (NIV). In the Septuagint (LXX), or the Greek Old Testament in use at the time of the late Second Temple, *paradosis* also describes the ritual teachings that were handed down orally.[254]

For our discussion on 1 Corinthians 11, it is especially pertinent to see how Paul uses the term *paradosis* in his Epistles. He insists that the early churches should keep the

---

differences exist between the Corinthian branch and today's church. But even while honoring the historicity of first century Christianity, we can find Paul's powerful message illuminating and still applicable to Christian women who veil to pray.

[253] G. W. H. Lampe, ed., *A Patristic Greek Lexicon* (Oxford: Clarendon, 1995), 1014. Italics original. *Strong's New Exhaustive Concordance of the Bible* defines *paradosis* as "from; transmission, a precept; spec. the Jewish traditionary law" (Nashville, TN: Thomas Nelson Publishers, 1995), 67 of the Greek Dictionary section.

[254] The term *paradoseis* is found thirteen times in the New Testament, eight of which are in Matthew 15 and Mark 7, where Christ discusses the "traditions of the elders" with the Jewish scribes (Matthew 15:2, 3, 6; Mark 7:3, 5, 8, 9, 13; also see Galatians 1:14; Colossians 2:8; 2 Thessalonians 2:15, 3:6; and 1 Peter 1:18). Some of these *traditions* refer to ritual behavior found *not* in the written law, but in the 10,000 oral laws. Pharisees and others claimed that these oral laws began with Moses and were passed down for 1,500 years. Others may be new Christian ordinances as described in 1 Corinthians 11:2.

paradosis as their salvation depended on it (1 Corinthians 15:2-3). In reference to Paul's usage of *paradosis*, the *Theological Dictionary of the New Testament* explains, "The essential point for Paul is that it has been handed down (1C 15:3) and that it derives from the Lord (11:23)."[255] Elsewhere, Paul describes *paradosis* as teachings and rituals taught by apostolic leaders (1 Thessalonians 2:15, 3:6). Perhaps most applicable of all, in the same chapter that Paul discusses the veil, he states that he passed on the "ordinances / *paradosis*" in the same manner in which he received them from Christ: "I have received of the Lord that which also I delivered unto you" (1 Corinthians 11:23). In 2 Thessalonians 2:15, the apostle exhorts the saints to "stand fast, and hold the traditions [*paradosis* / ordinances] which ye have been taught, whether by word, or our epistle."

On the other hand, according to Paul, if the *paradosis* are initiated by the Greco-Roman philosophies or by himself, they are not valid (Colossians 2:8). He warned the saints, "withdraw yourselves from every brother that walked disorderly and not after the tradition [*paradosis* / ordinances] which he received from us" (2 Thessalonians 3:6). Paul uses "*paradosis*" to refer both to formal instruction and to teachings. For example, in Galatians 1:14, he uses *paradosis* to describe Jewish traditional practices or rites. It appears that his use of *paradosis* in 1 Corinthians11 and 15, comes from an earlier Christian tradition that predates him; these verses "have a fairly settled christological formula."[256]

Looking beyond Paul into in other early Christian sources, we find *paradosis* generally referring to unwritten sacred "tradition given by Christ, preached by apostles, guarded by

---

[255] G. Kittel, ed., Geoffrey W. Bromiley, translator, *Theological Dictionary of the New Testament* (Grand Rapids MI: Eerdmans Publishing, 1965), 6.172-173; Buchsel, "παραδοσις." In 1 Corinthians 11:23, Paul uses *paradosis* to imply the ordinance of the Lord's Supper.
[256] Ibid.

fathers."[257] These teachings handed down through word or example referred particularly to the sacrament of Jesus' Last Supper and "the later activities of the Twelve."[258] Initially, some held the *paradosis* more precious than Scripture (and other Christians, alongside Scripture), as they claimed that the Lord passed them on verbally. Most of this type of *paradosis* remained unwritten. The early Christians kept these rites and ceremonies secret "to enhance the dignity of the mysteries."[259] In the Christian historical tradition, *paradosis* comes up in liturgical usage. In that setting, *paradosis* became associated with the Christian institutions for communion, baptism, special prayers, oil of unction, triple immersion, and other early rites.[260]

The primitive Christian Church performed many sacred rites or ordinances, including baptisms for the living and the dead, the gift of the Holy Ghost, the sacrament of the Lord's Supper, sealing of marriages for eternity, washing feet, and prayer circles.[261] The early Christian leaders discuss these

---

[257] Lampe, ed., *A Patristic Greek Lexicon*, 1015. "Accepted tradition of church order and usage, as derived from apostles and handed on as norm of practice" (1014).

[258] Ibid., 1014-1015.

[259] Ibid., 1015. It was the "unwritten tradition" that lasted to even the post-Nicene father, John Chrysostom (c. AD 400), when he refers to *paradoiseis* as teachings transmitted by the Lord's apostles, often unwritten, but must be obeyed (1016).

[260] Ibid., 1015. Although the word was not limited to apostolic teachings throughout Greek literature (there it often relates to teaching in general—including rabbinic interpretation of Scripture, pagan religion, etc.), yet in the early Christian institutions, it carries a specific usage for "scriptural baptismal formula" or "making sign of cross, praying towards east, words of Eucharistic epiclesis, blessing of baptismal water, oil of unction, and candidate, as traditional practices." *Paradoiseis* was also used for orthodox doctrine, including false doctrine among the Christians. Later they used it for those doctrines "established by early fathers." Clement refers to *paradoiseis* as a title for a "Gnostic apocryphal work, *Traditions of Matthias*."

[261] Biblical examples of ordinances practiced in the primitive Christian church include the following Scriptures: "Else what shall they do which are baptized for the dead, if the dead rise not at all? why are they then baptized for the dead?" (1 Corinthians 15:29); "Repent, and be baptized every one of you in the name of Jesus Christ for the remission of sins, and ye shall receive

ordinances either as "sacraments" (in the Latin Church), or as "mysteries" (in the Greek Church).[262] Using both words, Origen (c. 248) wrote:

> When those who have been turned towards virtue have made progress and have shown that they have been purified by the Word, and have led as far as they can a better life—then (and not before) do we invite them to participate in our sacraments. . . . Whoever is pure not only from all defilement, but from what are regarded as lesser transgressions, let him be boldly initiated into the mysteries of Jesus. For they are properly made known only to the holy and pure.[263]

Fifty years earlier, Clement of Alexandria (c. 195) also emphasized the importance of worthiness in conjunction with the *paradosis* or ordinances: "the mysteries are not exhibited indiscriminately to everyone."[264]

Within this sacred sphere, several early texts mention these ceremonial rites in the early Church. Tertullian, in AD

---

the gift of the Holy Ghost" (Acts 2:38); "And as they did eat, Jesus took bread, and blessed, and brake [it], and gave to them, and said, Take, eat: this is my body . . ." (Mark 14:22); "Neither is the man without the woman, neither the woman without the man, in the Lord" (1 Corinthians 11:11); "give diligence to make your calling and election sure" (2 Pet.er 1:10); "Honour unto the wife . . . and as being heirs together of the grace of life" (1 Peter 3:7); "Whosoever therefore resisteth the power, resisteth the ordinance of God: and they that resist shall receive to themselves damnation" (Romans 13:2); and "Submit yourselves to every ordinance of man for the Lord's sake: whether it be to the king, as supreme" (1 Peter 2:13). Also see Hugh Nibley with Don E. Norton, ed., *Temple and Cosmos: Beyond This Ignorant Present* (Salt Lake City, UT: FARMS and Deseret Book, 1992), 313.

[262] Martin P. Nilsson, *Greek Popular Religion* (NYC, NY: Columbia University, Press, 1940), 42-43. The Greek word for "mystery / μυστήριον" in the ancient world referred to the "mystery or secret rite," as we see in the *Eleusinian and* Dionysian *Mysteries as well as others.*

[263] David W. Bercot, ed., *A Dictionary of Early Christian Beliefs* (Peabody, MA: Hendrickson Publishers, 1998), 573.

[264] Ibid.

198, described a service that included washing and anointing: "We have come out of the font, we are thoroughly anointed with a blessed oil."[265] A few years later in AD 210, Tertullian further described, "The flesh, indeed, is washed in order that the soul may be cleansed. The flesh is anointed so that the soul may be consecrated."[266] As Hugh Nibley observed, "The further back we go [in Christian history], the more prominent becomes the rite in the church."[267] Members of The Church of Jesus Christ of Latter-day Saints take particular interest in early Christian rites, as "we believe in the same organization that existed in the Primitive Church" (Articles of Faith 1:6). Both dispensations practice prayers in which women wear head coverings to represent their authority.[268]

> 11:3 *"But I would have you know, that the head of every man is Christ; and the head of the woman is the man; and the head of Christ is God."*

The first phrase of verse 3, *"but I would have you know,"* suggests that the saints had, at least partially, misunderstood Paul's previous instructions: "Keep the ordinances, as I delivered them to you" (1 Corinthians 11:2–3). Paul uses the phrase, "but I would / *thelō de,*" four times in this letter. Interestingly, he repeats this each time he corrects a misconception (1 Corinthians 7:32; 10:20; 14:5). Here the misconception dealt with why women covered their heads while praying and why men did not (1 Corinthians 11:4–11). His tone suggests that as if the saints of Corinth had a problem following this specific teaching.

Paul wants to correct this misunderstanding, but rather than merely restate the dress code on veils, he teaches an

---

[265] Ibid., 481.

[266] Ibid., 573.

[267] Hugh Nibley, *Mormonism and Early Christianity* (Provo, UT: FARMS, 1987), 46-47.

[268] Hugh Nibley, "The Early Christian Prayer Circle," *BYU Studies* 19, no. 1 (Fall 1978): 41-78.

important doctrinal background that underlines the veil imagery. He explains the series of relationships established from the order of creation: God-Christ-man-woman. Paul reviews that God is the *head* of Christ, who is the *head* of man, who is the *head* of woman. The word "head / *kephale*" has multiple meanings in both Greek and English, but most often refers to: 1) the physical head or body, and 2) figuratively, the "starting point."[269] According to the *Theological Dictionary of the New Testament,* the word "head / *kephale,*" as used by Paul in 1 Corinthians 11, deals with the relationship of man and woman "at the very foundations of their creaturehood."[270] Therefore, God the Father was the "starting point" or origin of Christ (John 20:17),[271] who was the "starting point" of man (3

---

[269] Wayne Grudem, "Does Kephal ("Head") Mean "Source" or "Authority Over" in Greek Literature? A Survey of 2,336 Examples," *Trinity Journal* ns 6.1 (Spring 1985): 38-59. Grudem, from the Trinity Evangelical Divinity School, argues against the definition of "source," but his study demonstrates that 53% of the 2,336 examples of ancient Greek Literature that he examined use "head" physically, and the next most common use, 23% of the texts use it figuratively to mean the "starting point" (51). Theologically, he prefers the definition found in 16% of the texts as a person of superior authority. I use "starting point" as synonymous with "origin."

[270] Gerhard Kittel, ed, *Theological Dictionary of the New Testament* (Grand Rapids, MI: Eerdmans Publishing, 1965), 3.679. I disagree with this dictionary's interpretation that "woman is the reflection of man to the degree that in her created being she points to man, and only with and through him to God." This speaks more of the perspective of the translators (writing for Nazi Germany) than Paul's text as he explains in 1 Corinthians 11:8-11.

[271] God the Father created Jesus' spirit body, His mortal body, and His resurrected body (see Luke 1:34-35; Acts 13:34). Latter-day Saints (LDS) believe that Jesus is the literal "Son" of God and the premortal Jehovah, God of the Old Testament (Mosiah 3:5-8). The Father then is the source of the Son. Because they define God and Christ through the Trinity, my description runs contrary to that of most Christian biblical scholars, who prefer the definition of superior authority or rank. The Council of Nicea was called in 325 AD to determine the relationship between God the Father and Jesus the Christ. The issue was not resolved, though, and over the next centuries it continued to divide the eastern and western versions of Christianity until the Eastern Orthodox and Roman Catholic (Universal) Churches were formed. Here, again, the perspective of the restored gospel possibly sheds new light specifically on the definitions of these verses and on Paul's writings in

Nephi 9:15), and man, via his side-rib, was the "starting point" of his helpmeet, woman (Genesis 2:22; Moses 3:23; Abraham 5:17).[272]

This relationship chain becomes the foundation of Paul's instruction here.[273] Three times in ten verses he uses different words to describe the genders' intertwining origins: woman originates from man, and a man-child comes from woman (1 Corinthians 11:3, 8, 12, NASB). He also repeats that God created man in His image (1 Corinthians 11:7). Looking at the argument as a whole, Paul discusses a symbiotic connection in which men and women have mutual responsibilities for one

---

general. From the perspective of the restoration, the Prophet Joseph Smith taught that truth was restored to each dispensation, so I stand on the assumption that Paul understood that Jesus was the literal Son of God, His Father, spiritually and physically. For the LDS view of the Father and Son, see Joseph Smith-History, 1:17; 3 Nephi 9:15; D&C 130:22.

[272] For many Trinitarian Christians, the Old Testament describes the source or creator of man as Jehovah Elohim (Genesis 1-2). For Latter-day Saints though, the pre-mortal Jesus was Jehovah. This allows LDS to make sense of this passage. Some Christian scholars question how Paul understood the Godhead, with the Father as the source of the Son, but it is not as confusing for those who deny the trinity. Elder Rulon S. Wells clarified during April Conference in 1931, "Who was it that created this world? Have we not read it was the Word that was with the Father in the very beginning, and that all things were made by him and without him was not anything made? He it was then that created the heavens and the earth. He it was then who, under the Father, created Adam and Eve and placed them as in the Garden of Eden. He it was, this Son of God, known then as Jehovah." See John 1:1-4; D&C 29:34.

[273] An alternative definition of "head / *kephale*" is "authority." As a result, some scholars, including Robert Allard, Mark Finney, and Ed Christian, see this section as Paul teaching the proper ecclesiastical relationships, beginning with God who presides over all, to Christ who presides over men, and men who preside over women. Robert E. Allard, "Freedom on your head' (1 Corinthians 11:2-16): A Paradigm for the Structure of Paul's Ethics," in *Word & World* 30, no. 4 (Fall 2010), 399-407. Mark Finney, "Honour, Head-coverings and Headship: 1 Corinthians 11.2-16 in its Social Context," in *Journal for the Study of the New Testament* 33, no.1 (2010). Also Ed Christian, "Prophets under God's Authority: Head coverings in 1 Corinthians 11:1-16," in *Journal of the Adventist Theological Society* 1, nos. 1-2 (1999) 291-95.

another.

This bears highlighting, as Paul does not make a case for male superiority. In the same section, he speaks of woman as privileged with authority and indispensable to men and vice versa (1 Corinthians 11:10, 11, 12). Outside of these verses (and a similar verse in Ephesians 5:23), every other one of the 49 New Testament references to "head / *kephale*," describes either a physical head or the Savior.[274] Yet many have interpreted this as saying men are to rule women. I do not find evidence for that in the Pauline Epistles at large, nor specifically in the context of 1 Corinthians 11. Whenever Paul refers to a "ruler," he uses other words—i.e., *"rulers /archon (Romans 13:3)*, "rule / preside / *proistemi*" (1 Timothy 3:5; 5:17), "rule / govern / *brabeuo*" (Colossians 3:15), and "rule / leader /*hegeomai*" (Hebrews 13:7, 17, 24)—not *kephale*.[275]

As we will see in a few verses, Paul does not encourage male dominance over females (1 Corinthians 11:11-12). Some of the transforming doctrines that the Lord restored denounced unrighteous dominion and superiority of any kind: "A servant is not greater than his master" (John 15:20 NIV; also 13:16), "whosoever of you will be the chiefest, shall be servant of all" (Mark 10:44), and "Good Master, what shall I do to inherit eternal life? And Jesus said unto him, Why callest thou me good? None is good, save one, that is God" (Luke 18:18-19; also see Matthew 19:16; and Mark10:17). Paul's verses on veiling women encourage a positive interrelationship among man, woman and God; they do not promote gender supremacy.

Paul's linear order or creation may sound demeaning to some modern readers.[276] However, He does not intend this as

---

[274] References in the New Testament where "head / *kephale*," speaks of the Savior are found in: Acts 4:11; Ephesians 1:22; 4:15; Colossians 2:10; 1 Peter 2:7.

[275] Timothy and Barbara Friberg, *Analytical Lexicon of the Greek New Testament* (Grand Rapids, MI: Baker Books, 2000), 77; "active rule over, be leader of." *Strong's New Exhaustive Concordance of the Bible* defines it, "first (in rank or power):—chief (ruler), magistrate, prince, ruler (16, #758).

[276] Catherine Thomas, CES Symposium, unpublished manuscript, 1992. "What makes all of this so hard in practice? It may seem unfair that the man

verses 10 and 11 discuss. His analogy applies specifically to the creation. In the ancient world, ideas that linked someone with deity were honorable and empowering. Paul does not suggest that women needed a detour or middleman in order to communicate with God. In the New Testament, both men and women pray directly to God the Father (Luke 11:1-2; Acts 1:14; 16:13; Romans 8:26; etc.); both men and women have access to the gifts of the Spirit (1 Corinthians 12:1-11); and both build the kingdom of God (1 Corinthians 12:12-31). Paul describes men and women as team players, not as competing individuals lined up in order of importance (1 Corinthians 12:7). Paul's orderly lineup does not need to disrupt the other scriptural admonition for men and women to work beside as "complement[s]," "help meet[s]," "counterpart[s]" (Genesis 2:18, HCSB, KJV, YLT), or "yokefellow[s]" (Philippians 4:3).[277] Christ, Peter, and Paul taught the need to work together in harmony with the goal of becoming one as joint heirs (John 17:21-23; 1 Peter 3:7; Romans 8:17).

Modern prophets similarly describe the goal of side-by-side spousal relationships. L. Tom Perry said, "The couple works together eternally for the good of the family. They are united together in word, in deed, and in action as they lead, guide, and direct their family unit. They are on equal footing. They plan and organize the affairs of the family jointly and

---

is subject to a perfect head, and the woman to an imperfect head. But how much humility the man must cultivate to hear the Lord's voice! And how much humility the woman must exercise to encourage and rely on her imperfect husband to make that connection. The man's presidency over the woman is designed to be as much of a tutorial for him as it is for the woman to submit to his presidency. A very fine tuning is required of each. The challenge of perfecting ourselves is great indeed, but the challenge of perfecting ourselves in a relationship is greater." Catherine Thomas points out the delicate innuendoes and powerful learning opportunities of this connection.

[277] By working in the same direction, seeking the same goals, and pulling with the same force, a couple can become unified. Whether this team effort is describes as an alignment from the order of creation, or as working side by side, the end result is the same; two mortals working together to serve God.

unanimously as they move forward."[278] Paul advocates mutually supportive relationships in this section (1 Corinthians 11:11), but first he describes the order of creation as a linear link to God in order to explain the symbolism behind women veiling during prayer.

11:4: "Every man praying or prophesying,
having his head covered, dishonoureth his head."

In verse 4, Paul frankly states, that men who cover their heads, either as a reflection of their Judeo-Greco-Roman backgrounds, or for any other reason, dishonor their "head" or God.[279] The idea behind "head covered" means something *"hanging down from the head"* like a veil that would cover the face, not a hat.[280] Paul uses the dual meaning for head: "Every man praying or prophesying, having his *head* [physically] covered, dishonoureth his *head* [figuratively]." In keeping with the creation narrative, Paul's injunction follows the reasoning that man was created in the image and glory of God, so when man communes with God, he should not veil his face, but acknowledge that affiliation (Genesis 1:27). By covering his face, a man would cover the image of God, thereby denying the power and dignity that the Creator bestowed upon him at creation. In other words, if a man worships with his face covered, he dishonors his starting point or origin. To do otherwise was to devalue his Christian beliefs. However problematic male head covering may have been, it appears that the bigger issue was that woman were not veiling their heads, as this becomes the subject for the next five verses.

---

[278] Elder L. Tom Perry, "Fatherhood an Eternal Calling," *Ensign* (May, 2004). The quote is preceded with, "Since the beginning, God has instructed mankind that marriage should united husband and wife together in unity. Therefore, there is not a president or a vice president in a family."

[279] For more information on men wearing veils in the first century AD, both the social and liturgical, see Mark Finney, "Honour, Head-coverings and Headship" *Journal for the Study of the New Testament* 33, no. 1 (2010).

[280] Jerome Murphy-O'Connor, *Keys to First Corinthians: Revisiting the Major Issues* (Oxford, New York: Oxford University Press, 2009), 143-144.

*11:5–6: "But every woman that prayeth or prophesieth with
her head uncovered dishonoureth her head:
for that is even all one as if she were shaven . . ."*

Paul's statement clarifies an enormous breakthrough in
worship for Christian women.[281] The apostle begins by
explicitly declaring that women prayed and prophesied in public
worship services of early Christian churches. This Christian
practice marked a distinct departure from Paul's previous
Pharisaic traditions.[282] At the time of the Second Temple, a
Jewess' religious experiences were sharply curtailed—from
pilgrimages to synagogue worship.[283] Not only did some rabbis
discourage women from speaking and worshiping in public,
they also discouraged women from leaving their homes,
learning The Law, speaking with men, or eating at the same
table with male visitors.[284] This example of women praying and
prophesying may refer to private, personal experiences, but the
larger context of "ordinances" suggests that they were part of a

---

[281] Clanton, *The Good, the Bold, and the Beautiful*, 23. See my Introduction,
"Synagogue."
[282] *Mishnah, Ketuboth* 6.6; *Gittin* 9.10. Jewish women were not allowed to
speak in their worship or synagogue, nor in any public gathering—in fact, a
husband could divorce his wife for speaking to another man (see chapter 6,
under "Divorce").
[283] *Mishnah, Kiddushin*, 4:13. See my introduction and chapter 1.
[284] Dan W. Clanton, *The Good, the Bold, and the Beautiful* (New York: T &
T Clark International, 2006), 23. Philo uses a simile to generalize women,
"cooped . . . up . . . like a woman who belongs at home." *De Specialibus
Legibus II* 33.124. *Mishnah, Sotah,* 3.4. "If a man gives his daughter a
knowledge of the Law it is as though he taught her lechery." It is feasible
that in that wealthy home, young girls were educated too, or else they may
have had the opportunity to overhear lessons. The Talmud mentioned a few
females who learned the oral laws. Witherington, *Women and the Genesis of
Christianity,* 7. Nosson Scherman, *The Mishnah: A New Translation with a
Commentary, Yad Avraham anthologized from Talmudic sources and classic
commentators* (Brooklyn, NY: Mesorah Publications, 1981), III.58; "A
father should not teach his daughter Torah because certain acumen is gained
from it which she may use to hide her immorality. . . . It is also possible that
she may use her knowledge of the Torah to attract men to her."

special congregational experience. It corresponds with Joel 2:28, where the Spirit pours out the gift of prophecy on both men and women as "your sons and your daughters shall prophesy."

Paul's choice of wording for "prophesy / *propheteuo* / to speak forth under inspiration" may refer to women giving sermons as well. In either case, it represents enormous liberation, as the whole idea of women participating in the public worship services was limited at the time.[285] Jewish men dominated the public world and confined women's worship primarily to their homes.[286] Outside of her home, a Jewess was to be unseen and unheard.[287] Paul's statement is an enormous step forward for women's communal worship.

In verses 5 and 6, Paul also explains why women, unlike men, cover their heads while participating in special prayers or prophesying. Paul's argument for women seems exactly the opposite of that for men. When a woman covers "her head / *kephale*" (physically), she shows honor and respect to "her starting point / *kephale*" (husband, Christ, and then God). To rephrase Paul's words, a man honored his relationship to God by uncovering his head, while a woman honored God by veiling her head. Paul explains this dichotomy in verse 7, but first he expresses his opinion that a woman's head without a covering

---

[285] Howard Clark Kee and Lynn H. Cohick, *Evolution of the Synagogue* (Harrisburg, PA: Trinity Press, 1999), 34, 96.

[286] Clanton, *Good, Bold, Beautiful*, 24; ; "From kosher laws to the recitation of the *shema,* from private prayer to Sabbath practices, not only would women have been present, they would have been active participants due to their dominance in the private, domestic sphere."

[287] Judaeus Philo, *Special Laws III.,* 7 vols. (London: William Heinemann, Ltd., 1967), 3.169, 171; "Marketplaces and council-halls, law-courts and gatherings, and meetings where a large number of people are assembled, and open-air life with full scope for discussion and action – all these are suitable to men both in war and peace. The women are best suited to the indoor life which never strays from the house . . . A woman then, should not be a busybody, meddling with matters outside her household concerns, but should seek a life of seclusion."

during certain prayers, is as disgraceful as shaving her head.[288]

> *11:7: "For a man indeed ought not to cover his head,*
> *forasmuch as he is the image and glory of God:*
> *but the woman is the glory of the man"*

In verses 7, Paul references both creation stories from Genesis chapters 1 and 2.[289] The first describes a male and female created "in the image of God" and both are given dominion over the earth (Genesis 1:26-27). The second has Adam naming all the animals, unable to find one equal or complementary to him until God takes part of his rib cage to create a "partner" (Genesis 2:20-22, NEB) or "his one before" (Genesis 2:20, TEB).[290] Modern revelation teaches of a spiritual creation before the physical creation, which may help clarify the

---

[288] Flavius Josephus, translated by William Whiston, *Josephus Complete Works: Wars* (Grand Rapids, MI: Kregel Publications, 1978), 2.15.1-n. Josephus mentions a woman named Bernice who shaved her head in conjunction with taking a Nazarite vow. Even though her vow was noble and voluntary, she was still publicly humiliated and shamed for the loss of her hair. This phrase from 1 Corinthians 11:6, had a dramatic effect in the late fourth century, when the early Church father Chrysostom wrote, "If thou cast away the covering appointed by the law of God, cast away likewise that appointed by nature." Chrysostom, *Homily XXVI*, "On the Veiling of Women," in *Nicene and Post-Nicene Fathers of the Christian Church*, ed. Philip Schaff, vol. 12, *Saint Chrysostom: Homilies on the Epistles of Paul to the Corinthians* (Oxford: Parker, 1891), 152. Chrysostom also felt that when women "abide within our own limits and the laws ordained of God, but to go beyond, is not an addition but a diminution" (ibid.). I feel Chrysostom misunderstood Paul by interpreting these verses to mean that men were to rule over women.
[289] Daniel Ludlow, ed., *Encyclopedia of Mormonism*, "Ancient Sources" (New York: Macmillan, 1992), 1.17.
[290] A more literal translation is found in the TEB, using side, not rib; "And YHVH ELOHIM made a deep sleep fall upon the *soil*-man, and he slept; and he took one from his sides, and he closed flesh under it. And YHVH ELOHIM built the side that he took from the *soil*-man into a woman, and he made her come toward the *soil*-man. And the *soil*-man said, 'This one this time—bone of my bones, and flesh of my flesh! To this one will be called "woman," because from a man this one was taken'" (Genesis 2:21-23).

dichotomy between the two Genesis accounts (D&C 29:32; Moses 3:5).

Paul references both of these creation stories, yet he does not follow the Genesis wording.

Genesis 1:27	1 Corinthians 11:7
God created man in his own image, in the image of God created he him, male and female created he them.	*. . . he is the image and glory of God*

Paul's refiguring of the creation helps us understand what he meant by the "glory of God."[291] Rather than using the *plural to* denote humanity, Paul deviates to use the single form of the word "man / *aner*" (Genesis 2:21–23; 1 Timothy 2:13),[292] to describe a linear connection with his Creator.[293]

---

[291] Although Paul deviates from the English versions of Genesis 1:27, perhaps his memory or copy of the text may have been different; thus he uses a singular man.

[292] E.A. Speiser, *The Anchor Bible Genesis* (New York: Doubleday, 1964), 7. Biblical commentaries often mention the plural nature of *Adam* in Genesis 1:26-27. For example, "Hebrew employs here plural possessives" Similarly, the *Word Biblical Commentary,* speaking of Genesis 1:26-27, explains that the "fluidity between the definite and indefinite form makes it difficult to know when the personal name 'Adam' is first mentioned. . . .The very indefiniteness of reference may be deliberate . . . 'mankind, humanity' as opposed to God or the animals. . . Adam, the first man created and named, is representative of humanity . . . clearly mankind in general, 'male and female,' not an individual is meant." Gordon J. Wenham, *Word Biblical Commentary* (Texas: Word Books, 1987), 32.

[293] Alonzo Gaskill, *The Savior and the Serpent: Unlocking the Doctrine of the Fall* (Salt Lake City, UT: Deseret Book, 2002), 110–125. Gaskill emphasizes that the symbols from the rib account foreshadow Jesus as the second Adam. Eve foreshadows the members of the Church for whom Christ dies. Both Adam and Jesus are wounded in the side to bring forth the life of Eve and the Church. Gaskill points out that the second creation story also teaches the plan of salvation. Adam typifies Christ with a wound in his side to produce Eve, who represents the Church members or fallen humanity. As Adam's wounded side produced mankind, so Christ's wounds provide the way for mankind to return to God the Father. Christ as the second Adam, and

Paul evidently wants to accentuate the "glory of man," as something different from the "glory of God" (1 Corinthians 11:7), which causes us to ask *why*? Reading this phrase within the context of this chapter, this letter, the Pauline corpus, and the New Testament at large, we can safely assume Paul does *not* mean that God created woman solely to glorify men, nor that man could use woman for his glory in a manipulative or disrespectful manner. We have no scriptural foundation to suggest that woman was created only for the use of man.

Although Josephus and many contemporaries of Paul disagreed,[294] Paul repeatedly states that woman is not inferior to man (1 Corinthians 11:7, 11). Understanding what Paul means by "the woman is the glory of man" (1 Corinthians 11:7) is vital to understanding why Paul thinks women should wear a veil during special prayers.

Narrowing in on the "glory of God," the passage in Moses 1:39 explains that God's work and glory is "to bring to pass the immortality and eternal life of man." The same can hold true for humanity's work and glory. The union of man and woman is crucial in that work and glory. The union is a glorious thing. Nevertheless, in the hierarchy of God, the glory of humanity should not overshadow the glory of God, and so glorious woman covers her face out of respect to God.

Paul describes woman as a symbol of human potential, since she facilitates the potential for human glory. Paul teaches that during this ordinance, when men and women commune with God through prayer and prophesy, the man takes on a vicarious role to represent the image and glory of God while a woman represents the image and glory of supplicating humanity. Man does not cover his face because he acts in the image of God. Woman, on the other hand, veils her face as a

---

as the Savior, champion's fallen humanity. Eve represents all those born of women, who become the Church and join Adam/Christ in a covenantal relationship." Gaskill emphasizes that the symbols from the rib account foreshadow Jesus as the second Adam (110-125).

[294] Josephus, *Against Apion*, II. 25. "'A woman is inferior to her husband in all things.'"

107

symbol of humanity (representing both genders in this sense). She should humbly acknowledge His divine glory by reverently and symbolically covering humanity's glory when she stands in the presence of God. This interpretation is consistent with the Scriptures that describe a woman or bride as a symbol of God's people or the church.[295]

11:8-9 "For the man is not of the woman; but the woman of the man. Neither was the man created for the woman; but the woman for the man."

According to Genesis, God created Eve so that a corresponding union could be formed with potential for increase and glory (Genesis 1:27; 2:18-23). Woman's arrival in Eden fulfilled the need for man's "counterpart" (YLT) or "authority corresponding to him" (ISV) or "a helper suitable for him" (NSB) or "help meet" (KJV). Significantly, God did not provide Adam immediately with a wife, but waited for Adam to name all the animals, whereupon he recognized his own need for an equivalent partner: "And Adam gave names to all cattle, and to the fowl of the air, and to every beast of the field but for Adam there was not found an help meet for him" (Genesis 2:20). It is as if God waited to introduce this important creation until Adam himself recognized his own inability as a single man: Adam recognized that he needed a copartner. "Eve was adequate for, or equal to, Adam. She wasn't his servant or his subordinate."[296]

In this sense, woman is "the glory of man" because she becomes the vehicle for humanity to gain a body furthering their potential glory.[297] God gave women the sacred trust to carry and grow embryos. This is why Adam named his wife "Life" or "Living," translated as "Eve / *Chavvah*." With this

---

[295] 1 Nephi 21:18; D&C 109:73-74; John 3:29; Revelation 21:9; Isaiah 50:1; 66:8; Jeremiah 33:11; etc.

[296] Bruce C. and Marie K. Hafen, "Crossing Thresholds and Becoming Equal Partners," *Ensign* (August 2007): 27.

[297] Ibid., 93.

unique responsibility to bring forth life, woman reflects the work of Christ himself. Just as Christ labored to create sons and daughters of God, so God designed a woman's body to create mortal sons and daughters.[298] But woman cannot do this alone. The physical creation of each human requires the work of woman and man working together as God planned.

Through the spousal relationship, a woman and a man became a mutually supporting entity. This may be misunderstood with many influential translations of Genesis 3:16, in which Eve is told, "Thy desire shall be to thy husband, and he shall rule over thee" (KJV). We now have other translations that clarify this as a joint responsibility "and he will rule *with you*" (TEB) or "he will govern *with you*" (emphasis added).[299]

Adam was no dictator.[300] The partnership is more important than either of the single entities. Only as a unified unit can either person experience lasting glory. God created Adam and Eve so that a glorious union could potentially be

---

[298] Jane Allis-Pike, "'How Oft Would I Have Gathered You As A Hen Gathereth Her Chickens': The Power of the Hen Metaphor in 3 Nephi 10:4-7," in Andrew C. Skinner and Gaye Strathearn, ed., *Third Nephi: An Incomparable Scripture* (Salt Lake City: Neal A. Maxwell Institute and Deseret Book, 2012), 57-74: "It may seem paradoxical that Christ would choose to compare himself to a hen, since he is neither a female nor a mother. However, Christ, as a god, is the only 'man' who can be compared with a woman, at least in her capacity to give birth."

[299] Personal correspondence with the translation team at *Power on High Ministries*. The KJV of Genesis 3:16, and the LXX, use "rule over," although, this biblical translation speaks more of the translators' belief, than of the text. According to the Hebrew scholar, Legrand Davies, the KJV translation of "rule over" in Genesis 3:16, is based on the last two letters of the sentence translated as "over her +" In Hebrew, the "beth" is a prefix or inseparable preposition. Hebrew Dictionaries include its meaning as: in, at, to, on, among, with, towards, according to, by, because of, on top of, beside, and about 20 other such meanings. All are valid, depending on the interpretation of the passage. Adam ruling "with" Eve, is in keeping with LDS doctrine outlined in D&C 132:19-20 (personal correspondence in author's possession).

[300] Bruce C. and Marie K. Hafen, "Crossing Thresholds and Becoming Equal Partners," *Ensign* (August 2007): 27.

formed. Again Paul highlights the chain of relationships, or order of creation established in verse 3, to establish the value of the woman as integral to God's plan.[301]

Allegorical View

Paul's words about the order of creation can also be interpreted allegorically. Later in this same Epistle, Paul refers to Jesus as the "last Adam" (1 Corinthians 15:45).[302] Early Christian writers built on this theme: "Eve is a type of the church as Adam is a type of Christ. As Eve was made out of a part of Adam, so the church is part of the Lord Jesus. The church is called His bride as Eve was Adam's bride."[303] Typologically, Adam and Jesus are wounded in the side to bring forth the life of Eve and the Church respectively. As Adam's wounded side produced Eve and thereby humanity, so Christ's wounds provide the way for mortals to return to God the Father. As the second Adam and as the Savior, Christ champions fallen humanity. Eve represents all those born of women, who become the Church and join Adam/Christ in a covenantal relationship. Furthermore, "Adam and Eve were commanded to be one, and, in like manner, Christ and His Church are to be one."[304] In this allegorical scenario, the Church (Eve) works through the mediator Christ (Adam) to become unified as the scriptural

---

[301] Hugh Nibley, *Old Testament and Related Studies* (Salt Lake City, UT: Deseret Book; Provo, UT: FARMS, 1986), 93.

[302] In addition to Paul's reference, Luke refers to two men as "son of God," Adam and Jesus (Luke 3:38; 22:70).

[303] Gaskill, *Savior and the Serpent*, 115; quoting Ambrose. It appears that Adam conveys the command to Eve, who walks by faith. Gaskill sees this as significant: "Again, according to scriptural accounts, Eve had less information than Adam—she could not see as clearly, as it were—and thus Adam was to be her guide, to whom she was to cling. Similarly, you and I have less information about the things of salvation than do Christ and His prophets—we labor under a veil, as it were—and hence they must be our guides, to whom we must cling. To take matters into our own hands is to bring heartache and trials into our lives (as Eve did metaphorically into hers)." Ibid., 119.

[304] Ibid., 114.

110

Bridegroom and Bride (Revelation 18:23; Isaiah 61:10; Joel 2:16).

Restored Perspective

Stepping outside the Pauline text for a moment, insights from the restoration also shed light on this perspective.[305] In this dispensation, Elder Bruce Hafen explains, "The concept of interdependent, equal partners is well-grounded in the doctrine of the restored gospel."[306] The partnership is more important than either of the single entities. With the restored understanding of vicarious work for the dead, the sealing of eternal partners may happen on either side of the veil. Men and women continue to progress and can be sealed by the Holy Spirit of Promise to fulfill their eternal potential (D&C 132:18-19). If mortals remain single in the afterlife, they cannot be completely glorified (D&C 132:17).

It is the mutuality of men and women that brings glory. Without the union of man and woman, their work of procreation and eternal glory cannot be achieved. The inter-reliance of the couple, unified to do God's work, allows them to develop into a glorified state. They jointly hold "the patriarchal priesthood," meaning, "the priesthood shared by husbands and wives who are sealed."[307] I think Paul refers to this glorious union in these verses (1 Corinthians 11:8-9).

> *11:10 "For this cause ought the woman to have power on her head because of the angels."*

---

[305] Elder M. Russell Ballard, *Conference Report*, April 2013.

[306] Bruce C. and Marie K. Hafen, "Crossing Thresholds and Becoming Equal Partners," *Ensign* (August 2007): 27.

[307] Ludlow, *Encyclopedia of Mormonism*, "Priesthood, Patriarchal," 3.1135. From the perspective of the restoration, "the patriarchal order of the priesthood is the right of worthy priesthood-holding fathers to preside over their descendants through all ages; it includes the ordinances and blessings of the priesthood shared by husbands and wives who are sealed in the temple."

In verse 10, Paul concentrates on the doctrine that this veil covering designates a woman's power and authority to act in that ordinance. Women become agents of authority or "power / *exousia.*" The KJV translates the word *exousia* in this case as "power," and the RSV as "veil." The NIV comes closest to the original Greek with the term "authority." 1 Corinthians repeatedly addresses the topic of authority—specifically, the need to respect authority, who has the authority, and what that authority is.[308] Here Paul returns to the subject again and focuses on women's authority to act in church worship. Clarifying even further, the YLT translation reads, "because of this the woman ought to have a token of authority upon the head, because of the messengers" (YLT).[309] Similarly, the *Anchor Bible* commentary describes the woman's veil as "a sign of the power received from the Lord (v.11) and of the dignity she has to worship and praise God in the presence of the angels."[310]

Paul returns to the creation theme in the last phrase of verse 10, referring to the angels that protect the creative order of Eden.[43] Not only do angels guard "the way of the tree of life" (Moses 4:31), but they also watch over woman and give her

---

[308] 1 Corinthians 7:37; 9:4-18; 11:10; 15:24.

[309] The translations of the KJV, NIV, NRSV, EVS, ASV, etc. all state that the veil refers to a *woman's authority* or *power.* Other loose paraphrases, like the Good News Bible from 1966, chose simple words for the benefit of children and foreigners—therefore not adhering as strictly to the original text—reading: "On account of the angels, then, a woman should have a covering over her head to show that she is under her husband's authority." Similarly, the Weymouth New Testament from 1903 reads, "That is why a woman ought to have on her head a symbol of subjection." However, these translations speak more of their culture than they do of the text.

[310] Joseph A. Fitzmyer, *The Anchor Yale Bible: First Corinthians* (New Haven, CT: Yale-Anchor, 2008), 417. Fitzmyer summarizes, "the genuine force of *exousia* is best brought out by the simple translation, 'a woman ought to have authority over her head,' in the sense that, in covering it she actively exercises control over it, 'so as not to expose it to indignity.'"

power "on her head" (1 Corinthians 11:10).[311] Perhaps in reference to these sentinel angels, Paul teaches that women need this sign of authority on their heads.[312] Covered with "authority / *exousia,*" it is possible that during worshipful prayer, the veil signaled the messenger angels to provide the woman with the word of God or prophecy. Or perhaps, when the woman wore her emblem of authority, it signaled to the angels that the mouthpiece was now ready to receive divine instruction to testify.[313]

Imparting the same gospel, though removed by a dispensation from Paul, Brigham Young notes that angels guard the entrance to heaven where both women and men give them "signs and tokens" to return to the presence of God.[314] President

---

[311] Another powerful image of a sacred veil is found in Exodus 26:33, "the veil shall divide unto you between the holy place and the most holy." The temple veil takes on the role of the Savior.

[312] David W. Bercot, ed., *A Dictionary of Early Christian Beliefs* (Peabody, MA: Hendrickson Publishers, 1998), 667. The early Christian father, *Tertullian* (c. 198), understood the angels referenced by Paul to be devils: "This refers to the event, when on account of 'the daughters of men,' angels revolted from God." Similar ideas spread throughout Christianity.

[313] Hans Conzelmann, *A Commentary on the First Epistle to the Corinthians* (Philadelphia, PA: Fortress, 1988), 189. As mentioned earlier, biblical scholars have very different interpretations of this passage. Without the perspective of the restoration, Conzelmann interprets these "angels" as fallen angels that originated from "sexually libidinous," from demons who had sex with mortal women. Reverend Lockwood quoted early Church fathers (Ambrose, Ephraim, and Primasius) who thought the angels referred to bishops or presbyters, but Lockwood argues that the New Testament usage of "angels" designates "supernatural beings." Lockwood, *1 Corinthians*, 374. In a different direction, the *Anchor Bible* commentary sees the angels as "guardians of order of nature and so are concerned with proper respect for God in worship." Orr and Walther, *1 Corinthians*, 261. These interpretations contribute to the "jumbled mess" of 1 Corinthians 11 (see footnote 251).

[314] Brigham Young, *Journal of Discourses* (London: Latter-day Saints' Book Depot, 1855), 2:31. When President Brigham Young dedicated the cornerstone of the Salt Lake Temple on April 6, 1853, he taught the saints about the role of angels in connection with their endowment. "Your endowment is, to receive all those ordinances in the House of the Lord, which are necessary for you, after you have departed this life, to enable you to walk back to the presence of the Father, passing the angels who stand as

John Taylor references these teachings of Paul's as he addresses women on similar truths about angels and gender:

> Thou hast obeyed the truth, and thy guardian angel ministers unto thee and watches over thee. Thou hast chosen him you loved in the spirit world to be thy companion. Now, crowns, thrones, exaltations, and dominions are in reserve for thee in the eternal worlds, . . . Thou wilt be permitted to pass by the Gods and angels who guard the gates, and onward, upward to thy exaltation in a celestial world among the Gods, to be a priestess queen upon thy Heavenly Father's throne, and a glory to thy husband and offspring, to bear the souls of men, to people other worlds (as thou didst bear their tabernacles in mortality) while eternity goes and eternity comes; and if you will receive it, lady, this is eternal life. And herein is the saying of the Apostle Paul fulfilled, that the man is not without the woman, neither is the woman without the man, in the Lord; that man is the head of the woman, and the glory of the man is the woman. Hence, thine origin, the object of thy ultimate destiny. If faithful, lady, the cup is within thy reach; drink then the heavenly draught and live.[315]

In addition to the ideas of John Taylor and Brigham Young, Joseph Smith's translation of this verse suggests another interpretation.

---

sentinels, being enabled to give them the key words, the signs and tokens, pertaining to the Holy Priesthood, and gain your eternal exaltation in spite of earth and hell."

[315] John Taylor, "The Mormon," August 29, 1857, in *Latter-day Prophets Speak: Selections from the Sermons and Writings of Church Presidents*, ed. Daniel H. Ludlow (Salt Lake City, UT: Bookcraft, 1993), 10. The cut portion reads, "and the way is opened for thee to return to the presence of thy Heavenly Father, if thou wilt only abide by and walk in a celestial law, fulfill the designs of thy Creator and hold out to the end that when mortality is laid in the tomb, you may go down to your grave in peace, arise in glory, and receive your everlasting reward in the resurrection of the just, along with thy head and husband."

Joseph Smith makes only one change to 1 Corinthians 11 in his inspired version: he changed the word "power" in verse 10, to "covering."[316] In Joseph Smith's mind, a woman was "to have *a covering* on her head because of the angels."[317] In this context, when female saints cover their heads with veils to pray and prophesy, they function as "priestesses'" with divinely acknowledged power. A priestess' veil becomes part of her "robes of righteousness" and opens the door to a female version of the ministry of angels (Moroni 7:29-33, 37; D&C 29:12; 109:76).

11:11-12: "Nevertheless neither is the man without the woman, neither the woman without the man, in the Lord. For as the woman is of the man, even so is the man also by the woman; but all things of God.

Paul ends his explanation by stressing the complete interdependence of men and women: woman was created from man, while man is born of woman. Paul's claim encompasses the Edenic creation and birth process. In this unique role, each mother opens the veil to mortality, just as Jesus opened the veil of immortality. A woman's womb symbolizes a veil of life as spirit children pass from heaven to earth through her. In this task, woman acts as a veil.

Verses 11 and 12 focus on the union within a husband-wife relationship. God organized this union as a covenant with Him (D&C 132:15). Hugh Nibley describes the covenantal partnership between God, a husband and wife as a system of checks and balances:

---

[316] Joseph Smith's translation of 1 Corinthians appears to have taken place in the early 1830s, over a decade before the temple endowment was revealed to the saints in 1842. Perhaps the prophet would have asked and received more clarification on these verses about women veiling during prayer after he introduced the endowment.

[317] Thomas A. Wayment, ed., *The Complete Joseph Smith Translation of the New Testament: A Side-by-Side Comparison with the King James Version* (Salt Lake City UT: Deseret Book, 2005), 272; emphasis added.

There is no patriarchy or matriarchy in the Garden; the two supervise each other. Adam is given no arbitrary power; Eve is to heed him only insofar as he obeys their Father—and who decides that? She must keep check on him as much as he does on her. It is, if you will, a system of checks and balances in which each party is as distinct and independent in its sphere as are the departments of government under the Constitution—and just as dependent on each other.[318]

Through this trio of unity we understand the qualifications of eternal relationships.

Paul seeks to strengthen the unity and mutuality among husbands, wives, and God. To do so, he has to combat a culture of divorce across the Roman Empire; historians estimate adults in the middle and upper classes had four to five divorces each.[319] In contrast to these disposable relationships, Paul promotes marital longevity through unity and kindness: "Let every man have his own wife, and let every woman have her own husband. Let the husband render unto the wife due benevolence: and likewise also the wife unto the husband . . . If any brother hath a wife . . . and she be pleased to dwell with him, let him not put her away" (1 Corinthians 7:2–3, 12-14). Consistently, Paul acknowledges the worth of women as equal to men. His request for a woman to wear a veil during ordinances has nothing to do with gender inequality and everything to do with her relationships and authority to participate in Christian ordinances.

---

[318] Nibley, *Old Testament and Related Studies*, 93.

[319] Stagg, *Woman in the World of Jesus* (Philadelphia, PA: Westminster Press, 1978), 86; Ben Wirtherington, *Women and the Genesis of Christianity* (NYC: Cambridge University Press, 1984), 20. David Instone-Brewer, *Divorce and Remarriage in the Bible: The Social and Literary Context* (Grand Rapids, MI: Eerdmans, 2002), 73. "Seneca complained that there are women who do not number the years by consuls but by husbands; they divorce to marry and they marry to divorce (*De beneficiis* 3.16.2l)."

11:13: "Judge in yourselves:
is it comely that a woman pray unto God uncovered?"

In this new Christian order, Paul teaches the primitive saints that women may pray or prophesy, and her head covering is the evidence of her authority to act in that manner. The word "comely / *prepo*" also means "to stand out, to be conspicuous, eminent, becoming, seemly, or fit." Paul concludes this subject by reminding the Corinthian saints, who had been disposed to contentions in the past (see 1 Corinthians 11:16), that they were not a law unto themselves on this matter. Paul calls for a unity of the faith among all the churches of God—even in the practice of women wearing veils when praying and prophesying. He asks the saints to take responsibility for themselves and judge if a veil worn during ordinances could signify the order of creation with divine relationships between God and mortals.

To summarize this section, within Paul's list of corrections to the Corinthian saints ("but I would have you know," 1 Corinthian 11:3), he expounds on the issue of women wearing veils during special prayers in early Christian ordinances (11:2). As he explains these principles, he recognizes and encourages the unity between husbands and wives. His instructions capture the order of creation—a fortifying link between women, men, Christ, and God—that endowed humanity with God's power. The woman's veil represents "power on her head" in the presence of angels (11:10). Essentially, Paul asks whether it is "not better to pray and prophesy with humility before God and with a sign of her authority?" For Paul, the sanction derived from the creation allows God's glory (referring to man) to pray unveiled; and by the same token, humanity's glory (referring to woman) should humbly commune with God veiled.

117

II. 1 Corinthians 14:31-35

Women Prophesy in Church Worship

Following Paul's discussion on a woman's veil, he spends three chapters teaching the appropriate use of the gifts of the Spirit (1 Corinthians 12-14). He exhorts the saints to prophesy in a manner to edify, exhort, "and comfort" one another (1 Corinthians 14:3). He also cautions the Corinthian saints that their public expressions of the gifts of the Spirit must be illuminating. These chapters sound as if their worship services were less than orderly. Some saints spoke in tongues without an interpreter, people spoke at the same time as others, and a general irreverence prevailed. Paul hopes to improve their public worship services by establishing order. He discourages the use of tongues without an interpreter, and encourages prophecy over speaking in tongues (1 Corinthians 14:4-5, 23-25).

In the adjoining chapters of 1 Corinthians 11-14, we find at least five sections in which the apostolic church leader follows the Lord's example by urging women as well as men to speak, teach, or prophesy (1 Corinthians 11:5, 12:7-11, 14:3-4, 24, and 31).[320] At times the KJV uses pronouns that hide the multiple gender implications of the Greek. For example, the KJV of 1 Corinthians 14:3 uses "he" while the Greek and most other English translations open the text to both genders, as we read in the NIV translation, "But the one who prophesies speaks to people for their strengthening, encouraging and comfort." Paul invites all saints to seek the gifts of the Spirit: "each one is given the manifestation of the Spirit to profit withal" (1 Corinthians 12:7, ASV); similarly, he speaks to both men and women to share the gift of prophecy in chapter 14.

---

[320] Also outside this Epistle, see Galatians 3:28; Philippians 4:2-3; and chapter 2 of this book.

14:31: For ye may all prophesy one by one,
that all may learn, and all may be comforted.

Public worship in early Christianity was filled with the outpouring of the gifts of the Spirit on men and women. Specifically, the gift of prophecy, can refer to foretelling the future, as well as exhorting, inspiring, and strengthening one another. In the apostolic church, all the saints were asked to join their testimonies and gifts to bless one another.

14:32-33: And the spirits of the prophets are subject to the
prophets. For God is not the author of confusion,
but of peace, as in all churches of the saints.

Repeatedly throughout this chapter Paul instructs the saints on reverence in their worship services. He asks them not to speak at the same time (14:23, 29-30), so that everyone can understand (14:11, 14-15, 19, 27-28), and to build the church (14:6, 26). Here in verse 32, he refers to prophets as a group of people. Acts 13:1 lists five prophets in a congregation of the early church: "Now in the church at Antioch there were prophets and teachers: Barnabas, Simeon called Niger, Lucius of Cyrene, Manaen . . . and Saul." The Old Testament also refers to groups of prophets (1 Samuel 10:10-13; 2 Kings 2:3, 5). Other Epistles refer to false prophets (2 Peter 2:1). Biblically, prophets represent all those who speak for God, or those who testify of Christ (Amos 3:7; 1 John 4:2-3; Revelation 19:10).[321] In this light, Paul asks all those who prophesy to share their testimonies in an orderly fashion.

14:34-35: Let your women keep silence in the churches:
for it is not permitted unto them to speak;
but they are commanded to be under obedience,

---

[321] The Prophet Joseph Smith also referred to prophets as those who testified of Christ. Ehat and Cook, ed., *The Words of Joseph Smith*, 10-11.

as also saith the law.
And if they will learn any thing,
let them ask their husbands at home:
for it is a shame for women to speak in the church.

These two puzzling verses seem to contradict Paul's previous support of women in 1 Corinthians 11:5, 14:31, and many others. Verses 34 and 35 stand out in glaring opposition to Paul's previous advice, and we are left to wonder why the text contradicts itself. When we find contradictory passages that stifle women's worship, we should examine them in light of other positive statements from the author and the Lord (and the seven points outlined in the "Introduction"). In an alternative interpretation by John Welch, we find more sensitive wording: "Women should be reverent (*sigatosan;* KJV, "keep silent") and not chatter (*lalein;* KJV, "speak"), but be supportive [KJV, "under obedience"]."[322] Another definition for "*sigatosan*" is "be at peace." However, even an examination of other reputable English translations does not resolve the blatant conflict of messages.

These two verses may be a tangential thought that fits into the broader section of 1 Corinthians' discussion on disorderly conduct in meetings. It is feasible to imagine that because the Greek and Jewish culture restricted many women in their public worship, perhaps the social freedom newly found in Christianity incited some women to speak or act beyond propriety (or at least beyond the previous norm). Were Corinthian women interrupting the meetings with questions? Do we have another translation that sheds light on this passage, or could the verse have been added later by a scribe? I want to examine these two possibilities.

---

[322] Welch and Hall, *Charting the New Testament*, 2002, 15-15.

NIS	NIV	JB
The women are to keep silent in the churches; for they are not permitted to speak, are to subject themselves, just as the Law also says. If they desire to learn anything, let them ask their own husbands at home; for it is improper for a woman to speak in church.	Women should remain silent in the churches. They are not allowed to speak, but must be in submission, as the law says. If they want to inquire about something, they should ask their own husbands at home; for it is disgraceful for a woman to speak in the church.	Women are to remain quiet in the assemblies, since they have no permission to speak: theirs is a subordinate part, as the Law itself says. If there is anything they want to know, they should ask their husbands at home: it is shameful for a woman to speak in the assembly.

The Joseph Smith translation (JST) modifies the meaning entirely by changing "speak" (KJV) to "rule" (JST): "it is not permitted unto them to rule in the church" (1 Corinthians 14:34).[323] It transforms the discussion from speaking to authority and ruling. Was the problem that women usurped authority? 1 Corinthians discusses authority repeatedly. Elsewhere, though, Paul explicitly supports female leaders (including Tabitha, Chloe, Phebe, Lydia, and Priscilla).[324] With the perspective of the JST change, it sounds like Paul has a particular kind of ruling in mind. One wonders what problems the Corinthian saints had that warranted this reprimand (and

---

[323] For more information on the Joseph Smith Translation see, Robert J. Matthews, *A Plainer Translation: Joseph Smith's Translation of the Bible— A History and Commentary* (Provo, UT: Brigham Young University), 1975.
[324] See chapter 2 and appendix 4.

other reproofs). Were they correcting the presiding elder? A few verses earlier, Paul instructs church members to listen respectfully when someone else is speaking ("hold his peace," 1 Corinthians 14:30). Not knowing the circumstances inhibits our full understanding.

The second—and most convincing—explanation to me is that perhaps these two verses were not written by Paul at all.[325] Evidence shows that they were added later by someone else. Greek textual scholars find that the most reliable and earliest manuscripts of 1 Corinthians do not include these two verses (1 Corinthians 14:34-35).[326] Furthermore, textual critics note a break in the flow of Paul's thought between verse 33 and 36, which also suggests that an editor added the two troublesome verses later as his own interpretation. It does not seem plausible that Paul would contradict himself within the same section of the same letter. These two verses also match the heretical view of women from the end of the first century and may have been added by a copyist or compiler a few decades later.[327]

Whenever there is a contradiction between two Scriptures, Latter-day Saints have the responsibility to compare biblical doctrine with the revelations of the restoration. In this case, women speak, teach, counsel, testify, exhort, and administer in the restored church. They may prophesy and pray as priestesses in their homes, church services, public gatherings, and temples. Joseph Smith revealed that women should be ordained "to expound Scriptures, and to exhort the church, according as it shall be given thee by [God's] Spirit" (D&C 25:7). However, women do not govern the priesthood leaders as pointed out in the JST version of 1 Corinthians 14:34.

---

[325] Or perhaps, as part of Paul's rebuttal, these words were added as a quotation from the slogans of the Corinthian elitists in a sarcastic tone (as Paul quotes their statement earlier in 1 Corinthians 7:1).

[326] By examining The Bible Society 1975 edition of *The* Greek *New Testament*, one can see which Greek manuscripts included these verses. Working with the Classical Greek scholars, we find that the oldest and most trusted biblical manuscripts do not include 1 Corinthians 14:34-35.

[327] Dianne Bergant, Robert J. Karris, ed., *The Collegeville Bible Commentary* (Collegeville, MN: Liturgical Press, 1989), 1129.

In conclusion, the apostolic church battled great diversity that affected the saints' ability to accept and live Jesus' teachings. In the Epistles we find evidence that the saints struggled with keeping doctrine pure—including accepting women as equal participants in worship. We find passages where the apostles tried to clarify and teach the principles and ordinances that Christ taught. However, in the currently available New Testament translations, we also find statements that contradict the Lord's teachings regarding women's worship. It leaves one to wonder if the text had been altered, or if the early leaders misunderstood the Lord's teachings. Fortunately, the majority of the Epistles encourage Christian women to join in public worship. Specifically, in 1 Corinthians, women are empowered to pray and prophesy as part of their devotion and sanctification.

Chapter 4
Marriage: From Arranging to Cohabitation

Whereas the first chapters looked at Christ's physical emancipation of women and the effect that had on women in the early Christian church, we now look at the spiritual power our Redeemer unleashed. His example and teachings rejuvenate not just women themselves, but all aspects of the world of women. These changes to family life were quieter and less obvious.

Just like the Jews who were so intent on finding a *conquering* Messiah to overthrow their Roman oppressors that they missed the Son of God who came as a *suffering servant* (Isaiah 49, 52, 53)—so too we may miss the subtle yet emancipating changes that Christ provided for family life if we only look for a gallant, daring liberator. Christ sowed new social and spiritual seeds that had the potential to provide a loving, nurturing, healthy family life, but in some cases took years and even centuries to germinate and bear fruit.[328]

---

[328] This slow germination may be attributed, in part, to the fact that very few people read the Lord's teachings for centuries. As soon as Christians began

This chapter provides a historical overview of how Jewish marriages began in the late Second Temple era. This protocol provides an insightful backdrop to familiar New Testament stories. Woven in between accounts of arranging marriages, betrothals, ceremonies and feasts, we find Jesus and His apostles planting empowering principles about personal revelation, the Atonement, the Holy Ghost, trials, and consecration.

Cultural and Scriptural Background

Jews honored marriage as a religious duty to fulfill God's commandment given in the Garden of Eden. Adam needed a "help meet" (KJV) or "a strength corresponding to him" (ISV) or "his one before" (Genesis 2:20, TEB[329]), because "it was not good that the man should be alone" (Moses 3:18). "Therefore, shall a man leave his father and his mother, and shall cleave unto his wife: and they shall be one flesh" (Genesis 2:24; Moses 3:24). The Old Testament persuades men to "live joyfully with the wife whom thou lovest all the days of thy life" (Ecclesiastes 9:9) and "rejoice with the wife of thy youth" (Proverbs 5:18).

Proverbs linked marriage with wisdom and heavenly approval: "Whoso findeth a wife findeth a good thing, and

---

regularly reading the New Testament, changes began culturally, politically, economically, and emotionally that allowed the Lord's word to grow in more hearts. Over time the Lord's words have borne fruit.

[329] The TEB translation of Genesis 2:20 includes a pre-Eden relationship between Adam and Eve. To better understand the context of this quote, here is the TEB of Genesis 2:18-20: "And YHVH ELOHIM said, "Not good—the soil-man being by himself, I will make for him a help, as his one before." And YHVH ELOHIM shaped from the soil every living thing of the field, and every flyer of the skies, and he made come toward the soil-man to see what he would call to it; and whatever the soil-man would call to it—each living life-breather—that was its name. And the soil-man called names to every animal, and to the flyer of the skies, and to every living thing of the field; and to Soil-Man he did not find a help, as his one before." The translation note for "his one before" reads, "one facing him, before or opposite him, as his corresponding counterpart."

obtaineth favor of the LORD" (Proverbs 18:22). Nearly a thousand years later, during the intertestamental period, we read the Jewish philosopher Ben Sira restating the importance of marriage with a slight variation: "Where there is no wife, a man will become a fugitive."[330] Later still, rabbis still felt strongly enough about marriage that they declared that a "Jew without a wife" is one of the groups "excommunicated by Heaven."[331]

At the time of the New Testament, marriage was a prerequisite for certain professions, "An unmarried man may not teach scribes . . . [nor] herd cattle."[332] Celibacy was uncommon among Jews, except among certain strict Essenes.[333] Polygamy was permitted, as it was in the Old Testament, yet it appears that most marriages were monogamous, probably for financial reasons.[334]

---

[330] Ben Sira, *Ecclesiasticus*, 36:30.

[331] *Babylonian Talmud, Pesahim* 113a. There were seven groups who were not eligible for heaven. The quote continues, "one who has a wife but no children; one who has children but doesn't raise them in the study of the Torah; one who has no phylacteries on his head or on his arm, no fringes on his garment, no mezuzah on his door; and one who won't put shoes on his feet." The Talmud instructed men to love their wives; "Who loves his wife as himself and honors her more than himself . . . to him the text refers, Thou shalt know that thy tent is in peace." *Babylonian Talmud: Yebamoth,* 62b.

[332] Jacob Neusner, *The Mishnah: A New Translation* (New Haven, CT: Yale, 1988), *Qiddushin,* 4:13a; 4:14a; Interesting in the middle of this rabbinic debate on teaching, one rabbi inserted, "nor may a woman teach scribes" (4:13b).

[333] Josephus, *Wars,* 2.8.2; *Antiquities,* 18.1.5. Josephus explained that some groups of Essenes viewed woman as unfaithful and remained celibate, while other Essenes married (*Wars,* 2.8.12). Also see Skolnik, *Encyclopaedia Judaica,* 6.511.

[334] Neusner, ed, *Judaism in the Biblical Period,* 437. "The Israelite kings openly practiced polygamy but were castigated for it (Deuteronomy 17:17). Prophets, priests, and other prominent biblical figures were monogamous. Social and economic obligations imposed on a husband to support each wife equally (Exodus 21:10)." At the time of the New Testament, polygamy was usually practiced only as a levirate marriage (marrying your departed next of kin's wife to raise up seed to the deceased, Genesis 38:8; Deuteronomy 25:5).

New Testament Examples

The New Testament unabashedly promotes marriage: "Marriage is honourable in all" (Hebrews 13:4). The word "honourable" can also be translated as "esteemed . . . beloved . . . dear."[335] The Gospels and Epistles are filled with noble examples of married couples who work together in furthering God's work (i.e., Mary and Joseph, Zacharias and Elisabeth, Zebedee and Salome, Simon Peter and his wife, Chuza and Joanna, and Priscilla and Aquila). The Lord's apostles urge "the younger women [to] marry, bear children, guide the house, give none occasion to the adversary to speak reproachfully" (1 Timothy 5:14).

Rather than rejecting the cultural marriage laws, Jesus reformed their relationships by teaching mutual respect and the need to change one's heart. He denounced anger and called for reconciliation. He taught them to love as He does (Matthew 5:24; 5:38-42, JST; John 13:34). He honored and respected women as equals of men (Matthew 9:22; 26:10; Luke 10:42; John 20:15-17, etc.). He taught principles to develop unity, love, trust, fidelity, mutuality, and service in marriage (John 13:34; 17:21-23; 1 Corinthians 11:11; Ephesians 5:28; Titus 2:4; etc.).

1. Arranged Marriages

Cultural Background

The Old Testament includes the story of an arranged marriage between Isaac and Rebekah (Genesis 24). The New Testament has no explicit account of an arranged marriage, but they are assumed to have taken place, as other sources from the era illuminate. One rabbi gave ultimate authority for matchmaking straight to God. He claims that since the creation of the world, God has kept busy as a marriage broker: "He sits

---

[335] Strong, *Exhaustive Concordance of the Bible,* 91; Greek dictionary for "honourable / *Timios* or *timiotatos*."

and makes matches, assigning this man to that woman and this woman to that man."[336]

The ultimate authority for arranging marriages may have come from God, but in practice, either the father, or next of kin, tightly controlled the arrangement of each child's marriage.[337] It was an extremely important duty of fatherhood: "Marry thy daughter well, and then shalt do a great work, and give her to a wise man."[338] The rabbis saw a well-matched couple as a guarantee for a stable home, which then led to a durable nation.[339]

The ideal healthy Jewish young man married at eighteen (although there are historical examples ranging from age thirteen to twenty-four).[340] The rabbis taught, "a man who does not marry by the age of twenty has sinned."[341] Displeasing God may have been bad enough, but if a Roman man were still single by age twenty-five, or a woman by age twenty, they had to pay an extra state tax.[342] The ideal Jewish girl married a little younger—usually between the ages of twelve to fifteen. The day after a girl's twelfth birthday, she was no longer a minor "young girl / na'rah;" and the day after she turned twelve and a half she could legally be married.[343] Given the young ages of their marriages, their culture of gender segregation, and their inexperience socially, it is not surprising that arranged marriages seemed the best cultural option.[344]

---

[336] *Midrash Genesis Rabbah* 68.4.

[337] *Mishnah*, *Ketuboth,* 4:4. "The father has authority over his daughter as touching her betrothal." Intercourse was the only way to cement a levirate marriage.

[338] Ben Sira, *Ecclesiasticus*, 7:27.

[339] Neusner, ed, *Judaism in the Biblical Period*, 223-224.

[340] *Mishnah, Avoth,* 5:21; *Kiddushin*, 29b. Glover, *Jewish Laws and Customs*, 231; Campbell, *Marriage and Family in the Biblical World,* 186, footnote 20. Neusner, ed, *Judaism in the Biblical Period*, 224.

[341] *Mishnah, Kiddushin,* 29b.

[342] Campbell, *Marriage and Family in the Biblical World*, 144.

[343] *Mishnah, Kiddushin,* 2.1; "A man may give his daughter in betrothal while she is still in her girlhood either by his own act or by that of his agent."

[344] Ben Sira, *Ecclesiasticus*, 26:10-11; 22:3. Ben Sira advised fathers to keep their daughters inside: "If thy daughter be shameless, keep her in straitly, lest

Every Jewish father or guardian had twelve years to find a spouse for his daughter. A girl under twelve / *q'tannah,* was completely under her father or guardian's control. But by age twelve, she was allowed to voice some of her desires.[345] Then came the important age of twelve and a half when she became "a maiden of full age / *bogeret.*" Supposedly, if the father waited until then to find her husband, he lost full control of the decision. After twelve-and-a-half, the daughter could reject her father's choice of a husband up to "four or five times."[346] Ideally, a compatible union was found before that magical age.

The father's task of arranging marriages became complicated by familial, financial and political motivations. Jewish etiquette dictated that marriages remained within specific social circles—gentry married gentry, laborers married laborers.[347] The lowest division of Jewish social hierarchy

---

she abuse herself through overmuch liberty. . . . a foolish daughter shall be to his loss." In a commentary on these verses, Violet Brunton interprets, "Woman did not go out in public alone. If your headstrong daughter wandered outside on her own, she would make you 'the talk of the town' by displaying her beauty to men (42: 11-12); an over-anxious father might well imagine her ..." John Snaith, *The Cambridge Commentary on the New English Bible—Ecclesiasticus* (New York: Cambridge University Press, 1974), 133. As discussed in chapter 1, young women were usually kept indoors, but if they were ever in the company of men, Ben Sira cautioned men to not look or linger if women were present, "Behold not everybody's beauty: and tarry not among women." Ben Sira, *Ecclesiasticus,* 42:12.

[345] *Mishnah, Yebamoth,* 13.1.

[346] *Mishnah, Yebamoth,* 13.1. The famous rabbi Hillel (60 BC to 20 AD), wrote much on the subject and dictated that a girl of twelve-and-a-half "may exercise right of refusal four or five times" in the selection of her husband. In reaction to this limit, the more lenient rabbinic school of Shammai retorted, "The daughters of Israel are no [such] ownerless property!" Shammai allowed the underage girl to stay in her father's home until "she is come of age," meaning the onset of puberty. See appendix 1 this book.

[347] Louis H. Feldman, Meyer Reinhold, *Jewish Life and Thought among Greeks and Romans* (Fortress Press, 1996), 13. By AD 388, the *Theodosian Code* 3.7.2 forbade Jews to marry Christians; "No Jew shall take Christian woman in marriage, neither shall a Christian marry a Jewess. Indeed, if anyone shall commit something of the kind, his crime shall be considered as adultery with the right to accuse allowed the general public."

allowed marriages between proselytes, freed slaves, and illegitimate children.[348]

In some situations, a son's desires could influence his father's decision. The Jewish historian Josephus (AD 37-101) advised young men who felt a fancy toward a young girl to "demand her in marriage of him who hath power to dispose of her, and is fit to give her away."[349] His language of "demand her" and "dispose of her" may have developed from a warped outcome of arranged marriages, which over the generations tended to make marriage into a market and women into a commodity.[350]

Years later, the financial vocabulary became more common as the Talmud speaks of its advantage to solicit the best wife:

> Let a man always sell all he has and marry the daughter of a scholar. If he does not find the daughter of a scholar, let him marry one of the daughters of the great men of the generation. If he does not find the daughter of one of the great men of the generation, let him marry the daughter of the heads of synagogues. If he does not find the daughter of the heads of synagogues, let him marry the daughter of a charity treasurer. If he does not find the daughter of a charity treasurer, let him marry the daughter of an elementary school-teacher.[351]

This hierarchy of professions also speaks of the financial nature of purchasing a bride that prevailed at the time. The wealthier the family, the more power one had to arrange a marriage.

---

[348] *Mishnah, Kiddushin* 4:1.

[349] Josephus, *Against Apion,* 2:25. The whole quote reads, "[Our law] commands us also, when we marry, not to . . . take a woman by violence, nor to persuade her deceitfully and knavishly; but demand her in marriage of him who hath power to dispose of her." Josephus should be credited for denouncing rape and deception, but his use of "demand her in marriage . . ." still sounds insensitive to a woman's feelings.

[350] Ben Sira, *Ecclesiasticus,* 36:26. Quotation is on page 43.

[351] *Babylonian Talmud, Pesah*, 49b.

Marriage within the Extended family

Fathers often arranged marriages within their extended families in order to ensure compatibility and preserve family property.[352] Especially if a young woman were an heiress (i.e., she had no brothers), Moses instructed her to marry within the family tribe to keep family inheritance constant (Numbers 36:1-12). If she did not, when she married and moved into her husband's family home, she lost her inheritance of property.

Closer to the time of the New Testament, the apocryphal book of Jubilees (c. 120 BC) recommended marriage with a cousin (Jubilees 4:15, 16, 20, 27, 28). Josephus includes several examples of marriages between an uncle and niece (although a marriage between and an aunt and nephew were forbidden).[353] Marriages with a sibling were forbidden as were other close kin.[354] Many families remained in the same location for generations, so marrying within the community often meant marriage within the extended family.

Marriage within the Priesthood Lineage

The highest honor for an Israelite daughter was to marry a descendant of Aaron, or secondly a Levite, so that her sons could hold the priesthood and serve in the temple.[355] The law

---

[352] Numbers 36:1-12; Ilan, *Jewish Women in Greco-Roman Palestine,* 77.

[353] Josephus, *Antiquities,* XVII.1:3; XVIII.5.4; XIX.9:1. *Wars* I.28:4; and marriage with a cousin *Wars* I.24:5 etc. Also see Alfred Kingsley Glover, *Jewish Laws and Customs* (Well, MN: WA Hammond, 1900), 230.

[354] Neusner, ed, *Judaism in the Biblical Period,* 441. The forbidden relationship of an aunt and nephew is also recorded: "Marriages between an aunt and nephew, marriage to a brother's wife or to a wife's sister while the wife is alive (even after a divorce), marriage to the wife of an uncle, marriage to a son or daughter in law, and marriage to someone already married."

[355] Jacob Neusner, *Sifre to Numbers: An American Translation and Explanation,* vol. 2 (Atlanta, GA: Scholars Press, 1986), *Numbers Seventy-Eight,* 1.S. *Mishnah, Kiddushin* 4:1. In the same social class as Levites are physically impaired priests from Aaron, and pure Israelites from any of the other tribes.

of Moses instructed those with priestly lineage to choose a virgin from a worthy Levite family (Leviticus 21:14).[356] This carried down to the time of the New Testament, where we read from Josephus, who was a priest himself, that a priest should find a bride with proper Levitical lineage "without having any regard to money, or any other dignities."[357] While a priest was allowed to marry the daughter of a Levite or pure Israelite, if a priest married the daughter of a priest, it conveyed a twofold honor.[358]

New Testament Examples

In Luke's account of the birth narratives, he carefully includes the detail that Zacharias the priest marries one "of the daughters of Aaron," the priestess Elisabeth (Luke 1:5).

---

[356] All male descendants of Jacob's son Levi held the Levitical priesthood, but the higher honor was given to those direct descendants from Aaron who held the Aaronic Priesthood. While Levites took care of the more secular tasks of running the temple, the priests performed the majority of the temple sacrifices. They acted as mediators between God and men at the altar by placing an animal on the altar and sprinkling its blood on the horns and corners of the altar (Leviticus 4:7, 25). Aaronic priesthood holders could function as priests, chief priests, or the one reigning high priest.

[357] Josephus, *Against Apion,* 1.7. The full quote reads, "He who is partaker of the priesthood must propagate of a wife of the same nation, without having any regard to money, or any other dignities. But he is to make a scrutiny, and to take his wife's genealogy from the ancient tables. And this is our practice not only in Judea, but wheresoever any body of men of our nation do live; and even there an exact catalogue of our priests' marriages is kept; I mean at Egypt and Babylon, or in any other place of the rest of the habitable earth, withersoever our priests are scattered; for they send to Jerusalem the ancient names of their parents in writing."

[358] Brown, *Birth,* 258. In the Old Testament priests were advised to marry within their tribe, "Let them marry to whom they think best; only to the family of the tribe of their father shall they marry" (Numbers 36:6). Women who were direct descendants of Aaron (as Elisabeth was Luke 1:5) were to marry in the Aaronic lineage to keep the priesthood lineage pure. Moses encouraged marriages within the same tribe, but by the time of Jesus, in general situations, this practice was not strictly followed.

Within the cultural context of arranged priestly marriages, this detail confirms that Zacharias' family obediently observed the guidelines of the Torah to keep their priesthood lineage pure.

Luke further provides more noble attributes of Zacharias and Elisabeth: "they were both righteous before God, walking in all the commandments and ordinances of the Lord blameless" (Luke 1:6). Luke probably emphasizes these details to combat the cultural baggage that taught that barrenness was a sin.[359] Zacharias and Elisabeth seem to bridge the old and the new covenant as they epitomize a devout Old Testament couple— even echoing Abraham and Sarah's infertility—while they bridge the new covenant as disciples and witnesses of the Promised Messiah.

Although the nativity narratives are silent on the ages of Mary and Joseph at their betrothal, we can infer that they follow the traditional rules, as Joseph is described as "just," which also means "equitable . . . innocent, holy . . . meet, righteous" (Matthew 1:19).[360]

Matthew chooses Joseph as his main character in his nativity narrative and in every reference portrays him as a conscientious, law-abiding Jew (Matthew 1:19-20, 24; 2:13, 19). This suggests that Joseph was less than twenty years old.

We are left to assume that the angel Gabriel visits Mary sometime between age twelve and fourteen, as she is already betrothed to Joseph but has not yet consummated their marriage: "the angel Gabriel was sent from God unto a city of Galilee, named Nazareth, to a virgin espoused to a man" (Luke 1:26-27).

Artists tend to depict Mary in her late teens or early twenties, but historical records from the time suggest she would have been closer to thirteen, a very young bride by modern standards. Nevertheless, God often calls and empowers youth as

---

[359] Read more on infertility as a punishment for sins in chapter 7, "childbirth."

[360] Strongs, *Exhaustive Concordance of the Bible,* 24, of the Greek Dictionary section *dikaios.*

His leaders, and Mary fits that pattern.[361] Artists also depict Joseph as much older with grey or balding hair, but this idea comes from a later tradition that developed around the theory that Mary was a virgin for life.[362]

Jesus did not eradicate arranged marriages, but He did plant principles with the potential to grow into the freedom of choice.[363] God initiates agency in the Garden of Eden: "thou mayest choose for thyself, for it is given unto thee" (Genesis 2:21, JST). Teachings on agency flow through the Old Testament: "Choose you this day, whom ye will serve . . . but as for me and my house, we will serve the LORD" (Joshua

---

[361] For example, the prophet Samuel (1 Samuel 3:8-11), David son of Jesse (1 Samuel 16:12-13), Nephi and Jacob sons of Lehi (1 Nephi 2:16; 2 Nephi 2:2-4), Joseph Smith (JS-H 1:7-20), etc.

[362] When the Roman church began teaching that Mary was a virgin for her whole life, they struggled with verses in Mark 6:3 and Matthew 13:55 that state that she had at least seven children; "Is not this . . . the son of Mary, the brother of James, and Joses, and of Juda, and Simon? and are not his sisters here with us?" To harmonize the biblical list of Jesus' siblings with the later Roman-Christian thought about Mary's virginity for life, a story developed that claimed Joseph was an older widower with children. This way he could have fathered the other six plus children mentioned, been widowed, and then married the young Mary without ever consummating their marriage. Those who claim that Mary remained a virgin for life have adopted the story that Mary merely raised several stepchildren. We have no scriptural evidence for this conjecture. The story is found in the apocryphal *Protevangelium of James* (also known as the *Nativity of Mary* or *Apocalypse of James*) that dates to the second century but appears to quote an older text. See appendix 3 for more information on the text.

[363] Interestingly, it is not until the Protestant reformation, when many people started reading the Bible, that we see many of Jesus' subtle teachings having a major social impact. Once the printing press brought the price of Bibles within an affordable range for people to own, and once a large portion of the population became literate, we find the Christian world reading the Bible. It is then that many emancipating teachings of Jesus took root. For example, those who came to the new world for religious freedom built their society on the teachings of the Bible. They read and implemented its teachings. As a result, over generations we see emancipating social changes for slaves, women, children, and society at large.

24:15).[364] In the New Testament Jesus gently tutors Martha on the importance of choice: "one thing is needful . . . Mary hath chosen that good part" (Luke 10:42). These subtle seeds of choice developed the power to grow into emancipation. Truth became the means to find freedom: "and the truth shall make you free" (John 8:32). Jesus chose His twelve apostles, and they in turn chose Stephen and others (Luke 6:13; Acts 6:5).

The apostles carry the message on: "whatsoever a man soweth, that shall he also reap" (Galatians 6:7-8). The greatest freedoms and opportunities of all come from choosing to follow God as Jesus exemplifies: "I seek not mine own will, but the will of the Father" (John 5:30); and He prays, "not as I will, but as thou wilt" (Matthew 26:39). The Lord also applies agency as He "learned . . . obedience by the things which he suffered" (Hebrews 5:7-8; also 11:25). Jesus, and his namesake Joshua, set the biblical stage for the freedom of choice.[365]

2. Betrothal

Cultural Background

The Jewish marriage ceremony took place in two stages, usually a year apart.[366] The Bible refers to the first half as either an "espousal" or "betrothal," yet no English word correctly identifies this first step of Jewish matrimony.[367] This unique Jewish custom described the beginning of the Jewish marriage

---

[364] Proverbs 1:29 rebukes the people's bad choices, "they . . . did not choose the fear of the LORD."

[365] Restoration Scriptures, though half the size of the Bible, have three times as many verses on agency—see topics including desire, obey, choose, free, judge, agency, freedom, prove, willing, opposition, etc.

[366] *Mishnah, Ketuboth* , 5:2 "a virgin is granted twelve months wherein to provide for herself." Also see Campbell*, Marriage and Family in the Biblical World,* 186.

[367] In Greek *"erusin"* and in Hebrew, *"'aras."* See Deuteronomy 28:23-30; 2 Samuel 3:14; Hosea 2:19-20; Matthew 1:18; Luke 1:27; 2:5; 2 Corinthians 11:2).

covenant. More than an engagement and more than a ceremony, the betrothal included making vows between the couple that were as binding as the marriage, but usually without the consumation.[368]

The betrothal included a legal marriage contract or *ketubah* drawn up as a purchase agreement of the husband's property: "a woman is acquired" by her husband.[369] Marriage became a financial purchase involving both the bride's and groom's families. The contract included the groom's payment of a "bride price." The minimum sum was 200 denarii for a virgin, with no maximum (a denarius was one day's minimum wage, thus 200 days' labor).[370] The groom paid this to the bride's father but the money eventually was to go to the bride if her husband died or divorced her without a religious cause (see section entitled "divorce" later in chapter 6). If the families were wealthy, the bride's father also paid the groom a dowry.

The monetary aspect of the marriage agreement brought up a debate between the rabbis about the *"difference between the acquisition of a wife and the acquisition of a slave."*[371] In addition to their similar workloads, wives and slaves or servants also overlapped legally, financially, and sexually.[372] A wife differed from a slave in that she kept the things she brought into the marriage as her "right of possession (but not of disposition)."[373] Also, if her husband died or divorced her, a

---

368 W.F. Albright and C.S. Mann, *The Anchor Bible Series-Matthew* (New York: Doubleday, 1971), 7; "the penalty for fornication with one person while betrothed to another was death for both guilty parties."

[369] *Mishnah, Kiddushin* 1:5. Eugene J. Lipman, *The Mishnah: Oral teachings of Judaism* (Norton, 1970), 192; "The text does not read, 'a man acquires a woman,' but deliberately says, 'a woman is acquired' to teach us that a woman can be married only with her knowledge and consent ... A Hebrew slave is acquired by money or by contract."

[370] *Mishnah, Ketuboth,* 4.7; 5.1.

[371] Jeremias, *Jerusalem,* 367. Also from Eugene J. Lipman, *The Mishnah: Oral teachings of Judaism* (Norton, 1970), 192.

[372] Gail Susan Labovitz, *Marriage and Metaphor: Constructions of Gender in Rabbinic Literature* (Lanham, MD: Lexington, Rowman and Littlefield, 2009), 59, 109, 133, 161.

[373] Jeremias, *Jerusalem,* 368.

wife received her "bride price," but a slave was not reimbursed if there were a death or dismissal. If kidnapped, a wife, and not a slave, had to be ransomed.[374] We are left to speculate on the difference of feelings.

Once the fathers or guardians agreed on a monetary contract, the families took the first step toward making the sacred marriage vows. Two witnesses recorded the transaction as the couple made their formal vows under a wedding tent or "canopy /*chuppah*."[375] The betrothal ceremony concluded with a prayer over a statutory cup of wine, which the couple drank. If the families had the means, a celebration followed. From the moment of the ceremony, the couple held their relationship as consecrated, as though they had wed. The betrothed girl could become widowed, divorced, and punished by death for adultery.[376] The ideal Jewish couple remained celibate during their betrothal.

New Testament Example

Joseph Vacillates

The New Testament records one betrothed couple: Mary and Joseph. When Joseph discovers Mary's pregnancy, he agonizes over his duty to divorce her for adultery, as they had already made their vows. "When as his mother Mary was espoused to Joseph, before they came together, she was found with child of the Holy Ghost. Then Joseph her husband, being a just man, and not willing to make her a publick example, was minded to put her away

---

[374] *Mishnah, Horayoth*. 3.7.

[375] Skolnik, *Encyclopedia Judaica,* 13.568. The bridal canopy was initially a tent or room where the wedding festival took place. However, in some cases, even without the formal wedding ceremony and feast, if two witnesses hear a bridegroom say to his betrothed, "Behold, you are consecrated to me with this cohabitation according to the law of Mosesand of Israel." Followed by cohabitation, the couple was considered married. Ibid., 13.570. One symbol of the wedding tent was a type of tabernacle where the couple came before God to make their covenants.

[376] *Mishnah, Ketuboth* 1.2; *Yebamoth,* 4:10; 6:4; *Gittin,* 6:2; also see Campbell, *Marriage and Family in the Biblical World,* 63, 221-222.

privily" (Matthew 1:18-19). The Gospels describe Joseph as an upright, virtuous descendant of David who obeyed the Mosaic law.

Joseph feels duty-bound to end his marriage contract until an angel of the Lord intervenes and provides freedom from his agony.[377] "Joseph, son of David, do not be afraid to take Mary as your wife; for the Child who has been conceived in her is of the Holy Spirit" (Matthew 1:20, ASB). Joseph's personal revelation not only liberates him from his obligations to the Mosaic law, but it also strengthens and empowers him with the knowledge that Mary was innocent and pure, that the Messiah was coming, and that he had an important role to play as the adoptive father of the Son of God.

One of the sanctioning seeds of emancipation that Jesus offers the world is the ability to receive personal revelation: "ask, and it shall be given you; seek, and ye shall find; knock, and it shall be opened unto you . . . . your Father which is in heaven give good things to them that ask him" (Matthew 7:7, 11). Later Jesus' disciples reiterate the theme, "If any of you lack wisdom, let him ask of God, that giveth to all men liberally, and upbraideth not; and it shall be given him" (James 1:5). God's answer to Joseph's conundrum of marriage or divorce offers hope to all who have deep questions. Jesus provides a tool to access the powers of heaven and liberation.[378]

3. Wedding Ceremony

Cultural Background

---

[377] Deuteronomy 22:20-21 states it a religious duty to stone a girl who was not a virgin at marriage.

[378] Sometimes current revelation contradicts past revelation. For example, the Israelites dietary laws are not repeated in the Word of Wisdom. With Abraham's sacrifice of Isaac, personal revelation trumped the earlier law of God. Similarly, Joseph of Nazareth had to break the Law of Moses to follow the angel's direction to marry Mary.

About a year after the betrothal, Jewish families prepared for the wedding ceremony. Wedding preparations culminated three days before the ceremony–which usually occurred on a Wednesday–when even the groom was required to devote himself to the preparations. [379] The bride adorned herself for her wedding by bathing, dressing, and putting on perfume. Her hair was left completely unveiled. This was the only public exposure of her hair in her adult life.[380] The bride and groom often wore a wreath or gold headdress. A procession of townspeople singing, dancing and carrying torches, paraded from the groom's home to the bride's home and back again. Once they arrived, the groom took his bride into his family home where the families had a wedding canopy or *chuppah* prepared.[381]

Under the canopy, the groom gave his bride a ring and completed their wedding vows: "You will be my wife according to the law of Moses."[382] Traditional promises were pronounced

---

[379] Campbell, *Marriage and Family in the Biblical World,* 206. Wednesdays were chosen as the day for a virgin's wedding. "This is explained in the Babylonian Talmud by the fact that the court sat on Thursdays and thus if the groom claimed that the bride had not been a virgin he could immediately complain to the court." Thursday was the wedding day for a widow so that her husband could devote three days to her before he returned to work. Skolnik, *Encyclopedia Judaica,* 13.566.

[380] *Mishnah, Ketuboth* 2.1; "She went forth [to the marriage] in a litter and with hair unbound . . ." (brackets in Danby's translation). Skolnik, *Encyclopedia Judaica,* 13.565; "Until the destruction of the temple both the bride and groom wore distinctive headdresses, sometimes of gold."

[381] Skolnik, *Encyclopedia Judaica,* 13.565.

[382] Campbell, *Marriage and Family in the Biblical World,* 190. A typical marriage contract or *ketubah* read as follows: "This *ketubah* before God and man that on this . . . day . . . the holy covenant of marriage was entered between bride-groom and his bride, at . . . Duly conscious of the solemn obligation of marriage the bridegroom consecrated to me as my wife according to the laws and traditions of Moses and Israel. I will love, honor, and cherish you; I will protect and support you; and I will faithfully care for your needs, as prescribed by Jewish law and tradition." The bride made the following declaration to the groom: "In accepting the wedding ring I pledge you all my love and devotion and I take upon myself the fulfillment of all the duties incumbent upon a Jewish wife." Neusner, ed, *Judaism in the Biblical Period,* 411.

by the husband—to redeem his wife if she were captured, to give their sons the *ketubah* upon the wife's death, to provide maintenance for their daughters until they were married, and, if the husband died, to require the sons to provide for their mother or else return the *ketubah*.[383] Ten men gathered to give a prayer or blessing.[384] The ceremony was finalized by a benediction over a cup of wine, and the bride became consecrated to the groom. Great rejoicing and feasting followed.

New Testament Example

One example of a wedding processional stands out in the Gospels: the parable of the ten virgins.[385] Matthew placed the

Parable of Ten Virgins

parable directly after the great prophecy of the Lord's Second Coming in order to illustrate the preparation needed for that great event (Matthew 24 and 25:1-13).[386]

The main character of this parable is the bridegroom, or "Son of Man" (Matthew 25:13).[387] In the parable, ten close unmarried friends of the bride wait for the arrival of the bridegroom.[388] Five of them join the joyous group of loved ones making up the bridegroom's processional, escorting the bride to his home for the wedding ceremony. If the procession occurred at night, the cultural practice of the time included bringing

---

[383] *Mishnah, Ketuboth* 4.12.

[384] *Mishnah, Megillah*, 4.3.

[385] The parable of the ten virgins is also referenced in modern revelations: D&C 33:16-17; 45:56-57; 63:54.

[386] Joseph Smith's translation of Matthew 24 changed the order of most verses, organizing the chapter to separate the Lord's Second Coming. It can be found in the Pearl of Great Price, as *Joseph Smith-Matthew*.

[387] In Matthew's typical style, he began, "then shall the kingdom of heaven be likened unto . . ." (Matthew 25:1). Matthew used this phrase, "kingdom of heaven" thirty-one times, and it is not mentioned anywhere else in the Bible. Daniel 2:44 uses the same words, but not the exact phrase, "In the days of these kings shall the God of heaven set up a kingdom."

[388] The Greek word for virgin, *parthenos*, also means the more general, unmarried young women.

torches or a lamp to light the way. Prudent people kept an extra flask of oil.[389]

The purpose of the parable was to use the marriage preparations and covenant as a symbolic backdrop to discuss the covenant criterion required to prepare spiritually and receive the Lord at His coming. Those who spiritually prepare to covenant with the Lord join His covenant people.[390] The Savior facilitates more light to shine on His covenant children to prepare them for His coming.[391]

The Doctrine and Covenants describes the virgins' lamps as a symbol of the Holy Spirit: "I spake concerning the ten virgins for they are wise and have received of the truth and have taken the Holy Spirit as their guide and have not been deceived—verily I say unto you, they shall not be hewn down and cast into the fire, but shall abide the day" (D&C 45:56-57). Modern revelation explains how that can happen: ". . . The power of my Spirit quickeneth all things. Wherefore, be faithful, praying always, having your lamps trimmed and burning and oil with you, that you may be ready at the coming of the Bridegroom" (D&C 33:16-17).[392] Jesus' teachings can

---

[389] The first pressing of olives produced the most precious oil for temple anointings, the second pressing for eating, and the third for light.

[390] Bruce A. Van Orden and Brent L. Top, eds., *The Lord of the Gospels*: *The 1990 Sperry Symposium on the New Testament*, 20. President Spencer W. Kimball explained: "'The kind of oil which is needed to illuminate the way, light up the darkness is not shareable. How can one share a tithing receipt; a peace of mind from righteous living; an accumulation of knowledge? How can one share faith or testimony? How can one share attitudes or chastity, or a mission? How can one share temple privileges and security? Each one must obtain that kind of oil for himself.' We must cultivate their own spiritual level of faith. To carry an empty vessel (church membership without covenants, without the Spirit) one is in severe self-delusion and doesn't admit it is empty."

[391] Scripture on the Lord's Second Coming include Matthew 24 (JST); Luke 21:25-28; D&C 45; also see D&C 34:6; 84:28; 128:24; 133:19, 25, 46; etc.

[392] In this parable and throughout the Scriptures, the Lord drew on the marriage covenant to represent His followers entering into a divine contract with Him. He describes membership in His kingdom, and marriage with Him. Isaiah 51:1, "Where is the bill of your mother's divorcement?" For

fill one with the Spirit (oil or anointing), leading one to become more Christlike.[393]

4. Wedding Feast

Cultural Background

If the families had the means, a weeklong feast followed the wedding ceremony (Genesis 29:27; Judges 14:10, 17). Friends and family of the bride and groom who had traveled from out of town, gathered for a reunion and feasting.[394] Meals were arranged at the homes of the bride and groom to strengthen family bonds between the two families. During the celebration, the ten men who gave the groom's blessings during the ceremony repeated it multiple times.[395]

New Testament Examples

The Gospel of John describes the "beginning of miracles" at a marriage feast. John carefully chose and crafted this account as the first of Jesus' seven miracles.[396] John describes

---

more marriage imagery between God and His people, also see Isaiah 54:6; Hosea 2:1-11; Malachi 2:14-15; etc.

[393] The name Christ, which is Greek for the Hebrew verb / *mashach* / messiah, means "to anoint." The Promised Messiah is the Anointed One who offers His anointing with those who become His sons and daughters.

[394] Michael L. Satlow, *Jewish Marriage in Antiquity* (Princeton, NJ: Princeton University Press, 2001), 178; "There are many stories about rabbis who make feasts for their sons (but almost never for their daughters), often at the home of other rabbis."

[395] Satlow, *Jewish Marriage,* 178. The blessings were not recorded until the time of the Talmud. There the blessings mentioned Adam and Eve, and the marriage metaphor between God and Zion.

[396] The other Gospels include many more of the Lord's miracles, but only the Gospel of John includes this story. The seven miracles mentioned in John are: Wedding at Cana (2:1); 4:46 Healing of official's son (4:46); Healing of paralytic (5:1); Multiplication of loaves and fishes (6:1); Walking on water (6:19); Healing blind man (9:1); Raising Lazarus from the dead (11:1). John also organized his Gospel to include seven sermons by Jesus. The number

Jesus' purpose in performing this miracle as a means "through which he revealed his glory" (John 2:11, NIV). It teaches the most emancipating message of the gospel: the power of the atonement.

Wedding at Cana

Christ's *first* miracle also testified of His *last* mortal miracle, His atoning sacrifice. John filled his Gospel with example after example of Jesus' superiority to the law of Moses.[397] Throughout John's retelling of the Lord's seven miracles and seven sermons,[398] he emphasizes that Jesus tore down the apostate or incomplete traditions to make room for a liberating restoration of truth.[399]

This miracle is layered in symbolism and typology for those who have eyes to see. The story begins at a wedding feast in Cana, a small town neighboring Nazareth. Coming from a culture that did not speak God's name out of respect, and

---

seven appears a favorite of Johnnanine literature as we also see seven used in the Book of Revelation in connection with: churches, spirits, golden candlesticks, lamps, stars, seals, horns, angels, trumpets, thunders, crowns, heads, and plagues.

[397] The Gospel of John does not mention Mary's name anywhere. The Gospel of Mark never uses the name of Jesus' legal father, Joseph.

[398] Raymond Brown, *An Introduction to the Gospel of John* (New York: Doubleday, 1997), 30. This leading Catholic scholar, finds seven discourses recorded in John's account during Jesus' ministry, prior to the Last Supper:
1. Born again—Nicodemus born of water and of spirit (John 2:2-21)
2. Living water—women at the well (John 4:10-26)
3. Jesus' work is His Father's work (John 5:20-47)
4. Bread of Life, eat my flesh, drink my blood (John 6:44-65)
5. Sabbath, righteous judgment, will of Father (John 7:16-29)
6. Light of the World (John 8:12-59)
7. Good shepherd, other sheep (John 10:1-30)

[399] For example, Jesus showed the incompleteness of the Jewish washings at the wedding of Cana, the false prejudices against race, gender, and sinners in Samaria with the woman at the well (discussed in chapter 1), and healing the lame and blind men on the Sabbath to communicate appropriate worship. The Lord restored doctrines and truth with each of the seven miracles in John.

coming in a Gospel where the author never mentions his own name, perhaps John, out of respect chose not to mention Mary by name. Or perhaps figuratively, John refers to Mary as "woman," hearkening back to Genesis where Eve is identified as "woman" (Genesis 2:22).[400] Whatever his motive, it was polite (John 19:26).

Extending proper generosity to guests was a serious obligation in the ancient world. In their culture, failing to do so would have been a breach of hospitality. Running short of wine had even led to lawsuits in the day.[401] The *modus operandi* recommended not serving all the wine initially for the guests, but holding some back for later, and serving the best first.

At the feast, Mary is concerned because they had run out of wine. The fact that Mary felt responsible for the wine suggests that the wedding may have been for one of Mary's close family relations.[402] She also directs the servants, "Whatsoever he saith unto you, do it," indicating that she held a position of responsibility at the feast (John 2:5).

Teaching Perspective. There are many different lenses that one can use to interpret this miracle. On a didactic level, there are some very clear and direct teachings. For example, Christ commands the servants, "Fill the water pots with water. And they fill them up to the brim" (John 2:7). This teaching has been used to emphasize the need to completely fill one's life with the word of Lord and with the Holy Ghost. Another specific teaching comes from Mary, who, as Christ's first disciple, specifically directs the servants to follow Christ: "Whatsoever he saith unto you, do it" (John 2:5). Mary's

---

[400] Raymond E. Brown, *The Gospel and Epistles of John: A Concise Commentary* (Collegeville, MN: The Order of St. Benedict, 1988), 28-29.
401 Kent Jackson, and Robert Millet, *Studies in Scriptures vol 5* (Salt Lake City, UT: Deseret Book, 1986), 113.
[402] Matthew 13:55 and Mark 6:3 list Mary's four sons and unnamed daughters. Some have speculated that this was Jesus' wedding, but age customs suggest that He would have married a decade earlier or even younger.

counsel can directly bless families as they do what the Lord directs.

Physical Perspective. On a physical level, Jesus changes water stored in stone vessels into wine: "There were set there six water pots of stone, after the manner of the purifying of the Jews, containing two or three firkins apiece" (John 2:6-7). The purifying pots held a lot of water—which in turn produces a lot of wine—108 to 150 gallons. That would have been from 2,000 to 3,000 servings! That amount would have provided plenty for a feast in Cana, plus a year's supply of wine for the couple.[403]

The curious nature of the water pots does not come from their size though, but their purpose. These pots are exceptional in that they are stone and thus, ritually "clean," unlike the normal clay, wood, or reed vessels that Jews considered "unclean" (Leviticus 11:33; and Mark 7:3-4; Isaiah 66:20). John specifically mentions that they are stone containers for Jewish ritual purification or ceremonial washings. He also points out the specific number, six.

Numerical Perspective. On a symbolic level, John frequently uses numbers figuratively, and this story was no exception.[404] Throughout his Gospel and Book of Revelation,

---

[403] Craig Evans, *Jesus and His World: The Archaeological Evidence* (Louisville, KY: John Knox Press, 2012), 13. The estimated population of Nazareth at the time is between 200 and 400. Cana may have been a similar size or smaller, which provides a basis for the number of wedding guests.
[404] We see John's uses of symbolic numbers especially in the book of Revelation (i.e., numbers seven, twelve, one hundred forty-four thousand, etc.). Alonzo Gaskill wrote, "It is the idea that anciently numbers were used as common symbols for ideas or beliefs . . . numbers were highly symbolic in biblical times. John uses them because he expects his readers to see the metaphorical meaning, rather than the literal number" (unpublished, *Commentary on the Book of Revelation*). The Bible itself defines some of the symbolism. Forty is the purification period (Leviticus 12:2-4, also see Genesis 7:4, 12, 17; 8:6; Exodus 16:35; 24:18; Matthew 4:2; Mark 1:13; etc.), seven is used for completeness. Multiples of twelve are often found for God's order (Revelation 7:5-8; 21:12, 14; Genesis 35:22; Exodus 24:24; Numbers 7:3).

he uses the number six to represent incomplete or imperfect (because six is one less than seven—the number of completion).[405] John uses six in triplicate—666—for the wicked beast as something totally imperfect (Revelation 13:18).

At the marriage in Cana, "there were six water pots of stone." John uses six to underscore that the Jewish purification was incomplete. The ritual washing of the lower Mosaic law–for which these pots are generally used–is imperfect in and of itself because its purpose was to prefigure a more perfect cleansing through the Messiah (Alma 13:16). Raymond Brown proposed that the six pots of water became complete only with Jesus' addition of *His* wine—symbolic of His blood—as the seventh ingredient.[406] Thus Mary's observation in John 2:3, "'They have no wine,' becomes a poignant reflection on the barrenness of Jewish purifications."[407] Likewise human purification becomes perfect only through Christ's atoning blood.[408]

To help us make this connection on a theological level, John mentions that the miracle happens on "the third day" (John 2:1).[409] This could refer to the third day of the wedding party, but it appears that John wants it to mean more as he specifically tells his readers to look for a way that the making of wine "revealed his glory" (John 2:11, NET).[410] The miracle is

---

[405] Seven develops its scriptural symbolism starting in Genesis with the days of creation. Seven is used throughout the Bible to represent something whole, finished, or perfect; see introduction, "Numbers with Biblical Symbolism."

[406] Brown, *The Gospel and Epistles of John,* 27.

[407] Brown, *Anchor: John I-VII,* 105.

[408] Jesus used wine as the symbol of His atoning blood both in his Bread of Life Sermon and the sacrament (John 6:54-56; Matthew 26:28; Mark 14:24; Luke 22:20).

[409] John used the "third day" for symbolic reasons, as a careful counting shows that this was actually the seventh day he references. John begins with Jesus' baptism as day one, and then lists five days up to the call of Philip. The next reference to time is, "the third day" which would be the seventh day (John 1:29; 35, 39, 43; John 2:1). Symbolically, Jesus' "third day" was the perfect day.

[410] The third day may also refer to the days after Philip's call (John 1:43).

recorded in this way to highlight the Savior's cleansing atonement, death, and resurrection.

Over half of the references in the four Gospels to the number three foreshadow or describe the time that Christ spent in the tomb.[411] A few sentences after the marriage at Cana, John includes Christ's prophecy, "Destroy this temple, and in three days I will raise it up" (John 2:19). It does not seem accidental that John includes these two symbolic references so close together in the narrative. It is as if John wants his readers to see the references to three as a revelation of Jesus' mission. Outside of the Gospel of John, the best example comes from Jesus' prophecy: "For Jonas was three days and three nights in the whale's belly; so shall the Son of man be three days and three nights in the heart of the earth" (Matthew 12:40).

Prophetic Perspective. On the prophetic level, the multiplying of wine at the wedding feast fulfills Messianic prophecies.[412] We read prophetic images of an abundance of wine in Proverbs 9:4-5, "Come, eat of my bread, and drink of the wine which I have mingled."[413] The miracle at the wedding of Cana answers this prophecy on one level. But on another level, the abundance of wine could have spoken of Christ's blood offering, symbolizing the sacrament wine, having the

---

[411] I found twenty-five references of "third" or "three" that spoke of the time Jesus' body lay in the tomb, or his mission, and twenty-three that spoke only to the number, with ten references that could be argued as a symbolic representation of Christ's death. See Matthew 12:40;13:33;15:32; 16:21; 17:4; 17:23; 18:16; 18:20; 20:3; 20:19; 22:26; 26:44; 26:61; 27:40; 27:63; 27:64; Mark 8:2; Mark 8:31; 9:5; 9:31; 10:34; 12:21; 14:5; 14:41; 14:58; 15:25; 15:29; Luke 1:56; 2:46; 4:25; 9:22; 9:33; 10:36; 11:5; 12:38;12:52; 13:7; 13:21;13:32; 18:33; 20:12; 20:31; 23:22; 24:7; 24:21; 24:46; John 2:1; 2:6; 2:19; 2:20; 12:5; 21:11; 21:14; 21:17.

[412] Alfred Edersheim, *Jesus the Messiah* (New York: Longmans, Green and Co, 1898), 163—calculated that the Old Testament includes 456 prophesies of the Messiah.

[413] Also the prophet Amos foretold of an abundance of wine in the Messianic era, "Behold, the days come, saith the LORD, that the plowman shall overtake the reaper, and the treader of grapes him that soweth seed; and the mountains shall drop sweet wine" (Amos 9:13-15).

enormous capacity to heal the sins of the world (Mosiah 3:11, 16; D&C 20:40). Prophetic images of atoning wine are reflected in Jacob's blessing to Judah, when he promises that his son's posterity would include a "lawgiver," who "bind[s] his foal unto the . . . choice vine; he washes his garments in wine, and his clothes in the blood of grapes" (Genesis 49:10-11). This Messianic prophecy speaks to the pain that Christ would undertake in His atonement—He "treadeth the winepress of the fierceness and wrath of the Almighty God" (Revelation 19:15).

Typological Perspective. On a typological level, Jesus' first miracle in Cana–turning water to wine–is reminiscent of Moses' first miracle as a prophet–turning water to blood in Egypt (Exodus 7:19). Both miracles typify Christ's atonement, although, both the miracle of Moses turning ponds, rivers, and streams into blood, and the miracle of Christ turning water into wine pale in comparison to the transformation of water into blood in Christ's body as a means of bringing to pass the salvation of humanity. The typological significance of these miracles is that they help the reader to reflect upon and better understand the process and beauty of the Atonement. When Jesus suffers in Gethsemane, "he sweat was as it were great drops of blood falling down to the ground" (Luke 22:44; also see Mosiah 3:7). The water from Christ's body (his sweat) literally turns to blood as He took upon Himself the pains and sins of the world.

The symbols of this first miracle at the wedding in Cana proclaim Jesus' glory on several levels—historical, physical, symbolic, numerical, theological, prophetic, and typological. They all seem to converge on the need to apply Jesus' enabling purification through His atoning blood. Jesus provides His abundant new wine for disciples to enjoy "immortality and eternal life" (Moses 1:39). And like the vessels of water, when incomplete human vessels allow Jesus to enter their lives, they change and became purified into something better. Elder Neal A. Maxwell observes, "While the wine produced in the miracle at Cana is long gone, Jesus' blessings, both personal and universal, continue with us to this very day. . . . His working out of the miracle of the Atonement gives us each everlasting blessings."[414]

Two Symbolic Marriage Feasts

In the New Testament, Jesus' prophesies twice of His Second Coming using a marriage feast as the background. Making and renewing covenants are often tied to feasts in the ancient world.[415] Jesus uses marriage feasts as a teaching tool to continue the Old Testament figurative relationship between God (the husband) and Zion or Jerusalem (His bride).[416]

1. A Marriage for the King's Son
(Matthew 22; also see D&C 58:11; Luke 14:16-24)

In this parable, Jesus describes the preparations for a royal wedding to which a king first invited the expected guests, but when He "sent forth his servants to call them that were bidden to the wedding: and they would not come" (Matthew 22:2-3).[417] Shockingly, the king's guests reject his invitation even though they would have probably been individuals of high standing in

---

[414] Neal A. Maxwell, *Even As I Am* (Salt Lake City, UT: Deseret Book Co., 1982), 7. ". . . How blessed we are to have 'proofs' of the longevity of His Lordship!"

[415] All three of the great Jewish feasts were to renew their covenants. The Passover feast is the great covenant feast (Exodus 12:43; Numbers 9:12; 2 Kings 23:21; Nehemiah 8:13-9:3; etc.).

[416] Also, modern revelation uses a wedding feast to symbolize Jesus' Second Coming; "After that cometh the day of my power; then shall the poor, the lame, and the blind, and the deaf, come in unto the marriage of the Lamb, and partake of the supper of the Lord, prepared for the great day to come" (D&C 58:11).

[417] After Matthew's unique introduction the storyline is similar to the text found in Luke 14:16-24, but without the wedding setting. Interestingly, Luke places a different marriage venue a few verses ahead where the text warns against self-righteousness, "When thou art bidden of any man to a wedding, sit not down in the highest room; lest a more honourable man than thou be bidden of him" (Luke 14:8).

the kingdom (Matthew 22:4-7). Such disrespect for a royal summons may sound unlikely, but the ungrateful guests embody the chosen people, specifically the Jews, who reject Jesus.[418] Then the king invites all those on the streets, "and gathered together as many as they found, both bad and good" (Matthew 22:10).[419]

The parable adopts the biblical imagery of a feast, representing the completeness and richness of life in God's kingdom (Isaiah 25:6; Revelation 19:7-10).[420] The opulence of the feast includes a fattened calf, slaughtered and prepared. The parable mentions the slaughtered animal three times (Matthew 22:4, 8).[421] This is important because Jesus becomes the fattened calf of "the sin offering," even "a great and last sacrifice" or "red heifer" that will carry the sins of the world (Leviticus 9:8; Alma 34:10; Numbers 19:2). Or does the preparation and slaughter suggest an eschatological urgency of the Lord's Second Coming? The feast is ready now—will the guests come while it is still available? Either interpretation invites the reader to come and join the wedding feast.

---

[418] Raymond Brown, Joseph Fitzmyer, Roland Murphy, *The New Jerome Biblical Commentary* (Englewood Cliffs, NJ: *Prentice Hall,* 1990), 665.

[419] God's generous invitation opens the doorway for the gospel message to go to the Gentiles as they may represent the outcasts.

[420] Marriage, childbirth, widowhood, and divorce also took on symbolic attributes in the Bible. Isaiah 62:5 offers a good example, "As the bridegroom rejoices over the bride, so shall thy God rejoice over thee." The first few chapters of Jeremiah use marriage symbols of betrothal, divorce, and reconciliation to describe the covenant relationship between Jerusalem and God; "I remember thee, the kindness of thy youth, the love of thine espousals . . . but thou hast played the harlot with many lovers; yet return again to me, saith the LORD" (Jeremiah 2:2; 3:1). In addition to God's marriage with Zion, we read of the birth of God's son, Israel, "You have seen how the Lord your God bore you as a man bears his son" (RSV Deuteronomy 8:5; also see Hosea 11:1; Jeremiah 31:9). The Old Testament refers to Zion and Jerusalem as the bride of Jehovah based on symbolism of their covenant together and Israel always as their son. John Schmitt, "Gender Correctness and Biblical Metaphors: The Case of God's Revelation to Israel," *Biblical Theological Bulletin* 26, 1996, 99-102.

[421] In the parable of the two brothers or prodigal son, we see another "fatted calf" who was slain for the prodigal (Luke 15:27-28).

At the end of the story, after the outcasts from the streets arrive at the feast, "both bad and good" (Matthew 22:10), the king sorts out his guests:

> And when the king came in to see the guests, he saw there a man which had not on a wedding garment: And he saith unto him, Friend, how camest thou in hither not having a wedding garment? And he was speechless. Then said the king to the servants, Bind him hand and foot, and take him away, and cast him into outer darkness; there shall be weeping and gnashing of teeth. For many are called, but few are chosen (Matthew 22:11-14).

This guest did not conform to the king's dress code nor did he meet the requirements of the kingdom. Refusing to put on the clean wedding garment may represent one's refusal to apply the Lord's atonement. The word atonement means among other things, "to cover, purge, to make reconciliation."[422] Or perhaps the King requires the guests to wash and dress in his "robes of righteousness" (D&C 29:12) as a symbol of their repentance, but some refuse to repent.[423] The parable

---

[422] Hugh Nibley, *Approaching Zion,* 558-559. "The basic word for atonement is *kaphar*, which has the same basic meaning in Hebrew, Aramaic, and Arabic, that being 'to bend, arch over, cover; . . . to deny, . . . to forgive, . . . to be expiated, . . . renounce.' The Arabic *kafara* puts the emphasis on a tight squeeze, such as tucking in the skirts, drawing a thing close to one's self. Closely related are Aramaic and Arabic *kafat*, meaning a close embrace, which are certainly related to the Egyptian *hpet,* the common ritual embrace written with the ideogram of embracing arms. It may be cognate with the Latin *capto*, and from it comes the Persian *kaftan*, a monk's robe and hood completely embracing the body. Most interesting is the Arabic kafata, as it is the key to a dramatic situation. It was the custom for one fleeing for his life in the desert to seek protection in the tent of a great sheik, crying out, '*Ana dakhiluka*,' meaning 'I am thy suppliant,' whereupon the Lord would place the hem of his robe over the guest's shoulder and declare him under his protection." We see this image in the Book of Mormon too (see 2 Nephi1:15; 4:33; Alma 5:24).

[423] Perhaps it means that the King of Kings extends His invitation to sinners, but expects them to repent in order to enter the banquet or His Kingdom. Matthew repeated the Lord's call for righteous obedience in the Sermon on the Mount (Matthew 5-7).

distinguishes between God's invitation and God's reward. He invites all, but only a "few are chosen"—those who willingly repent of their sins and accept the complete "covering" of the Atonement (Matthew 22:14).[424]

2. Marriage Supper of The Lamb (Revelation 19:7-9)

The second allegorical marriage feast comes from the book of Revelation and teaches about enduring to the end. This parable has only two characters: The Lamb, representing Christ, and his bride, representing the church. Christ hosts the wedding supper of the Lamb "at His second coming when he symbolically claims his bride, the faithful members of his church."[425] By that time the church or "wife hath made herself ready" (Revelation 19:7) and "it was given to her to clothe herself in fine linen, bright and clean; for the fine linen is the righteous acts of the saints" (Revelation 19:8, ASV).[426] John the Revelator explains that the bride's fine white linen is made from righteous living.

The clothing description of white linen corresponds to the clothing worn by priests when serving in the temple (Exodus 39:27-42; Leviticus 6:10; Ezekiel 44:17-26).[427] On the Day of

---

[424] This includes the need to obey God's commandments, and enter into His ordinances (D&C 121:34-37; also see D&C 49:26; 52:16; 97:25; 138:58; Mormon 7:5).

[425] Ludlow, *Encyclopedia of Mormonism*, 2.860; D&C 109:73-74.

[426] Parry, *Temples of the Ancient World*, Tvedtnes, "Priestly clothing in Bible Times," 671, 677. Priests replaced their every-day garb and donned sacred vestments (Exodus 28:40) which figuratively removed the priest from this world and prepared him to enter the presence of God. As with most religious ritual, symbols underlined their priestly clothing to portray righteousness and purity.

[427] Ezekiel 44:17-26 describes the priestly linen clothing worn in Solomon's Temple, grooming standards, and their dietary restrictions from wine: "When they enter in at the gates of the inner court. . . . they shall be clothed with linen garments . . . linen bonnets upon their heads, and shall have linen breeches upon their loins . . . and when they go forth into the utter court . . . they shall put off their garments wherein they ministered, and lay them in the holy chambers, and they shall put on other garments; and they shall not

Atonement, before the high priest went into the Holy of Holies, he changed from his colorful robe into "holy garments" of white linen to commune with God at the veil (Leviticus 16:23).[428] At the wedding supper in Revelation 19, the sacrificial Lamb provides the pure clothing of sanctification for all who had proven worthy to attend the wedding, or the sealing of the saints. At that time, the bride or the church may wear the priestly temple clothing as she goes before the Lord.

The feast symbolizes the blessings of the covenant, "Blessed are they which are called unto the marriage supper of the Lamb . . . . Come in unto the marriage of the Lamb, and partake of the supper of the Lord, prepared for the great day to come" (Revelation 19:9). Modern revelation further teaches that the marriage of the Lamb will take place in the New Jerusalem on Mount Zion (3 Nephi 20:22; D&C 84:2).[429]

---

sanctify the people with their garments. Neither shall they shave their heads, nor suffer their locks to grow long. . . . Neither shall any priest drink wine, when they enter into the inner court. . . . And they shall teach my people the difference between the holy and profane, and cause them to discern between the unclean and the clean."

[428] Leviticus 16:4, 32, "He shall put on the holy linen coat, and he shall have the linen breeches upon his flesh, and shall be girded with a linen girdle, and with the linen mitre shall he be attired: these are holy garments; therefore shall he wash his flesh in water, and so put them on. . . . And the priest, whom he shall anoint, and whom he shall consecrate to minister in the priest's office in his father's stead, shall make the atonement, and shall put on the linen clothes, even the holy garments." Also see Leviticus 16:23.

[429] Restoration Scriptures on the marriage supper of the Lamb build on John's theme as they describe the rich and learned, wise and noble who are invited before "the day of my power; then shall the poor, the lame, and the blind, and the deaf, come in unto the marriage of the Lamb" (D&C 58:6-12). While dedicating the Kirtland Temple, the Prophet Joseph Smith prayed that the saints would prepare to rise and meet Christ; 'That our garments may be pure, that we may be clothed upon with robes of righteousness, with palms in our hands, and crowns of glory upon our heads, and reap eternal joy for all our sufferings" (D&C 109:76). The metaphorical marriage covenant is used as the image to describe eternal joy—in all its emancipation.

5. Cohabitation

Cultural Background

The last stage of finalizing a marriage was consummation: "A wife is acquired in three ways. . . . She is acquired by money, by writ, and by intercourse."[430] The latter was the only way to confirm a levirate marriage.[431] Old traditions speak of displaying the "tokens of virginity" or blood-stained bed sheets after the wedding night (Deuteronomy 22:13-21).[432] This ancient practice provided evidence of the bride's virginity to protect her family against lawsuits.[433] Though we have little evidence that by the end of the Second Temple era anyone displayed their blood stained sheets, it appears that a young woman was still expected to be a virgin on her wedding night.

Bed and Board

Different Jews interpreted the importance of the connubial relationship in various ways. Josephus limited marital

---

[430] *Mishnah, Kiddushin*, 1:1; Louis M. Epstein, *The Jewish Marriage Contract: A Study in the Status of the Woman in Jewish Law* (Clark, NJ: Lawbook Exchange, 2004), 11.

[431] *Mishnah, Kiddushin*, 1:1.

[432] Campbell, *Marriage and Family in the Biblical World, 46.* Epstein, *Jewish Marriage*, 13. After a study of Jewish marriage contracts, Epstein concluded that consummation "became a real legal factor in the marriage." There is also evidence of this in Deuteronomy where sexual contact led to marriage, "If a man find a damsel that is a virgin, which is not betrothed, and lay hold on her, and lie with her, and they be found; Then the man that lay with her shall give unto the damsel's father fifty shekels of silver, and she shall be his wife; because he hath humbled her, he may not put her away all his days" (Deuteronomy 22:28-29; also 21:11-13). The ideal followed the prescribed order—first money, a contract, and then consummation. Yet, in the ancient Israelite world, if intercourse occurred first, the couple was still considered married for life.

[433] Paul J. Achtemeier, *Harper Collins' Bible Dictionary* (San Francisco, CA: HarperCollins, 1996), 1205.

intimacy "only for . . . procreation."[434] Similarly Tobit reads, "thou gavest to him Eve for a helper. And now, Lord, thou knowest that not for pleasure's sake, but solely for the desire of children, I take a sister to wife."[435] Philo agreed with Genesis that Adam "knew" his wife sexually, but felt the patriarchs' children came directly from God, without intercourse.[436] The same philosopher supported marriage, even to the degree of counseling warriors to marry any captured young girls. But out of compassion for a captive's feelings, Philo added, "leave her alone for thirty days, and allow her without fear of disturbance to mourn . . . after this, live with her as your lawful wife."[437]

At the time of Herod's Temple, most couples married in their teens and lived into the groom's family home for the first few years. This meant the young bride needed to work alongside her mother-in-law to maintain the house. In addition to the myriad of household chores—from harvesting to cooking and carding to weaving—the young bride also had to learn how to please her mother-in-law. Many homes included multiple generations living under the same roof. If the young husband was able to earn enough for a private home, the couple often moved next door.

Wife

A young girl entering marriage not only had to learn to meet the needs of a new family, but also had to learn to obey

---

[434] Josephus, *Against Apion,* 2.25; "What are our laws about marriage? That law owns no other mixture of sexes but that which nature hath appointed, of a man with his wife, and that this be used only for the procreation of children." He censures homosexuality as it is unable to produce children. Child bearing takes a prominent position in his list of values.

[435] Tobit VIII, Vulgate translation.

[436] Philo, *De Cherubim,* XII, 41. "The helpmeets of these men are called women, but are in reality virtues."

[437] Philo, *On the Virtues,* 111f. "Holiness requires that she who is to enter a husband's bed, not as a hired harlot, trafficking her youthful bloom, but either for love of her mate or for the birth of children, should be admitted to the rights of full wedlock as her due."

her new master. In devout Jewish households, a new husband claimed his new title: "rab" or "rabbi," which meant "master," "my great one," or "honorable sir." His wife used this title to express her servile relationship to him.[438]

A young bride went from acting as a servant to her father to acting as a servant to her husband: "She continues under the authority of the father till she enters into the control of the husband at marriage."[439] As the philosopher Philo summarized, "wives must be in servitude to their husbands, a servitude not imposed by violent ill-treatment but promoting obedience in all things."[440] Also from a book of historical fiction from that era, God gives the instruction, "Thus saith the Lord; I did not create thy wife to command thee, but to obey."[441] Many Jewish records describe a similar servant-master inequality between the genders, where a husband acts as a master and his wife an obedient servant.[442]

Husband

The most fundamental duty for a Jewish man was to rule his home.[443] The husband owned all the property in the home—including any land, goods, and people (Numbers 26:55).[444] He was the legal voice and had legal responsibility to care for his household (Jeremiah 35:6-10; Proverbs 6:20). That responsibility also carried obligations to his wife that included:

---

[438] Jeremias, *Jerusalem,* 369.

[439] *Mishnah, Ketuboth* 4:5.

[440] Judaeus Philo, *Philo* (Boston, MA: Harvard University Press, 1954), 9. 425; "On the Embassy to Gaius."

[441] Robert H. Charles, ed., *The Apocrypha and Pseudepigrapha of the Old Testament* (Oxford, England: Clarendon Press, 1913), 2.134. "The Lord said: . . . thy wife shall tremble when she looketh upon thee." This account comes from the Jewish Pseudepigrapha, written by professional Jewish scribes sometime between 200 BC and 100 AD.

[442] Stagg, *Woman in the World of Jesus*, 34.H.

[443] Skolnik, *Encyclopedia Judaica*, "Family" 6.691.

[444] Skolnik, *Encyclopedia Judaica*, 6.92, "Family: Functions of family members."

"providing food, clothing, shelter, and medication and fulfilling his connubial duty."[445] If he did not accomplish these duties, his wife could demand before a court that he provide them.[446]

New Testament Examples

The New Testament has many diverse family units. They differ in size, age, nationality, social standing, and relationship.[447] The four Gospels describe the Lord interacting in several family units, quietly teaching values through His example, especially the values of compassion, selflessness, impartiality, mercy, and love. Peter's mother-in-law lived with Peter's family in Capernaum. When Jesus visited them, He noticed that the older woman was ill with a fever; "He touched

---

[445] *Mishnah, Horayoth,* 3.7. The husband must try to save his wife if she were taken captive. The *Mishnah* outlines the order in which family members should be redeemed. Consistent with ancient Jewish thought, a husband's life was saved first, but a woman was clothed first; "A man must be saved alive sooner than a woman, and his lost property must be restored sooner than hers. A woman's nakedness must be covered sooner than a man's and she must be brought out of captivity sooner than he. When both stand in danger of defilement, the man must be freed before the woman."
[446] *Mishnah, Ketuboth,* 4:8-9; 5:6-8.
[447] The New Testament includes many examples of dynamic couples and various family units that biblical readers will recognize, including:
- Zacharias, Elisabeth, and their son John
- Mary and Joseph, Jesus, James, Joses, Simon, Judas, and daughters
- Zebedee and Salome, their sons "of thunder"—James and John
- Simon Peter and his wife, his mother-in-law, and brother Andrew
- Jairus and his little daughter
- Siblings Mary, Martha, and Lazarus
- A centurion and his servant
- A blind man and his parents
- A Syrophenician mother and her possessed daughter
- John Mark, his mother Mary, and Uncle Barnabas
- Chuza and his wife Joanna
- Priscilla and Aquila
- Eunice, her son Timothy, her mother Lois, and her Greek husband
- A widow and her son
This list is not exhaustive, but shows the diversity of biblical family life.

her hand and the fever left her" (Matthew 8:15, NIV). The Lord exemplifies awareness of other's needs and service. A man with leprosy begged the Lord for His attention, and "Jesus moved with compassion" touched and healed him (Mark 1:41).

We see another example of the Lord's compassion as He approached the city gate of Nain. Jesus came upon a funeral procession and observed a widow mourning the loss of her only son. In Luke 7:13, we read that the Lord "had compassion on her, and said unto her, Weep not." After comforting her, He did all within His power to help her. Jesus had compassion again on the families that follow him for three days by providing nourishment for them (Mark 8:2). The Lord's awareness of others' needs, His selfless service, compassion, and action teach values that can bless all those who follow His example.

The Lord renounces selfishness and inspires impartiality in relationships: "A servant is not greater than his master" (John 15:20 NIV; also13:16). Furthermore, He urges service by introducing an additional recipient: "Inasmuch as ye have done it unto one of the least of these my brethren, ye have done it unto me" (Matthew 25:40). The word "brethren" here, and in many of cases in the KJV, often refers to both genders as "fellow believers" or "brothers and sisters" (NET). The Lord's universal message applies to both husbands and wives, siblings and parents, friends and foes.

In the Beatitudes, Jesus plants even more spiritual seeds that potentially strengthen family bonds. He calls on His disciples to extend mercy and to become peacemakers (Matthew 5:7, 9). Later in the Sermon on the Mount, the Lord teaches the need to communicate and forgive:

> If you are offering your gift at the altar and there remember that your brother or sister has something against you, leave your gift there in front of the altar. First go and be reconciled to them; then come and offer your gift" (Matthew 5:23-24, NIV).

All these behavioral models required a cultural paradigm shift, which opened the way for sweeter family relationships.[448] Following the example of their Lord, the apostolic church also taught much about the mutuality of marriage which we will discuss next in chapter 5.

---

[448] A few other verses from the Gospels that promote families are: Matthew 1-2; 5:32; 7:11; 18:2-5; 19:14; 9:36-37; 10:14-15; 9:47; 18:16-17; 22:2; Mark 10:11-12; Luke 1-2; 15:6; 16:18; 20:34; John 2:2; 8:39 14:21; 19:27.

Chapter 5
Mutuality in Marriage
As Taught by Apostles

Notwithstanding the way that Jesus honored women and children, some sections of the New Testament Epistles leave the reader questioning the role of marriage in the early apostolic church. Generally speaking, the New Testament Epistles provide positive support and endorsement of marriage.[449] A husband and wife should love and respect each other (Ephesians 5:33). Husbands should honor their wives "as being heirs together of the grace of life" (1 Peter 3:7). A wife should love and stay with her husband and children (1 Corinthians 7:10; Titus 2:4). Paul chose church leaders who were "the husband of one wife, having children who believe, . . . above reproach as God's steward, not self-willed, not quick-tempered, not addicted to wine, not pugnacious, not fond of sordid gain, but hospitable, loving what is good, sensible, just, devout, self-

---

[449] Tradition credits apostles Peter and Paul as the only two authors that speak specifically on spousal relations in the Epistles. However the authorship of several Epistles is debated by scholars. A few of the letters that include discussions of marriage include: Romans 7; 1 Corinthians 7; 1 Timothy 4-5; Ephesians 5; Hebrews 13; 1 Peter 3.

controlled" (Titus 1:6-8; NASB, also 1 Timothy 3:2). Divorce was also discouraged (1 Corinthians 7:11; Mark 10:4-8), except in certain circumstances (1 Corinthians 7:15; Matthew 5:32).

However, there are a few verses in the Epistles that elicit questions about early Christian teachings on marriage. When the apostles' writings seem inconsistent with Christ's restored truths about women and marriage, then they are either in error, or we need to take a closer look. This chapter addresses these apparent inconsistencies about marriage. It looks at three passages in 1 Peter 3, 1 Corinthians 7, and Ephesians 5, all of which deserve an explanation. It does this by including the context for the apostles' writings and by presenting the passages in a variety of translations.[450] It also compares the biblical apostles' writings with those of latter-day apostles. This deeper examination confirms that the early Christian church did in fact endorse Christ's emancipation of women and revolutionary ideas about the mutuality of marriage in a joint partnership.

I. 1 Peter 3:1-9

In this Epistle, Peter included a nine verse code of conduct for marriages.[451] The chief apostle gave advice on what to do if

---

[450] It is not just the translation that conveys different meaning, but it helps. President J. Reuben Clark wrote, "[I hope to] provoke in some qualified scholars having a proper Gospel background, the desire and determination to go over the manuscripts and furnish us, under the influence and direction of the Holy Ghost, a translation of the New Testament that will give us an accurate translation that shall be pregnant with the great principles of the Restored Gospel. We shall then have a reliable record of the doings and sayings of our Lord and Master Jesus Christ." J. Reuben Clark, *Why the King James Version* (Salt Lake City, UT: Deseret Book, 1956), viii–ix.

[451] The Epistle of first Peter was probably written during Peter's Roman imprisonment before AD 64. It appears that a scribe (Silas or Mark) wrote it for Peter as it is written in elegant Greek with no traces of "Semitisms" (Hebraic or Aramaic phrases). In this Epistle, Old Testament Scriptures are quoted from the Greek Septuagint which also suggests that the writer was more comfortable with Greek than Hebrew. Joseph Smith must have admired Peter's Epistles as he is quoted as saying, "Peter penned the most

a wife converted to Christianity but her husband did not (1 Peter 3:1), how to become unified through cooperation without fear or intimidation (1 Peter 3:6), and how to live with compassion and kindness toward one's spouse (1 Peter 3:8). Peter's brief commentary begins, however, with a few words that seem inconsistent with Christ's liberating teachings on women. The first verse is the most difficult to understand.

1 Peter 3:1

KJV	NEB	Welch-Hall[452]
Likewise, ye wives, be in subjection to your own husbands; that if any obey not the word, they also may without the word be won by the conversation of the wives.	In the same way you women must accept the authority of your husbands so that if there are any of them who disbelieve the gospel they may be won over, without a word being said.	A wife's obedience to her un-Christian huband may influence the husband.

The first step in understanding this verse is to look at its context. In the previous verses Peter discusses Jesus' perfect submission to His perfect Father.

> Christ suffered for you, leaving you an example, that you should follow in his steps, "He committed no sin, and no deceit was found in his mouth." When they hurled their insults at Him, He did not retaliate; when He suffered he made no threats. Instead, He entrusted Himself to Him who judges justly . . . now you have returned to the Shepherd and Overseer of your soul (1 Peter 2:21-25, NIV).

---

sublime language of any of the Apostles" (Smith, *History of the Church,* 5:392).

[452] Welch and Hall, *Charting the New Testament,* 15-15, offers a paraphrase, not literal translation.

Just as Jesus responded to difficulties without retaliation and strove for perfect unity with the Father, the verse in 1 Peter 3:1 explains that a husband and wife should strive for unity. Peter appeals to women to work together with their husbands—whether or not their spouses are Christian. Indeed, Peter understood that a wife's example had the potential to inspire a husband, and boost his understanding and acceptance of the gospel.

Sometimes this section in 1 Peter is denounced for what seems a misogynist attitude. Part of that impression comes from the translators' choice of "subjection" or "submission" for the Greek *hupotasso*. Peter uses *hupotasso* six times in this letter and the KJV translators use "submit" or "subject." Examples include, "submit yourself to every ordinance" (1 Peter 2:13, also 2:18); and later, "Likewise, ye younger, submit yourselves unto the elder. Yea, all of you be subject one to another, and be clothed with humility: for God resisteth the proud, and giveth grace to the humble" (1 Peter 5:5).

Hupotasso is a favorite word across the Epistles, where we find it forty times in various forms, most of which are from Paul. (In fact, Paul's uses *hupotasso* in his spousal code of conduct sections from Colossians 3:18-19 and Ephesians 5:21-24, just as Peter does here.[453]) This word was initially a Greek military term meaning "to arrange in a military fashion under the command of a leader." But more applicable here, it also developed a *nonmilitary* meaning, "a voluntary attitude of

---

[453] Paul's family code of conduct sections in Ephesians 5:21-24 and Colossians 3:18-19 overlaps with 1 Peter 3, so we do not repeat those definitions in the last section of this chapter. One important detail needs to be pointed out. Ephesians 5:22 KJV reads, "Wives, submit to your husbands as to the Lord." But the Greek verb is not placed there. "The oldest manuscripts omit 'submit yourselves,' supplying it from" the previous verse where Christians were to submit together in unity to God. *Jamieson-Fausset-Brown Bible Commentary* (Grand Rapids, MI: Zondervan, 1961), Ephesians 5:22. The oldest manuscripts read, ". . . wives, to your own husbands, as to the Lord."

giving in, cooperating, assuming responsibility, and carrying a burden."[454]

The New Testament uses this word, *hupotasso,* to communicate cooperation—not controlling domination. The message of cooperating in mutuality by assuming responsibility would have left flabbergasted both the Jews and Greco-Romans of the time.

> This requirement was the new, radical idea that Christian husbands also were to love and submit to their wives rather than control them. Perhaps this concept of mutual submission was so radical for the Christians that the church eventually lost sight of this teaching and reverted to the behavior of the surrounding culture—insisting only on the submission of wives, but not that of husbands . . . the mutuality and equality of the first couple were forgotten.[455]

In a family setting based on this Christian principle, both husband and wife engage in this voluntary cooperative order between God and each other—not from fear or controlling oppression, but out of love and a desire for unity.

God gave both men and women different supporting roles to play in the synergistic spousal relationship. In their different roles, they each submit at different times. The Lord told Abraham to submit to his wife's counsel in Genesis 21:12 (regarding Hagar). Both roles are equally important, and both genders must develop humility, selflessness, sacrifice, and love as prerequisites for Eternal Life.

Submission to God's plan for families focuses on love, cooperation and harmony. Yielding to what is best for the whole family curbs pride and self-centered behaviors. Elder Boyd K. Packer described a modern application of this teaching both in the church and marriage: "In the church there is a distinct line of authority . . . in the home it is a partnership with

---

[454] Bromiley, *TDNT*, viii.41, *hypotassetai.*
[455] Parales, *Hidden Voices: Biblical Women,* 132.

husband and wife equally yoked together, sharing in decisions, always working together."[456] The goal is unity.

The next verse of Peter's code of-conduct offers the means whereby an unbelieving spouse might come to accept Christ's gospel.

1 Peter 3:2

KJV	NJB	NAS	Welch-Hall[457]
While they behold your chaste conversation coupled with fear	When they see the reverence and purity of your way of life	As they observe your chaste and respectful behavior	By her chaste conduct coupled with respect.

The KJV word "conversation" in verses 1 and 2 actually comes from the Greek "*anastrophe* / manner of life, conduct, behavior." Modern English translations use a derivation of "behavior," rather than the KJV "conversation."[458] Peter admonished a Christian wife to love and respect her husband— even if he is not a Christian. Peter gave husbands the same counsel in verse 7: "Likewise, husbands, live with your wives in an understanding way, showing honor to the woman . . ." (NIV). But first, Peter illustrated his point with the biblical example of Abraham and Sarah.

Peter held up Sarah and Abraham as the model unified couple.[459] He called women to become "daughters" of Sarah by following her example.[460] Her example is that she voluntarily

---

456 Boyd K. Packer, "The Relief Society," *Ensign* (May 1998), 73.
457 Welch and Hall, *Charting the New Testament,* 15-15.
458 RSV, NEB, JB, NAS, NIV, NEB, etc.
459 1 Peter quotes Genesis 18:12 from the Greek Septuagint (LXX).
460 Jesus and John the Baptist teach a similar idea—Jesus in John 8:39, "If ye were Abraham's children, ye would do the works of Abraham;" and John 1:12; "But as many as received Him, to them gave He power to become the

took responsibility to achieve unity by cooperating. Women become daughters of Sarah as they live as Sarah did. Looking at verses 3, 4, and 5 together, Peter asked women to adorn their character with goodness as Sarah did, rather than worrying about outward adornments.

1 Peter 3:5-6

KJV	NJB	NAB
For after this manner in the old time the holy women also, who trusted in God, adorned themselves, being in subjection unto their own husbands: Even as Sara obeyed Abraham, calling him lord: whose daughters ye are, as long as ye do well, and are not afraid with any amazement	That was how the holy women of the past dressed themselves attractively—they hoped in God and were submissive to their husbands; like Sarah, who was obedient to Abraham, and called him her lord. You are now her children, as long as you live good lives free from fear and worry.	For this is also how the holy women who hoped in God once used to adorn themselves and were subordinate to their husbands; thus Sarah obeyed Abraham, calling him lord. You are her children when you do what is good and fear no intimidation.

Verse 6 presents a new verbal difficulty. Here Sarah called her husband Abraham "master" or "lord." Her use of this title insinuates a lack of equality between spouses, a kind of dominion different from cooperation. But in the ancient world, referring to a husband as "lord" was a common practice and

---

sons of God." For John the Baptist statements also see Matthew3:9; Luke 3:8; and later by Paul in Galatians 3:7.

people often used formal titles in conversation. The word had a hierarchical meaning but was also a common way to refer to a man.[461] In the Judaic world of Jerusalem at that time, "the wife was obliged to obey her husband as a servant would a master—the husband was called *rab* [short for rabbi]—indeed this obedience was as a religious duty."[462] This passage reflects cultural differences between our time and theirs and does not negate Peter's underlying principles that encouraged couples to express mutual love and offer selfless service to one another.

It is interesting to note, however, that the Lord addressed people by their names: Mary, Martha, and Lazarus, His apostles, and with special significance, Mary Magdalene at the tomb (John 20:16). Furthermore, two of the Gospels describe Jesus correcting someone who addressed Him with an honorific title: "a man ran up to him and fell on his knees before him. 'Good teacher,' he asked, 'what must I do to inherit eternal life?' 'Why do you call me good?' Jesus answered. 'No one is good—except God alone' (Mark 10:18 NIV; also Matthew 19:16-17). Our Savior called his friends by their names and reserved venerating titles for God.

Verse 6 ends with Peter's clarifying instructions to Christian women: "fear no intimidation" (NAB). Other translations seem to promote greater emotional strength: "let nothing terrify you" (RSV) or do not "give way to fear or worry" (JB). In the Roman Empire and Jewish world, many women lived in fear of their husbands. Arranged marriages were not necessarily built on a foundation of love, and a wife was often considered her husband's servant or property.

Wives were completely dependent on their husbands for substance, and too often were the victims of their wrath. As we will discuss in chapter 6, when a husband became upset at his

---

[461] Bauer, *A Greek–English Lexicon of the New Testament,* 459. The Greek New Testament uses "lord / *kurios*" for both God and humans. The latter is used for "one who has come of age and controls his own property . . . master of the house . . . designation of any person of high position . . . the husband in contrast to the wife . . . of a father by his son."
[462] Jeremias, *Jerusalem,* 369.

wife, he could easily divorce her—even for something as minor as burning his toast. The threat of divorce left some wives paralyzed in a state of fear.[463]

It appears that Peter wanted Christian women to free themselves from fear, including fear of incurring their husbands' wrath and from inhibiting worry. He counseled women that they should perform their duties toward their families and society without trepidation or intimidation. Even more stunning against the backdrop of the New Testament setting, the Lord's message empowered women in their divine roles.

To support women to act with confidence, Peter next instructs husbands to honor their wives.

1 Peter 3:7

KJV	NEB	Welch-Hall[464]
Likewise, ye husbands, dwell with them accord - ing to knowledge, giving honour unto the wife, as unto the weaker vessel, and as being heirs toget- her of the grace of life that your prayers be not hindered.	In the same way, you husbands must conduct your married life with understanding: pay honour to the woman's body, not only because it is weaker, but also because you share together in the grace of God which gives you life. Then your prayers will not be hindered.	A husband should live according to revealed truth, giving honor to his wife, as a tender, instr- ument and also recogniz- ing that they will be heirs together of the gift of life.

---

[463] Ben Sira, *Ecclesiasticus*, 25:26. Charles, *The Apocrypha and Pseudepigrapha of the Old Testament*, 2.134. Stagg, *Woman*, 34.
[464] Welch and Hall, *Charting the New Testament,* 15-15.

It is hard to determine what the author meant by women as "a tender instrument" or "the weaker vessel" (1 Peter 3:7). [465] One translation proposes a physical definition with "weaker than you are" (GW). Generally speaking, females have smaller bone structure and less muscle mass than males.[466] Yet Peter's overall message was not about anatomy. He wants husbands to support and be considerate of their wives. Just as Peter praised Sarah for honoring her husband, he asks husbands to honor their wives. His message throughout this passage is for spouses to cherish each other.

In 1 Peter 3:7, Peter prefaced his explanation with the phrase, "according to knowledge" of truth—which included the revelation that spouses can become "heirs together" through the eternal nature of marriage.[467] Even though "eternal marriage" and "celestial marriage" are not phrases found in the New Testament, 1 Peter 3:7 alludes to that principle with the phrase, "being heirs together of the grace of life."[468] When a husband

---

[465] Strong, *Exhaustive Concordance of the Bible,* 81. Greek dictionary for "vessel / *skeuos*: . . . implement, equipment or apparatus," or figuratively, "a wife as contributing to the usefulness of the husband." For an overview of use in the New Testament see Mark 11:16; Luke 8:16; Acts 9:15; 10:11; 1 Thessalonians 4:4; 2 Timothy 2:21.

[466] John Elliott, *Anchor Bible, 1 Peter* (NYC, NY: Doubleday & Random House, 2000 reprint), 568. Even before scientific precision measured these genetic issues, Aristotle made a similar observation, "For the divine made one strong and the other weaker so that the latter would be more protected as a result of her timidity and the former more ready to defend as a result of his manliness . . . the one provides things from the outside, the other preserves the things inside."

[467] "Heirs together" also speaks of receiving one's calling and election, which Peter mentions in 2 Peter 1:10. The Prophet Joseph taught this was an ordinance only given to worthy couples (Ehat and Lyndon W. Cook, *Words of Joseph Smith,* 209). The word, *gnosis* is defined as: "knowledge signifies in general intelligence, understanding: the general knowledge of Christian religion, the deeper more perfect and enlarged knowledge of this religion, such as belongs to the more advanced, especially of things lawful and unlawful for Christians; moral wisdom, such as is seen in right living."

[468] Bauer, *A Greek–English Lexicon of the New Testament,* 340. The definition for "life / *zoe*" includes: "1) life in a physical sense . . . 2)

169

and wife become "heirs together," both have the potential to receive exaltation (D&C 131:1-4; 132:19-25).[469] Peter teaches this concept of becoming heirs of eternal life at least four other times (1 Peter 3:7; 2 Peter 1:10; Romans 8:17; Titus 3:7).[470] Joseph Smith learned that this gift is only given to married couples who are sealed by the Holy Spirit of Promise (D&C 132:19). With the sealing, the power and blessings of the patriarchal priesthood are "shared by husbands and wives who are sealed in the temple."[471]

Verse 7 ends with a warning that a husband cannot communicate with God if he does not communicate respectfully with his wife.[472] This concept is a radical shift from rabbinic teachings of the time that discouraged open and honest communication between husband and wife. Conversations were severely limited with all women, both within the family and without. The Mishnah taught that speaking to women was a waste of time and could be morally dangerous. [473]

Peter burst these cultural barriers by insisting that developing harmony in personal relationships was necessary in order to experience harmony with God in prayer. Both the Lord and His apostles urged couples to communicate, make amends, respect and listen to each other—in order to foster the Spirit of God in relationships as well as in prayer (i.e., Matthew 5:23-24; 25:40; etc.). Peter concluded his instructions on marriage by

---

supernatural life belonging to God and Christ which believers will receive in the future, but which they also enjoy here and now."

[469] Ezra Taft Benson, "What I Hope You Will Teach Your Children about the Temple," *Ensign* (Aug 1985): 9.

[470] Larry E. Dahl and Donald Q. Cannon, *Encyclopedia of Joseph Smith's Teachings* (Salt Lake City, UT: Bookcraft, 1997), "Degrees of Glory." Ehat and Cook, *Words of Joseph*, 211. Joseph Smith taught that all prophets and apostles taught from the perspective of knowing the fullness of truth. Also see D&C 132:5, 7, 13, etc.

[471] Ludlow, *Encyclopedia of Mormonism*, "Priesthood, Patriarchal," 3.1135.

[472] Smith, *History of the Church,* 1.131. Joseph Smith could not receive revelation when out of harmony with Emma.

[473] *Mishnah, Avoth* 1:5. As quoted in chapter 1, "Communication." *Babylonian Talmud, Nedarim.* 20a.

reiterating the primacy demonstrated by the Savior and the Father in 1 Peter 2:21-25, and by the Savior's command at the Last Supper: "Be one" even as "I and my Father are one" (John 17:22; 10:30).

1 Peter 3:8-9

KJV	NET	NIV
Finally, be ye all of one mind, having compassion one of another, love as brethren, be pitiful, be courteous: Not rendering evil for evil, or railing for railing: but contrariwise blessing; knowing that ye are thereunto called, that ye should inherit a blessing.	Finally, all of you be harmonious, sympathetic, affectionate, compassionate, and humble. Do not return evil for evil or insult for insult, but instead bless others because you were called to inherit a blessing.	Finally, all of you, be like-minded, be sympathetic, love one another, be compassionate and humble. Do not repay evil with evil or insult with insult. On the contrary, repay evil with blessing, because to this you were called so that you may inherit a blessing.

Peter focused on the qualities of love, meekness, and courtesy necessary for believers in their marriages and in every other interaction, both inside and outside of the church, with friends or with strangers (1 Peter 3:11-17). The Master teaches that Christians no longer live the old law of "an eye for an eye" but, as disciples of Christ, they must return good for evil, kindness for cruelty, and forgiveness for pain (Matthew 5-7). Peter carried on Jesus' message and emphasized that love, compassion, humility, and unity were especially crucial in marriage. It appears that many of the early church members needed to learn the significance of applying charity in spousal relations because Paul gives similar counsel.

II. 1 Corinthians 7

Like Peter's comments on marriage, Paul's advice to the Corinthians includes passage that call for close examination. His advice on spousal unity (7:3), false practices (7:2-11), and child rearing in mixed-faith marriages (7:12-16) are placed between efforts to correct two deviant sexual behaviors: in chapter 6, he tackles the libertines who argued that everything sexual was permissible; and in chapter 7, he speaks to the ascetics who stood on the other end of the sensual spectrum, contending that anything sexual should be forbidden.

The first half of 1 Corinthians 7 contains several challenging verses, starting with verse 1.

1 Corinthians 7:1

KJV [JST]	NIV	ISV
Now concerning the things whereof ye wrote unto me [JST saying]: It is good for a man not to touch a woman [?].	Now for the matters you wrote about: "It is good for a man not to have sexual relations with a woman."	Now about what you asked: "Is it advisable for a man not to marry.

Most translations clarify that verse 1 is a restatement of a question the Corinthians had asked—not a statement of Paul's opinion. [474] While we do not hot have background for the

---

[474] Smith, *History of the Church,* 5:261. The Prophet Joseph gave his advice on how to understand scriptural passages, "I have a key by which I understand the Scriptures. I enquire what was the question which drew out the answer." Paul answered at least six questions in the second half of 1 Corinthians—each identified by his formula, *"now concerning"* or *"now touching."* 1) 7:1 on marriage and divorce, 2) 7:25 on virginity; 3) 8:1 food offered to idols; 4) 12:1 Spiritual Gifts; 5) 16:1 collection for Jerusalem; 6)

Corinthians' question, Paul's response in verse 2 shows that he strongly disagrees with the original statement about "touching" or having sexual relations with women

1 Corinthians 7:2

KJV [JST]	NIV	ISV
Nevertheless, [JST: I say] to avoid fornication, let every man have his own wife, and let every woman have her own husband.	But because of immoralities, each man is to have his own wife, and each woman is to have her own husband.	Let every man have his own wife, and let every woman have her own husband to marry.

In verse 2, Paul censured immorality and championed marriage. The KJV word "fornication" is taken from the Greek "*pornea,*" which means all illicit sexual relations. As discussed in chapter 3 of this book, Corinth had the reputation as one of the sexual capitals of the ancient world—the phrase "to play the Corinthian" meant to visit a house of prostitution, and to be "a Corinthian business man" described a whoremonger.[475] Given this cultural context, it is not surprising that Paul spent much of his letter to the Corinthians addressing the law of chastity.

Paul clearly spoke out in favor of marriage and openly supported marital intimacy, deeming it meaningful, if for nothing else than to assist in living the law of chastity.

16:12 Apollo. There were other questions that Paul answered without the same introductory formula (i.e., 7:17; 9:1).

[475] John L. McKensize, *The Dictionary of the Bible* (NYC, NY: Touchstone, 1995, MacMillian, 1965), 149.

KJV [JST]	NIV
Let the husband render unto the wife due benevolence: and likewise also the wife unto the husband. The wife hath not power of her own body, but the husband: and likewise also the husband hath not power of his own body, but the wife.	The husband should fulfill his marital duty to his wife, and likewise the wife to her husband. The wife does not have authority over her own body but yields it to her husband. In the same way, the husband does not have authority over his own body but yields it to his wife.

Paul used this opportunity to teach the potential of physical and emotional unity between husband and wife. He spoke positively and candidly about intimacy within the bonds of marriage (also 1 Corinthians 7:28).[476] Within reason, each spouse should serve their companion's private needs. This might be difficult to discern in the KJV, which discreetly cloaked Paul's word choice as, "benevolence," but the RSV uses more vivid language, "conjugal rights." In verse 5, Paul asks couples to give themselves selflessly to each other.

---

[476] Ruden, *Paul Among the People,* 101. "Paul comes up with something altogether new: husbands and wives must have sex with each other on demand, because they both need it—it's the reason they got married. According to these verses [1 Corinthians 7:3-5] they may need it equally. The rules for marriage treat human sexuality as a part of nature that needs expression" (also see Ruden, 107-108) Paul's Christian teachings on sex stand in contrast to his contemporary, Josephus, who taught that sex was for procreation only. See footnote 434.

1 Corinthians 7:5

KJV [JST]	NIV	Aramaic Bible
Defraud ye not [JST "part ye not"] one [JST "from"] the other, except it be with consent for a time, that ye may give yourselves to fasting and prayer; and come together again, that Satan tempt you not for your incontinency.	Do not deprive each other except perhaps by mutual consent and for a time, so that you may devote yourselves to prayer. Then come together again so that Satan will not tempt you because of your lack of self-control.	Do not deprive one another except when you both agree in a time which you devote to fasting and prayer, and you shall again return to pleasure, lest Satan tempt you because of the desire of your bodies.

Paul developed his ideas on the importance of physical intimacy in marriage by directing couples to "not deprive" (NIV) or "not refuse one another" their "conjugal rights" (1 Corinthians 7:5, 3, RSV). This fulfilled the command given to Adam and Eve to be "one flesh," which Jesus also repeated (Genesis 2:24; Matthew 19:5-6; Mark 10:7-8). The only exception to this, in Paul's opinion, was a period of abstinence if they jointly "consent / *sumphonos* / a harmonious agreement or compact." His use of "time / *kairos*" refers to an "opportune or seasonable time, the right time, or a limited period of time.[477] The last word in verse 5, "incontinency / *akrasia*," is

---

[477] *Mishnah, Ketuboth,* 5.6. The *Mishnah* stipulated that a period of abstinence should last no longer than a week to six months month depending on the circumstances: "If a man vowed to have no intercourse with his wife, the School of Shammai say: [She may consent] for two weeks. And the School of Hillel say: For one week [only]. Disciples [of the Sages] may continue absent for thirty days against the will [of their wives] while they occupy themselves in the study of the law; and laborers for one week. The

usually translated "lack of self-control."[478] Basically, Paul teaches that it is unwise to abstain from sex for too long in marriage or one might be tempted to have sex with someone else. In a straightforward manner, Paul advocated sexual relations within marriage—unless a reciprocal decision was made for a short period of abstinence.

Paul prefaced the next section with a disclaimer—it was only his opinion and not a "commandment" from God.

1 Corinthians 7:6-8

KJV [JST]	NIV	Aramaic Bible
But I speak this by permission, and not of command-ment. For I would that all men were even as I myself. But every man hath his proper gift of God, one after this manner, and another after that. I say therefore to the unmarried and widows, It is good for them if they abide even as I.	I say this as a concession, not as a command, I wish that all of you were as I am. But each of you has your own gift from God; one has this gift, another has that. Now to the unmarried and the widows I say: It is good for them to stay unmarried, as I do.	I say this as to the weak, not by commandment. For I wish that all people might be like I am in purity, but every person is given a gift from God, one in this way and one in that way. But I say to those who do not have a wife and to widows, that it benefits them if they should remain as I am.

duty of marriage enjoyed in the Law [Exod. 21:10] is: every day for them that are unoccupied; twice a week for labourers; once a week for ass-drivers; once every thirty days for camel-drivers; and once every six months for sailors" (brackets included in the Danby translation).

[478] The New Testament uses this word only one other time—Jesus denounces the *Pharisees*, "they are full of extortion and excess / *akrasia*" (Matt 23:25).

Paul's disclaimer is needed, as the difficult passage brings up several questions. After Paul spoke positively about marriage from verses 2 to 5, his statement in verse 8, that "it is good for them to stay unmarried, as I do," seems odd—especially in light of the entire Pauline library which repeatedly supports mutuality in marriage (1 Corinthians 11:11; Ephesians 5:21-6:4; Colossians 3:18-21; 1 Timothy 2:15).[479]

At this point one may wonder if Paul were currently a widower. [480] Although the early saints knew Paul's marital status at the time, we do not. We do know that he was a strict Pharisee before his conversion to Christianity (Philippians 3:5) and claimed to obey all The Law, which included marriage. In verse 8, Paul explained that being a missionary was like being unmarried or widowed. All these roles demand sexual self-restraint. In this light, Paul called for celibacy in the limited context of missionary service or "consent for a time" (1 Corinthians 7:5). Keep in context that just a couple of sentences earlier, Paul defended marital sex as something good and needed (1 Corinthians 7:3-5).

Another explanation may be found in his statement regarding having a "proper gift of God" found in verse 7. Perhaps this refers to a spiritual gift (which Paul elaborates on in 1 Corinthians 12:1) or a calling in the church (1 Corinthians 14:12; 1 Timothy 4:14; 2 Timothy 1:6). He also alludes to his missionary call in verse 22. So perhaps this "gift" was a missionary call to travel–something that would require separation from one's spouse for a time, and therefore temporary celibacy. If this were the case, then his directive on celibacy may be consistent with his previous counsel on

---

[479] The NRSV footnote of 1 Corinthians 11:11 reads, "*In the Lord,* in Christ, thus among Christians, *Not independent of man . . . of woman* suggests mutuality, and some interpreters believe equality as well." Even though this commentary suggests equality is a higher aim, in my thinking mutuality should be the goal.

[480] Anderson, *Understanding Paul,* 104. "One tendency here is to see Paul as a widower, serving the Lord rather than remarrying. But another option is persuasive; he was using himself as an example of sexual self-control" (1 Corinthians 7:7).

marriage if the former were written specifically for those called as missionaries for a specific period of time.

1. Corinthians 7:9

KJV [JST]	ISV	Aramaic Bible
But if they cannot contain, let them marry: for it is better to marry than to burn [JST better to marry than that any should commit sin].	However, if they cannot control themselves, they should get married, for it is better to marry than to burn with passion.	But if they do not endure, let them marry. It is beneficial for them to take a wife rather than to burn with lust.

In verse 9, the JST emphasized the need for self-control by changing "burn" to "commit sin." Most translations infer sexual desires.[481] Paul asked missionaries to focus on the Lord's work—with or without a wife.

Next Paul turns to the subject of divorce. He points out that this is no longer his opinion. In the Sermon on the Mount, Jesus asked His chosen disciples to live the celestial law of marriage where eternal spouses do not separate (Matthew 5:32 ". . . saving for the cause of fornication"). In contrast to this higher law, in Jewish society divorces were easily obtained (as we will discuss in chapter 6).[482] Under their law, "a man takes a wife and possesses her. She fails to please him because he finds something obnoxious about her, and he writes her a bill of divorcement, hands it to her, and sends her away from his house" (Deuteronomy, 24:1).[483]

---

[481] Bruce, *Corinthians,* 68. Jews used "burn" as an idiom for one who fell into fornication and therefore would "burn" in *Gehenna* / hell.
[482] Jeremias, *Jerusalem,* 371.
[483] Skolnik, *Encyclopedia Judaica,* "Divorce: In later Jewish Law" 5.711.The translation is unique to the *Encyclopedia Judaica.*

In the Roman world divorce was so common that historians estimate most adults (in the middle and upper classes) had four to five divorces each. [484] We see the influence of the Roman divorce culture infiltrating the Jewish culture through people like Herod the Great who married ten times, and his son Herod Antipas who married his brother's ex-wife.[485] Paul deplored these societal norms and promoted Christ's higher law of forgiveness and love.

1 Corinthians 7:10-11

KJV [JST]	ISV	Aramaic Bible
And unto the married I command, yet not I, but the Lord, Let not the wife de-part from her husband: But and [JST removes and] if she depart, let her remain unmarried, or be reconciled to her husband: and [JST changes to "but"] let not the hus-band put away his wife.	To the married I give this command (not I, but the Lord): A wife must not separate from her husband. But if she does, she must remain unmarried or else be reconciled to her husband. And a husband must not divorce his wife.	To married people I give this command (not really I, but the Lord): A wife must not leave her husband. But if she does leave him, she must remain unmarried or else be reconciled to her husband. Like-wise, a husband must not abandon his wife.

[484] Stagg, *Woman in the World of Jesus,* 86; Wirtherington, *Women*, 20.
[485] Herod Antipas was the tetrarch of Galilee and Peraea during Jesus' ministry. He first married the daughter of the King of Arabia, but left her to take his brother Philip's wife, Herodias. John the Baptist rebuked them, which put in motion his beheading.

Paul's encouragement to work things out in marriage offered the empowering hope of reconciliation, repentance, and forgiveness. Verse 11 included the option to "be reconciled" after a divorce. The law of Moses limited divorced reconciliation, to the extent of forbidding remarriage to a woman that a man had previously divorced in certain cases.[486] But Paul called for reconciliation—which could refer to a variety of associations between divorced couples—all of which may offer healing. Christ's higher laws extend even to divorced partners: "Blessed are the peacemakers" (Matthew 5:9-10).

In verses 12 through 14, Paul returns to his own advice on the same question that Peter dealt with, namely, interfaith marriages. In this new religion, both apostles valued marriage to the degree that they discouraged tearing apart families, even if the couple held different religious beliefs.

When the Prophet Joseph Smith "translated" or revised these verses, he received further revelation about the problems Paul addressed (now recorded in D&C 74).[487] He learned that the Corinthians had a specific question about how a Jewish-Christian couple should raise their children. The core issue was how to raise children when one spouse still wanted to raise the children under the law of Moses.[488]

---

[486] According to Deuteronomy 24:1-4, once a Jewish man divorced his wife, if she remarried, but was left alone again (either by death or divorce), the first man could not remarry her.

[487] D&C 74 was received on January 25, 1832. See verses 1, 5-7.

[488] D&C 74:2, "the unbelieving husband was desirous that his children should be circumcised and become subject to the law of Moses, which law was fulfilled." According to section 74, Christianity teaches the saints that the law of Moses was not required for their children's salvation. If a couple raised their children living the laws of Moses (sometimes summarized as "circumcision"), it ignored Christ's role in fulfilling The Law. The dispute dealt with devout Jews believing that they were actually saved through the law of Moses. They feared that by neglecting details like circumcision, they would be doomed to *Gehenna* / hell. Paul wanted this Jewish teaching "done away" (D&C 74:6). Christian doctrine declared that children are "holy being sanctified through the atonement of Jesus Christ" (D&C 74:7). Mormon 8:8 repeated this.

180

1 Corinthians 7:12-14

KJV [JST]	ESV	Aramaic Bible
But to the rest speak I, not the Lord: If any brother hath a wife that believeth not, and she be pleased to dwell with him, let him not put her away. And the woman which hath an husband that believeth not, and if he be pleased to dwell with her, let her not leave him. For the unbelieving husband is sanctified by the wife, and the unbelieving wife is sanctified by the husband: else were your children unclean; but now are they holy.	To the rest I say (I, not the Lord) that if any brother has a wife who is an unbeliever, and she consents to live with him, he should not divorce her. If any woman has a husband who is an unbeliever, and he consents to live with her, she should not divorce him. For the unbelieving husband is made holy because of his wife, and the unbelieving wife is made holy because of her husband. Otherwise your children would be unclean, but as it is, they are holy.	But to others I am saying, not my Lord, if there is a brother who has a wife who is an unbeliever and she is willing to stay with him, let him not leave her. And whichever wife has a husband who is not a believer, and he is willing to stay with her, let her not leave her husband. That man who is an unbeliever is sanctified by the wife who believes, and that woman who is not a believer is sanctified by the husband who believes, otherwise their children are defiled, but now they are pure.

Paul felt so strongly about this that he "wrote unto the church, giving unto them a commandment, not of the Lord, but of himself, that a believer should not be united to an unbeliever;

except the law of Moses should be done away among them"
(D&C 74:5). Paul called on Christian parents to work as hard as
they could to teach their children the truth—which in this case
meant that Christ fulfilled The Law.

In verse 15, Paul gave an exception regarding when divorce
was appropriate. Christ indicated in both the Sermon on the
Mount and His conversation with the Pharisees, that the only
exception for a divorce was sexual sin.[489] But Paul added
another exception, namely, in cases when a saint's non-
believing spouse left the marriage.

1 Corinthians 7:15

KJV [JST]	NET	Aramaic Bible
But if the unbelieving depart, let him depart. A brother or a sister is not under bondage in such cases: but God hath called us to peace.	But if the unbeliever wants a divorce, let it take place. In these circumstances the brother or sister is not bound. God has called you in peace.	But if he who does not believe separates, let him separate. A brother or sister is not in bondage in such cases. God has called us to peace.

If reconciliation did not work, then Paul did not want a divorced
Christian to feel under the bondage of breaking God's law. In
such cases, Paul counsels the divorced spouse to seek God's
"peace." Paul defines what he meant by "God's peace" in
another letter: "And God's peace shall be yours, that tranquil
state of a soul assured of its salvation through Christ, and so
fearing nothing from God and content with its earthly lot, of

---

[489] Matthew 5:32; 19:3, 9; Mark 10:2, 11, 12; Luke 16:18.

whatsoever sort that is" (Philippians 4:7, Amplified Bible). In the Jewish world, divorce carried a heavy stigma, and Paul hoped for healing through Christ for those who had experienced a divorce. The same still holds true.

Paul continues to address the issue of mixed faith marriages in hope that believing spouses could be an influence in teaching the gospel of Christ to their family.

1 Corinthians 7:16

KJV [JST]	NIV	Aramaic Bible
For what knowest thou, O wife, whether thou shalt save thy husband? or how knowest thou O man, whether thou shalt save thy wife?	How do you know, wife, whether you will save your husband? Or, how how do you know, husband, whether you will save Your wife?	For what do you know, woman, if you will save your husband, or you, man, if you will save your wife?

This verse on interfaith marriages is less confusing if we clarify which spouse is the believer. For example, "How do you know, [believing] wife, if you might convert your [non-believing] husband, or you, [believing] husband, might convert your [non-believing] wife?" (NIV). Paul hopes that by living Christ's teachings, the believing spouse could bless his or her household and bring others to Christ—who could ultimately save them.

3) Ephesians 5:25-33

The Epistle to the Ephesians speaks about a husband's and wife's obligation to love each other. In the middle of the Epistle, the author includes a Christian family code of conduct, with a beautiful section on mutual love and respect between spouses.

KJV [JST]	NIV

Husbands, love your wives, even as Christ also loved the church, and gave himself for it; 26) That he might sanctify and cleanse it with the washing of water by the word, 27) That he might present it to himself a glorious church, not having spot, or wrinkle, or any such thing; but that it should be holy and without blemish. 28) So ought men to love their wives as their own bodies. He that loveth his wife loveth himself. 29) For no man ever yet hated his own flesh; but nourish-eth and cherisheth it, even as the Lord the church: 30) For we are members of his body, of his flesh, and of his bones. 31) For this cause shall a man leave his father and mother, and shall be joined unto his wife, and they two shall be one flesh. 32) This is a great mystery: but I speak concerning Christ and the church. 33) Nevertheless let every one of you in particular so love his wife even as himself; and the wife see that she reverence her husband.

Husbands, love your wives, just as Christ loved the church and gave himself up for her 26) to make her holy, cleansing her by the washing with water through the word, 27) and to present her to himself as a radiant church, without stain or wrinkle or any other blemish, but holy and blameless. 28) In this same way, husbands ought to love their wives as their own bodies. He who loves his wife loves himself. 29) After all, no one ever hated their own body, but they feed and care for their body, just as Christ does the church— 30) for we are members of his body. 31) "For this reason a man will leave his father and mother and be united to his wife, and the two will become one flesh." 32) This is a profound mystery—but I am talking about Christ and the church. 33) However, each one of you also must love his wife as he loves himself, and the wife must respect her husband.

Of note, the Epistle speaks more about a husband's duty to love his wife than it does the wife's duty to her husband. The author uses ninety-two Greek words instructing men, and only forty words of guidance to women.[490]

From verses 25 to 31, the author reaches back to scripture from three different dispensations that spoke of love that he combines with marriage. It starts with Jesus' higher law, known as the "new commandment" that He taught at His Last Supper: "love one another; as I have loved you" (John 13:34). The author adds the promise that if the couple abides in love, Jesus will sanctify their marriage. Next he applies part of the Mosaic law of love: "thou shalt love thy neighbour as thyself" (Leviticus 19:18) to marriages by teaching husbands to "love [your] wives as [your] own bodies" (Ephesians 5:28). Then Ephesians 5:31 returns to the creation account as a template for marriage: "a man leave his father and his mother, and shall cleave unto his wife" (Genesis 2:24).

Paul uses the word "love" three times in these verses.[491] Although the Greeks had four different words for love, Paul elaborates on "charity / *agape* / love" and gives it a special definition in Christianity.[492] He fills an entire chapter by

---

[490] Parales, *Hidden Voices: Biblical Women*, 130.

[491] There are four "prison letters" supposedly written when Paul was on "house arrest" (c.AD 61-63), that share many similarities: Colossians, Philemon, Ephesians and Philippians. When the New Testament was canonized, tradition credited Ephesians as Pauline, though modern biblical scholars doubt this. Textual scholars question the authorship of Ephesians because it does not send personal greetings, nor does it appear that the audience knew the author personally (1:15; 3:2-3; 4:21). This absence is especially odd as Paul was a missionary in Ephesus for three years just prior to his first Roman imprisonment. The letter may have also been a circular letter written to a larger audience as nowhere in the Epistle does it state it was to the Ephesians.

[492] Greek had at least four words to express love: *eros* for erotic love; *storge* for affection or parental love; *philo* for friendship or brotherly love; *agape* for self-sacrifice or according to the Gospel of John, God's pure love. The latter two words are used interchangeably by many Greek authors. But Paul appears to separate them with his exposé on *agape* as charity in 1 Corinthians 13:3-13.

quoting an older document that enlarged its meaning.[493] A portion of 1 Corinthians 13 became a handbook of instructions on how to internalize charity with the motivating claim that charity was "the greatest" gift of the Spirit (1 Corinthians 13:13).[494] The prophet Mormon cited a similar passage and added, "Charity is the pure love of Christ" (Moroni 7:47). In Ephesians 5:25-33, the author uses the same word, "*agapao /* love." By adding this special definition for charity, these verses in Ephesians becomes even more powerful: "the husband has *pure love* toward his wife, as Christ has *pure love* for the Church."[495]

The passage ends with a call for spouses to join in a modified system of checks and balances in marriage: [496] "let each one of you love his wife as himself, and let the wife see that she respects her husband" (Ephesians 5:33, ESV). The overriding message not only in Ephesians 5:33, but throughout the New Testament, is for saints to love their spouses and respect each other. The same message is preached in Christ's restored church.

Latter-day Prophets and Apostles On Marriage

The Lord restored the emancipating work to heal family relations and elevate women and children again as part of this dispensation of the fullness of times (D&C 76:95). Modern Scripture honors marriage as a divine law. The Lord echoed

---

[493] Anderson, *Understanding Paul,* 117. There is evidence that the citations on "charity" from 1 Corinthians 13 came from an earlier Christian record of Jesus' sayings. Bishop Clement of Rome wrote a letter around AD 97 quoting, "love endures all things" and nine other statements about love— quoting Jesus—not quoting Paul. Furthermore, Jesus gave parallel priority to love in John 13:35 and 14:15. If this were a document from Jesus' sayings, it helps us understand why Mormon also quoted it in Moroni 7.

[494] The Greek word, "*agape /*love" is translated in the New Testament 86 times as "*love,*" 27 times as "*charity.*"

[495] Welch and Hall, *Charting the New Testament,* 15-15.

[496] Nibley, *Old Testament and Related Studies*, 93. Quote on page 125.

biblical passages when He told the restored church, "Thou shalt love thy wife with all thy heart, and shalt cleave unto her and none else" (D&C 42:22). Marriage "is ordained of God" (D&C 49:15). Spouses comfort and forgive each other (D&C 25:5; 132:56); the "twain shall be one flesh . . . that the earth might answer the end of its creation" (D&C 49:16). The eternal potential of marriage is outlined in D&C 132:19:

> . . . if a man marry a wife by my word, which is my law, and by the new and everlasting covenant, and it is sealed unto them by the Holy Spirit of promise, . . . [they] shall inherit thrones, kingdoms, principalities, and powers, dominions, all heights and depths—then shall it be written in the Lamb's Book of Life, . . . and shall be of full force when they are out of the world; and they shall pass by the angels, and the gods, which are set there, to their exaltation and glory in all things, as hath been sealed upon their heads, which glory shall be a fulness and a continuation of the seeds forever and ever.

It is clear from these statements that part of the restoration of all things included eternal covenantal marriage relationships.

In addition, the Lord revealed to the Prophet Joseph Smith principles of leadership that wives and husbands should likewise apply to their family relationships: "the powers of heaven cannot be controlled nor handled only upon the principles of righteousness . . . no power or authority can be maintained . . . only by persuasion, by long-suffering, by gentleness and meekness, and by love unfeigned" (D&C 121:36-41). This principle has extra meaning in light of the patriarchal priesthood that both spouses share jointly.[497]

In the restored church the family unit stands paramount, and in the ideal family, a wife and husband work together at the head of their family: "Every father is to his family a patriarch and every mother a matriarch as coequals in their distinctive

---

[497] Ludlow, *Encyclopedia of Mormonism*, "Priesthood, Patriarchal," 3.1135. In this book see page 188 and footnotes 502, 307, and 471.

parental roles."[498] As Elder Russell M. Nelson explains, a husband and wife's "stewardships, equally sacred and important, do not involve any false ideas about domination or subordination."[499] Similarly, Elder L. Tom Perry teaches that in marriage there is "not a president or a vice president. The couple works together eternally for the good of the family . . . They are on equal footing."[500]

The aim for such a marriage and family is sanctification. As a husband and wife serve the Lord and submit their will to Him, they become one in purpose.[501] The Lord chose to submit in love to those in political power to die for humanity. Following this example, God called spouses to acquiesce selflessly in love to each other to become more Christlike. As they serve each other and are valiant in their testimonies of God, they in turn receive the greatest blessings restored in the gospel: through the patriarchal priesthood. This is the "fulness of the priesthood, which is the highest order of priesthood, [and] is attained only through an eternal union of male and female."[502] Whether that marital relationship is developed in this life or the next, prophets have promised that these blessings of exaltation will come to all worthy saints.[503]

---

[498] James E. Faust, "The Prophetic Voice," *Ensign* (May, 1996): 6. Also see Gordon B. Hinckley, "The Family: A Proclamation to the World," *Ensign* (November, 1995).

[499] Russell M. Nelson "The Sacred Responsibilities of Parenthood," *Ensign* (Mar 2006): 29-30.

[500] L. Tom Perry, "Fatherhood, an Eternal Calling," *Ensign* (May 2004), 71. The quote continues, "They plan and organize the affairs of the family jointly and unanimously as they move forward."

[501] Valerie Hudson, Richard Miller, "Equal Partnership in Marriage," *Ensign* (April, 2013). "Latter-day Saint theology teaches that gender difference does not superimpose a hierarchy between men and women: one gender does not have greater eternal possibilities than the other."

[502] Ludlow, *Encyclopedia of Mormonism*, "Priesthood, Patriarchal," 3.1137. The quote continues, ". . . sanctified by the sealing ordinances in a temple of the Lord and ratified by the Holy Spirit of promise (D&C 132:18-19). Those so united, who honor their covenants with each other and the Lord, will in the Resurrection inherit exaltation and eternal life."

[503] Joseph Fielding Smith, *Doctrines of Salvation*, 2.76. "You good sisters, who are single and alone, do not fear, do not feel that blessings are going to

In conclusion, by breaking away from their Judaic and Greco-Roman cultures, the writers of the New Testament launched a new vision for mutually supportive and loving marriages. The Lord and His apostles taught disciples about relationships by focusing on charity and unity. A close, caring, selfless, happy relationship in marriage was different from anything in the neighboring cultures—as different as Jesus' new commandment, or turning the other cheek (John 13:34; Matthew 5:39). It became a "part of the Christian charter."[504]

Jesus came to empower humanity on many levels. In restoring the importance of spousal and family connections, He unveiled the symbiotic relationship between God and humanity. If families do not love and serve each other, not only do they ignore each other, they also "did it not to me" (Matthew 25:45; D&C 42:38). Jesus demonstrated through His own love and care that religious life intimately connects human relations.

Christ emancipated women and families from oppressive cultural baggage. We find evidence of the changes He brought in the early Christian church writings. The Epistles attributed to the apostles confirm and continue the teachings of Jesus in the Gospels describing marriage in a revolutionary way. Though some of the Epistles seem incompatible with Christ's teachings on marriage, when we take a closer look at seemingly troublesome passages and examine them in the light of restored truths, we find support for Christ's innovations related to women and marriage.

---

be withheld from you. You are not under any obligation or necessity of accepting some proposal that comes to you which is distasteful for fear you will come under condemnation. If in your hearts you feel that the gospel is true, and would under proper conditions receive these ordinances and sealing blessings in the temple of the Lord; and that is your faith and your hope and your desire, and that does not come to you now; the Lord will make it up, and you shall be blessed-for no blessing shall be withheld."

[504] Ruden, *Paul Among the People,* 102.

Divorce and widowhood in the Jewish world of the first century were often emotionally and financially devastating. Understanding this context allows us to understand better the power and relevance of Christ's parables and teachings. It also helps us to see some of the subtle ways in which Christ and His apostles modified these traditions in order to emancipate women, marriages, and families. We will see this as we look at this chapter's examples of unfulfilled marriage, divorce, and widowhood in the New Testament.

Unfulfilled Marriage

Cultural Background and Baggage

Literature from the late Second Temple era speaks of both happy and unhappy marriages.[505] As Ben Sira expounded, "A

---

[505] Ben Sira, *Ecclesiasticus*, 26:1-4. An example of a happy relationship comes from a paraphrasing of Proverbs 31: "Happy is the husband of a good

good wife is a good gift; she shall be given into the bosom of him that feareth God." [506] Nevertheless, right after this positive statement, later scribes slipped in a negative example: "An evil wife is a plague to her husband. What is the remedy? Let him drive her from his house [i.e., divorce her], and he shall be healed from the plague of her."[507] Philo offers examples of happy marriages when he looks back at the patriarchs. Sarah, Rebekah, and Leah are the examples of virtuous women, but he speaks of no positive examples of women in his day.[508]

Most late Second Temple writings now available describe unfulfilled marriages. Rarely was the spousal relationship associated with joy.[509] A man's drooping hands and weak knees came from "the wife who does not make her husband happy."[510] This account did not acknowledge the husband's attitude, responsibility, nor accountability for his own feelings. Ben Sira spoke far more of the pain of having an "evil" or "wicked" wife than of any pleasure they shared.

The term "evil wife" had a broad definition as one who broke the commandments, including one who did not silently submit to her husband's control.[511] Ben Sira defines a "wicked woman" as one who socializes outside of her home: "Give the

---

wife: for the number of his years is double. A virtuous woman rejoiceth her husband: and shall fulfill the years of his life in peace. A good wife is a good portion, she shall be given in the portion of them that fear God, to a man for his good deeds. Rich or poor, if his heart is good, his countenance shall be cheerful at all times."

[506] Ben Sira, *Ecclesiasticus,* 26:3.

[507] Arthur Ernest Cowley, Adolf Neubauer, ed; *The Original Hebrew of a Portion of Ecclesiasticus* (Oxford England: Oxford University-Clarendon Press, 1897), 24.

[508] Philo, *On the Cherubim; and on the Flaming Sword.* Part 2, XII.

[509] *Philo,* Yonge, trans., 160. Philo describes a slave who wanted to remain with his master for life as saying, "I have loved my master, my wife, and my children. . ." Yet, in the complete collection of Philo's writings, joy and wife / woman are never linked, but he speaks of joy in other settings. One of those was the patriarch Joseph's joy in being reunited with his family again in Egypt.

[510] Ben Sira, *Ecclesiasticus*, 25:23b.

[511] Charles, *The Apocrypha and Pseudepigrapha of the Old Testament,* 2.134.

water no passage; neither a wicked woman liberty to gad abroad. If she go not as thou wouldn't have her, cut her off from thy flesh. . . . The wickedness of a wife changes her appearance, and darkens her face like that of a bear. Her husband takes his meals among the neighbors."[512] Ben Sira bemoaned, "An evil wife is an ox yoke which chafes; taking hold of her is like grasping a scorpion . . . Any wound, but not a wound of the heart! Any wickedness, but not the wickedness of a wife![513] Elsewhere he continues, "I would rather dwell with a lion and a dragon than dwell with an evil wife."[514] He continues to blame an "evil wife" for causing "a dejected mind, a gloomy face and a wounded heart."[515]

After the time of the New Testament, rabbis labeled a man "wicked" if he did not control his wife. For example, a husband was "wicked" if he allowed his wife to "go outside with her head uncovered . . . and she spins in public and baths with men."[516] One has to wonder if they really felt that spinning in the fresh air was as immoral as bathing with men. Supposedly, by going outside without being veiled, a woman used seditious behavior to persuade men to look at her, inviting adultery. Later rabbis made a list of supposed "sins" (including idleness) that were a breech in fidelity, as they would lead to adultery.[517]

For many, a wife had value and significance inasmuch as she enabled her husband to keep God's commandments to

---

[512] Ben Sira, *Ecclesiasticus*, 25:12-18. He continues, "[the husband] cannot help sighing bitterly. Any iniquity is insignificant compared to a wife's iniquity; may a sinner's lot befall her! A sandy ascent for the feet of the aged—such is a garrulous wife for a quiet husband."

[513] Ben Sira, *Ecclesiasticus*, 26:7, 25:13. The preceding verse reads: "There is grief of heart and sorrow when a wife is envious of a rival, and a tongue-lashing makes it known to all" (27:5-6).

[514] Ben Sira, *Ecclesiasticus,* 25:16.

[515] Ben Sira, *Ecclesiasticus*, 25:23a.

[516] *Babylonian Talmud, Gittin* 90 a, b: "This corresponds to the way of a bad man who sees his wife go out with her hair unfastened and spin cloth in the street . . . with her armpits uncovered and bathe with the men. . . . Such a one it is a religious duty to divorce, as it says, because he hath found some unseemly thing in her … and he sendeth her out of his house."

[517] *Mishnah, Ketuboth,* 5:5.

marry and raise a family.[518] A wife became a means to an end—
the end being posterity. Also tied to the commandments, an
unhappy union was seen as the cause that led men to break
God's laws.

> Anyone who marries a woman unsuitable for him violates
> five negative commandments: "Do not take vengeance"
> (Leviticus 19:18), "Do not bear a grudge," "Do not hate
> your brother" (19:17), "and you shall love your neighbor
> as yourself" (19:18), "that your brother may live with
> you" (25:36), and the consequences are nothing less than
> removing fertility and increase from the world.[519]

Husbands blamed their wives for their own behaviors and
attitudes. A lack of personal responsibility prevailed in
unfulfilled marriages.

New Testament Examples of Changes by Jesus

This cultural backdrop of blaming the woman is needed
when we look the story of the woman taken in adultery (John
8:3-11).[520] The scenario offers an example of another one of
Jesus' emancipating tools. The scene falls on
Jesus' visit to Jerusalem for the Feast of the
Tabernacles—which included the Torah
reading for the punishment of adultery. The
scribes and Pharisees attempted to ensnare Jesus by setting up
another "no win" situation.

Woman Accused of Adultery

The whole encounter appears to be a farce. If the woman
were "in the very act," where was the guilty man? The law of
Moses required both parties be stoned (John 8:5; Leviticus

---

[518] *Philo*, Yonge, trans., 272. "And *what is the duty of man* except most
firmly to believe those things which *God* asserts?" Later rabbis counted 613
commandments from the Torah and ten thousand oral laws. See introduction,
"Oral Laws and Commandments."
[519] Ilan, *Jewish Women in Greco-Roman Palestine,* 79.
[520] This story is missing from the best Greek manuscripts of the Gospel of
John. Some place it in Luke's Gospel (where the Greek matches better).

20:10). Most commentaries view the woman as a pawn used by the scribes and Pharisees to trap Jesus. The accuser posed a question that would violate a law with either answer: "This they said, tempting him, that they might have to accuse him" (John 8:6). If Jesus released the woman, He broke the law of Moses; if He had her killed, He violated the Roman law.[521] Or perhaps the Pharisees wanted to test Jesus' prophetic ability? In any case, the battle of the Jews against the Romans played a large part in the Jewish anticipation and acceptance of the Messiah.

Jesus refused to play their games and "stooped down, and with His finger wrote on the ground, as though he heard them not" (John 8:6). In Roman legal practice, the judge first wrote the sentence and then read it aloud.[522] Jesus' answer put the burden back on His questioners. As Jesus turned the situation around, the woman was no longer on trial—they were. "He that is without sin among you, let him first cast a stone at her" (John 8:7). Jesus' example silently spoke to the importance of avoiding unrighteous judgment. He spoke of hypocrisy, and He spoke of forgiveness. The accusers left the scene either because Jesus pricked their own consciences or He did not respond as they had hoped.

The scene closed in climactic drama: the "sinful and the Sinless" alone together.[523] Regardless of whether the charges were made up, Jesus acted as a serene judge balancing justice and mercy. He did not condone the sin but offered the great challenge, "sin no more!" (John 8:11). Only when one forsakes sin can God completely rejuvenate one with His Spirit and love.

---

[521] The law of Moses states that anyone—male and female—caught in adultery is to be stoned (Leviticus 20:10; 22:15; as well as Ezekiel 15:38-40). Another question not answered in John's narrative is whether the Sanhedrin already tried the woman in their standard practice and why they wanted Jesus to duplicate or validate their verdict. The Roman law is outlined by Brown, *The Anchor Bible: John I-XII,* 337.

[522] Ibid., 334. Many have speculated on what Jesus wrote. An old Christian tradition, traced to Jerome, suggests that Jesus wrote the sins of the accusers in the dirt. Another connects the finger/handwriting of judgments with Daniel 5:24. All are speculation; the author is silent.

[523] John Milton, *Paradise Lost* (London: Collins, 1874), 98.

Divorce

Cultural Background and Baggage

First century marriages seemed doomed to fail—
beginning with an arranged union to appease financial and
social motives, a segregated lifestyle, lack of communication,
unequal opportunities, authoritarian habits, and a master-slave
relationship.[524] For centuries before and after the New
Testament, divorce resulted in social disgrace for Jewish men,
woman, and children. The Old Testament refers to divorce as
treachery against one's companion and a breach of the covenant
(Malachi 2:10-16). In the same way, a few centuries later,
during the intertestamental period, the Apocrypha warned that a
man who "breaketh wedlock . . . shall be punished" by God.[525]
This communal disapproval lasted until well after the Second
Temple period, where we read a mournful lamentations on
divorce "ye cover the altar of the Lord with tears, with weeping
and with sighing, insomuch that he regardeth not the offering
any more, neither receiveth it with good will at your hand."[526]
This section covers the *who, why,* and *how* of divorce, and
"what" it meant to women.

Who: A Husband's Right

During the Second Temple era, divorce was the unilateral
choice of the husband. Later Jewish law enumerated five

---

[524] See chapter 1, "Communication" pages 27-28.
[525] Ben Sira, *Ecclesiasticus*, 23:18-21; "A man that breaketh wedlock, saying
thus in his heart, Who seeth me? I am compassed about with darkness, the
walls cover me, and no body seeth me; what need I to fear? the most High
will not remember my sins: Such a man only feareth the eyes of men, and
knoweth not that the eyes of the Lord are ten thousand times brighter than
the sun, beholding all the ways of men, and considering the most secret
parts. He knew all things ere ever they were created; so also after they were
perfected he looked upon them all. This man shall be punished in the streets
of the city, and where he suspecteth not he shall be taken."
[526] *Babylon Talmud*, *Gittin* 90b.

exceptions when a woman could leave her husband: "[If] he that is afflicted with boils, or that has a polypus, or that collects dog excrements, or that is a coppersmith or a tanner."[527] Some diseases or professions were so vile that a wife was not expected to stay in the same environment as her husband. That said, it was a rare event when a woman left her husband. Ben Sira believed that the repercussions for a woman's leaving one marriage and entering into another brought curses for generations.[528]

Why: Uncleanness

A man could "put away" his wife if she transgressed the law of Moses or any Jewish custom (Matthew 19:3-9), as well as for relatively trivial mistakes.[529] How, where, and to whom she spoke, what she wore, cooked, or cleaned could all potentially lead to a divorce. Not only were her words and actions culpable, but she was also held responsible for her husband's emotional and romantic feelings.[530] The rabbis detailed hundreds of examples of what they felt were "just causes" for a man to divorce his wife. They divided their legal

---

[527] *Mishnah*, *Ketuboth* 7.10. One of the exceptions when a woman could leave her husband included being married to a tanner. The smells associated with tanning were so abhorrent that no one was expected to live in the same place. Yet, Acts 9:43-10:32 refers to the apostle Peter staying with Simon the tanner. Was it the only place available to Peter? Was Simon humbled through his profession to make him more open to receive Christianity?

[528] Ben Sira, *Ecclesiasticus*, 23:22. "Thus shall it go also with the wife that leaveth her husband, and bringeth in an heir by another. For first, she hath disobeyed the law of the most High; and secondly, she hath trespassed against her own husband; and thirdly, she hath played the whore in adultery, and brought children by another man. She shall be brought out into the congregation, and inquisition shall be made of her children. Her children shall not take root, and her branches shall bring forth no fruit. She shall leave her memory to be cursed, and her reproach shall not be blotted out."

[529] *Mishnah Gittin* 1-9. Under Roman law, a Roman woman could instigate a divorce.

[530] Ben Sira, *Ecclesiasticus*, 25:21; "Stumble not at the beauty of a woman and desire her not for pleasure."

196

grounds to justify a divorce into two major categories: 1) a religious duty, and 2) legal vindication of the husband.

—*Divorce as a Religious Duty.* The law of Moses allowed a husband to divorce his wife if he found "some uncleanness in her" (Deuteronomy 24:1). Over a thousand years later the rabbis categorized exactly what they interpreted as "unclean." If a wife violated one of the causes outlined on this list, the husband had a "religious duty" to divorce her without paying her *ketubah* (the "bride price").[531] Rabbis from the early first century AD interpreted this verse in two different ways. Either "uncleanliness" related to adultery, which was punished by death,[532] or "uncleanliness" included anything displeasing to the husband.[533] In the latter category, five forms of a wife's "uncleanliness" required divorce: 1) childlessness, 2) feeding her husband untithed food, 3) having intercourse during her menstrual cycle, 4) not preparing a dough-offering, or 5) not fulfilling a vow.[534] The latter case of fulfilling a vow became tricky because a wife did not have sole control of her religious vows—her husband did.[535]

---

[531] See chapter 4, "Marriage." The *ketubah* was a sum of money prescribed at the marriage settlement, as the price the groom had to pay his bride if he divorced her, thus allowing her to have something to live on for a period of time.

[532] Genesis 20:6; 26:10; Leviticus 20:10, 22; Deuteronomy 22:22, 24. *Mishnah Gittin,* 9.10. School of Shammai (who probably lived from 50BC to 30 AD) limited "uncleanliness" to adultery.

[533] *Mishnah, Gittin,* 9:10. The School of Hillel (60 BC-AD 20) claimed that anything "unclean," included anything displeasing or unbecoming to the husband.

[534] *Mishnah, Ketuboth* 7.6.

[535] As part of their religious worship, Israelite men and women made vows to consecrate their lives to God, or in the words of the Old Testament, to "bind" their souls "with a bond" (Numbers 30:2). Moses gave husbands jurisdiction over vows made by their wives (Numbers 30:8, 13). On the surface, this aspect of the law of Moses appears to restrict the autonomy of women. If done with genuine love and concern for the individual, though, the Mosaic law could foster cooperation and unity among family members. Moses taught that a father or husband, as the head of a family, should be intimately involved in his loved ones' lives and should give them spiritual

Even though "childlessness," or infertility, plagued Old Testament prophets—Abraham and Sarah, Jacob and Rebekah, Elkanah and Hannah, to name a few—the rabbis felt authorized to dictate when infertility became a "religious duty" for divorce:

> If a man took a wife and lived with her for ten years and she bore no child, he may not abstain [any longer from the duty of propagation]. If he divorced her she is permitted to marry another, and the second husband may also live with her [no more than] ten years. If she miscarried [the period of ten years] is reckoned from the time of her miscarriage.[536]

Though not everyone lived this, those men who followed the oral laws felt it was politically correct for a man to divorce his wife for infertility.[537]

—Divorce as legal vindication. The *Mishnah* includes a long list of "just causes" for a man to divorce his wife. Ben Sira counseled husbands, "Allow . . . no boldness of speech in an evil wife. If she does not go as you direct, separate her from yourself."[538] The rabbinical debate included that a woman should be divorced for burning her husband's bread or dinner,[539]

---

direction. A well-known biblical vow is that of a Nazarite. Numbers 6:1-2 states that both men and women can "separate themselves to vow a vow of a Nazarite." We see examples of that in Manoah's wife and Samson's mother (Judges 13), in Samuel (1Samuel 1:11), and John the Baptist (Luke 1:15). There were also vows of abstinence (Numbers 30), vows of commitment (Genesis 28:20), a voluntary or a free-will offering (Leviticus 7:16), vows to fight (Numbers 21:2), and monetary vows (Deuteronomy 23:21). For more see Tony W. Carledge, *Vows in the Hebrew Bible and the Ancient Near East* (Sheffield, England: JSOT Press, 1992), 12.

[536] *Mishnah*; *Yebamot* 6:6 (brackets original to translation). The schools of Hillel and Shammai decided a wife or husband could fine the other for not cohabitating once a week. *Ketuboth* 5:6-7.

[537] Philo, *Special Laws,* 3.35. "Those who marry maidens in ignorance at the time of their fitness or unfitness for successful delivery of children, and, when they learn much later on through their childlessness that they are barren, do not send them away, deserve our pardon."

[538] Ben Sira, *Ecclesiasticus*, 25:25-26.

[539] *Mishnah*, *Gittin* 9.10. "If she spoiled a dish for him, for it is written, because he hath found in her indecency in anything."

"spinning in the street" (which included her doorway) or "speaks to any man."[540] Other objections, "if spittle is found on the bed curtain," or "if shoes lie under the bed." (The shoes and spittle were evidence that a stranger had been there.[541])

Threats of divorce controlled nearly every detail of behavior. If a woman "speaks inside her house so that her neighbors hear her voice," she was labeled a "scolding woman" which was cause for divorce.[542] Perhaps the most arbitrary, Rabbi Akib (ca. AD 120-140) rationalized, "even if he found another fairer than she, for it is written, 'And it shall be if she find no favour in his eyes,'" he felt a divorce was justified.[543]

How: Obtaining a Bill of Divorcement

The divorce process itself was simple: the husband wrote a "bill of divorcement" that included a date, his signature, and witnesses' names.[544] The bill of divorcement may be written with anything or on anything—"ink, caustic, red dye, gum, copperas, or with whatsoever is lasting . . . on an olive-leaf or on a cow's horn (and he must give her the cow) or on the hand of a slave (and he must give her the slave)."[545]

Even though the divorce process was simple, most Jews remained married. Financial and social restraints kept marriages together. Husbands had to pay a minimum of 200 days' wages to their wives if the divorce was due to "legal vindication." More emotionally costly, the social contamination deterred the spread of divorce.[546] These restraints allowed Jewish marriages

---

[540] *Mishnah, Ketuboth* 6.6.

[541] *Babylonian Talmud, Yebamoth,* 24b-25a. "Only the woman lying face upwards could have spat on that spot. Intercourse may therefore be suspected."

[542] *Mishnah, Ketuboth* 6.6. Abba Saul justified divorce "if she curses his parents in his presence."

[543] *Mishnah,* Nashim, *Gittin,* 9.10.

[544] *Mishnah,* Nashim, *Gittin* 1-9. *Gittin* 2.4. "All [men] are qualified to write a bill of divorce, even a deaf-mute, an imbecile, or a minor" (*Mishnah, Gittin,* 2.4).

[545] *Mishnah,* Nashim, *Gittin,* 2.3.

[546] Jeremias, *Jerusalem,* 371.

to remain intact more frequently than Greco-Roman marriages, but the constant threat disabled their relationships.

What this Meant to Women

The unilateral threat of divorce overshadowed Jewish marriage relationships with insecurity and distrust.[547] This relentless intimidation left many women living in an environment of fear. Those wives lived in constant anxiety over the possibility of offending their spouses and thereby facing destitution and social disgrace. To avoid that, a wife tried to comply with every demand her husband made. Circumstances like these stunted marriage unions that should have had the potential for security, confidence, and love.

New Testament Examples

The social restrictions from the late Second Temple period fated marital relationships to fall short of their divine potential. Yet the Savior restored truths to help unfulfilled marriages and offered healing to wounded spouses. In the case of divorce, Jesus denounced the current customs and returned marriage to its paramount position. When the Pharisees tried to entice Jesus, "tempting him" into a debate on the emotional topic of divorce, He refused to deal with the minutiae of their oral laws (Matthew 19:3, Mark 10:2). Instead He reinstated one of the four commandments given in the Garden of Eden: "What God hath joined together, let not man put asunder" (Mark 10:9 echoing Genesis 1:28; 2:24). Luke 16:18 recorded a still stronger condemnation against divorce: "whosoever putteth away his wife and marrieth another, committeth adultery; and whosoever marrieth her that is put away from her husband

---

[547] Ben Sira, *Ecclesiasticus*, 25:26. The Greco-Roman world differed where many adults married and divorced four or five times. See appendix 2.

committeth adultery" (see also Matthew 5:32). Jesus restored the paradisiacal law.[548]

These higher decrees are still the ideal in Jesus' restored church: "Thou shalt love thy wife with all thy heart, and shalt cleave unto her and none else" (D&C 42:22). However, we do not live in a paradisiacal world, and living prophets allow divorced persons to remarry in temples without the charge of adultery.[549] In this dispensation, remaining married is not necessarily the best option (D&C 10:63).[550] The Edenic archetype stands as a goal, but if divorce does occur, disciples of Christ should forgive seventy times seven and not cast stones (Matthew 18:22).

Within this cultural context of divorce, we can appreciate the social scar that an infertile couple carried. It makes Zacharias and Elisabeth seem all the more admirable for remaining married even after decades of childlessness (Luke 1:7, 18). Luke emphasized that they "had God's approval" as they "followed all the Lord's commands and regulations perfectly" (Luke 1:6, GW). They

Zacharias and Elisabeth

---

[548] Paul repeated it for the apostolic church, "Let not the wife depart from her husband ... let not the husband put away his wife" (1 Corinthians 7:10-11).

[549] The law of marriage outlined in Matthew 5 and 3 Nephi 12, is not currently applied in the LDS church. One is not considered an adulterer if one marries twice. Even though the Lord's high law is a noble ideal, the challenges and sins of this generation do not allow some to live this law fully. Modern prophets allow temple cancellations and do not hold couples who marry after a divorce guilty of adultery. All who earnestly try to receive First Presidency approval are allowed to enter into the temples of God and are pronounced clean.

[550] Theoretically, reconciling marital difference is best, but in practice it is often difficult to incorporate. Many devoted Christians "do not now live in the kind of family situation they desire or deserve." Elder Bruce Hafen lamented, "Of course Church doctrine encourages marriage and discourages divorce, but marrying is not always under our control, and there are times when divorce is the better choice. Our Church leaders have long taught that, despite divorce or being single, no eternal blessing, even celestial glory, will be denied those who are true and faithful." Bruce C. Hafen, "Marriage, Family Law, and the temple," J. Reuben Clark Law Society Annual International Broadcast, January 31, 2014, Salt Lake City, UT.

endured the emotional pain of wanting children, the social shame of barrenness, and the spiritual confusion of why their prayers had not been answered. Through it all, they did not submit to the oral traditions that governed divorce, but instead held to the higher law given to Adam, for a husband to "cling to his wife" (Genesis 2:24, ISV). The years of trials that they endured before John the Baptist's birth must have refined them and their relationship with God (D&C 122:7).

The example of Zacharias and Elisabeth personifies the principles of obedience and sacrifice. They endured their trial and developed during the process of purification. They set an example of fidelity to each other and God, while overcoming social pressures. The Lord promises to exalt those who follow Him, no matter how difficult the trials and disappointments of life become: "For my Father's will is that everyone who looks to the Son and believes in him shall have eternal life, and I will raise them up at the last day" (John 6:40, NIV). God offers eternal emancipation to the obedient.

Widowhood

Cultural Background

When a woman's husband died, for the first time in her life, she was not beholden to anyone. As a child, her father had control over her, and that charge was transferred to her husband upon marriage. The *Mishnah* speaks of widowhood as synonymous with a woman's freedom: "A wife . . . can get her freedom by divorce, or through her husband's death."[551] This freedom was not relished, though, as it often resulted in abject poverty. For this reason, most Jewesses did not remain widows for long. There were tax incentives, too. In an attempt to bolster the families among Roman citizens, Caesar Augustus enacted reforms to legally and financially pressure fertile widows and

---

[551] *Mishnah, Kiddushin,* 1:1.

divorcees to remarry within two years.[552] He added a penalty tax to citizens who were widowers and divorcees who did not have at least three children.[553]

When a widow remarried, the minimum "bride price" or *ketubah,* paid for her was half that of a virgin.[554] Usually second marriages remained in the same social circle as first marriages.[555] Also a widow did not uncover her head on the wedding day as she had previously, because she was no longer a virgin. To ensure some form of a marriage celebration for a widow, the rabbis suggested that the ceremony take place on Thursdays, thus allowing the new husband to "rejoice with her for three days."[556] If an older widow did not remarry, she often returned to the home of her father, brother, or son for economic support (Genesis 38:11; Leviticus 22:13).

The law of Moses called for the children to honor their fathers and mothers—which included a reversal of roles when the children needed to take care of their aging parents, especially widowed mothers; "Hearken unto thy father that begat thee, and despise not thy mother when she is old" (Proverbs 23:22; also Exodus 20:12; Deuteronomy 5:16). Mosaic laws also called for the community to care for widows: ". . . the widow(s), which are within thy gates, shall come, and shall eat and be satisfied; that the LORD thy God may bless thee" (Deuteronomy 14:29; also 24:17-22; 26:12-13; Isaiah 1:17; Jeremiah 22:3). Yet in practice this did not always happen (Mark 12:42).

---

[552] Witherington, *Women and the Genesis of Christianity,* 23. For more, see appendix 2, page 304.

[553] Jackson J. Spielvogel, *Western Civilization 7th ed.* (Belmont, CA: Thomson & Wadsworth, 2009), volume 1, 152; "Augustus also revised the *tax* laws to penalize bachelors, *widowers,* and *married* persons who had fewer than three children."

[554] *Mishnah*, *Ketuboth,* 1.2.

[555] Except for the high priest, who was not allowed to marry a widow according to Leviticus 21:14.

[556] *Mishnah*, *Ketuboth* 1.1. "A virgin should be married on a Wednesday and a widow on a Thursday, for in towns the court sits twice in the week, on Mondays and on Thursdays; so that if the husband would lodge a virginity suit he may forthwith go in the morning to the court."

But during the Second Temple era, a few wealthy Jews found their way out of this responsibility. The Gospel of Mark referred to this practice as "corban."[557] In the parlance of the time, corban referred to an early commitment to donate one's estate to the temple or some other religious purpose upon one's death. From the moment of promising the future donation, corban immobilized all assets for anyone other than the man himself. This meant the greater family's needs were ignored. The problem lay in not assisting aged widows or other needy family members who were still alive. This donation enabled a man to use his funds while he was alive for himself, while ignoring the needs of his extended family, all the while, appearing noble in the eyes of the community.

New Testament Example

The early Christian leadership showed a particular concern for widows, which stemmed from their Master's example. All three synoptic Gospels record Jesus condemning the Jewish leaders for not caring for widows: "Woe unto you, scribes and Pharisees, hypocrites! for ye devour widows' houses, and for a pretense make long prayer: therefore ye shall receive the greater damnation" (Matthew 23:14; also see Luke 20:46-47). Luke seems particularly interested in the

Luke

downtrodden and social outcasts. He authored half of the references to widows in the New Testament.[558] Luke called attention to their plight of loneliness, dependency, and destitution. He included the report of The Twelve acknowledging the widows' neglect "in the daily ministration" that led to the calling of seven valiant men to oversee their needs (Acts 6:1).

---

[557] Josephus, *Against Apion,* I.22. "Corban . . . declares what a man may call a thing devoted to God."

[558] Luke 2:37; 4:25, 26; 7:12; 18:3, 5; 18:3; 20:47; 21:2, 3; Acts 6:1; 9:39, 41. Luke's examples in Acts demonstrate how Christ's high regard for women was passed on to the apostolic church.

Luke and Mark both recorded the story of the well-known, though unnamed, widow and her offering at the temple (Mark 12:42; Luke 21:2). They place the story during the last week of Jesus' life as He taught in the "Court of the Women," a 200-square-foot temple courtyard where men, women, and children were allowed to worship.[559] Around the perimeter ran a covered colonnade with thirteen containers, each labeled for its own charitable contributions. These pots were narrow at the top and wide at the bottom like a trumpet, and hence were called "trumpets."[560] Donors placed their offerings in the appropriate trumpet, thus sparing them any public interaction with the sacrificing priest. Jesus pointed out the widow as she generously donated her all—two mites—into the temple treasury: "All of these people have given what they could spare. But she, in her poverty, has given everything she had to live on" (Luke 21:4, GW). Luke and Mark emphasized the public display of the rich man's donation, although the message that Jesus underscored had little to do with money. He teaches the importance of giving one's all in worship—no matter how meager that offering.

Widow's Mite

The Lord chose a widow to illustrate this point—not the high priest, or an Aaronic priesthood holder, or a rabbi, but a destitute single woman. He chose her in part for her poverty, but most of all for her devotion and complete consecration to the Lord. She became another female witness of another restored truth. Her full consecration shows her love and trust in God to provide for her. She went to a holy place to consecrate her time and means to His service. Unlike her culture that

---

[559] The synoptic Gospels (Matthew, Mark, and Luke) place everything that happened in Jesus' Jerusalem ministry in the last week of His life. Their Gospels only include one trip to Jerusalem, so everything Jesus did in Jerusalem was telescoped into that time frame. John, on the other hand, includes several trips to Jerusalem, including three for Passover. John spreads the Jerusalem events in Jesus' life over the course of the three-year ministry (i.e., the cleansing of the temple is done at the beginning of his ministry). John's chronology is generally more trusted.

[560] Alfred Edersheim, *Temple and its Ministry and Services as they were at the time of Christ* (Grand Rapids, MI: Wm. B. Eerdmans, 1886 reprinted 1987), 48.

ignored her needs, Jesus pointed her out as a great example and will reward her for it. Just as He noticed this widow's donation, He also notices every sincere sacrifice of time, talent, and energy, no matter the size.

In addition to honoring a widow by using her as an exemplar, Christ also preached against those who took

| Corban | advantage of widows. He condemned corban because it removed a man's financial responsibility

to his kin. He began his condemnation of corban by quoting The Law:

> Moses said, Honour thy father and thy mother, and, Whoso curseth father or mother, let him die the death: But ye say, If a man shall say to his father or mother, "It is Corban," that is to say, a gift, by whatsoever thou mightest be profited by me; he shall be free. And ye suffer him no more to do ought for his father or his mother; making the word of God of none effect through your tradition (Mark 7:10-13).

This censure empowered families and especially widows by placing a man's responsibility to his relatives ahead of his social standing and philanthropic donations.

| James | Another church leader, James, the brother of the Lord, also speaks out in behalf of widows

when he teaches, "Pure religion and undefiled before God and the Father is this, to visit the fatherless and widows in their affliction, and to keep himself unspotted from the world" (James 1:27).

| Paul | The apostle Paul devoted nearly an entire chapter in his short first letter to Timothy, to the needs of

widows. One wonders if Timothy had a congregation of widows under his care. Paul asks the church members to step up their care to "honor widows who have no other family members to care for them" (1 Timothy 5:3 ISV). Paul rebukes those who do not take care of widowed family members (5:8). He counsels the widows to put their "hope in God and continue night and day to pray and to ask God for help" (1 Timothy 5:5, NIV).

Jesus calls His disciples to meet the physical, emotional, and spiritual needs of widows and others in need. He condemns the selfish and liberates the needy with instructions to meet

Poor in Spirit

other's needs. He also empowers those in need: "blessed are the poor in spirit, who come unto me; for theirs is the kingdom of heaven. And again, blessed are they that mourn; for they shall be comforted" (Matthew 5:5-6, JST). Widows held a special place in Jesus' ministry, and He set the example for His disciples to likewise acknowledge them and meet their needs.[561]

Women and Mourning

Cultural Background and Baggage

From the moment of a death, family and friends of the deceased united in ritualized mourning. The first seven days of mourning were known as *Shiva*, a time when "they were prohibited from conducting business or doing other work, from bathing, cutting the hair, engaging in sexual relations, wearing leather shoes, or otherwise engaging in pleasurable activities."[562] Wailing and dramatic expressions of sorrow were carried out by hired mourners who were usually women (although there are also records of professional male mourners). They beat their breasts, tore their hair, clapped their hands, and ripped their clothing to show distress.[563] The KJV often uses the word "weep" when referring to the mourning at death, but the

---

[561] Jeffery R. Holland, *"Care for the Poor," Ensign* (Nov 2014). "In our day, the restored Church of Jesus Christ had not yet seen its first anniversary when the Lord commanded the members to 'look to the poor and … needy, and administer to their relief that they shall not suffer' [D&C 3835]. Note the imperative tone of that passage—'they *shall* not suffer.' That is language God uses when He means business.

[562] Neusner, ed., *Judaism in the Biblical Period,* "mourning."

[563] In addition, there were certain rules for those in mourning. For example, you cannot cut your hair for thirty days. Steinberg, *Encyclopedia of Jewish Medical Ethics*, 954.

Greek is better translated as "wail" (Mark 5:38; 14:72; 16:10; Luke 22:62; John 11:31, etc.).

The *Mishnah* recorded the prescribed precedent for husbands who lost a wife: "Even the poorest Israelite should hire not less than two flutes and one wailing woman."[564] A hired "wailing woman" cried and shrieked to dramatize sorrow. The hired mourner dressed in sackcloth, wept overtly, howled for hours, and threw dirt on her head.[565] Initially, this tradition was meant to show remorse, but it evolved into meaningless theatrics and status symbols.

New Testament Example

In John 11, the description of mourning at the death of Lazarus lies in sharp contrast to the practices of the day. It is a story of sincere, heartfelt grief. The story demonstrates how honest grief can lead to peace and hope through Christ. It is a story of the Lord's compassion and the power of His teachings. Martha and Mary faced a devastating loss when their brother Lazarus died.[566] The name of their home town,

| Raising Lazarus |

Bethany, was appropriately known as the *house of the afflicted* (John 11:17 JST; Luke 10:38-42).[567]

When Lazarus first became ill, his sisters sent for Jesus, who had spent the winter east of the Jordan River in

---

[564] *Mishnah Ketuboth,* 4.4; quoting Rabbi Judah (born AD 135) who codified the *Mishnah.*

[565] 1 Maccabees 2:14, 3:47 includes a description of a Jewish man and his family morning his wife; "And Mattathias and his sons tore their garments, and they covered themselves with haircloth, and they lamented greatly . . . And they fasted on that day, and they clothed themselves with haircloth, and they placed ashes on their heads, and they tore their garments." We see a related style of mourning used for repentance in Jonah 3:6-8 and Matthew 11:21.

[566] Matthew 26:6 and Mark 14:3 both mention another male figure, belonging possibly to the home of Lazarus, Mary, and Martha—"Simon the leper." Feasibly, Simon may have been their father, Martha's spouse, or another family member either deceased or living elsewhere due to his leprosy.

[567] Freedman, *Eerdmans' Dictionary of the Bible,* 168.

Perea (John 10:40; 11:3).[568] When Jesus heard about Lazarus' illness, He said, "This sickness is not unto death, but for the glory of God, that the Son of God might be glorified thereby" (John 11:4; repeated for emphasis again in 11:40). If Jesus were only performing the miracle to heal a dear friend, He would have gone immediately, but He had other motives. And while He delayed, Lazarus died.

His timing emphasized His priority to teach in addition to heal. He told His disciples that He waited to go "to the intent ye may believe" (John 11:15).[569] As with all miracles, the timing is especially important. Many Jews believed the spirit of the deceased stayed near the dead body for three days, so Jewish tombs were usually sealed after three days. Because Jesus delayed His healing until the fourth day, no one could doubt that Lazarus was completely dead (John 11:6).

No longer beset by misplaced priorities, though desperate for the Lord's arrival, Martha waited near the road and was the first to greet Jesus. John includes parts of the

| Mary and Martha's Faith |

Lord's conversation with Martha—a conversation that set the stage for the theme of resurrection. Christ says to her, "I am the resurrection, and the life" (John 11:25). To which Martha replies: "Yea, Lord: I believe that thou art the Christ, the Son of God, which should come into the world" (John 11:27). Martha developed a firm

---

[568] In the winter, following the Feast of Dedication, Jesus left Palestine and stayed in Perea (John 10:40). The boarder for Perea is only twenty-five miles from Bethany. Now, in early spring, shortly before the Passover, Jesus will cross the Jordan River again back into Judea. Symbolically, Jesus retraces Israel's path and crosses from "the world" to "the Promised Land" where he will soon unite with His Father. Raymond Brown sees this miracle as the conclusion of the first half of the Gospel of John (sometimes described as the Book of Signs) and acts as an introduction to the second half—Jesus' passion and resurrection (Brown, *The Gospel and Epistles of John,* 61; *Anchor Bible*: *John I-XIII*, 420).

[569] Jesus assured his disciples "Our friend Lazarus sleepeth; but I go, that I may awake him out of sleep / exupnizo" (John 11:11). The Greek word for "sleepeth" is *koimao* and is used 18 times in the New Testament. Usually it really means to fall asleep, and only once is it translated "death," so it is understandable why the disciples became confused.

testimony that Jesus is the Christ / Messiah, which gave her grounding even during this time of sorrow (see similarities to Peter's testimony in table 1 of chapter 1). She may not quite understand everything that will happen to her brother, but she believes one thing with certainty— Jesus is the promised Messiah—and that is all we *really* need to know. Ironically, restoring Lazarus' life spurred the Sanhedrin to plot Jesus' death (John 11:53).

Martha Testifies

When Mary arrives, she falls down at the Savior's feet and weeps—a good place for all disciples to meet Him. (We find most of Mary's interactions with Jesus in the same position.) The Lord's reaction to Mary's sorrow is one of the most touching scenes in the Bible: "When Jesus saw her weeping . . . he was intensely moved in spirit and greatly distressed, and . . . . Jesus wept (John 11:33, 35, NET). When Jesus joins her in weeping, it validates the need to "mourn with those that mourn" (Mosiah 18:9).[570] Although He knew full well that Lazarus would rise, he still fully engaged with her in her grief. Also, before He performed the miracle, Jesus looked upward and thanked His Father for hearing Him (John 11:41-42; also John 17:1; Matthew 14:19). Then "He cried with a loud voice, Lazarus, come forth. And he that was dead came forth" (John 11:43-44).

Although Lazarus would later die, Jesus opened the door for him and all children of Adam and Eve to have immortality

---

[570] Twice among the Nephites Jesus also expressed love through tears of gratitude and compassion (3 Nephi 17:5-7, 10). "In the midst of their prayers and full faith, and the blessing of their children, Jesus himself wept after exclaiming, 'And now behold, my joy is full' (3 Nephi 17:20-22). Also God wept during Enoch's vision (Moses 7:28). In daily life such joyful tears are the release of the long strain of expectation, the fulfillment of hope. One would hardly expect Jesus to lack the emotions expressed by idealistic mortals. So a significant dimension of Third Nephi is the Lord of experience. Christ's character there has substance and actuality" (Wilford Griggs, ed., *Apocryphal*, 93). One apocryphal source speculates, "Lazarus came back to life just twelve seconds after Jesus spoke or in sketching Lazarus' later career as 'treasurer of the church at Philadelphia' and dying 'when 67 years old, of the same sickness that carried him off when he was a younger man at Bethany" (ibid.).

(Mormon 9:13; D&C 138:14). Jesus himself becomes "the first fruits of them that slept," the first resurrected being (1 Corinthians 15:20).[571] He teaches this to Martha in Bethany: "I am the resurrection, and the life: he that believeth in me, though he were dead, yet shall he live: And whosoever liveth and believeth in me shall never die" (John 11:25-26). Mary and Martha believed Him, which allowed them to express sincere and honest grief in contrast to their extreme cultural practices that thwarted the Spirit.[572] Jesus provided liberation from death, physically and spiritually, for each person born on earth—but for the here and now, He also teaches healing precepts that bring hope and peace in times of sorrow.

---

[571] This verse comes from the greatest chapter in the New Testament on the resurrection: "For since by man came death, by man came also the resurrection of the dead. For as in Adam all die, even so in Christ shall all be made alive" (1 Corinthians 15:21-22). Filled with the universality of that great hope, Paul wrote to the Corinthian saints, "O death, where is thy sting? O grave, where is thy victory? The sting of death is sin; and the strength of sin is the law" (15:55-16).

[572] Richard G. Scott, *Ensign,* November 2009; "The inspiring influence of the Holy Spirit can be overcome or masked by strong emotions, such as anger, hate, passion, fear, or pride. When such influences are present, it is like trying to savor the delicate flavor of a grape while eating a jalapeño pepper. Both flavors are present, but one completely overpowers the other." Similarly, at the same conference, Vicki Matsumori taught, "If we provide a still and quiet time each day when we are not bombarded by television, computer, video games, or personal electronic devices, we allow that still, small voice an opportunity to provide personal revelation and to whisper sweet guidance, reassurance, and comfort to us" (Vicki Matsumori, *Ensign,* November 2009).

Chapter 7
Children: From Childbirth to Vocation

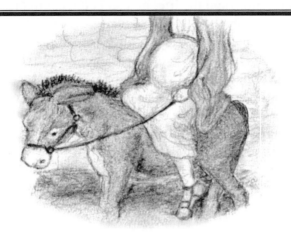

The world of women consisted mainly of interacting in their homes with children and servants.[573] This chapter looks specifically at the social background of children and the next chapter, slaves or servants. In most homes, children shared the same category of work as servants or slaves.[574] The New Testament uses the word *pais* synonymously for child, servant, and slave (i.e., the centurion's servant, Jairus' daughter, the lunatic, children crying in the temple, etc., are all identified by the same Greek word).[575] Each had to stand up in the presence of their master or father "to greet him, and perhaps even to bow down before him. He [the child or slave] could not stand or sit

---

[573] Paula S. Fass, *The Routledge History of Childhood in the Western World* (NYC: Routledge, 2013). Jewish family life was also subjected to certain Roman laws. For more see appendix 2.

[574] *Philo*, Yonge, trans., 2.116. When Philo looked back on Abraham's marriage to Hagar he perceived her dual relationship of slave and child, "[When] he calls her handmaiden, he confesses both facts, both that she is a slave and also that she is a child; for the name of the handmaiden suits both these circumstances." In Hagar's case, the young servant girl also had the role of wife.

[575] Matthew 8:8, 13; 17:18; 21:15; Luke 8:51; also see Matthew 12:18; Luke 1:54; 1:69; 2:43; 7:7; 9:42; etc.

in his place, speak in his presence, contradict him, or respond sharply to him. This was the way of the Torah."[576]

The discussion in this chapter on children begins with childbirth and birth defects, and then turns to how they were raised, disciplined, educated, socialized, and apprenticed.

Childbirth

Cultural Background and Baggage

The Old Testament places enormous value on children: offspring are divine creations in the image of God and endowed with dominion over the earth (Genesis 1:26-27). Devout Jewish couples welcomed children as a blessing from God, "an heritage of the LORD" (Psalms 127:3). The oldest commandment known in Eden promoted childbirth: "God said unto them, Be fruitful, and multiply, and replenish the earth" (Genesis 1:28). All children were welcomed in abundance: "Thy wife shall be as a fruitful vine by the sides of thine house: thy children like olive plants round about thy table" (Psalms 128:3).

Bringing children into the world was an act of co-creation with God.[577] Thousands of years after Eden, rabbis debated what exactly this commandment meant. Josephus claimed that the sole purpose of marriage was to multiply and replenish the earth.[578] The rabbinic school of Hillel (60 BC to 20 AD) elaborated on how many children one should have and concluded each couple should have at least one boy and one girl who lived. At the same time, the school of Shammai interpreted this to mean that each couple was to have at least two boys.[579] Male children were generally preferred: "As soon as a male

---

[576] Shaye J. Cohen, *From the Maccabees to the Mishnah* (Philadelphia, PA: Westminster Press, 1987), 122.

[577] Campbell, *Marriage and Family in the Biblical World,* 80.

[578] Josephus, *Against Apion,* 2.199. Levirate marriage, in particular was only for procreation.

[579] *Mishnah, Yebamoth* 6.6.

comes into the world peace comes into the world."[580] Woman
played the key role in fulfilling the commandment to bear
children, and felt responsible if it did not happen.

The absence of children was considered not only a
tragedy, but also a divine chastisement.[581] As mentioned in
chapter 6, a man had the duty to divorce his wife after ten years
of infertility.[582] Yet fertile women bore children at a great cost.
Of the women whose age of death is known, 54 percent died in
their childbearing years.[583] This does not mean they all died in
childbirth, but probably a large percentage did. Some rabbis
had a warped perspective and blamed a woman's death during
childbirth on specific sins: "For three transgressions do women
die in childbirth: for heedlessness of the laws of the menstruant
[sic], the dough-offerings, and the lighting of the [Sabbath]
lamp."[584] Children were precious, in part, because few lived.
Anthropologists estimate that one third of the babies born at this
time died in the first year of life, and one half of the survivors
died by the age of ten.[585]

---

[580] *Babylonian Talmud, Niddah,* 14 III.15, credited to rabbis Isaac and
Ammi. Campbell, *Marriage and Family in the Biblical World,* 145, 125. For
a Jew, it was a heinous sin to kill a baby because of gender. But in the
Roman sphere, there are letters in which a husband instructed his wife to
"expose" (leave it outside to die) their baby after birth if it were a girl, but
raise it if it were a son (Stagg, *Woman in the World of Jesus,* 85-86).

[581] Hennie J. Marsman, *Women in Ugarit and Israel: Their Social and
Religious Position in the Context of the Ancient Near East* (Boston, MA:
Brill Academic Publishers, 2003), 196. Across the ancient Near East, "being
blessed with children was regarded more important than the possession of
riches . . . Childlessness was connected with sin . . . A barren woman was
considered a pitiful person" (192, 196; 197).

[582] Luke 1:25; 2 Esdras 9:45; "I prayed to the Most High. Then after thirty
years, my God answered my prayer and had mercy on my distress; he took
not of my sorrow and granted me a son. What happiness he gave to my
husband and myself and to all our neighbors! What praise we gave to the
Mighty God!" Psalms 113:9, "He maketh the barren woman to keep house,
and to be a joyful mother of children. Praise ye the LORD."

[583] Ilan, *Jewish women in Greco-Roman Palestine,* 118.

[584] *Mishnah, Shabbath,* 2.6.

[585] Campbell, *Marriage and Family in the Biblical World,* 143. Christian
Laes claims that less than fifty percent of those lived fifteen years. *Children*

New Testament Example

The Lord and His apostles adopted the image of childbirth to speak of the emancipating spiritual cleansing of "being born again" (John 3:3-8 1 Peter 1:23). The phrase, "born again" has a double meaning in Greek—"anew" as well as "down from above," or "from the top." The symbolism of a rebirth is clear and powerful. Giving birth requires sacrifice, pain—often nigh unto death—water, and blood. Out of these come life and exquisite joy. The same elements emulate, albeit in a minuscule degree, Jesus' suffering to bring forth our eternal lives. As a result of Jesus' agony, blood, and sacrifice, sons and daughters of Adam and Eve can find emancipation from their fallen immortal state. Jesus uses these birth symbols when teaching Nicodemus, "Except a man be born of water and of the Spirit, he cannot enter into the kingdom of God" (John 3:5; also see Moses 6:59–60). Jesus' freedom from our fallen immortal state offers us immortality and the potential of eternal lives.

By emphasizing *rebirth*, the importance of a *natural birth* as the chosen people loses significance. Some Jews believed that, as descendants of Abraham, they were saved automatically from eternal torture (Luke 3:8; 16:24).[586] But Jesus corrected this falsehood by teaching that our natural birth is not enough to enter the Kingdom of God: "Think not to say within yourselves, We have Abraham to our father: for I say unto you, that God is able of these stones to raise up children unto Abraham" (Matthew 3:9). In its place, the Lord explained, "That which is born of the flesh is flesh; and that which is born of the Spirit is spirit" (John 3:6; also see Moses 6:59-60). The more one accesses the Spirit of the Lord, the more one can appreciate God's liberating forgiveness.

---

in the Roman Empire: Outsiders Within (New York: Cambridge University Press, 2011).

[586] Brown, *Birth,* 68. "The import of the Hebrew is that in Abraham's seed all the peoples of the earth will bless themselves or invoke blessings on another."

In addition to the emancipation of being born by the Spirit, the New Testament begins with the most sacred moment in the history of the world up to that point—Jesus' birth. It was the most important birth in the history of the universe. Only the Gospels of Matthew and Luke speak of this hallowed event (Matthew 1-2; Luke 1-2).[587] The miraculous birth of the Lord included many ironies that speak to the liberation of women and outcasts. The first witnesses in the New Testament were those who usually were not allowed to act as legal witnesses in their society—women and shepherds.[588] One of those, a poor young virgin gave birth to the Son of God in a makeshift barn-cave because the locals did not understands the significance of the birth.[589] Yet the birth set in motion the earthly mission of the Savior, which ended in the greatest emancipation of all: the redemption of sin and death so that Adam and Eve's posterity might eat of the tree of life without their sins.[590]

Jesus' Birth

---

[587] Mark and John's Gospel do not mention Jesus' birth, but begin chronicling His life at the baptism. Yet, 1 Nephi 11:20, also references it.
[588] Josephus, *Antiquities,* IV.8:15; *Mishnah, Shebuoth,* 4:1.
[589] Brown, *Birth of the Messiah,* 401-402.
[590] Nearly all the ideas in Luke's and Matthew's nativity narratives have double meanings as Jesus' birth prefigures His death and resurrection. We may have missed some of these powerful foreshadowing and their subsequent liberation. Seven illustrations follow:
1. Matthew introduced the child Jesus as Emmanuel, "God with us." After His Resurrection, He recorded Jesus' empowering promise, "I am with you always" (Matthew 1:23; 28:20).
2. The infancy accounts are filled with angelic visitations (Matt 1:20, 2:13, 19, Luke 1-2), and so is the Lord's passion and resurrection (Matthew 28:2-5; Luke 22:43; 24:23).
3. Joseph had trouble finding a place to deliver the Son of God, and retreated with Mary away from the crowds to an animal stall, probably in a cave. The lack of room for the Lord's birth foretells of His life and death, "the Son of Man hath not where to lay his head" (Matthew 8:20), including His burial in a borrowed tomb or cave (Matthew 27:57-60). Isaiah 33:16 prophesied of His birth and death locations, "He will dwell in a high cave of strong rock" (LXX Isa 33:15). Ironically, during Christ's mission very few recognized Him as their Promised Messiah, and few found room in their hearts for Him. But those who did, found freedom from their sins.

Birth Defects

Cultural Background and Baggage

Jews mistakenly assumed that God caused birth defects, illness, accidents, afflictions, or a child's premature death because of sin.[591] Likewise, they interpreted healthy births as a sign of righteousness, and held the misconception that God rewarded a woman's righteousness by removing her labor pains.[592] When Josephus retold the story of Moses' birth, he repeated this myth by telling that Moses' mother, Jochebed, delivered Moses without pain as a divine reward for her righteousness.[593] Somehow they failed to understand the

---

4). Three times Luke stressed that Mary wrapped her Son and where she laid Him; " . . . wrapped him in swaddling clothes, and laid him in a manger" (Luke 2:7, 12, 16); or in a modern translation, "she wrapped him in bands of cloth, and laid him in a feeding trough" (Luke 2:7, WEB). To wrap or swaddle a baby was a sign of parental care—even King Solomon was swaddled. Mangers were often moveable large rocks with a trough carved out or else "a cavity in a low rock shelf." Luke's message also emphasizes the fulfillment of Isaiah 1:3, "The ox knows its owner, and the donkey knows the manger of its lord, but Israel has not known me." At his death Jesus was again wrapped in linen and placed on another rock shelf (John 19:40-41).
5). The birth and death accounts include unusual signs in the heavens as a witness of the great events (Luke 2:9; Matthew 2:2, 9, 27:45, 51).
6). The Magi offered gifts traditionally for a king, and Jesus is crowned and mocked as a king of the Jews (Matthew 27:29, 31, 41).
7). Wicked men sought to kill both the baby and man (Matthew 2:19, 20; 21:15; 27:1–2). Herod sought to "destroy" Jesus at night (Matthew 2:13-14). And "the chief priests and the elders" worked through the night to persuade "the multitude that they should ask Barabbas and *destroy* Jesus" (Matthew 26:47–56; 27:20). For more details and sources see Lynne Hilton Wilson's article: *"Jesus' Atonement Foretold through His Birth"* in Richard Holzapfel and Kent Jackson eds., *To Save the Lost: An Easter Celebration* (Provo, UT: Religious Studies Center, 2009), 103.
[591] Avraham Steinberg, ed., *Encyclopedia of Jewish Medical Ethics* (Jerusalem Israel: Feldheim, 2003), 34, "Any illness may result from sin."
[592] Steinberg, *Encyclopedia of Jewish Medical Ethics*, 171.
[593] Josephus, *Antiquities,* II. 9:4; Jochebed "the mother's labor was such as afforded a confirmation to what was foretold by God; for it was not known

concept that even righteous people suffer—consider prophets like Job and Abraham.

Jewish legends perpetuated a false impression of birth defects.[594] Their society incorrectly presumed that physical imperfections made one a sinner, because priests with birth defects were not allowed to serve at the altar of the temple: "No man that hath a blemish of the seed of Aaron the priest shall come nigh to offer the offerings of the LORD made by fire" (Leviticus 21:21, 17-23). These misinterpretations emotionally and spiritually crippled both those with blemishes as well as their mothers, who were often blamed for them.[595] Related to the same erroneous belief, rabbis interpreted Exodus 20:5, "I the LORD thy God am a jealous God, visiting the iniquity of the fathers upon the children unto the third and fourth generation of them that hate me," to mean that the sins of the parents could leave a mark on their infant.[596] Not only did those with disabilities have to live with their limitations, but also with the social stigma that they may be guilty of a grievous sin. Sometimes the disabled were blamed for their disability.

The rabbis debated whose fault birth defects were: the parents or child?[597] For example, the Talmud claimed that blindness was a "punishment for specific sins—such as the taking of bribes, feigning blindness, negligence in feeding the poor, improper behavior during cohabitation, and faulty education for one's son or pupil."[598] The "improper behavior" included keeping one's eyes open during conception. Blindness was so heinous that some felt it was better to kill the infant.[599]

---

to those that watched her, by the easiness of her pains, and because the throes of her delivery did not fall upon her with violence."

[594] Steinberg, *Encyclopedia of Jewish Medical Ethics*, 107.

[595] *Mishnah, Shabbath,* 2.6. Rabbis blamed the cause of death during childbirth on the sins of the mother.

[596] Brown, *The Anchor Bible: John I-XII,* 371.

[597] Margaret Barker, *Creation: A Biblical Vision for the Environment* (London and NYC: T & T Clark, 2010), 232.

[598] Steinberg, *Encyclopedia of Jewish Medical Ethics*, 107.

[599] Ibid., 106; "Blindness was a very common condition in antiquity. Throughout the bible where human blemishes are cited, blindness is always mentioned first. A blind person in ancient cultures was considered very

Changes by Jesus

Jesus deplored the prejudices that further crippled those already physically or mentally challenged. Again He reversed their cultural perception. Outward defects had nothing to do with inward cleanliness and vice versa: "Woe unto you, scribes and Pharisees, hypocrites! for ye are like unto whited sepulchres, . . . ye also outwardly appear righteous unto men, but within ye are full of hypocrisy and iniquity (Matthew 23:27-28). He teaches His disciples that they should avoid sin—not avoid those people with blemishes to the degree that "if thine eye offend thee, pluck it out, and cast it from thee: it is better for thee to enter into life with one eye, rather than having two eyes to be cast into hell fire. Take heed that ye despise not one of these little ones" (Matthew 18:9-10).

Jesus corrected the fallacy that birth defects were the result of sin when he healed the man born blind.[600] This concept was so entrenched in their beliefs that even Jesus' disciples needed correction. When they saw the blind man,

| Healing The Blind |

they asked, "Master, who did sin, this man, or his parents, that he was born blind?" (John 9:2). Clearly, a belief in some type of pre-earthly existence underscored the disciples' question (as does Jeremiah 1:5; Job 38:4, 7; Psalms 82:6).[601] Without denouncing pre-mortal existence but attacking the heresy, "Jesus answered, Neither hath this man sinned, nor his parents: but that the works of God should be made manifest . . . As long as I am in the world, I am the light of the world" (John 9:3, 5).

---

lowly and was the subject of scorn, ridicule and even death. A newborn determined to be blind was not allowed to survive. If the blindness was not recognized until he grew up, he became a beggar."

[600] Steinberg, *Encyclopedia of Jewish Medical Ethics*, 106. "In antiquity, blind people filled the cities and temples as alms collectors. Most blind people did not reach their potential, were considered worthless to society, were frequently hungry and sometimes starved to death. Blindness was universally considered to be a great tragedy, and mostly as punishment for sin."

[601] The Church of Jesus Christ of Latter-day Saints' doctrine of a pre-mortal life is not generally shared by Jews or Christians currently.

219

Jesus then made a mud paste by spitting "on the ground, and made clay of the spittle, and he anointed the eyes of the blind man with the clay, And said unto him, Go, wash in the pool of Siloam" (John 9:6-7). Jesus subtly evoked the Genesis creation accounts by working with "clay" and identifying Himself as the "light of the world" (John 9:5, 7; Genesis 1:3).[602] Society told this man that his birth defect was a result of sin, but Christ did not lay that blame on him. Instead, He empowered him with the opportunity to exert the faith to be healed. Jesus assisted him to develop faith by sending him on a journey to wash off the clay in the pool of Siloam. The name, Siloam, means "sent" (John 9:7).[603] Jesus was the *One sent from God* who in turn sent the blind man on a journey to receive his sight.[604] Jesus healed the man of blindness, but he was not fully healed until he was fully converted by "the One Sent."

The healed man did not return to find Jesus, possibly because he or did not know how to find Him or he was distracted. So Jesus sought him out—as He does with all of us with myopia. When Jesus found him, a precious conversation developed which completed the man's healing. Jesus asked him "Dost thou believe on the Son of God?" The man still in spiritual darkness asked, "Who is he, Lord that I might believe on him? (John 9:36). Jesus' poignant answer reemphasized the miracle, "Thou hast both seen him, and it is he that talketh with

---

[602] The clay also reflects Enoch: "And the Lord spake unto Enoch, and said unto him: Anoint thine eyes with clay, and wash them, and thou shalt see" (Moses 6:35).

[603] Different archeologists have labeled more than one pool in Jerusalem as potentially as Siloam, but a blind man would be challenged to get to any of them on his own. In Solomon's Temple, the Levites retrieved water in a golden pitcher from Siloam (*Shiloah* in Hebrew) on the "last and great day of the feast" of Tabernacles to pour over the sacrifice, in memory of the rock of Rephidim (John 7:37; Exodus 17:1-6). Brown, *Gospels and Epistles of John,* 56. It was also to this pool that the Lord pointed and cried, "If any man thirst, let him come unto me and drink" (John 7:37).

[604] The early Church Fathers Tertullian and Augustine saw the pool of Siloam as symbolic of baptism and used this story of healing the blind man to prepare converts for baptism (Brown, *The Anchor Bible: John I-XII,* 380-1).

thee" (John 9:37). The man's faith and spontaneous worship was touching: "Lord, I believe. And he worshipped him" (John 9:38).

The healed man and the Pharisees should have recognized this miracle as a sign of the promised Messiah.[605] Isaiah prophesied that only One could "open the blind eyes, to bring out the prisoners from the prison, and them that sit in darkness out of the prison house" (Isaiah 42:7).[606] Perhaps the Jews missed the miracle's significance because they were looking for a conquering perfect Messiah,[607] not one who broke their Sabbath laws.[608] A Jewish oral law banned spitting in the dirt

---

[605] While the Old Testament prophets raised the dead, healed the lame, closed the heavens, opened the seas, and miraculously provided food—no one but the promised Messiah could heal the blind. Mark 8:22-26; 10:46-52, also gives two examples of Jesus healing the blind.

[606] Also see Isaiah 42:6-7; Psalms 146:8; Exodus 4:11; Mosiah 3:5.

[607] Mark Harding, *Early Christian Life and Thought in Social Context* (NYC: T&T Clark International, 2003), 323. The Messianic hope of the time was outlined by the *Psalms of Solomon* (69-40 BC) and focused on a conquering Messiah: "He will have Gentile peoples serving him under his yoke, and he will glorify the Lord publically in the whole world. He will pronounce Jerusalem clean . . . He will have nations come from the ends of the earth to see his glory . . . He will be a righteous king over them, taught by God, there will be no unrighteousness among them during his reign, because everyone will be holy, and their king will be the Lord Messiah . . . And he himself will be free from sin, in order to rule such a great people. He will expose officials and drive out sinners by the strength of his word.

[608] Jacob Neusner, *The Mishnah: Religious Perspectives* (Boston, MA: Brill, 1999), 119; "One may not perform an act of healing on the Sabbath." Several oral laws also prohibited healing on the Sabbath. If one dislocated a joint or broke a bone on the Sabbath the oral laws forbad one to set the fracture because once in place the victim's body would work to heal itself, thus breaking the Sabbath. *Mishnah, Shabbath,* 22:6. "They may not . . . set a broken limb. If a man's hand or foot is dislocated he may not pour cold water over it, but he may wash it after his usual fashion." One could take out a thorn with "a sewing-needle" as long as the needle was not used for sewing. Ibid, 17:2. Certain foods, like Greek hyssop, were often used for medicinal purposes, so they made a law not to spice foods with it on the Sabbath as it might be a means for healing. Ibid., 14:3. On the other hand, a rabbi Meir gave permission to use certain cures on the Sabbath: "a nail of one that was crucified" to cure a festering wound, or a locust's egg to cure an ear ache, or a jackal's tooth to cure sleepiness (if the jackal were alive)

221

on the Sabbath because it could be considered "cultivating," which was one of the thirty-nine forms of work forbidden on the Sabbath.[609]

Each of the seven miracles that John's Gospel mentions, show Jesus tearing down a falsehood and demonstrating a sign of his Messiahship (John 20:30). Jesus repeatedly performed miracles on the Sabbath to tear down the erroneous laws that were strangling the day of rest.[610] In this case, Jesus also enabled the healed man (and all those who believed in the miracle), not only with sight, but also with faith. That position of empowerment to see Him "eye to eye" is available to all who are blinded in some way and need healing and sanctification by His Light (Isaiah 52:8). John 9 chronicled Jesus' assault of

---

and sleeplessness (if the jackal were dead). Ibid., 6:10. These folk-medical treatments were permissible, but no general cures.

[609] Rabbis redefined the fourth commandment, "remember the Sabbath day, to keep it holy" (Exodus 20:8), to include "forty save one" forbidden forms of work on the Sabbath. (1) sowing, (2) ploughing, (3) reaping, (4) binding sheaves, (5) threshing, (6) winnowing, (7) cleansing crops, (8) grinding, (9) sifting, (10) kneading, (11) baking, (12) shearing wool, (13) washing, (14) beating, (15) dyeing, (16) spinning, (17) weaving, (18) making two loops, (19) weaving two threads, (20) separating two threads, (21) tying [a knot], (22) loosening [a knot], (23) sewing two stitches, (24) tearing in order to sew two stitches, (25) hunting a gazelle, (26) slaughtering or (27) flaying or (28) salting, (29) curing its skin, (30) scraping it or, (31) cutting it up, (32) writing two letters, (33) erasing in order to write two letters, (34) building, (35) pulling down, (36) putting out fire, (37) lighting fire, (38) striking with the hammer, and (39) taking aught from one domain into another. Ibid, 7:2 (numbers added). They elaborated on each of those 39 types banned forms of labor to fill the entire second division in the *Mishnah* (tractate of *Moed: Shabbath*). For example, the *Mishnah* forbade "carrying" on the Sabbath. So the next level of micromanagement included what was included in "carrying" (i.e., a handful of straw, a dried fig's bulk of foodstuff, a piece of leather, enough red clay to make a seal, carrying a dead man out of his house on a couch, and biting finger nails or pulling out a hair). *Mishnah, Shabbath,* 7:4; 8:3, 8.5, 10.5, 6.

[610] The New Testament writers recorded stories of twenty-six healings by Jesus (some count more, others less due to duplicates). It appears that the Gospel authors and the Lord Himself, deliberately healed on the Sabbath many times. Eight Sabbath healings are specifically mentioned (Matthew 8:14; 12:9-13; Mark 1:21-28, 29-31; 3:1-6; Luke 4:33-39; 6:6-11; 13:10-17; 14:1-6; John 5:1-15; 7:23; 9:1-13).

several incorrect doctrines, starting with a misunderstanding of birth defects, Sabbath laws, and ending with accepting the Savior as the Light of the World.

Parenting Children

Cultural Background and Baggage

From the time of Adam, God commanded fathers and mothers to "teach . . . unto your children, that all men, everywhere, must repent, or they can in no wise inherit the kingdom of God" (Genesis 6:59, JST; Moses 6:57; also see 6:61-62; Deuteronomy 4:10; 6:7, 11:19; Psalms 34:11, etc.). The Lord repeated the sacred responsibility to Aaron, "teach the children of Israel all the statutes which the LORD hath spoken unto them by the hand of Moses" (Leviticus 10:11). Jewish parents often named their children using words that expressed their faith and aspirations for them.[611]

One of the patriarchal duties passed down from the Old Testament included blessing one's children. Isaac blessed Jacob and Esau (Genesis 27:27-40), Jacob blessed his twelve sons (Genesis 49:28), and Moses blessed his congregation, "Consecrate yourselves today to the LORD, even every man upon his son, and upon his brother; that he may bestow upon you a blessing this day" (Exodus 32:29). Regardless of the children's ages, God commanded them to respect and honor their parents (Exodus 20:12; Deuteronomy 5:16).

During the time of Herod's Temple, children were considered a blessing, in part because they served their fathers and were an economic advantage. By the age of five or six, children in the country contributed to the family coffers by gathering firewood and working in the vegetable garden.[612] Children washed their father's face and feet, dressed and fed him.[613] Children and servants both took orders from their

---

[611] Campbell, *Marriage and Family Life in the Biblical World,* 53.
[612] Campbell, *Marriage and Family life in the Biblical World,* 81.
[613] Jeremias, *Jerusalem,* 154, 363-364.

masters and gave their time to please them. Fathers dictated what and where their children ate, how they were educated, what vows they made, and collected any money they found or earned.[614] Jewish children under age twelve were identified as minors. According to the oral Mosaic tradition, children, as minors, were not liable in court or legal matters until "age thirteen and one day," but "liability for heavenly punishment begins at twenty years of age."[615]

Rabbis also gave fathers specific directions when raising a son: "He must circumcise him, redeem him, teach him the *Torah*, take a wife unto him, and teach him a trade."[616] Unlike girls, boys were impelled to go to synagogue for study and worship and to Jerusalem for pilgrimage feasts (Passover, Pentecost, and Feast of the Tabernacles or Booths).[617] Most Jewish families in Palestine lived in an agricultural environment, which often meant that a child worked beside his or her father on the land as a financial necessity.[618] If food or money became scarce, a Jewish father had the legal right to sell his children (under the age of twelve) and his wife into slavery.[619] Patriarchal control over children left little room for the modern idea of child labor laws or children's rights.

The plight of Jewish children during this era was not entirely grim. Parents devoted much time and effort to their children, especially in their infancy. Mothers nursed their babies for at least eighteen months, usually twenty-four months,

---

[614] *Mishnah, Ketuboth,* 4:1-2, 4; 5:6; Jeremias, *Jerusalem,* 368.

[615] Steinberg, *Encyclopedia of Jewish Medical Ethics*, 682. "The rabbinic divisors disagree as to whether or not the father is punished for his son's sins committed before age thirteen because of poor training or, contrariwise, whether or not the son is punished for his father's sins."

[616] Babylonian Talmud, *Kiddushin*, 29a. The rabbinic commentary added a post script, "Some say he must teach him to swim also." The ideal Jewish man started providing for his family around the age of twenty: "20 to pursuing a career." *Mishnah*, *Avoth* 5:21.

[617] For more see appendix 1.

[618] Thurston, *Women in the New Testament*, 15-16.

[619] *Mishnah, Ketuboth,* 3.8. "She that is a minor is subject to right of sale . . . if she is passed her girlhood she is not subject to right of sale."

and some doubled that time.[620] Fathers also sacrificed for them, as Ben Sira remembered: "The father waketh for the daughter when no man knoweth, and the care for her taketh away his sleep, when she is young, lest she pass away the flower of her age, and when she is married, lest she should be hateful."[621]

Jews from the time of the late Second Temple era interpreted Moses' commandments on raising children in their own way. For example, Moses teaches that children should "honour thy father and thy mother" (Exodus 20:12); and from the time of Solomon, "My son, hear the instruction of thy father, and forsake not the law of thy mother" (Proverbs 1:8).

Yet these two commandments received a different spin in Ben Sira's interpretation: he felt children were to honor their fathers and recognize the rights of their mothers.[622] He asserted that God would atone for children's sins and hear their prayers if they showed ample respect to their fathers: "Whoever honors his father atones for sins, and whoever glorifies his mother is like one who lays up treasure. Whoever glorifies his father will have long life, and whoever obeys the Lord will refresh his mother."[623] Ben Sira mentions both parents repeatedly, yet he required a higher level of respect for fathers than for mothers.

To protect their children's chastity, the best Jewish parenting practices kept children, especially girls, indoors as much as possible.[624] This may have initially been motivated by

---

[620] *Babylonian Talmud, Kethuboth,* 60a.; *Nedarim,* 2.1. Also see, Ilan, *Jewish Women in Greco-Roman Palestine,* 121.

[621] Ben Sira, *Ecclesiasticus,* 42:9.

[622] Ben Sira, *Ecclesiasticus,* 3:2 "For the Lord honored the father above the children, and he confirmed the right of the mother over her sons."

[623] Ben Sira, *Ecclesiasticus,* 3:3-9. "For kindness to a father will not be forgotten, and against your sins it will be credited to you; in the day of your affliction it will be remembered in your favor; as frost in fair weather, your sins will melt away. . . . he will serve his parents as his masters. Honor your father by word and deed, that a blessing from him may come upon you, For a father's blessing strengthens the houses of the children, but a mother's curse uproots their foundations."

[624] Ben Sira, *Eccleasiasticus,* 42:10-11. Ben Sira told fathers to guard their daughter "in her virginity lest she should be corrupted, and be found with child in her father's house: and having a husband, lest she should misbehave herself, or at the least become barren. Keep a sure watch over a shameless

a desire of protection, but the means that many patriarchs justified to achieve it potentially crippled agency and love. With children rarely in public, their infrequent presence was unfamiliar and often looked down on. As adults were not accustomed to having children in public settings, they often considered children a nuisance and in need of frequent corrections.[625] Ben Sira counseled children to "discipline the mouth" or to be silent, just as he did to women.[626] Children were also considered powerless and governed by their elders.[627]

Changes by Jesus

Initially entrenched in the Jewish culture, Jesus' disciples attempted to remove children from public gatherings. All three synoptic Gospels tell the story of when the disciples rebuked those who brought children to Jesus: "Then were there brought unto him little children, that he should put his hands on them, and pray: and the disciples rebuked them" (Matthew 19:13; Mark 10:14; Luke 18:16). Mark added, "When Jesus saw it, he was much displeased" (Mark 10:14). It appears that the disciples were so laden with their cultural baggage that they could not instinctively feel the value of nurturing children. Jesus' response turned the social hierarchy upside down: "Suffer the little children to come unto me, and forbid them not: for such is the kingdom of God" (Mark 10:14; Luke 18:16).

---

daughter: lest at any time she make thee become a laughingstock to thy enemies, and a byword in the city, and a reproach among the people, and she make thee ashamed before all the multitude."

[625] Ben Sira, *Ecclesiasticus,* 42:5. "But of these things, be not ashamed . . . of frequent correction of children, and of smiting an evil-disposed servant."

[626] Ben Sira, *Ecclesiasticus,* 23:7-15. "Hear, my children [concerning] the discipline of the mouth, He that keepeth [it] will not be ensnared. But the sinner is ensnared by his lips, And the reviler and the arrogant will stumble through them. . . . There is a manner of speech that is to be compared with death . . . Accustom not thy mouth to unseemly manner [of speech], For there is a sinful thing in that" (brackets in original).

[627] Richard N, Holzapfel, Eric D. Huntsman, Thomas A. Wayment, *Jesus Christ and the World of the New Testament* (SLC, UT: Deseret Book, 2006), 117.

Children who had been treated as servants in their homes were now acknowledged as citizens of celestial realms.

Jesus inverted the cultural hierarchy of the home by honoring children, not masters. Mark's Gospel recorded the Lord tenderly embracing a child as an example for all to follow: "when he had taken him in his arms, he said unto them, Whosoever shall receive one of such children in my name, receiveth me" (Mark 9:36-37; similar to Luke 9:48). This restored an empowering truth about the value of children. Another time Jesus reversed the social ranking with even more clarity: "And Jesus called a little child unto him, and set him in the midst of them, And said, Verily I say unto you, Except ye be converted, and become as little children, ye shall not enter into the kingdom of heaven. Whosoever therefore shall humble himself as this little child, the same is greatest in the kingdom of heaven" (Matthew 18:2-4).

> Jesus Embraces a Child

In the Lord's order, the wealthy, robe wearing, educated, wise ones receive Jesus' warning, not His acclaim: "Beware of the scribes, which desire to walk in long robes, and love greetings in the markets, and the highest seats in the synagogues, and the chief rooms at feasts . . . the same shall receive greater damnation" (Luke 20:46-47). He revered serving others, not dictating orders. Jesus' values jump off the pages of Scripture: He loves children. He treats them sensitivity. He serves them. He taught that the kingdom of heaven will be made up of pure humble servants. Disciples follow the Lord's example with interactions with children.

Jesus attacked the practice of selling one's wife or child into slavery by using it as a deplorable example in one of His parables: "But forasmuch as he had not to pay, his lord commanded him to be sold, and his wife, and children, and all that he had, and payment to be made" (Matthew 18:25). The parable continues to show the master softening as he "was moved with compassion," and forgives the man's gargantuan debt so that the debtor's family did not have to be sold into slavery (Matthew 18:27).

> The Parable of the Unmerciful Servant

227

Jesus often exaggerated details of His parables for their storytelling value, and here the sum of moneys involved is magnified to prove his point. The first man owed ten thousand talents—the equivalent of billions of dollars today. In the historical setting, Josephus recorded that the total value of Herod's Temple treasury was ten thousand talents. [628] It would have been impossible for one man to accumulate this debt at that time. But Jesus used the backdrop of slaves, debt, and prison to describe the size of His atonement. No matter how enormous our debt, God can forgive and emancipate those in His debt.

When we look at Jesus' healing miracles, we find several illustrations of His sensitive compassion towards children. Across the four Gospels we find seventeen healings of adults and at least six of children.

1) Roman centurion's servant or child (Matthew 8:5-13; Luke 7:1-10)
2) Jairus' daughter (Matthew 9:18-26; Mark 5:22-24, 38-43; Luke 8:41-42, 49-56)
3) Canaanite woman's daughter (Matthew 15:21-28; Mark 7:24-30),
4) Boy with devil (Matthew 17:14-21; Mark 9:17-29; Luke 9:38-43)
5) Widow's son raised (Luke 7:11-17)
6) Nobleman's son at Capernaum (John 4:46-54)

---

[628] Andrew Teasdale, "Herodian Times and Historical Backgrounds: Herod the Great's Building Program," *BYU Studies* (fall 1996-97): 36.3. "Thus, the unforgiving servant may in fact represent the king or the temple high priest into whose hands God had entrusted the keeping of that huge amount of sacred wealth. No one else in Judea could conceivably have held that kind of money. Thus, the political upshot of the parable may well be this: despite the great debts and offenses of the rulers of the temple against God, they can be readily forgiven by God, so long as they beg his forgiveness and worship him. When asked, however, to be generous to a commoner in need of a small amount, the rich rulers of the temple will be unmoved, and as a consequence, they will be held personally accountable for the loss of the entire temple treasury."

The raising of Jairus' beloved daughter demonstrates not only the Lord's care of children, and power over death, but also shows Him rejecting another social custom that encumbered the Jews' spiritual sensitivity. In Luke's account, as the Lord

| Jairus' Daughter |

arrived at the death bed, an entourage of mourners had begun wailing: "And all wept, and bewailed her" (Luke 8:52).[629] Once the Lord restored a peaceful home, "He took the damsel by the hand,   and said unto her, Damsel, I say unto thee, arise" (Mark 5:41).

As discussed in chapter 6, Jewish mourning had become a ritualized dramatization.[630] A hired "wailing woman" cried hysterically, shrieked for hours, dressed in sack cloth, threw dirt on her head, and made a frenzied theatrical demonstration. In addition to raising the little girl from the dead, Jesus' example teaches the [631] Jesus saw the howling as a mockery of grief and not conducive to the Spirit, so "he put them all out" (Luke 8:54). In addition to raising the little girl from the dead, Jesus' example teaches the inappropriateness of insincerity. His removal of the irreverent mourners stripped off yet another layer of cultural baggage that offended the Spirit. By so doing, Jesus teaches that those who mourn have a greater potential to receive the Spirit or Comforter in peace and sincerity. Those who mourn can be lifted by the Spirit at the sacred moment when loved ones pass through the veil from the second estate. Following Jesus' example allows the Spirit to touch mourners for their own needed healing.[632]

---

[629] See chapter 6, "Widowhood." Also Paul similarly asked the dramatic mourners to leave the room before he raised Tabitha in Acts 9:40-42.

[630] *Mishnah, Ketuboth,* 4.4; quoting Rabbi Judah who codified the *Mishnah* (born AD 135).

[631] 1 Maccabees includes a similar description of a Jewish man and his family mourning; "And Mattathias and his sons tore their garments, and they covered themselves with haircloth, and they lamented greatly . . . And they fasted on that day, and they clothed themselves with haircloth, and they placed ashes on their heads, and they tore their garments" (2:14, 3:47). Jonah 3:6-8 and Matthew 11:21 related this style of mourning for repentance, too.

[632] In a similar account in Luke 7:11-17, the Lord raised the widow's son on the way to the grave.

Discipline

Cultural Background and Baggage

Jewish literature on childrearing from this era included a spectrum of advice on how to discipline children. On one end of the spectrum we read, "Lay not a hand in violence . . . on tender children."[633] Ben Sira counseled fathers to spend time with their children in worthwhile pursuits: "Instruct thy son, and labor about him, lest his lewd behavior be an offence to thee."[634] Working beside a child allowed for shared meaningful experiences. Discipline was the duty of the father. There must have been parents who offered generous gifts to their children, as Jesus acknowledged, "If ye then, being evil, know how to give good gifts unto your children . . .," leaving us with the hope that many did love their children (Matthew 7:11).

On the other end of the spectrum, we find very sever corporeal punishment used to disciple. Ben Sira preached that the way to teach children to fear God was to discipline them physically: "Stripes and correction are at all times wisdom."[635] He elaborated by giving several suggestions to wise or "loving fathers" to "not spare the rod," and "break him in and beat him sound while he is still a child."[636] He continued:

> He that loveth his son, frequently chastiseth him, that he may rejoice in his latter end . . . A horse not broken becometh stubborn, and a child left to himself will become headstrong. Give thy son his way, and he shall make thee afraid: play with him, and he shall make thee sorrowful.

---

[633] Walter T. Wilson, *The Sentences of Pseudo-Phocylides* (Gottingen and Berlin: Hubert & Co., 2005), 162. Also "Be not rash with your hands; bridle wild anger" (ibid., 115). *Pseudo-Phocylides* is a Greek apocryphal account that claimed an earlier authorship. The lack of Hebraic citations and the use of the Septuagint, as well as other textual and linguistic details, have led scholars to date it between 100 BC and AD 100.

[634] Ben Sira, *Ecclesiasticus*, 30:13 (modernized spelling).

[635] Ben Sira, *Ecclesiasticus,* 22:6.

[636] Ben Sira, *Ecclesiasticus*, 30:1, 2, 12; "He who disciplines his son will find profit in him."

Laugh not with him, lest thou have sorrow, and at the last thy teeth be set on edge. Give him not liberty in his youth, and wink not at his devices. Bow down his neck while he is young, and beat his sides while he is a child, lest he grow stubborn, and regard thee not, and so be a sorrow of heart to thee.[637]

It appears that Ben Sira felt a father should manifest his love through chastening, suppression, control, physical punishment, and a lack of play and laughter. Discipline was also used to keep children, women, and servants submissive.[638] One purpose of discipline was to teach a child to respect or fear their authorities and God. Ben Sira further teaches that it was better to have a child "that feareth God, than a thousand ungodly children. And it is better to die without children, than to leave ungodly children."[639]

Changes by Jesus

Jesus vehemently denounced those who hurt children: "Whoso shall offend one of these little ones which believe in me, it were better for him that a millstone were hanged about his neck, and that he were drowned in the depth of the sea" (Matthew 18:6; similar to Mark 9:42 and Luke 17:2). The Greek verb used for "offend / *skandalizo*" (KJV) also meant "entrap, i.e., trip up . . . entice to sin, apostacy."[640] The Lord equated a death sentence as better place than life for those who leads a child to doubt their innate faith in God, or who teaches a child to sin. Intentionally teaching children falsehoods and extinguishing their faith is a serious sin.

The Lord liberated children and also those who are shackled with the baggage of violence. He also teaches the abused to stand up for themselves, while still being willing to

---

[637] Ben Sira, *Ecclesiasticus,* 30:1, 8-12.
[638] Jeremias, *Jerusalem,* 371-375.
[639] Ben Sira, *Ecclesiasticus,* 16:3-4.
[640] Strong, *Exhaustive Concordance of the Bible,* 81; Greek dictionary for "offend / *skandalizo*."

forgive: "If thy brother trespass against thee, rebuke him; and if he repent, forgive him" (Luke 17:3). The liberating principle of forgiveness unlocks one imprisoned by emotional pain, scars,

| Forgive |

and fear. By applying forgiveness, even to those who have wronged one, the wounded victim is enabled to heal and grow from the experience (D&C 122:7). The Lord taught the reciprocal nature of learning to forgive: "if ye forgive men their trespasses, your heavenly Father will also forgive you" (Matthew 6:14; similarly in Mark 11:26; Luke 6:37). Those who have wounds that need healing from abuse can be restored by implementing Jesus' power-filled words and atonement.

Discipline also included forgiveness. The apostle Peter thought he was being munificent by suggesting that Christians should forgive others seven times—as the Jews limited forgiveness to three offences.[641] But "Jesus said to him, 'I do not say to you up to seven times, but up to seventy times seven'" (Matthew 18:21-35). The Lord then illustrates what He meant with the parable of a king who wished to settle accounts with his servants. Jesus teaches a very different principle from the way Peter understood it. To the Lord, forgiveness is not quantitative but qualitative.[642]

Rather than correcting with harsh discipline, the Lord restored truths that had the power to motivate change and bring those He taught closer to the Spirit. The Savior's goal in disciplining the errant world was to restore, not to destroy: "When he went ashore he saw a great crowd, and he had compassion on them, because they were like sheep without a shepherd. And he began to teach them many things" (Mark 6:34). He teaches principles that strengthened His disciples to correct their own behavior. When necessary, He still called for repentance, but Jesus spoke and acted with love and encouragement (John 8:11; 13:34-35). Discipline should restore

---

[641] Rabbis interpreted Amos 1:3 and Job 33:29 as "twice and thrice." Bruce R. McConkie, *The Mortal Messiah: From Bethlehem to Calvary* (SLC, UT: Deseret, 1981), 3.91.

[642] Alfred Edersheim, *Jesus the Messiah*, 125.

peace: "Blessed are the peacemakers: for they shall be called the children of God" (Matthew 5:9).

The apostles confirmed that the best way to foster change was to teach the words of God: "All scripture is given by inspiration of God, and is profitable for doctrine, for reproof,

> Discipline by Teaching

for correction, for instruction in righteousness" (2 Timothy 3:16; John 7:17). Jesus used story-telling or parables to condemn sin and to change His listeners for the better. From Mark's perspective, "But without a parable spake he not unto them: and when they were alone, he expounded all things to his disciples" (Mark 4:34).

Children's Education

Cultural Background and Baggage

Jews valued education. A child's education differed depending on his or her gender, wealth, and location. Girls studied mainly domestic skills from their mothers, while all young men who had the capacity and the means studied to read the Law. Ecclesiasticus called on fathers to take the role as teacher: "He that instructeth his son shall be praised in him, and shall glory in him in the midst of them of his household. He that teacheth his son, maketh his enemy jealous, and in the midst of his friends he shall glory in him."[643]

Boys

Local rabbis welcomed the most promising young men in the community to the synagogue, their homes, or *yeshiva* when the boys reached age five to begin their education of The Law.[644] Rabbis summarized an ideal boy's education and subsequent life:

---

[643] Sirach, *Ecclesiasticus*, 30:2-3.

[644] Jews often studied the Scriptures in their own language. "Inscriptions dug up by archeologists show that even in Jud[ea] Jews knew and used some Greek—how much is hard to say, but half of all Judean Jewish inscriptions

5 to Scripture, [645]
10 to *Mishnah,*
13 to fulfilling commandments,
15 to Talmud,
18 to the bride chamber, [646]
20 to pursuing a career, [647]
30 to authority,
40 to discernment,
50 for the counsel,
60 to be an elder,
70 for grey hairs,
80 for special strength,
90 for bowed back,

---

from Jesus' time are in Greek. Jesus and his followers probably knew some Greek terms, phrases and ideas, though the rabbis prohibited the study of Greek philosophy." The Dead Sea Scrolls also include Hebrew biblical scrolls. Scholars wonder if Stephen were Samaritan, as he cites the Samaritan Torah. However, "*variants* of the *Hebrew* biblical text, as the Dead Sea Scrolls have revealed, were more widespread than previously appreciated." Tremper Longman III, David E. Garlandintor, *The Expositor's Bible Commentary, rev. ed 10, Luke-Acts* (Grand Rapids, MI: Zondervan, 2009). David Peterson, *Acts of the Apostles* (Grand Rapids, MI: Eerdmans, 2009), 272. "There are several examples of Stephen's modifying biblical texts, using a fragment from another context to amplify and explain the significance of what he is alluding to or quoting. Acts 7:5 uses a portion of Deut 2:5."

[645] Each community had as many Scripture scrolls as they could afford. After the five books of The Law, the most frequently cited scrolls in the New Testament were Psalms and Isaiah.

[646] *Mishnah, Kiddushin,* 29a. Young men pursuing their education had to balance the timing of their marriage with their studies. Rabbis debated which should come first. Reading their debate gives a feel for what these men thought of marriage: "If one must study and is about to marry, he studies first and marries later. But if he cannot do without a wife, he marries first, and then he studies. Rab[bi] Yehuda said in the name of Samuel: the law is that he marries first and studies later. Said Rabbi Yohanan: What? with a stone around his neck he can study the law?"

[647] *Mishnah, Kiddushin,* 4:14. Once a young man received his religious education, the *Mishnah* instructed fathers to teach their sons a skill, but not "a craft that is practiced among women." The Jews sharply separated their occupational choices by gender.

234

100 as a corpse.[648]

This superlative summary of life fit only the most healthy, advantaged, and brightest Jewish males. Yet the list is helpful to see the value that Jews placed on education—especially in religious matters—and marriage.[649] When not in school or studying, sons helped with the family chores. This was not the case in wealthy or aristocratic homes where servants or slaves took over the children's work so that their education could broaden into Greek or a host of other topics.[650]

Girls

A Jewish girl's education centered on the domestic arts learned at home. Mothers taught their daughters to spin, weave, cook, tend their younger siblings, and do needlework.[651] Girls learned these skills quickly, as they were usually betrothed for marriage at twelve years old. In addition to learning how their mothers ran a home, they also learned from their mothers-in-law for the first few years of marriage, since the young bride and groom lived with the groom's family.

---

[648] *Mishnah, Avoth* 5:21. Each translation differs slightly. One reads, "twenty for pursuing a vocation, at the age of thirty for entering into one's full vigor, at the age of forty for understanding, at the age of fifty for counsel, at age sixty one attains old age." Philip Blackman, *Mishnayoth,* (New York: The Judaica Press, 1963), 537. The last item at the end of the ideal man's life was longevity. The length of life fits into historical possibilities. Pliny (a Roman philosopher, writer, and naturalist, who lived during the time of the New Testament) reported ninety people living in his area who were "at least 100 years" old. Alessandro Launaro, *Peasants and Slaves: The Rural Population of Roman Italy—200BC to AD 100* (New York City, NY: Cambridge University Press, 2011), 186. As a biblical reference points, King Herod died at age 69 or 70, Caesar Augustus at 76, but Anna lived to over 100, according to one reading of Luke 2:36.

[649] Josephus, *Life* 2; *Jewish War* 2.8.2-13.

[650] In addition to learning the religious law, sons (and occasionally daughters) of wealthy Jews also studied Greek, math, and science.

[651] Jeremias, *Jerusalem,* 363. Some fathers also intervened in different aspect of their daughter's education as Philo suggests: "The husband seems competent to transmit knowledge of the laws to his wife, the father to his children, the master to his slaves" (Philo, *Hypothetica,* 7:14).

Between the time of the Solomon's Temple and Herod's Temple, unhealthy cultural changes demeaned girls and women, curtailing their ability to learn and contribute. We see the influence of cultural baggage penetrating into the field of girls' education in the rabbinical interpretations of Old Testament passages. For example, Exodus 35:25 underscored the importance of the domestic art of spinning: "All the women that were wise-hearted did spin with their hands." But centuries later, rabbis interpreted this verse depreciatively: "a woman has no wisdom except in handling her spindle."[652]

Another more significant scriptural comparison, deals directly with a girl's education. The prophet Jeremiah called on women to learn from the Scriptures: "hear the word of the LORD, O ye women, and let your ear receive the word of his mouth, and teach your daughters" (Jeremiah 9:20). Once the women learned their Scriptures, Jeremiah called on them to teach their daughters.

However, six hundred years later, rabbis debated whether their daughters should be allowed to study the law of Moses. Although some rabbis in the *Mishnah* permitted a father to "teach scripture to his sons and daughters,"[653] later writers recorded misogynist thoughts like this: "And you shall teach them to your sons—not your daughters."[654] "If a man gives his daughter a knowledge of The Law it is as though he taught her lechery."[655] "A father should not teach his daughter Torah because certain acumen is gained from it which she may use to hide her immorality. . . . It is also possible that she may use her

---

[652] Ilan, *Jewish Women in Greco-Roman Palestine*, 191. Skolnik, *Encyclopedia Judaica*, 6.323.

[653] *Mishnah, Nedarim* 4.3.

[654] Babylonian Talmud, *Kiddushin,* 29b.

[655] *Mishnah, Sotah,* 3.4. Rabbi Eliezer spoke out against educating women more than most rabbis, perhaps because he suffered under the tongue of his well-educated wife. His wife was the sister of the leader of the Sanhedrin, Gamaliel. It is feasible that in that wealthy home, young girls were educated too, or else they may have had the opportunity to overhear lessons. The Talmud mentioned a few females who learned the oral laws. Wirtherington, *Women and the Genesis of Christianity,* 7.

knowledge of the Torah to attract men to her."[656] Not quite as restrictive, another rabbi argued that a girl should know the punishments of adultery. For this purpose, he said, "A man ought to give his daughter a knowledge of The Law."[657] If females were not to learn the full Law, it is not surprising that the *Mishnah* prohibited them from being teachers.[658] Cultural baggage like this kept the vast majority of Jewish girls illiterate.

Changes by Jesus

Jesus also valued education, and He provided the example of the ideal path of Christian maturation. However, unlike the above male checklist of accomplishments, our Lord's path is a process of becoming "complete in goodness, as your Heavenly Father is complete" (Matthew 5:48, WNT). The process is consistent across gender, class, and age. It includes learning humility, gratitude, obedience, sacrifice, empathy, forgiveness, faith, hope, and charity. A dispensation later the Lord further revealed resources for learning: "seek ye out of the best books words of wisdom; seek learning, even by study and also by faith" (D&C 88:118).[659]

The Lord's ideal education allows freedom from ignorance, emancipation from sin, and enablement to draw on His powers. Internalizing all these qualities allows a disciple to

---

[656] Nosson Scherman, *The Mishnah: A New Translation with a Commentary, Yad Avraham anthologized from Talmudic sources and classic commentators* (Brooklyn, NY: Mesorah Publications, 1981), III.58.

[657] *Mishnah, Sotah,* 3.4.

[658] *Mishnah, Kiddushin,* 4:13; ". . . nor may a woman be a teacher of children." The same passage also prohibits single men from teaching: "An unmarried man may not be a teacher of children."

[659] The breadth of the Lord's learning extends to "things both in heaven and in the earth, and under the earth; things which have been, things which are, things which must shortly come to pass; things which are at home, things which are abroad; the wars and the perplexities of the nations, and the judgments which are on the land; and a knowledge also of countries and of kingdoms—That ye may be prepared in all things when I shall send you again to magnify the calling whereunto I have called you" (D&C 88:79-80).

"come unto Christ and be perfected in Him, and deny yourselves of all ungodliness" (Moroni 10:32).

John the Baptist & Jesus

In Luke's description of childhood, we see the young John the Baptist and Jesus developing into the perfect man. Luke carefully crafted a parallel pattern for the education of two boys.[660]

John the Baptist	**Jesus**
And the child grew, and waxed strong … in spirit (Luke 1:80).	And the child grew, and waxed strong in spirit, [661] filled with wisdom and the grace of God was upon him (Luke 2:40)

Luke added a double portion of virtues to God's Firstborn.[662] More than any other mortal, God endowed Jesus with complete or perfect wisdom and grace. [663] After the Lord

---

[660] Fitzmyer, *Luke I-IX*, 419, "The infancy narrative continues in the spirit of traditional Jewish piety. This episode tells of the circumcision, naming, and manifestation of Jesus and is the parallel to the circumcision, naming, and manifestation of John" (also see 372). Luke's Parallel Structure comparing John the Baptist and Jesus:
1. Annunciations by Gabriel (Luke 1:5-25; compared to 1:26-38)
2. Greetings of Elisabeth and Mary (Luke 1:39-45; compared to 1:46-56)
3. Birth, circumcision, naming, or announcement (Luke 1:57-66; compared to 2:1-21)
4. Declaration of Destiny (Luke 1:67-79; compared to 2:21-38)
5. Growth (Luke 1:80; compared to 2:39-40, 52)

[661] Actually, the KJV is unique in including the word "spirit" in this parallel phrase for Jesus. Even translations taken from the same Greek text do not include "spirit" in Luke 2:40 (i.e., RSV). The absence may be accidental, or else a scribe may have been unwilling to confirm that Jesus had to grow in the Spirit (Brown, *Birth,* 469).

[662] Philo, *Special Laws,* II.123-139. The Mosaic laws of inheritance allowed the oldest son to receive twice or a "double portion" of what the other sons received (Deuteronomy 21:17). If there were three sons, with 400 denarii available—the inheritance would be divided by four so the oldest son received 200 and the others 100. For an example see 2 Kings 2:9.

[663] Luke highlights Jesus' unique quality of "grace / *charis*" or "favor / *charis.*" The King James Bible used two different English words, but the Greek is the same. "*Charis*" was a significant word for the New Testament

turned twelve, Luke added to his commentary on Jesus' education: "And Jesus increased in wisdom and stature, and in favour with God and man" (Luke 2:52). Those who strive to follow Jesus' educational path are empowered as they seek for wisdom, physical, spiritual, and social growth.

While the Jews emphasized religious learning from their rabbinic commentary of The Law, Jesus called on men, women, and children to learn from the source of The Law: "learn of me; for I am meek and lowly in heart: and ye shall find rest unto your souls" (Matthew 11:29). Jesus includes children in the audience when He teaches, heals, and feeds over five thousand in Galilee (Matthew 14:21) and similarly for the four thousand (Matthew 15:38). These young girls and boys, along with the adults, are nourished physically and spiritual through the Bread of Life.

| "Learn of me" |

The Lord made an educational transformation when He revealed truths "unto babes" that older folks could not learn (Matthew 11:25). He turned the education roles utterly around and called on His disciples not only to learn meekness and purity from children, but also to "become as a child" (Matthew 18:3; similarly Luke 18:17). The Savor promised those who learn from Him, that they "will become children of your Father in heaven" (Matthew 5:45, ISV). It is significant that the highest reward attainable is the position of a child in the Father's kingdom.

Vocation

Cultural Background and Baggage

---

authors as it has multiple innuendos and meanings they repeated it over 150 times. It "denotes effective divine power." James D. G. Dunn, *Romans 1-8* (Dallas, TX: Word Books, 1988), 17. Jesus' development was gradual and he gained favor as he developed; "he received not of the fulness at first, but continued from grace to grace, until he received a fulness; And thus he was called the Son of God" (D&C 93:13-14).

An important aspect of a young man's growth included an apprenticeship or some other means to become self-supporting and provide for a family. From the time of Adam, God taught the need to work: "Adam began to till the earth, and to have dominion over all the beasts of the field, and to eat his bread by the sweat of his brow, as I the Lord had commanded him. And Eve, also, his wife, did labor with him" (Moses 5:1). The LDS scripture cannon include nearly one thousand references to "work," establishing an unmistakably strong labor ethic.

One rabbi felt that a father who "does not teach his son a trade, teaches him to rob." And then the rabbinic banter erupted, "Teaches him to rob? How is that?—we may say: as though he taught him to rob."[664] Another rabbi argued, "I should lay aside every trade in the world and teach my son only Torah. . . . It keeps him from all evil when he is young, and it gives him a future and a hope when he is old."[665]

The vast majority of Jewish men in Palestine worked in some agriculturally based occupation. Ninety percent of Jews living in Palestine at the time of the New Testament had a vocation that supported farming or fishing villages.[666] Neither farming nor fishing were considered prestigious vocations.

The most esteemed professional positions were those for the educated: the head of the synagogue, a scholar, or an elementary school teacher.[667] The most prestigious jobs maintained a man's religious cleanliness and avoided contamination by Gentiles, blood, disease, or death (Leviticus 10:10; Isaiah 52:11; Ezekiel 44:23).

---

[664] Babylonian Talmud, *Kiddushin*, 29a.

[665] *Mishnah, Qiddushin*, 4:14m, r; the quote continues: "For a man eats its fruits in this world, and the principle remains for the world to come. But other trades are not that way. When a man gets sick or old or has pains and cannot do his job, lo, he dies of starvation. But with the Torah it is not that way" (4:14 n-q).

[666] Thurston, *Women in the New Testament*, 15-16. Unfortunately, those who left first-hand historical writings from this era were the literate aristocracy, the minority who lived in urban settings. Readers must take this into account when reading first hand writings.

[667] *Babylonian Talmud, Pesah*, 49b.

240

The *Mishnah* taught that it was more important to have a clean and honest trade than a high-paying one:

And let him pray to him to whom belong riches and possessions. For there is no trade which does not involve poverty or wealth. For poverty does not come from one's trade, nor does wealth come from one's trade. But all is in accord with a man's merit . . . a man should not teach his son to be an ass driver, a camel driver, a barber, a sailor, or a herdsman, or a shopkeeper. For their trade is the trade of thieves . . . the best among physicians is going to Gehenna, and the best of butchers is a partner of Amalek.[668]

Certain professions were shunned because of their dishonest or "unclean" reputation, like a dung-collector, copper smelter, tanner, goldsmith, peddler, weaver, tailor, and bath attendant.[669]

Herdsmen were another example of those untrusted, because so many shepherds deceitfully allowed their herds to feed on other men's property.[670] Judaic courts of law would not accept a shepherd's witness as legitimate.[671] Even though we find positive references to shepherds in the Bible—such as King David and Psalms 23:1, "The LORD is my shepherd; I shall not want"—when we read later rabbinic literature we find

---

[668] *Mishnah: Qiddushin*, 4:14. Gehenna was hell and Amalek a pagan nation.

[669] Jeremias, *Jerusalem,* 304-305.

[670] Jeremias, *Jerusalem,* 305; ". . . A similar suspicion weighed on herdsmen who did not enjoy a very good reputation. As proved by experience, most of the time they were dishonest and thieving; they led their herds on to other people's land, and pilfered the produce of the herd. For this reason it was forbidden to buy wool, milk, or kids from them." Also see Brown, *Birth,* 420.

[671] Josephus, *Antiquities,* IV.8:15; *Mishnah, Shebuoth,* 4:1. The list of unacceptable witnesses include ten classes of people: women, slaves, minors, lunatics, deaf, blind, wicked, contemptible, relatives and interested parties. Shepherds fell among the wicked as they grazed their flocks on other's lands.

"unfavorable references to herdsmen," labeling them "dishonest and thieving."[672]

Tax collectors were included among the "wicked" who were not allowed to act as a witness because they were suspected of collecting more money than their due and falsely attributed taxable items.[673] Supposedly, Theocritus, a third century Greek poet was asked what the worst wild beast was, and he answered, "On the mountains, bears and lions; in the city, publicans."[674] The Jews felt even more strongly because a publican worked for the Romans and had to affiliate with gentiles, so Jews labeled publicans as sinners (Matthew 21:31; Mark 2:15l Luke 15:1; etc.). They tried to avoid marriages with them: "Take not a wife out of a family where there is a publican, for they are all publicans."[675]

Changes by Jesus

An ideal Christian was not defined by his vocation, skills, nationality, or rank but by the condition of his or her heart and faith: "Now the end of the commandment is charity out of a pure heart, and of a good conscience, and of faith unfeigned" (1 Timothy 1:5). Ironically, the vocational outcasts are often highlighted in the New Testament as righteous, humble, devoted followers of God. Jesus himself chose to adopt the symbol of "the good Shepherd" (John 10:11, 14; also Hebrews 13:20; 1 Peter 5:4) and the Good Samaritan (Luke

---

Good Shepherd & Samaritan

---

[672] Jeremias, *Jerusalem,* 306, also see 305, 374.

[673] Skolnik, *Encyclopedia Judaica,* 21.116.

[674] Fredric William Farrar, *The Life of Christ* (New York City: Dutton, 1874), 247.

[675] Ibid., The Romans hired tax collectors in each region to enforce their 1% income-tax, 1/10 ground tax on production, a poll or head tax levied on all men over fourteen and girls over twelve up until age sixty-five, and an "indirect tax," which covered imports and exports that crossed a major street or harbor. The tax ranged from 2.5% to 12.5%, providing plenty of room for favors or extra charges or partiality. Edersheim, *Jesus the Messiah,* 133. Eerdmans, *Dictionary of the Bible,* 1278; Bromiley, *The International Standard Bible Encyclopedia,* Hagner, "Tax Collectors," 741-743.

10:33-35).[676] Rarely did the key figures in the New Testament fall into the category of holding a privileged Jewish vocation—in reality, the opposite was true (except for a few men like Saul/Paul in the apostolic church).

Jesus' followers often came from the less than desirable social groups (for example, tax collectors and soldiers from Matthew 8:5-13; 9:1-13, and Simon the tanner from Acts 9:43-10:32). The Gospels name half of The Twelve apostles' occupations: Four to six were fisherman (Peter, Andrew, James, John, and possibly Thomas and Nathaniel / Bartholomew from John 21:1-3), one tax collector (Matthew / Levi), [677] and one familiar enough with finances to act as treasurer (Judas Iscariot). Usually a son inherited the occupation of his father, so we assume that Zebedee, the father of James and John, was also a fishermen, that Saul's father was a tent maker; and that Jesus followed Joseph's footsteps as a builder (either a stonemason, craftsman, or carpenter[678]).

John the Baptist's Teachings on Vocation

When the publicans and Jewish soldiers came to John the Baptist and asked him for counsel, he did not tell them to change their occupations—even though both groups came from the socially unclean end of the Jewish professional continuum:

> Then came also publicans to be baptized, and said unto him, "Master, what shall we do?" And he said unto them, "Exact no more than that which is appointed you." The

---

[676] John W. Welch, "The Good Samaritan: A Type and Shadow of the Plan of Salvation," *BYU Studies* 38, no. 2 (1999): 50-115.

[677] The apostle Levi (Luke 5:27, 29) son of Alphaeus (Mark 2:14), is often equated with Matthew (Matthew 9:9). John Welch argues that one did not name a child Levi unless they were of the Tribe of Levi. This opens the question, was the apostle a tax collector for the temple rather than for Rome (private discussion with John Welch).

[678] The Greek word used in Mark 6:3, specifies a builder, "Is not this the carpenter / *tekton* / builder?" Stone is more prolific in Palestine than lumber, so much of the building was done stonemasons. Mark 6:3 could have been translated, "Is not this the stonemason?"

soldiers likewise demanded of him, saying, "And what shall we do?" And he said unto them, "Do violence to no man, neither accuse any falsely; and be content with your wages" (Luke 3:12-14, with quotation marks added).

Instead of condemning their livelihoods, John the Baptist emphasized their need for integrity, kindness, and less about their pay scale. Lineage and profession were not important. As John the Baptist taught, "Therefore bear fruit in keeping with repentance; And do not presume to say to yourselves, 'We have Abraham as our father,' for I tell you, God is able from these stones to raise up children for Abraham'" (Matthew 3:8-9).

Jesus' Teachings on Consecration

The Scriptures advocate hard work, with an emphasis on the Master's work. The Lord pled with his disciples to prioritize their time and means: "Lay not up for yourselves treasures upon earth, where moth and rust doth corrupt, and thieves break through and steal; But lay up for yourselves treasures in heaven" (Matthew 6:19-20). He transformed the vocational hierarchy by teaching that the most worthwhile work disciples can perform is to follow Him. Those who followed Him clothed, fed, and served others (Matthew 25:34-40).

The Lord elevated "apprenticeships" from *money making* to *kingdom building*. Jesus asked the fishermen to leave their nets and "Follow me, and I will make you fishers of men" (Matthew 4:19; Mark 1:17). At the end of His mission, He called His apostle to "Feed my lambs . . . Feed my sheep" (John 21:15-17). He repeated similar counsel to this dispensation: "I say unto all the Twelve: Arise and gird up your loins, take up your cross, follow me, and feed my sheep" (D&C 112:14). The membership was also called to share the good news, "The thing which will be of the most worth unto you will be to declare repentance unto this people, that you may bring souls unto me, that you may rest with them in the kingdom of my Father" (D&C 15:6; also 16:4-

6). This call is not tied to gender or age, but desire (D&C 4), as the Master will enable all who choose this path.

Christ also spoke against garnering wealth when a rich man asked Him how to "inherit eternal life" (Mark 10:17; Luke 18:18). Jesus answered by first addressing the need to obey the commandments (Mark 10:19). The man justified himself: "Master, all these have I observed from my youth" (Mark 10:20). Jesus admired the young man's past obedience and saw into his heart, "beholding him loved him" (Mark 10:21). So Jesus attempted to teach a higher law: "One thing thou lackest: go thy way, sell whatsoever thou hast, and give to the poor, and thou shalt have treasure in heaven: and come, take up the cross, and follow me" (Mark 10:21). [679] But the rich man "went away grieved: for he had great possessions" (Mark 10:22).

The rank of the world is not the rank of heaven, and Jesus lamented, "How hardly shall they that have riches enter into the kingdom of God!" (Mark 10:23). Money becomes a problem when it becomes one's cherished desire: "where your treasure is, there will your heart be also" (Luke 12:34). Jesus clarified that misplaced priorities became a function of one's heart: "A good man out of the good treasure of his heart bringeth forth that which is good; and an evil man out of the evil treasure of his heart bringeth forth that which is evil" (Luke 6:45).[680]

Apostles' Teachings on Self Sufficiency

It was very important to the early missionaries and apostles that they not be a burden on the church. Paul felt so strongly about taking responsibility to provide for himself and family that he asserted, "If any provide not for his own, and

---

[679] In the parallel account in Matthew 19:21, the citation begins, "If thou wilt be perfect."

[680] The Book of Mormon also addresses this in Jacob 2:19, "And after ye have obtained a hope in Christ ye shall obtain riches, if ye seek them; and ye will seek them for the intent to do good—to clothe the naked, and to feed the hungry, and to liberate the captive, and administer relief to the sick and the afflicted."

especially for those of his own house, he hath denied the faith, and is worse than an infidel" (1 Timothy 5:8). Part of that included using one's means generously to care for those in need as the church collected funds for the poor (Luke 12:33; Acts 10:4; Romans 15:26; etc.).

The apostles taught the need to give even to one's enemies: "Therefore if thine enemy hunger, feed him; if he thirst, give him drink" (Romans 12:20). The Jerusalem Christians lived a form of the law of consecration built on a strong foundation of work and faith (Acts 2:44-45). They knew that "The earth is the Lord's, and everything in it" (1 Corinthians 10:26; Psalms 24:1) and thus acted as accountable stewards—not owners—of their means.[681] From the principles of agency, generosity, and love, the early saints across the empire donated their means to support their fellow saints in need (Romans 15:25-27). They strove to have no poor among them (Deuteronomy 15:4).

---

[681] Steven C. Harper, "'All Things Are the Lord's": The Law of Consecration in the Doctrine and Covenants" in Andrew H. Hedges, J. Spencer Fluhman, and Alonzo L. Gaskill, ed., *The Doctrine and Covenants: Revelations in Context* (Provo and Salt Lake City: Religious Studies Center, Brigham Young University, and Deseret, 2008), 212–128.

Chapter 8
Servitude: From Slaves to Students

This chapter provides a cultural overview of servitude during the late Second Temple period, as it related to family life. Many of New Testament examples demonstrate the Lord elevating the underprivileged and teaching the emancipation of love, faith, hope, service, and forgiveness. Jesus turned the traditional social hierarchy upside down by honoring those who served: "he that is greatest among you shall be your servant" (Matthew 23:11). He did not call for emancipation of servitude, instead He taught masters to serve.

Cultural Background and Baggage

Much of the social order of the Roman Empire stemmed from the servant-master relationship. It saturated their culture and infiltrated the lives of women and children.[682] A census across the Roman Empire from AD 47 documented that one-third of the population was enslaved or worked as servants.[683] Some large cities had higher percentages, including Jerusalem, which recorded that fifty-percent of the population were

---

[682] Ben Sira, *Ecclesiasticus,* 3.1,7, "Listen to me your father, O children; and act accordingly, that you may be kept in safety. . . . He will serve his parents as his masters." Jeremias, *Jerusalem,* 369; "The wife was obliged to obey her husband as she would a master."

[683] Bromiley, *The International Standard Bible Encyclopedia*, Bartchy, "Servant" 4.420. Tim G. Parkin, *Old Age in the Roman World: A Cultural and Social History* (Baltimore, MD: John Hopkins, 2003), 183. As a reference point from United States history, as early as 1690, half of the population in the Carolina colonies was enslaved. Edwin Gaustad and Leigh Schmidt, *The Religious History of America* (San Francisco: HarperCollins, 2004), 103. Across the Roman Empire, at different times, estimates range between six and sixty million people were slaves. Junius P. Rodriguez, *The Historical Encyclopedia of World Slavery* (Santa Barbara, CA: ABD-CLI, 1997), 7.548.

servants or slaves. To fully appreciate how many slaves there were, a normal middle-class Roman citizen owned eight slaves.[684] The only families that did not have a servant in the Greco-Roman world were those in hopeless poverty. There is evidence that some slaves even owned a slave of their own.[685] Many people chose servitude over starvation and sold themselves into slavery for the benefit of room and board.[686]

Slaves vs. Servants

In both Greek and Hebrew, the same word describes a servant and a slave, though a servant and a slave were treated quite differently.[687] Many of the slaves were war prisoners or "booty" from Rome's foreign conquests.[688] Some servants were paid, others were merely given bed and board in lieu of wages. Some were treated with respect, others were terribly abused. The trademark of a slave was scars across his or her back from whippings.[689] Masters considered slaves their personal property, and as such, slaves had no legal rights of their own to demand justice. A master's personal property included slaves, servants, wives, and children.[690]

---

[684] Heshey Zelcher, *A Guide to the Jerusalem Talmud* (Universal Publishers, 2002), 92. "The middle class citizens often owned eight slaves, the rich from five hundred to a thousand, and an emperor as many as twenty thousand."

[685] Bromiley, *The International Standard Bible Encyclopedia,* 4.544.

[686] Keith Crim, ed. *The Interpreter's Dictionary of the Bible* (Nashville, TN: Abingdon, 1976), Supplementary volume 830.

[687] The Greek New Testament used *doulos* for slave and servant, and in Hebrew the Old Testament, *'ebed.*

[688] Campbell*, Marriage and Family in the Biblical World,* 135. Many Greco-Roman slaves served only for a specified time to pay their debts. Like a servant, some slaves were paid and could buy their freedom from their owners. If the slave enjoyed a good relationship with his master, upon his release, the master often helped the slave financially to start up a new life on his or her own. Once male or female slaves were free in the Greco-Roman world, they could become shopkeepers, artisans, or domestics. A freed slave could take the plebeian name of his/her former owner as his clan name.

[689] Rawson, ed., *Marriage, Divorce, and Children in Ancient,* 161.

[690] Neusner, *The Economics of the Mishnah*, 65. "The household encompassed the householder, Jacob Neusnerother employees utilized as

Although many Jews were sold into slavery during times of persecution, in ideal circumstances, Jews did not enslave fellow Jews.[691] (The Essenes forbade keeping any servants, due to their strict interpretation of The Law which prohibited slavery, so they worked and lived "all in common."[692])

However, when economic need demanded it, male and female Jews worked for other Jewish families. After six years of labor, the Torah provided a means that a poor man could escape the cycle of indentured servitude: "If thou buy an Hebrew servant, six years he shall serve: and in the seventh he shall go out free for nothing" (Exodus 21:2).[693] The sabbatical year included freeing slaves (Deuteronomy 15:12; Leviticus 25:39-42). In the Roman world slaves were released by age thirty.[694] Many were given their freedom prior to that age.[695]

---

needed, as well as his livestock, movables, and real property. The householder's will reigned supreme, and his decisions governed."

[691] Zelcher, *A Guide to the Jerusalem Talmud,* 92; "Following both major revolts by the Jews of Israel against the Roman empire in the year 70 and 135, hundreds of thousands of Jews were killed, or sold as slaves."

[692] Philo, *Hypothetica* 11.4. "None of them allows himself to have any private property . . . but they put everything into the public stock and enjoy the benefit of them all."

[693] The law of Moses stipulated that if a male servant received a wife from his master, he could not take his wife or children with him when released: "If he came in by himself, he shall go out by himself: if he were married, then his wife shall go out with him. If his master have given him a wife, and she have borne him sons or daughters; the wife and her children shall be her master's, and he shall go out by himself" (Exodus 21:3-4). This is where the situation became tenuous. Many men chose to remain in the employ of someone else rather than leave their family. So The Law added, "And if the servant shall plainly say, I love my master, my wife, and my children; I will not go out free: Then his master shall bring him unto the judges; he shall also bring him to the door, or unto the door post; and his master shall bore his ear through with an aul; and he shall serve him for ever" (Exodus 21:5-6). The pierced ear was often filled with a hoop, so that servant for life was known by a hoop in his ear.

[694] Bromiley, *International Standard Bible Encyclopedia,* 4.545. Campbell, *Marriage and Family in the Biblical World,* 135. Some sources record a release at age thirty, others thirty-five or forty. The process releasing a slave was known as manumission.

[695] Ibid. "Pertinent inscriptions indicate, however, that large numbers, approaching 50 percent, were set free prior to their thirtieth year."

Generally, most servants were treated like serfs in the feudal system.[696] Servants who worked in the city often had a higher standard of living than poor free men who worked in the country off the land. Not all were subordinate either—especial those that served as tutors, physicians, nurses, managers of the household, and close companions.[697] Some owners treated their house servants or slaves as part of the family, gave them a comfortable living, and mourned over them when they died.[698] Yet, when the *Mishnah* listed the order that one should redeem family members if taken captive, servants and slaves are not even mentioned.[699]

In the Jewish world, Philo defended those in this lesser class on the social ladder and called for mutual respect: "Unless you treat your servants with gentleness, do not treat those of the same rank as yourself socially. Unless you behave decorously to your wife, never bear yourself respectfully to your parents. If you neglect your father and your mother, be impious also towards God."[700] Despite a low social status, Philo called for similar treatment toward servants, slaves, a wife, and parents.[701]

Changes by Jesus

Jesus attacks the "master-servant" social mentality as He teaches the principles of partiality, fairness, and freely serving: "The disciple is not above his master, nor the servant above his lord" (Matthew 10:24). His apostles resumed the message of fairness: "Masters, give unto your servants that which is just

---

[696] Rodriguez, *The Historical Encyclopedia of World Slavery,* 7.555.

[697] Bromiley, *International Standard Bible Encyclopedia,* 4.544.

[698] Winer, *Life in the Ancient World*, 176.

[699] *Mishnah, Horayoth.* 3.7.

[700] *Philo,* Yonge, trans., 2,172.

[701] Ibid., 252. When hospitality was needed, everyone pitched into help. Philo explained "For no one in the house of a wise man is ever slow to perform the duties of hospitality, both women and men and slaves and freemen, are most eager in the performance of all those duties towards strangers; therefore, after having feasted and delighted, not so much with that was set before them, as with the good will of their entertainer, and with his excessive and unbounded zeal to please them."

and equal; knowing that ye also have a Master in heaven" (Colossians 4:1). The Lord overturned the social ladder: "whosoever of you will be the chiefest, shall be servant of all" (Mark 10:44).

Again and again Jesus praised those who voluntarily served their fellowmen as the model behavior, "Blessed is that servant, whom his lord when he cometh shall find so doing" (Luke 12:43). Jesus was less concerned about abolishing slavery than He was about developing both masters and slaves into good stewards: "Well, thou good servant: because thou hast been faithful in a very little, have thou authority over ten cities" (Luke 19:17). As the mortal sense of equality is warped—all must trust in God's omniscience—He will reward generously.

Luke tells of a servant who became a beloved family member: "A certain centurion's servant, who was dear unto

> Centurion's Servant

him, was sick, and ready to die. And when he heard of Jesus, he sent unto him the elders of the Jews, beseeching him that he would come and heal his servant" (Luke 7:3). Jesus healed the servant from a distance, giving verbal praise to the centurion's faith and nonverbal affirmation to the centurion's love for his servant: "I have not found so great faith, no, not in Israel" (Luke 7:9).

Jesus did not discriminate by rank, and He healed a slave as readily as He did the daughter of the synagogue's leader. His parables were filled with stories of servants—sometimes as the good example, sometimes as the bad (Matthew 18:26-32, 25:26-30; Mark 12:4; Luke 20:10-11). One's caste was not an issue, but how one behaved within one's role is what mattered. Repeatedly, Jesus tore through layers of false traditions, bigotry, and bias that paralyzed relationships. He liberated His future followers to eradicate prejudices and injustices.[702]

Jewish Female Slaves

---

[702] Many of the Lord's teachings did not find their fruition until people began reading the Bible and adopted His messages. The seeds of truth He planted have taken millennia to germinate and grow.

Cultural Background and Baggage

Unlike her male counterparts, a Jewess slave owned by a Jewish man was rarely liberated every seven years. Earlier Israelite history set the precedent for this: "If a man sell his daughter to be a maidservant, she shall not go out as the menservants do" (Exodus 21:7). Female slaves were identified as the property of their masters and thus available for sexual use.[703] Rabbi Hillel admitted, "Whoever multiples female slaves multiplies promiscuity and whoever multiplies male slaves multiplies thieving."[704]

If a slave girl were set free, she could not marry another Jew because most female slaves were no longer virgins, her options in the Jewish culture was slavery or prostitution. Many Jewish bondswomen chose to remain domestic servants and concubines, rather than the alternative.

Unfair as it may sound, the Torah provided a means where the master could actually divorce a slave-wife: "If she please not her master, who hath betrothed her to himself, then shall he let her be redeemed . . . he hath dealt deceitfully with her" (Exodus 21:8). In the Old Testament, polygamy was also practiced with a slave-wives (i.e., Hagar, Zilpah, Bilhah). If a Jewish man consummated a marriage with a servant girl but then took another wife, The Law instructed that he must continue to provide for the servant-wife: "her food, her raiment, and her duty of marriage, shall he not diminish. And if he do not these three unto her, then shall she go out free without money" (Exodus 21:10-11).

New Testament Example

The Gospel of Luke shares a sweet dimension of servitude at Jesus' annunciation. When the angel Gabriel came to Mary and revealed God's plan for His Son's birth, she willingly

---

[703] Thurston, *Women in the New Testament,* 23. In the Roman world, "female slaves could also be sent out to work as prostitutes. Children born to slave women were her owners' property."

[704] Bromiley, *International Standard Bible Encyclopedia,* Q-Z, 545.

submitted: "Behold the handmaid of the Lord; be it unto me according to thy word" (Luke 1:38). "Handmaiden" comes from

| Mary the Handmaid of the Lord |

the Greek word for a female slave / *doule*. Mary committed to be the Lord's servant in whatever He required. She basically said, "I will do anything you ask, I will do everything within my power to fulfill your plan." She was also saying, "I am willing to carry your child." What remarkable faith—and it was not blind! In that society, she would not have used the word "handmaiden / *doule*" lightly.

With the vast number of servants—and as barely a child herself—Mary probably had an idea of what it meant to be a servant or slave. Likewise, she probably knew the consequences of being a disobedient slave. Coming from a culture where young girls were generally kept indoors, where communication with a betrothed was limited, where children were equated with slaves, and where adulteress and unwed mothers were stoned; Mary's humble acquiescence to become God's handmaiden is even more moving.

Runaway Slaves

Cultural Background

Though both the Jews and Romans had a built-in date for freedom for their slaves, there was enough torture and abuse that many slaves ran away. The law of Moses provided mercy for a runaway slave. If the fugitive asked for refuge in a new community, all were to welcome him and "not oppress him" or return him to his last owner (Deuteronomy 23:15-16).

In the Roman Empire, though, runaway slaves became such a problem that laws were created to keep them in submission. Decrees called for a runaway to be returned to the owner, yet cases show some slaves were killed.[705] Caesar

---

[705] Christopher J. Fuhrmann, *Policing the Roman Empire: Soldiers, Administration, and Public Order* (Oxford, England: Oxford University Press, 2012), 24. If a slave's master was not found, the slave was assumed to be the murderer and crucified.

Augustus enacted a law to kill all the slaves in the household if there was evidence that a master was killed by a slave.[706] If slaves were the lowest level on the social ladder, a runaway slave was "subhuman . . . a lost cause."[707]

If and when runaway slaves were found, they were often branded on their foreheads with "an 'F' for fugitive."[708] History speaks of a cruel, concerted effort in "Roman fugitive-slave hunting." The slave masters "bore the basic onus of recovering their runaways, [and] employed harsh methods to deter the escape of slaves who were considered disobedient or flight risks. These measures might include heavy chaining, permanent disfigurement from identifying brands, intentional scars, and most commonly, tattooed letters."[709]

Changes by Christianity

Paul wrote about finding a runaway slave. In his shortest Epistle, he composed a beautiful chiasmus to Philemon, one of his early Christian converts from Colossae. The impetus to write his friend came from finding Philemon's
runaway slave while Paul was in Rome. When he came in contact with a new Christian covert,
Onesimus, Paul learned that he was a runaway slave of none other than Paul's old friend Philemon.

As an apostle and Roman citizen, Paul thought it wisest to send the runaway back to his owner, accompanied by Paul's letter requesting ample forgiveness and fellowship for the prodigal, Onesimus. The law called for the runaway to return to slavery, but as a Christian, Paul asked his friend to treat the returning slave as he would treat the apostle: "receive him as

---

[706] Fuhrmann, *Policing the Roman Empire*, 23-24. "Fear of a large-scale slave uprising was probably a significant motive behind the Roman state's measures against slave flight. . . . In one controversial case under Nero, more than four hundred slaves were executed."

[707] Ruden, *Paul among the People,* 156. A runaway slave "bore all of the loathing and fury . . . that come when absolute privilege is disappointed."

[708] Douglas Connely, *Forgiveness: Making Peace with the Past* (Madison, WI: InterVarsity Press, 2005), 61.

[709] Fuhrmann, *Policing the Roman Empire,* 29.

myself" (Philemon 1:17). Paul pressed Philemon to welcome Onesimus back no longer as a slave, but as a friend in the gospel without retribution: "If he hath wronged thee, or oweth thee ought, put that on mine account . . . I will repay it" (Philemon 1:18-19). Paul requested emancipation for Onesimus: "[I have] confidence in thy obedience I wrote unto thee, knowing that thou wilt also do more than I say" (Philemon 1:21). It appears that Paul took extra care with this delicate subject, as he carefully crafted the entire letter as poetry used puns and word play with their names.[710] The Scriptures are silent as to what happened to Onesimus after he left Paul.[711]

---

[710] Onesimus means profitable; Philemon means loving, or friendship. The Chiasmus is adapted from Welch-Hall, *Charting the New Testament*, 15-20.
A Epistolary (1–3)
  B Paul's prayers for Philemon (4)
   C Philemon's love, faith, and hospitality (5–7)
    D Paul could use his authority (8)
     E But prefers to make supplication (9–10)
      F Onesimus a convert of Paul's (10)
       G Paul has made Onesimus profitable (11)
        H Receive Onesimus as Paul's own bowels (12)
         I Paul retained Onesimus as Paul's minister in the bonds of the gospel (13)
          J Without Philemon's willing consent Paul will not require Philemon to take Onesimus
          J' Perhaps the reason Onesimus left was so that Philemon could take Onesimus back forever as a fellow saint (15)
         I' Not as a servant but as a brother in the Lord (16)
        H' Receive Onesimus as Paul's own self (17)
       G' Paul will repay any wrong Onesimus has done (18–19)
      F' Philemon indebted as a convert to Paul (19)
     E' Paul makes supplication to Philemon (20)
    D' Although he could ask for obedience (21)
   C' Paul requests hospitality of Philemon (22)
  B' Philemon's prayers for Paul (22)
A' Epistolary—Good wishes (23–25)
[711] Colossians 4:9 also mentioned a Christian named Onesimus. Orthodox Christians and others claim a man named Onesimus became a bishop in Ephesus, though which Onesimus was that?

Master Teacher-Student Relation

Cultural Background

Servitude also had a place in the academic setting of a master teacher and pupil relationship in the Judeo-Greco-Roman settings. Out of devotion to one's teacher, a student often chose to do everything for his master that a slave would usually do.[712] In order to spend more time with his teacher, a disciple helped his master get dressed, eat, wash his face—everything except foot care. Even a master teacher did not have his pupils or disciples take off his sandals and wash his feet because it was too demeaning a task for anyone but a slave or a child.

Changes by Jesus

The prophet John the Baptist alluded to this teacher-student relationship when referring to the Savior. John illustrated his relationship to Jesus, when he acknowledged, "One mightier than I cometh, the latchet of whose

John the
Baptist

shoes I am not worthy to unloose." It was as if he humbly and poignantly confessed, "I'm not worthy to be the Messiah's student or disciple, let alone worthy to act as His slave" (paraphrasing Luke 3:16).

This same background also sheds light on why Peter so vehemently opposed Jesus' offer to wash his feet: "Never shall You wash my feet!" (John 13:8, NASB). Peter could not fathom asking his beloved Master—whom he believed was the Son of

---

[712] Judith R. Baskin and Kenneth Seeskin, *The Cambridge Guide to Jewish History, Religion, and Culture* (New York, NY: Cambridge University Press, 2010), 313. "The intentional community of the Rabbis was centered on the master-disciple relationship; through this link between teacher and student, the full import of life according to the Torah of Moses could be appreciated and acquired. . . . Students would apprentice with a master, often for many years, learning direct teachings and observing how a rabbinic Jew was to behave. These explicit and inferred rules governed all aspects of human life, from ritual matters and legal rulings to ethical maxims and daily behaviors."

God—to act as his slave. But Jesus had higher things to teach: "You do not realize now what I am doing, but later you will

| Jesus Washes Feet |

understand. . . . If I wash thee not, thou hast no part with me" (John 13:7-8, NIV).[713] Irrepressible and impassioned Peter immediately submitted to the Lord's will: "not just my feet but my hands and my head as well!" (John 13:9, NIV). Peter had learned through previous experience that his Master transformed social norms: the poor in spirit will become rich, the meek will inherit the earth, and the persecuted will inherit the heavens (Matthew 5:1-8). The Lord's new lesson revolutionized the tiered social strata. In contrast to the cultural norm, in divine kingdoms, masters serve.

Finally, Jesus himself took on the role of the suffering servant as Isaiah prophesied.

He hath no form nor comeliness; and when we shall see him, there is no beauty that we should desire him. He is despised and rejected of men; a man of sorrows, and

| Suffering Servant |

acquainted with grief: and we hid as it were our faces from him; he was despised, and we esteemed him not. Surely he hath borne our griefs, and carried our sorrows: yet we did esteem him stricken, smitten of God, and afflicted. But he was wounded for our transgressions, he was bruised for our iniquities: the chastisement of our peace was upon him; and with his stripes we are healed (Isaiah 53:2-5).

---

[713] The Lord restored "the washing of feet" as an ordinance to the Prophet Joseph Smith. The prophet then shared it with the saints in the Kirtland Temple in 1836. See, Dean C. Jessee, compiled and ed., *The Personal Writings of Joseph Smith* (Salt Lake City, UT: Deseret Book, 1984), 181. "In the Kirtland Temple in 1836, after attending to the ordinance of the washing of the feet, Joseph Smith said he had 'completed the organization of the church, and…[had given] all the necessary ceremonies' (*History of the Church*, 2:432). However, four days later, he was given greater keys of authority and knowledge which he did not confer on the leaders of the Church until the Nauvoo period (see D&C 110)." Ehat Cook, *Words of Joseph Smith*, 140.

This servant was not treated as a member of the family, loved, or admired. He was not even acknowledged or honored "in his own country," but His own people abused and tortured Him (Mark 6:4). Though Jesus never sinned, He willingly took the punishment of others without complaint.

> He was oppressed, and he was afflicted, yet he opened not his mouth: he is brought as a lamb to the slaughter, and as a sheep before her shearers is dumb, so he openeth not his mouth. He was taken from prison and from judgment: and who shall declare his generation? for he was cut off out of the land of the living: for the transgression of my people was he stricken. And he made his grave with the wicked, and with the rich in his death; because he had done no violence, neither was any deceit in his mouth. Yet it pleased the LORD to bruise him; he hath put him to grief: when thou shalt make his soul an offering for sin, he shall see his seed, he shall prolong his days, and the pleasure of the LORD shall prosper in his hand. He shall see of the travail of his soul, and shall be satisfied: by his knowledge shall my righteous servant justify many; for he shall bear their iniquities (Isaiah 53:7-11).

Isaiah's prophecies about the righteous servant were fulfilled in the life of Jesus of Nazareth.[714]

The Lord chose to serve rather than be served. He teaches the importance of service by His example and words, "If anyone would be first, he must be last of all and servant of all" (Mark 9:35, ESV). Jesus identifies himself as the servant of all: "For even the Son of man came not to be ministered unto, but to minister, and to give his life a ransom for many" (Mark 10:45). Jesus honors those who served voluntarily out of love. He denounces any kind of authoritative self-aggrandizement: "And whosoever shall exalt himself shall be abased; and he that shall

---

[714] Isaiah 49:16 and 52:13-14 also include prophecies about a "suffering servant" that have been attributed to the promised Messiah.

humble himself shall be exalted" (Matthew 23:12). Jesus also valued relationships with children: "Let the little children come to me and do not try to stop them, for the kingdom of heaven belongs to such as these" (Matthew 19:14, NET). This was a radical departure from the cultural practice in the ancient Jewish world. By turning the cultural pecking order on its head, Jesus teaches that: "God is no respecter of persons" (Acts 10:34). God rewards a man for his humility not for his pride, and for his selfless service not his social status.

Conclusion

Jesus' example and teachings counteract social bigotry that inhibit human respect and family unity. The cultural baggage of the ancient worlds had not only caused a gulf between fellow humans, but also between humanity and God. God shattered cultural restrictions and taught that all Christians should treat all humans equally.[715] From the time of Jesus' birth to the apostolic church, God elevated women and children to a place of dignity.

At the same time Jesus planted subtle seeds of truth that, when nurtured, have the potential to develop into respectful relationships founded on mutual support and love. All who internalize Jesus' teachings can receive freedom from their own culture or other baggage by "relying wholly upon the merits of him who is mighty to save" (2 Nephi 31:19; also Alma 7:14; 34:18; D&C 133:47; Isaiah 63:1).

Because all fall short, Christ will repair the breach between humanity and God, and between fellow human beings. His healing power comes as pure love. The work of becoming "one" through love opens up wonderfully brilliant possibilities. It potentially restores the promise of Eden—to live sublimely in the presence of God alongside those who are most dear to us.

---

[715] Parales, *Hidden Voices: Biblical Women*, 50. In Parales opinion, the Lord "died to end relationships of dominance and submission based on power structures (Matthew 20:20-28)."

Appendix 1
Political, Social and Religious Changes in Judea during the Intertestamental Era

Although this book deals with the era of the New Testament, this appendix provides some historical context to help the reader understand how and why things became the way they were by the time of the New Testament. Between the Old and New Testaments, political, religious, and social changes altered the way women were treated and how religion was perceived. This appendix briefly touches on six areas of change that affected Jewish families in the first century—changes to: politics, the law of Moses, women, family life, messianic hope, and temple rituals.

1. Political Changes

In 332 BC, Alexander the Great conquered Judea. For the next three centuries, Hellenistic rulers governed Israel.[716] The Jews were allowed to continue to practice their religion as they pleased until 170 BC. At that point, Antiochus IV arrived in Jerusalem and severely persecuted the Jews. He marched into the city, burning, killing, and plundering everyone and everything.[717] He decimated the Jewish leadership and

---

[716] Wylen, *Jews in the Time of Jesus*, 49. After Alexander's death, his empire was divided between his two generals: Ptolemy in Egypt (from 301 to 200 BC), and Seleucids in Syria-Mesopotamia (from 200 to 140 BC). These dynasties bordered Israel and vied for the right to govern her. The Ptolemies did not restrict Jewish religious affairs.
[717] Skolnik, *Encyclopaedia Judaica,* 2.203. Antiochus IV was a Seleucid ruler.

removed the priesthood line of authority.[718] He killed Jews who did not renounce the Torah and eat pork. Most upsetting, Antiochus IV sacked Zerubbabel's Temple, installed images of pagan gods, rededicated the temple to a Greek god, and performed sexual rites in the temple court.[719]

Rather than submit to Antiochus IV's demands, a few devout Jews, known as the *Hasidim* (pious ones)*,* went into hiding in the foothills of Judea. One of those, a priest named Mattathias the Hasmonean, began a revolt with the help of his five sons. In the Apocrypha, *Book of Maccabees*, Mattathias gathered Jewish support against the Syrian assassins by crying out, "Let everyone who is zealous for the law and supports the covenant come out with me!" (1 Maccabees 2:27). His son Judas led their supporters to victory in the ensuing three-year guerrilla war. Judas earned the nicknamed *Maccabee*, or "hammer," hence the rebellion's name: the Maccabean Revolt. At the end of the revolt, another one of Mattathias' five sons became the next high priest in Jerusalem.

As soon as the priests retook possession of their sacred city in 165 BC, cleansed Zerubbabel's Temple. 1 Maccabees 4:37-40 reads:

> The entire army assembled, and they went up to Mount Zion. They saw the temple laid desolate and the altar profaned and the gates burned and the courts overgrown with plants as "in a thicket" or "like one of the mountains" and the chambers laid in ruins. They rent their garments and made great lamentation and put on ashes. They prostrated themselves upon the ground and sounded the signal trumpets and cried out to Heaven.[720]

---

[718] F. F. Bruce, *New Testament History* (New York: Doubleday, 1969), 3. Since the time of King David, the Zadok family held the office of high priest (2 Samuel 8:17; 15:24-29; 1 Kings 1:39; Ezekiel 44:15; 48:11; Nehemiah 11:11; etc.). But in 171 BC, an ardent Hellenizer named Menelaus bribed his way into the office of high priest.

[719] Jonathan A. Goldstein, *1 Maccabees: A New Translation with Introduction and Commentary* (Garden City, NY: Doubleday-Anchor Bible, 1976), 277; 156-157.

[720] Ibid., 272.

After rebuilding the altar and purifying the sanctuary, they made new sacred vessels. The priests prepared the Holy Place by returning a menorah, table for shewbread, and incense altar to their traditional positions. The priests purified themselves and prepared to offer sacrifices for the temple's rededication (1 Maccabees 4:41-53). Unfortunately, no fire came down from heaven to burn the sacrifices as it had for Moses' Tabernacle and Solomon's Temple; no sign of the Divine Presence was visible (Exodus 40:34-38; 2 Chronicles 7:1-3). The Hasmonaean family of priests decided to move ahead in faith and determination and made their own fire (1 Maccabees 4:50-61; 2 Maccabees 10:1-8).

In a later rabbinic tradition, another story developed that associated a miracle with the rededication of the Second Temple. Traditionally, the dedication was to last for eight days (Leviticus 8:35-9:1, 5). But the legend claims that the priests did not have enough sacred oil to light the menorah for more than one day.[721] Miraculously, the cruse of oil lasted for all eight days, giving continuous light to the temple.[722] The rabbis described the miracle of the enduring light as the sign that God had accepted their efforts. Jews remember the miracle during Hanukah or "festival of lights."

Following Mattathias' and his sons' deaths, the Hasmonean dynasty and other priestly families kept the temple functioning under Greek and Roman rule. Because the Jews felt outnumbered by the growing Gentile population in their land, the Hasmoneans sought to expand their numbers by annexing another Semitic line, the Idumeans, their distant cousins

---

[721] Ibid., 283; "The legend of the miraculous cruse of oil is probably derived from the old prayer *'Al hannissim* as understood by the rabbi. . . . First Maccabees, now rejected by pious Jews, told only of victories. Though, Second Maccabees told of miracles, it, too, if known, could be rejected as a work in Greek and as unreliable because of the author's well-intentioned pious fictions."

[722] Ibid. Jewish feasts remembered miracles: Passover with the miraculous freedom from Egypt; Pentecost with Moses' miraculous meeting with God on Mount Sinai; and later rabbis associated miraculous shelters with the Feast of Tabernacles.

through Isaac's son Esau, who lived in southern Palestine.[723] Their expansion was not sufficient, and in 63 BC, the Roman general Pompey conquered Palestine. The Romans maintained control of Palestine until 300 AD.

In 47 BC, Julius Caesar gave the right to govern Judea to one of his friends, Antipater. Antipater's family traced their genealogy though the Idumean race, who had been adopted into Judaism a century earlier. Antipater became governor of Galilee in 47 BC. His second son, Herod (73-4 BC)[724] replaced him in Galilee. After several astute political moves and a marriage to the Jewish princess, Mariamne Hasmonean, Herod became king of Judea in 37 BC.[725] The Jews did not receive him willingly, and much blood was shed before Herod gained control.

Even though the Jews despised Herod, he became known as Herod the Great. His skills in engineering and manufacturing were unparalleled in ancient Israel, and he was renowned throughout the ancient world for his ingenious and grandiose building projects. In addition to reconfiguring Mount Moriah in order to double the size of the Second Temple and its

---

[723] Benedikt Eckhardt, ed. *Jewish Identity and Politics Between the Maccabees and Bar Kokhba*: *Supplement to the Journal for the Study of Judaism* (Leiden, Netherlands: Brill, 2011), 100-101. There is much debate as to whether or not the "Hasmonean expansion" of the Idumeans was a voluntary or forced conversion to Judaism.

[724] Ernest L. Martin, *The Birth of Christ Recalculated, 2nd Ed.* (Pasadena, CA: Foundation for Biblical Research, 1980). Herod, has a questionable death date as Martin elaborates. It is often estimated at 4 BC, because Josephus said it followed an eclipse and preceded Passover. Many scholars fix the eclipse of 12-13 March 4 B.C., as Herod's death date. However, Martin rejects that date in favor of one of the other solar and lunar eclipses near that time: "(1) Night of 15-16 September, 5 B.C.; (2) Night of 12-13 March, 4 B.C.; (3) Night of 9-10 January 1 B.C.; and (4) Early evening of 29 December, 1 B.C." Also see S. Kent Brown, Wilfred Griggs, H. Kimball Hansen, "Book Review: April Sixth," *BYU Studies, vol. 22* (Summer 1982), 3.356.

[725] Skolnik, *Encyclopaedia Judaica,* 9.32. Herod demonstrated his political savvy in his ability to ingratiate himself to different rulers. Initially he developed a friendship with Julius Caesar, followed by one with Cassius, Marc Antony, and later with Caesar Augustus.

courtyards,[726] he also engineered amazing water supplies to Jerusalem, the Judean Desert, and Masada, Antonia, and the Herodion. He designed and constructed elaborate fortresses and elegant cities such as Caesarea Maritima, which is particularly impressive because of its distinctive deep-water harbor.[727]

Josephus described Herod the Great as pathologically jealous (for example, he killed his wife Mariamne and his sons whom he saw as potential usurpers).[728] In another demonstration of paranoia, he disassembled the Jews' religious ruling council, the Sanhedrin, in order to protect his political control. King Herod robbed the office of high priest from the ancient lines of Aaron by arbitrarily dismissing and appointing new high priests as his political puppets as often as he wished.[729] Herod appointed and dismissed his high priest and several chief priests depending on their political willingness to work with him, not on their religious integrity.[730] This stripped the high priest's office of its sacred nature. The natural outcome of this new order was rivalry between the chief priests for the powerful ruling position of high priest. Looking back on this time, the Talmud apologized: "In the First Temple, the high-priests served, the son succeeding the father, and they were eighteen in number. But in the Second Temple they got the high-priesthood for money; . . . they destroyed each other by

---

[726] Josephus, *Antiquities,* XV.11.5; *Wars.* V.5.1

[727] Ehud Netzer, *The Architecture of Herod the Great Builder* (Tübingen: Mohr Siebeck, 2006).

[728] Josephus, *Antiquities,* XVIII, 3-22. Herod ended up marrying ten women who gave him fifteen sons and daughters.

[729] Moses directed Aaron, Eleazar, and each of his other worthy descendants to serve, in turn, as sole reigning high priest for his lifetime (Numbers 3:32; 4:16). During the Babylonian captivity, Ezekiel called those priests who descended from King David's late high priest, Zadok (1 Kings 1:32-34; 1 Chronicles 16:39), to keep their lineage pure; "Neither shall they take for their wives a widow, nor her that is put away [divorced]: but they shall take maidens of the seed of the house of Israel, or a widow that had a priest before" (Ezekiel 44:22).

[730] Jeremias, *Jerusalem,* 159.

witchcraft, so that some reckon 80 high-priests during that period."[731]

These and several other upheavals in political and religious leadership left the Jews divided in their loyalties. The Jews from the late Second Temple era splintered into various opposing groups: Pharisees, Sadducees, Essenes, Zealots, Hasidim, Sicarii, and others.[732] Each group claimed that its interpretation of the Torah was accurate, and the first four sects in the list evolved into the major parties during the time of the New Testament. The pharisaic rabbis lived a strict interpretation of Moses' laws and codified thousands of additional oral laws. The Sadducees comprised the temple aristocracy, with a literal interpretation of The Law that they recorded in their "book of Decrees."[733] The Essenes rejected the authority of the temple priests as corrupt, and left society to create holy communities based on Levitical purity.[734] Zealots fixated on overthrowing Roman occupation of Judea. In between all this diversity, most Jews longed for the re-emergence of a prophet or promised Messiah and freedom from Roman rule.

2. Changing Views of Women

With the growing importance of the oral laws, the intertestamental period also saw a change in opinion towards women's roles. By the time of the New Testament, we find a blatant difference in the attitudes toward women from those expressed in the Old Testament.[735] To explore those differences we will compare a few of the writings on women from the Old Testament with the Apocrypha.

The book of Genesis shows examples of wives and daughters who were allowed to lead Israel (Judges 4:4-8), move freely in public life (Ruth 1:22), look after sheep (Genesis

---

[731] *Jerusalem Talmud, Yoma* 1.1.
[732] David Noel Freedman, ed., *Eerdmans Dictionary of the Bible* (Grand Rapids, MI: Eerdmans Publishing, 2000), 712.
[733] Skolnik, *Encyclopaedia Judaica,* 15.455.
[734] Ibid., 6.511.
[735] Bromiley, *International Standard Bible Encyclopedia*, 1.1093.

29:6), draw water (Genesis 24:13; also 1 Samuel 9:11), visit each other (Genesis 34:1), and talk with men (Genesis 24:15-21; 29:11; also 1 Samuel 9:11-13). Great wives and mothers were venerated as exemplars, including five women identified as prophetesses.[736] One of those, the prophetess Deborah, also served as a judge (Judges 4-5). Another prophetess, Hildah, counseled kings (2 Kings 22:14-19). In short, opportunities for women in the Old Testament were liberal in comparison to a Jewess' options during the period of the New Testament.

The Old Testament honored many women by recording their stories. One such story is that of Ruth, the Moabitess convert, who chose to leave her people to worship Jehovah, which, in turn, supported her mother-in-law: "for whither thou goest, I will go; and where thou lodgest, I will lodge: thy people *shall be* my people, and thy God my God" (Ruth 1:16). Ruth also initiated her marriage to Boaz, who replied: "Fear not; I will do to thee all that thou requirest: for all the city of my people doth know that thou art a virtuous woman" (Ruth 3:11). Both King David and the promised Messiah are descendants of the union of Ruth and Boaz.

Another example of a noble female character from the Old Testament is Queen Esther who stood up for her people and her convictions before the Persian king (Esther 7). Her uncle testified of the hand of the Lord in her opportunity to save her people, "who knoweth whether thou art come to the kingdom for such a time as this?" (Esther 4:14).

Many other Old Testament writers spoke highly of women. Solomon eulogized a virtuous wife in Proverbs 31, leaving a clear picture of what the king valued in womanhood. For twenty verses he emphasized her independence, self-motivation, industry, service, virtue, preparedness, wisdom, and

---

[736] Prophetesses mentioned in the Old Testament: Miriam (Exodus 15:20), Deborah (Judges 4:4), Hildah (2 Kings 22:14), Noadiah (Nehemiah 6:14), and Isaiah's wife (Isaiah 8:3).

qualities as a partner. Isaiah praised nurturing mothers who possess attributes of God (Isaiah 49:15; 66:13).[737]

The Apocrypha stories are less well known, so they will receive a little more detail here. The book of Judith records an example of a strong woman who helped rebuild the Jewish nation after the Babylonian exile in the fifth century. Judith, the widow of Manasses, is an ancient type of "Joan of Arc" (Judith 8:7). She promised to deliver her nation from the Assyrians and volunteered for military service.[738] The leaders in Jerusalem trusted her to lead them, even as a woman. She discreetly kept her Judaic purity by avoiding forbidden foods and maintaining her chastity. She also gained the trust of the enemy. According to the story, our heroine got Nebuchadnezzar's general drunk and then cut off his head. In gratitude for saving the nation, the high priest Joakim personally blessed Judith (15:8). The book ends with a lengthy hymn of praise to Judith (16:1-17).[739]

Another book in the Apocrypha, Second Maccabees, praises a mother for upholding The Law and honored her as an example for all to see: "Now the mother was to be admired above measure, and worthy to be remembered by good men" (2 Maccabees 7:20). She and her seven sons resisted the tyranny of the Syrians by facing a cruel death rather than eat pork.

[She] who beheld seven sons slain in the space of one day, and bore it with a good courage, for the hope that she had in God: She bravely exhorted every one of them in her own language, being filled with wisdom: and joining a man's heart to a, woman's thought She said to them: I know not how you were formed in my womb: for I neither gave you breath, nor soul, nor life, neither did I frame the limbs of

---

[737] James H. Charlesworth, "Did Any Author in the Biblical Tradition Imagine God Having Female Breasts?" (Princeton, NJ: 2015), unpublished paper, in author's possession.

[738] This is one of the historical mistakes in the book—mixing up the Assyrian and Babylonian captivities of Israel. For more problems with the historicity of the text, see Michael D. Coogan, ed., *The New Oxford Annotated Apocrypha: New Revised Standard Version, 4th ed.* (England: Oxford University, Press, 2010), 31–36.

[739] Judith 16:6-9. 2.

every one of you. But the Creator of the world, that formed the nativity of man, and that found out the origin of all, he will restore to you again in his mercy, both breath and life, as now you despise yourselves for the sake of his laws (2 Maccabees 7:21-23).

After watching the Syrians torture six of her sons, the overlord asked the mother to convince her youngest son to deny his faith so that he could live to be rich. Instead this noble woman upheld her faith and encouraged her son to do so as well.

Bending herself towards him, mocking the cruel tyrant, she said in her own language: My son, have pity upon me, that bore thee nine months in my womb, and gave thee suck three years, and nourished thee, and brought thee up unto this age. I beseech thee, my son, look upon heaven and earth, and all that is in them: and consider that God made them out of nothing, and mankind also: o thou shalt not fear this tormentor, but being made a worthy partner with thy brethren, receive death, that in that mercy I may receive thee again with thy brethren (2 Maccabees 7:27-29).

Because of this courageous act, the last son and mother were tortured until they, too, died. The text honors all eight family members for their bravery, faith, and integrity.

Later intertestamental writings do not share this positive view of women. One text in particular, *Ecclesiasticus,* borders on misogyny. Living in Jerusalem during the second century BC, Joshua Ben Sira worked as a scribe and sage and had a long-lasting influence. Archeologists and historians have found copies of Ben Sira's text preserved in Masada, and in the Dead Sea Scrolls, Septuagint, Apocrypha and Talmud.[740] His proverb style writings include statements that demean women. It appears he was unhappy in his marriage as he wrote things like:

There is no poison above the poison of a serpent, and there is no wrath above the wrath of a woman. . . . [There is] little malice like the malice of a woman. May the lot of the wicked fall upon her.

---

[740] Skolnik, *Encyclopedia Judaica,* 3.376-377. Ben Sira's *Ecclesiasticus,* is also known in Greek as *Sirach,* or the *Wisdom of Sirach* as described earlier.

As a sandy ascent to the feet of the aged,
So is the woman of tongue to a quiet man.
Fall not through the beauty of a woman,
And be not ensnared by what she possesseth;
For hard slavery and a disgrace it is,
[If] a wife support her husband.
A humbled heart and a sad countenance
And a heart-wound, is an evil wife.
Hands that hand down, and palsied knees
For a wife that maketh not her husband happy.
From a woman did sin originate,
And because of her we all must die.
Give not water an outlet,
Nor power to a wicked woman.
If she go not as thou would have her
Cut her off from thy flesh.[741]

These verses and the rest of his book leave the reader assuming that the author believed that an ideal wife was a silent servant who submitted to all her husband's commands and only spoke to praise him.

3. Changes to Family Life

Between the two Testaments, many Jewish leaders reacted against the growing female freedoms allowed in Hellenistic society. Even though the Jews tried to remain a separate people, after they returned from their Babylonian captivity that became more and more challenging as the Greeks Hellenized the Mediterranean world from the fourth century on. By the time of the Second Temple, the majority of the Jews lived outside of Palestine.[742] At the same time, within Palestine, Gentile

---

[741] Ben Sira, *Ecclesiasticus,* 25:15-26. Richard Green Moulton's translation of the same verses reads, "Throw not thyself upon the beauty of a woman, and desire not a woman for her beauty. There is anger, and impudence, and great reproach, if a woman maintain her husband."

[742] *Encyclopædia Britannica Online*, s. v. "Diaspora", accessed March 23, 2015, http://www.britannica.com/ EBchecked/topic/161756/Diaspora. Going

neighbors brought some degree of Hellenization and Romanization to the Jewish homeland. In order to maintain their old traditions and protect themselves from outside ideas, they developed a public and private division of life, with women living inside and men outside. Their houses were also arranged to discourage females from contact with any males outside their own homes. This female isolation and male domination generated a negative image of women over time.[743]

The seemingly pious practice of separation, the lack of communication between genders, and unrighteous dominion snuffed out the God-given marital mandate from Eden that directed husbands and wives to become "help meets" or co-equals: "And the LORD God said, *It is* not good that the man should be alone; I will make him an help meet for him . . . Therefore shall a man leave his father and his mother, and shall cleave unto his wife: and they shall be one flesh" (Genesis 2:18, 24). At the end of Joachim Jeremias' treatise on *Jerusalem at the Time of Jesus*, he summarized, "We have therefore the impression that Judaism in Jesus' time also had a very low opinion of women, which is usual in the Orient where she is chiefly valued for her fecundity, kept as far as possible, shut away from the outer world, submissive to the power of her father or her husband, and where she is inferior to men."[744] Generally speaking, by the time of the late Second Temple, women were not valued as equals with men, but viewed like servants.

4. Changes in the Messianic Hope

---

back to the sixth century BC, only a portion of the Jews returned to Palestine after the Babylonian captivity. "The largest, most significant, and culturally most creative Jewish Diaspora in early Jewish history flourished in Alexandria, in the first century BC, forty percent of the population was Jewish. Around the first century AD, an estimated 5,000,000 Jews lived outside Palestine, about four-fifths of them within the Roman Empire, but they looked to Palestine as the centre of their religious and cultural life."
[743] See page 25, and chapter 1 "Segregation."
[744] Jeremias, *Jerusalem*, 359-376.

During the intertestamental period, rabbis and scribes combed through their Scriptures for promises of the coming Messiah. They looked for a conquering Messiah who would rid them of their foreign overlords. Rabbis counted 456 prophesies of the Messiah in the Old Testament.[745] They collected prophecies that anticipated His coming, like the *Psalms of Solomon,* which was written during the late Second Temple period.

> See, Lord, raise up for them their king, the son of David,
> In the time which thou knowest, O God.
> To reign over Israel thy servant;
> And gird him with strength to shatter the unjust rulers…
> He will possess the nations, to serve beneath his yoke;
> He will glorify the Lord with the praise of all the earth,
> He will cleanse Jerusalem in holiness, as it was of old,
> That the nations may come from the ends of the earth to see his glory,
> Bringing as gifts her sons who had fainted,
> And to see the glory of the Lord with which God has glorified her.
> A righteous king, taught by God, is their ruler, And
> there will be no unrighteousness among them all his days,
> For all will be holy, and their king the Anointed Lord.[746]

Exactly what they expected in their promised Messiah differed between Jewish groups and even *within* those groups.

---

[745]Walter C. Kaiser, *The Messiah in the Old Testament* (Grand Rapids, MI: Zondervan, 1995), 29. "In some 558 rabbinic writings there are 456 separate OT passages used to refer to the Messiah." The following numbers differ, but some claim the Pentateuch has seventy-five prophecies testifying of the coming Messiah, the Prophets 243, and the writings 138. Carl E. Armerding, W. Ward Gasque, ed., *A Guide to Biblical Prophecy* (Eugene, OR: Wipf and Stock, 2001), 87.

[746] *Psalms of Solomon,* 17:23, 32-36, quoted by F. F. Bruce, *New Testament History* (New York: Doubleday, 1969), 126. "The Psalms of Solomon have commonly been regarded as Pharisaic compositions, but they may more generally express the sentiments of any pious community cherishing the hope of Israel."

Jews from the late Second Temple era could not agree if the promised Messiah was connected with the house of David (Genesis 49:10; Numbers 24:17; Micah 5:2), or the house of Joseph,[747] or the priestly house of Aaron (as the Essenes thought).[748] Zechariah 4:11-14 describes two anointed ones or Messiahs, often interpreted as one Messiah from Aaron.[749] Another interesting tie to Aaron comes from Elisabeth. The only reference we have in Scripture to Mary's blood lineage is through her kinswoman Elisabeth, "of the daughters of Aaron," (Luke 1:5, 36). Both New Testament genealogies give a lineage for Joseph (not Mary), and through different lineages, claim that Joseph was a descendant of David (Matthew 1:1, 16; Luke 3:23, 31). As an adopted son, Jesus would have claimed his father Joseph's pedigree.[750] However, if Mary shared a blood line with Elisabeth, then Jesus may also have had an Aaronic blood line. Further evidence for this premise comes from an ancient document that listed Nazareth as a designated village where priests lived.[751] Uncertain as this hypothesis is, it

---

[747] Israel Knohl, "The Messiah Son of Joseph," *Biblical Archaeology Review* (Sept/Oct 2008; vol. 34, no. 5), 58. There are Judaic traditions that speak of a Messiah ben Joseph. This idea is stated in the Babylonian Talmud, and also in a three-foot stone dating from around the first century BC that records the Messiah son of Joseph giving signs to David.

[748] S. Kent Brown, Richard Neitzel Holzapfel, *Between the Testaments: From Malachi to Matthew* (2010), 197.

[749] Coogan, *Oxford History of the Biblical World*, 189. Some Christians often interpret this as being fulfilled in the Aaronic line through John the Baptist and the Davidic line through Jesus of Nazareth. Amy-Jill Levine, Dale C. Allison Jr., John Dominic Crossan, eds., *The Historical Jesus in Context* (Princeton, NJ: Princeton University Press, 2006), 113.

[750] Brown, *Birth,* 89. At the time of the Second Temple, Jews traced their lineage through their paternal line. An adopted child would have assumed his new father's genealogy. Because the two genealogies have more differences than similarities, some Bible readers rationalize that one is for Joseph and the other Mary—but this is neither scripturally nor culturally valid. "Even at first glance, however, this solution cannot be taken seriously: a *genealogy* traced through the mother is not normal in Judaism."

[751] Fitzmyer, *Luke I-IX*, 343. Even though Nazareth is not mentioned in the Old Testament, "a Hebrew inscription found in 1962 . . . listed the twenty-four priestly courses and the villages or towns where they were resident" with *Nsrt,* or Nazareth, as one of them.

purports that Jesus' parentage also rendered Him both Priest and King (Hebrews 4:14).

The hope of a messiah waxed and waned over the years.[752] Writings from the Dead Sea Scrolls describe three special Messiahs that represent, respectively, the "kingdom, priesthood, and prophecy."[753] By the time of the New Testament, we know of many who were primed and eagerly waiting for the Davidic Messiah's arrival (i.e., Simeon the temple-goer in Luke 2:25-35; Anna the prophetess in Luke 2:36-38; the two disciples on the road to Emmaus in Luke 24:21; John and Andrew, who were first disciples of John the Baptist, as recorded in John 1:41; etc.). The angel who appeared to the shepherds announced the Messiah's birth, "Today in the town of David a Savior has been born to you; he is the Messiah, the Lord" (Luke 2:11, NIV). Three decades later, locals debated, "Others said, 'He is the Messiah.' Still others asked, 'How can the Messiah come from Galilee?'" (John 7:41, NIV). Yet others, like Andrew, recognized the fulfillment of the prophecies and felt a witness that Jesus was the promised anointed one. Excitedly, Andrew shared the news with his brother Peter, "'We have found the Messiah' (which means Christ)" (John 1:41, ESV).

5. Changing The Law with 10,000 Oral Laws

Many Jews, the Pharisees in particular, believed that the Mosaic law would save them eternally. During the Second Temple period, some Jews became obsessed with micromanaging each detail of the 613 commandments recorded in Genesis, Exodus, Leviticus, Numbers, and Deuteronomy (also known as The Law, Pentateuch, or Torah). They dissected

---

[752] Skolnik, *Encyclopaedia Judaica,* 14.111. "In the time of the Second Temple there was a greater variety of messianic figures than later."

[753] Ibid., "These two figures, the priest and the king, are important for the eschatology of the Dead Sea Sect. . . . The third figure occurring in the Dead Sea Scrolls with the two messiahs is the prophet of the Last Days. Thus, in the Dead Sea Scrolls there are three messianic figures." LDS see the Prophet Joseph Smith as fitting the latter role. Also see 1 Maccabees 14:41.

Moses' laws into ten thousand additional commandments known as the oral law. The Pharisees respected the oral laws as Scripture: "the authoritative interpretation of the Written Law."[754] The rabbinic tradition claimed that the oral laws were handed down from Moses as instructions on how to fulfill the commandments written in the Torah. Different groups of Jews interpreted them differently, and the *Mishnah* includes examples of different pharisaical schools of thought arguing over different ways to interpret The Law.[755]

God created The Law for a holy people, to prepare them to receive their Messiah (i.e., Isaiah 40:3; Malachi 3:1). Yet the Jews who accepted the oral laws as divine emphasized the minutiae of The Law, which often distracted them from seeing God's overall purpose (2 Nephi 11:4; 25:24-27; Jacob 4:5). Over time, the oral laws became so important to the Pharisees that they "circumvent[ed] the Written Law."[756] They dedicated their lives to keeping each detail in order. The extra particulars of the oral laws restricted agency and brought an attitude of judgment and slavery to the oral laws. As one Jewish historian described, the oral laws became "the yoke of the kingdom of Heaven."[757]

The oral laws affected, and in some cases crippled, the family unit. The daily routine of the home was tightly controlled by detailed boundaries. Every aspect of home life—from food preparation, cleaning, washing, eating, to Sabbath observance and one's sex life—was governed by hundreds of laws. Some families concentrated more on how they washed their hands than on how they applied God's central direction—

[754] Ibid., 15.454.
[755] *Mishnah, Yadaim,* 4:7, "The Sadducees say, 'We cry out against you, O ye Pharisees, for ye declare clean an unbroken stream of liquid.' The Pharisees say, 'We cry out against you, O ye Sadducees, for ye declare clean a channel of water that flows from a burial ground.'. . ."
[756] Ibid., 15.456.
[757] Ibid., 15.456.

to "love thy neighbour as thyself: I am the LORD."(Leviticus 19:18).[758]

The New Testament often refers to the oral laws, or traditions of the elders, in a negative light (Matthew 15:3-6; Mark 7:5-13; Galatians 1:14). Jesus condemned them for crowding out the "weightier *matters* of the law, judgment, mercy, and faith" (Matthew 23:23). Luke 11:42 uses stronger language to denounce the oral laws: "Woe to you Pharisees, because you give God a tenth of your mint, rue and all other kinds of garden herbs, but you neglect justice and the love of God" (NIV, also Matthew 23:23). Not only did the oral laws distract them from living God's higher laws, it also blinded them from recognizing and receiving their promised Messiah.

6. Changing Temple Ritual

Temple worship also changed from Moses' Tabernacle to Herod's Temple. As Herod's building project tripled the size of the temple and its courtyards, and the Jewish population grew and spread around the Roman Empire, temple worship adapted for the diverse population. The greater size gave a greater message—the God of the Jews is important. According to the law of Moses, God commanded each healthy Israelite to come to the temple to worship (Exodus 23:14; Deuteronomy 16:16-17). At the time of the late Second Temple, from all around the Roman world, Jews in the Diaspora made a pilgrimage to Jerusalem. The most devout Israelites made an annual pilgrimage to Jerusalem to offer sacrifice on their holy days. More specifically, by the time of Herod's Temple, they came for at least one of the three week-long feasts each year in the spring, early summer, and fall: Passover (Pesach), Weeks or Pentecost (Shavuot), and Tabernacles or Ingathering (Sukkot)—the most important being Passover.

---

[758] Wilfried Warnin, *Literary Artistry in Leviticus* (Leiden, Netherlands: Brill, 1990), 14. Leviticus 19:18 is claimed as the summit or chiastic center and heart of the Torah. This verse is the climax of the "Holiness Code."

Jews prized their temple above all other places of worship. The Jews felt the temple mount in Jerusalem was the center of the earth.[759] The Psalmist wrote:

> On the holy mount stands the city he founded;
> The LORD loves the gates of Zion
> More than all the dwellings of Jacob.
> Glorious things are spoken of you.
> O city of God (Psalms 87:1-3, NRSV).

The temple, and even more specifically the Holy of Holies within the Sanctuary, was the most sacred place in the world to a Jew. The *Mishnah* outlined "ten degrees of holiness" to describe their temple precincts.[760]

> The land of Israel is holier than all lands ...
> The walled cities [of the Land of Israel]
> Within the wall [of Jerusalem] is more holy
> The temple Mount is more holy ...
> The rampart is still more holy
> The Court of the Women is still more holy
> The Court of the Israelites is still more holy
> The Court of the Priests is still more holy
> Between the porch and the altar is still more holy than it
> The sanctuary is still more holy than it ...
> The Holy of Holies is still more holy than they.

Jews carefully differentiated their divisions of sacred space. Ancient temples represented the principle of ordering the universe.[761] Their reverence for their temple reverberates throughout the text as it illustrates the central role that Jerusalem and the temple held for them—with a special devotion for the Holy of Holies where the high priest symbolically entered into the Lord's presence.[762]

---

[759] Charlesworth, ed., *Jesus and Temple,* 3.

[760] *Mishnah, Kelim,* 1:6-9.

[761] Hugh Nibley, *Temple and Cosmos* (Salt Lake City, UT: FARMS, Deseret Book, 1992), 42, 15, 19. "Civilization is heirocentric, centered on the holy point of the temple. . . . The temple is also an observatory. That is what a *templum* is—a place where you take your bearings on things."

[762] During the time of Solomon's Temple, the Bible referred to the inner sanctuary of the Holy of Holies as "the oracle" (1 Kings 6:31).

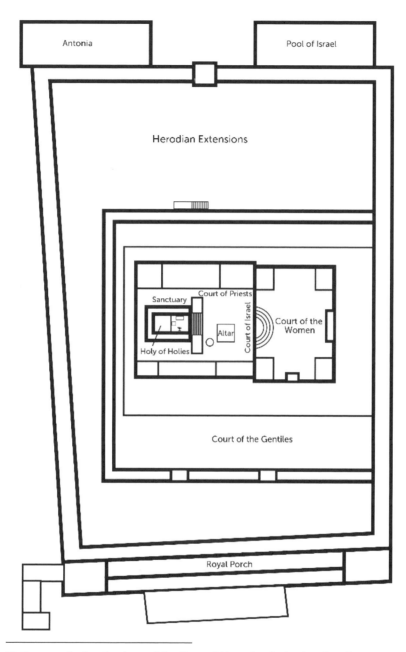

Unfortunately, by the time of the Second Temple, the Holy of Holies was empty—no Ark of the Covenant, no budding rod, no manna, no tables of The Law, no book of the covenant. Yet, after the destruction of Herod's Temple, Jews faced the Holy of Holies when they prayed in remembrance of that holy space.

Priesthood Ministers

At the time of the New Testament, temple workers included all healthy male descendants of Jacob's son Levi in the Levitical priesthood. Among the Levites, a higher position of honor was given to those direct descendants of Aaron. Aaronic priesthood holders could function as priests, chief priests, or the high priest. The hierarchy of offices was organized as follows:

A. One Reigning High Priest

B. Chief Priests: The captains of the temple[763]

    1. Cultus: leaders of the 24 weekly divisions/courses[764]
    2. Custody of the temple: temple overseers
    3. Temple finances: three treasurers

C. Priests: ~7,200[765] divided into twenty-four weekly courses each of four to nine daily courses

D. Levites: ~9,600[766] divided into 24 weekly courses as:

    1. Singers and musicians
    2. Temple servants and guards

Levites took care of the more secular tasks of running the temple—acting as the temple police, gatekeepers, tax collectors,

---

[763] See Introduction, under "Sadducees."

[764] In Hebrew, "course" is also "company." Brigham Young used the same pattern to divide the pioneers into "companies" as they paralleled the history of Israel walking to their promised land.

[765] Jeremias, *Jerusalem*, 200, 198-206. Supposedly, four families of priests returned to Jerusalem from Babylon, each containing just under 5,000 men, for a total of approximately 18,000 priests available to serve in Zerubbabel's Temple. This represented only a fraction of the priests who remained in Babylon or lived across the Diaspora.

[766] The number of temple workers was dramatically reduced from the 38,000 Levites of Solomon's day (1 Chronicles 23:3), or the 22,000 of Moses' day (Numbers 3:39).

janitors, fire keepers, and musicians.[767] They served at the temple between the ages of twenty-five and fifty, according to Numbers 8:24-25 (or starting at twenty, according to 1 Chronicles 23:24). The male descendants of Aaron performed the majority of the temple sacrifices, and began their priestly service at the age of thirty, finishing at age fifty (Numbers 4:3, 23, 35). Priests acted as mediators between God and men as they served at the altar. They placed a slain animal on the altar and sprinkled its blood on the horns and corners of the altar (Leviticus 4:6-7, 24-25). At the time of Herod's Temple, these priests served in the temple for five weeks a year: one week every six months, plus during the three weeks associated with the three major Israelite pilgrimage feasts: Passover, Pentecost, and Tabernacles or Booths.

On each day of their temple duty, the priests gathered before sunrise to wash in a purifying mikveh bath, dress in white linen, and receive their temple assignments for the day. When they assembled, they prayed and recited a confession of their faith: the Ten Commandments (Exodus 20:3-17) and the *shema* (Deuteronomy 6:4-9; 11:13-21; Numbers 15:37-41). To determine his daily assignment, each priest put his unique token or lot in a dish. Five lots were selected for the most important assignments of the day. The priests believed that the Lord, or his angel, would draw out the token belonging to the priest that God wanted to serve that day.[768] The assignments included:

1) Cleanse the altar and prepare a fire for the burnt animal offering[769]

---

[767] David Noel Freedman, ed., *Eerdmans Dictionary of the Bible* (Grand Rapids, MI: Eerdmans Publishing, 2000), 804. Interestingly, the singers taught and interpreted The Law as they recited it in song. Levites were also in charge of "the furniture and utensils, the flour, wine, oil, incense, and spices"—everything required for the service (1 Chronicles 9:29, NIV; 9:26-32; 23:24-29)."

[768] Edersheim, *Temple,* chapters 7 and 8.

[769] *Mishnah, Tamid,* 2:3. For the sacrificial altar they used "only olive wood and wood of the vine." For the incense altar, "fine pieces of fig wood" (2:5).

2) Sacrifice the lamb, catch the blood, sprinkle it seven times, cleanse the candlestick and altar incense, and carry the animal's limbs to the ramp

3) Burn incense in the Holy Place and offer the priestly prayer

4) Place the daily meat offering on the altar

5) Offer incense in the afternoon in the Holy Place

When selecting the priest to light the incense in the Holy Place, only those descendants of Aaron who had not yet had the opportunity were allowed to submit their lot. Lighting the incense on the golden altar was the most honored position among the priests. The smoke from the incense symbolized prayer as a "cloud of odors rose up before the Lord."[770] This opportunity may have been the only time in a priest's life that he entered into the holy sanctuary.[771] This twice-daily ritual fulfilled the commandment given to Aaron to burn incense "every morning ... [and] at even . . . perpetual incense before the Lord throughout your generations" (Exodus 30:7-8). The afternoon incense offering was lit at the ninth hour (3:00 in the afternoon), which was also known as "the time of prayer" (see Acts 3:1; Daniel 9:21).[772] Offering the incense symbolized Israel's accepted prayers and became the most solemn part of the temple service.[773]

---

[770] Edersheim, *Temple*, 167; and Revelation 8:1, 3, 4.

[771] Other priests may be selected by the incense lighter, to help him remove the ashes from the incense alter in the Holy Sanctuary. Also, once a week, a priest replaced the shewbread in the Sanctuary.

[772] Angel Gabriel visited Daniel during a time of prayer (Daniel 9:21), and Elijah received fire to consume his offering on Mount Carmel—"at the time of the offering of the evening sacrifice" (1 Kings 18:36).

[773] David Bercot, ed. *A Dictionary of Early Christian Belief: A Reference Guide to More Than 700 Topics Discussed by the Early Church Fathers* (Peabody, MA: Hendrickson, 1998), 660. Bridging from the old covenant to the new, the early Christian Clement of Alexandria (c. 195) also understood

The chief priests at the time of Herod's Temple were often wealthy Sadducees who received their positions through political favors. Initially, the office of the high priest was given to the first-born or worthy son of the reigning priest, who then served for life (Numbers 3:32; 4:16; Ezra 7:5). But as mentioned above, under Roman rule, during the late Second Temple, the high priest's office was arbitrarily chosen from among the chief priests. No longer was the position lifelong or associated with lineage. This most important priesthood position became a short-term political delegation that was hotly contested among the chief priests.

As outlined in the law of Moses, the office of the high priest held the responsibility to ensure that the temple rites ran according to God's direction (Exodus 28:28-30; Leviticus 6:22; 16:32; etc.). The high priest offered sacrifice for the people's sins, and figuratively bore "the iniquity of the holy things, which the children of Israel shall hallow in all their holy gifts" (Exodus 28:38).

Day of Atonement

Once a year on the Day of Atonement, the high priest had the sacred honor to act as an intercessor for his people by communing with the Lord through the veil and entering into the Holy of Holies (Leviticus 16; Hebrews 9:6-7). He prepared for that day by a week of purification, sacred washings (or a mikveh bath) and clothing while residing in the temple precincts.[774] According to the law of Moses, the high priest then performed seven solemn rituals in the sanctuary, which included blessing the children of Israel and taking their names before the mercy seat (Exodus 28:29-30).[775] On that day, the

---

"that blended incense that is mentioned in The Law is that which consists of many tongues and voices in prayer."

[774] *Mishnah, Moed: Yoma*, 1.

[775] First, the high priest sacrificed a bullock as a vicarious sin offering for "himself, and for his house" (Leviticus 16:6; also 4, 11). Second, he passed through the veil into the Holy of Holies with coals to burn "sweet incense beaten small, . . . that the cloud of incense may cover the mercy seat that is

high priest's responsibilities symbolized the sacred journey into heaven as he washed in the Holy Place, was anointed with holy oil, clothed in priesthood robes, offered sacrifices, released the scapegoat, and entered into the Lord's presence. The high priest then changed out of his white holy garments in the sanctuary and returned to the courtyard in his colorful high priestly robe, representative of, or symbolic of, returning to earth.

With the changes made during the late Second Temple era to the office of high priest, this holy day lost its sacred authority. The Essenes were especially upset about the changes in priesthood and the impurity it brought to the temple.[776]

Temple Sacrifices

Temple sacrifices were the height of religious worship for Jewish men and women during the Second Temple. Sacrifices were symbols to communicate the Lord's message of

---

upon the testimony, that he die not" (Leviticus 16:12-13). He left the most holy room to collect the bullock's blood. Once the smoke filled the Holy of Holies, he returned to perform the third ritual by sprinkling the bullock's blood on—and before—the mercy seat seven times (Leviticus 16:15). Sprinkling seven times represented the complete or perfect cleansing from the throne of God. Fourth, he brought two young goats into the sanctuary that had previously been selected for this sacred day, "one lot for the LORD, and the other lot for the scapegoat" (Leviticus 16:8). After sacrificing the LORD's goat, he brought its blood through the veil and repeated the sprinkling seven times on and before the mercy seat (Leviticus 16:14-15). Fifth he made "an atonement for the holy place, because of the uncleanness of the children of Israel, and because of their transgressions in all their sins: and so shall he do for the tabernacle of the congregation" (Leviticus 16:16). Sixth, he brought the scapegoat out and "la[id] both his hands upon the head of the live goat, and confess[ed] over him all the iniquities of the children of Israel, and all their transgressions in all their sins, putting them upon the head of the goat" (Leviticus 16:21). This goat was led "away by the hand of a fit man into the wilderness" as the scapegoat, or the sin bearer (Leviticus 16:21-22). Seventh, the high priest recited the blessing from Numbers 6:24-26, verbalizing the *tetragrammaton* or name of God, "YHWH."

[776] Skolnik, *Encyclopaedia Judaica,* 6.511. "On the evidence of the Dead Sea Scrolls, they deemed themselves the only true Israel and regarded the religious observance of other Israelites, and especially in the temple, as corrupt."

redemption.[777] Leviticus, the third book of Moses, acted as a priesthood instruction manual for sacrifices from Moses' Tabernacle until the destruction of Herod's Temple. It outlines two general types of sacrificial offerings: obligatory (sin and trespass), and voluntary (burnt, peace/wave, and meal/cereal).[778] Within the category of voluntary offerings, we read of peace offerings that were offered in thanksgiving (Leviticus 3:1-17; 7:11, 29; etc.). "When the three offerings— sin, burnt, and peace—were offered together, they symbolized respectively the progression from atonement through sanctification to fellowship with the Lord. Thus the law of sacrifice was instituted to point men to Christ and finally to sanctify them."[779]

Each morning and evening, the Israelites were commanded to offer a lamb. Moses taught them in Exodus 29:37-43, that as they did, God would meet them at the altar, speak to them, and sanctify them:

> . . . Whatsoever toucheth the altar shall be holy. Now this is that which thou shalt offer upon the altar; two

---

[777] Blood sacrifice was taught "from the days of Adam down to the resurrection of Christ" (Alma 40:18). An angel taught Adam, "This thing is a similitude of the sacrifice of the Only Begotten of the Father, which is full of grace and truth. Wherefore, thou shalt do all that thou doest in the name of the Son, and thou shalt repent and call upon God in the name of the Son forevermore" (Moses 5:7-8). The Lord instigated sacrifices to look "forward to the coming of Christ, considering that the law of Moses was a type of his coming" (Alma 25:15). Yet few who sacrificed to fulfill The Law realized their symbolic rituals (Galatians 5:4).

[778] Loris DeMarco, *Sweeter Than Honey* (Winston-Salem, NC: Salem Publishing Solutions, 2009), 123.One of the words used for sacrificial offerings found in Leviticus 1:3 and 7:16, is in Hebrew, *qorban* or *korban* (קרב). "The roots of this word share ties with 'close' 'to draw near,'" and 'approaching.'" This etymology explains that the sacrifice was a means to draw near to God.

[779] Kent Jackson and Robert Millet, eds., *Studies in Scripture*, 5: 241. A peace offering was also called a wave offering because the priest solemnly waved it before the Lord (Exodus 29:24, 26, 27; Leviticus. 7:28-30; 8:27; 10:14; etc.). Wave offerings also included a sheaf of barley offered as the first fruits during Pentecost or Passover (Leviticus 23:10-20).

lambs of the first year day by day continually. The one lamb thou shalt offer in the morning; and the other lamb thou shalt offer at even . . . This shall be a continual burnt offering throughout your generations at the door of the tabernacle of the congregation before the LORD: where I will meet you, to speak there unto thee. And there I will meet with the children of Israel, and the tabernacle shall be sanctified by my glory.

The Mosaic law designed sacrifices and temple worship to draw Israelites closer to God.[780]

Temple Worship for Woman and Families

According to the Law of Moses, families could bring their own animals to the temple for sacrifices (Leviticus 3:6). Theoretically, women could offer many of the sacrifices that men did (Exodus 35:29). Additionally, women were required to offer one for purification after childbirth (Leviticus 12:2-4),[781] after monthly menses (Leviticus 15:28-30), and if suspected to have committed adultery (as a "jealousy offering" Numbers 5:18-26).

However, by the time of Herod's Temple, most offerings were reduced to simply paying for the desired sacrifice. The Mishnah recalled that a woman was not required to be present at the temple for her offering—as long as she paid the money for her sacrifice, she became purified.[782] If women chose to go to the temple, they could observe but not participate. This was one of the changes that affected the Israelites of the

---

[780] Edersheim, *Temple,* 107. "This idea of substitution, as introduced, adopted, and sanctioned by God Himself, is expressed by the sacrificial term rendered in our version [KJV], 'atonement,' but which really means covering, the substitute in the acceptance of God taking the place of, and so covering, as it were, the person of the offerer." Also see Leviticus 17:11; Psalms 32:1-2; 84:9.

[781] See chapter one.

[782] Mishnah, *Qiddushin* 1 :7 "The observance of all the positive ordinances that depend on the time of year is incumbent on men but not on women."

intertestamental period. Some women still chose to worship at Herod's Temple; the New Testament records that the prophetess Anna and mother Mary did so regularly (Luke 2:22-24, 37, 41).

Another change in Herod's Temple was the addition of a sixty-eight-square-yard court called the Court of the Women. This courtyard was open to all clean Israelites, male or female, young or old, but it was the only sacred place women or children could go—as the other holy courts were reserved for men, Levites, and priests. Women were to stay along the edges to segregate them from the men. The Court of the Women is probably where the twelve-year-old Jesus spoke to the "doctors" (Luke 2:46), where Jesus often taught (Mark 12:35; Luke 18:47; 20:1; John 7:14; 8:2, 20), and where He saw the widow pay her two mites in the treasury (Mark 12:41-43; Luke 21:1).[783]

---

[783] Edersheim, *Temple,* 26. The Court of the Women also housed the treasury. Thirteen trumpet-shaped containers lined the perimeter of the courtyard where worshipers paid for their sacrifices. The chief priest over the treasury labeled each vessel with the price for each sacrifice that day.

Appendix 2
Greco-Roman Family Life
Within the New Testament

This appendix will briefly look at five aspects of the Greco-Roman world that relate to family life in the New Testament. It does not purport to provide an overview of the Roman world at the time of the Apostolic church, but only touches on significant historical connections with the Greco-Roman world that help one understand the New Testament better: 1) Hellenism, 2) Caesars and Domestic Reforms, 3) Population and Life expectancy, 4) Greco-Roman Family Life, and 5) Religious life.

1. Hellenism

The Greco-Roman world had a major influence on the culture and writing of the New Testament. The Greek penetration or Hellenization of the Euro-Asian-African world had been in progress for three hundred years before Christ's birth. The extensive conquest by Alexander the Great (356-323 BC) started the process of unifying the Mediterranean portions of the three continents under one academic language: Greek. The use of a single language had a unifying effect on the Empire. It opened the doorway for multicultural communication in religion, philosophy, science, art, and business. For this reason, the authors of the New Testament wrote in Greek.[784]

───

[784] Ben Whitherington, *History, Literature, and Society in the Book of Acts* (New York: Cambridge University Press, 1996), 327. Luke may have been the only Gospel written in the author's mother tongue. Luke/Acts has the best Greek in the New Testament, with Hebrews as the closest competition (which one tradition holds was translated by Luke from Paul's Hebrew).

Friction grew as Greek philosophy came into contact with Judaic ideals. This caused trouble when the Jews would not alter their customs, values, and theology to fit with Hellenized cosmopolitan ideas as other conquered nations did.[785] The Jews reacted against the rising tide of hedonism by digging deeper into their own peculiar beliefs. Almost like a pendulum swinging to opposite poles, as the Greco-Romans gave more public opportunities to women, the Jews kept them more at home. We see this in dress: as the Greco-Roman women wore less clothing, the Jews covered their women more completely.

Yet over time, and in spite of the devoted efforts of the conservative Jewish leaders, some aspects of Greek thought did infiltrate Jewish homes. One of the best examples of this is the fact that Jewish scribes translated their holy writings (The Law, Prophets, and Writings) into Greek (LXX) allowing greater accessibility by the Jews living across the Empire.

Not all Greek and Roman ideology was hedonistic, and many aspects of Hellenism left a positive stamp on the world. Their advances in engineering, architecture, literature, and the arts continue to bless the world. We also see that breakthroughs in individual rights for men, women, and children happened during this time. The New Testament Epistles are sprinkled with names of Greco-Roman women.[786] Yet, in the women's Hellenized public world, "there was no approved public forum for any kind of women's self-expression" from politics to the arts and religion.[787]

---

[785] Bromiley, *International Standard Bible Encyclopedia*, L. Morris, "Hellensism," 2.680. "The cosmopolitans never could understand the obstinacy with which the provincials clung to their narrow outlook."
[786] Sarah Ruden, *Paul Among the People: The Apostle Reinterpreted and Reimagined in His Own Time* (New York: Pantheon Books, 2010), 81.
[787] Ibid., 80. That said, we still understand that "No Greeks or Romans thought women should participate in government. . . . They had ritual functions. Some were priestesses. All citizen women took part in public ceremonies from time to time, on special occasions. They watched, or made the motions and spoke the traditional words (if any). . . . A few women created literature, but not for reciting in public. . . women elbow[ed] into discussions in the street."

2. The Caesars and Domestic Reforms

During his forty-five-year reign (31 BC to AD 14), [788] Caesar Augustus fostered a revival of Roman tradition, established peace, supported business and industry, made taxation more equitable, and enacted legislation to foster stronger families. From an ancient eastern perspective, Augustus did much to strengthen Roman family life. Prior to his reign, Roman fathers had the power of life and death over their wives and children.

Between 18 BC and AD 9, Augustus enacted laws that encouraged marriage and the production of children. [789] If a Roman woman had three living children, she was rewarded by being released from guardianship—an imposed condition where women had an older male guardian watching over and advising them. [790] (A non-Roman woman needed four children for the same benefit.) Also, having children improved the chance to inherit relatives' or friends' property. Augustus decreased the amount of money a childless husband could inherit from his progenitors. He also allowed politicians to hold an office longer if they had children—one year for each child. [791]

---

[788] Jacob Abbott, *History of Julius Caesar* (New York and London: Harpers, 1899), 230. Initially the Senate appointed Julius Caesar a leader for a short period of a ten-year reign. In 44 BC they made him ruler for life and gave him the title, "Father of his Country."

[789] Campbell, *Marriage and Family in the Biblical World*, 144. As touched on in chapter 4, Augustus fined a married couple if they did not have a child by the time the wife was twenty and the husband twenty-five years old. Thurston, *Women in the New Testament*, 22. We still find unequal punishments between gender under Augustus' government. Adultery became a public offense only for women, as it posed a threat to a citizen's succession and property inheritance.

[790] Mary R. Lefkowitz and Maureen B. Fant, *Women's Life in Greece and Rome: A Source Book in Translation,* 2nd ed. (Baltimore, MD: John Hopkins University Press, 1992), 101. Quoting from Roman law, "Guardians are appointed for males as well as for females, but only for males under puberty, on account of their infirmity of age; for females, however, both under and over puberty, on account of weakness of their sex as well as their ignorance of legal matters."

[791] Campbell, *Marriage and Family in the Biblical World,* 150.

Augustus tried to strengthen the family by reviving morality in the Roman Empire and promoting chastity.[792] He forbade "bequest" marriages and tightened divorce laws in an attempt to strengthen the family.[793] He fined widows and divorcées for remaining single over two years if they were still fertile, and had not yet had three children.[794] Yet, he was unable to stop the tide of immorality that plagued Roman life.[795]

Augustus also attempted to rectify other social values. He stimulated traditional religion in Rome by adding Julius Caesar's name (his adopted father) to the list of Roman deities. He bolstered the official religion by building eighty-two temples throughout the Empire. Those temples housed festivals as the mainstay of religious life. He encouraged small home-run businesses by intentionally wearing wool clothes made by his wife and daughter, thus advertising his plan to re-establish traditional ideas. He also instituted reforms for slaves that improved their conditions throughout the Empire. Augustus did much to create a healthier family life, but his new legislation

---

[792] Ann Witherington, *Women and the Genesis of Christianity* (Reprint, New York: Cambridge University Press, 1990), 22-23. The previous edition was under the first name Ben.

[793] George A. Buttrick, *The Interpreter's Dictionary of the Bible*, "Roman Empire," 4.105-106. As mentioned earlier, he also fined males and females for remaining single past certain ages. Witherington, *Women and the Genesis of Christianity,* 23. The only Roman women not required to marry were the Vestal Virgins, women over fifty, or those with three children.

[794] See chapter 6.

[795] Ibid. "In his social reforms, the Emperor Augustus promoted the cults advocating chastity, childbirth, and strong familial bonds. Coupling this with Augustus' effort to legally force widows and divorcées to marry, as well as the fine he placed on both males and females for remaining single past accepted ages, we can see how much Augustus desired to eliminate public and private situations where women were independent of men." Initially Augustus granted a grace period of eighteen months for remarriage without a fine, but that was extended to two years. Suetonius claimed it was three years, but this is not supported elsewhere. Karl Galinsky, *Augustan Culture: An Interpretive Introduction* (Princeton, NJ: Princeton University Press, 1996), 131. Mireille Corbier, "Divorce and Adoption as Roman Familial Strategies," in *Marriage, Divorce, and Children in Ancient Rome*, eds. Beryl Rawson (England: Oxford University Press, 1991), 47-78. The question of whether Jews living in Judea were taxed does not have a clear answer.

still fell short of gender equality, chastity before marriage, and fidelity during marriage.

Caesars from the New Testament Era

During the period of Jesus' life and the apostolic church, eight emperors ruled the Roman world. From Augustus to Domitian, each Caesar intersected in some aspect with Christians mentioned in the New Testament. We will briefly look at each one and how they fit into the scriptural history.

TABLE: 3

Caesar	Reign	Verses	Connection with New Testament
Augustus Caesar 63 BC- AD 14	31BC- AD 14	Luke 2:1	Luke draws attention to the ironic political dichotomy between Augustus and Jesus. Luke introduces Jesus as heir to "the throne of his father David," the Son of God and Savior of the world (Luke 1:32, 35, 47; 2:11)— all of which challenged Augustus' political propaganda. Posthumously, the Roman senate declared Julius Caesar a god. So Augustus used the titles of "son of god," "prince of peace" and "savior of the world" as Julius' adopted son and the one who ended the Empire's civil wars. His birth became the new year. Luke contrasts Augustus with the humble birth of the actual Savior. The true King will not be of this world. The real Savior did not tax the whole world but rather offered the universal gifts of forgiveness and resurrection.

Tiberius Caesar Augustus 42 BC–AD 37	AD 14-37	Matt 22:17,21 Mark 12:17 Luke 3:1; 20:25, 23:2 John 19:12,15	Luke linked Tiberius with the only exact date in the New Testament, the beginning of John the Baptist's preaching: "in the fifteenth year of the reign of Tiberius Caesar" (Luke 3:1). Some claim this was a sabbatical year, which allowed many farmers to take the time off to hear this "voice of one crying in the wilderness" (Luke 3:4). Jesus referred to Tiberius when he said, "Render to Caesar."
Caligula Gaius Caesar Augustus Germanicus AD 12-41	AD 37-41		Caligula's rule marked the first time a Caesar set out to persecute the Jews. Josephus recorded, "Gaius did not demonstrate his madness in offering injuries only to the Jews at Jerusalem, or to those that dwelt in the neighbor-hood, but suffered it to extend itself through all the earth and sea, so far as was in subjection to the Romans, and filled it with ten thousand mischiefs." Gaius' "mischiefs" included torturing women and reproaching womanish behavior in men.
Claudius or Tiberius Claudius Caesar Augustus Germanicus 10 BC–AD 54	AD 41-54	Acts 11:28; 18:3	Acts 11:28 tells of a "great dearth … in the days of Claudius Caesar." He reigned during the last decade recorded in Acts. Initially, he acted conciliatory toward the Jews, though later expelled them from Rome for rioting (Acts 18:3).
Nero Claudius Caesar Augustus Germanicus AD 37–68	AD 54-68	Acts 25:12; 26:32; 27:24; 28:19	In 64 AD, Nero instigated an imperial persecution of Christians by burning Rome and blaming it on them. When Paul "appealed unto Caesar," he most likely appealed to Nero (Acts 25:12; 26:32; 27:24; 28:19). Probably, Paul's two-year house arrest fell

291

			under Nero's reign. In AD 66, Nero put his military commander Vespasian in charge of the war against the Jews. Origen, Tertullian, and Eusebius blamed Nero for Peter's and Paul's martyrdoms (c. AD 67-68).
Vespasian Imperator Caesar Vespasianus AD 9 –79	AD 69-79		After a year of civil war, four Caesars claimed authority. Ultimately, the military commander Vespasian who conquered Jerusalem took the throne. In AD 66, Vespasian began the siege of Jerusalem, but left his son Titus to conquer Judea in AD 70. Vespasian restored peace to Rome throughout his decade long reign.
Titus Imperator Caesar Vespasianus Augustus A.D 41-81	AD 79-81	Matt 24: 1-2	Titus, with four legions of soldiers from Alexandria, held the siege and conquered Jerusalem. He ordered the destruction of Herod's Temple in AD 70, as prophesied by Jesus in Matthew 24:1-2. Titus had a famous love affair in Judea with a Bernice, who was the daughter of Herod Agrippa I, and sister of Agrippa II (Acts 25:13, 23; 26:30). She supposedly joined Titus in Rome to continue their affair for a time.
Domitian Imperator Caesar Domitianus Augustus AD 51-96	AD 81-96	Rev 1:9	Domitian is described as a despot. He proclaimed himself, "lord and god." Tradition credits him with throwing the apostle John into a vat of boiling oil. Supposedly, when John came out unscathed, Domitian sent him to the prison isle of Patmos where John received his apocalyptic vision described in the book of Revelation (Revelation 1:9). [796]

---

[796] Information in this chart was taken from: Brown, *Birth*, 415; Raymond Brown, *Christ in the Gospels of the Liturgical Year* (Collegeville, MN: Liturgical Press, 2008), 115; Fitzmyer, *Luke I-IX*, 455; Josephus, *Antiquities,*

3. Population and Life Expectancy

During the latter half of the New Testament, historians estimate that twenty million people lived in the Roman Empire, ten percent of whom were Jews.[797] The average life expectancy throughout the Empire was 25 to 35 years.[798] Many people lived into their seventies and a few made it to 100, but with a high infant mortality rate, the average life expectancy age decreased.[799] Only half of the children survived the first ten years of life. One-third of the babies who survived birth died during their first year of life. This means that a woman would need to have an average of five pregnancies to keep the population stable. Although children were encouraged for the growth of society, they did not have an easy life. As the historian Christian Laes explained, in the overpopulated city of Rome, possibly one third of the children were affected by poverty and thus suffered from "filth, hunger, and violence."[800]

XIX. 1.1, 1.5, 2.5; *Wars,* III 9:8; Matthew Bunson, *Encyclopedia of the Roman Empire, rev. ed.,* (NYC: Infobase Publishing, 2002)*,* 521; Anderson, *Understanding Paul.* 362-363.

[797] Launaro, *Peasants and Slaves: The Rural Population of Roman Italy*, 47. The census of AD 47 counted just shy of six million male citizens (32). The rural population estimates follow. Table compares the different low count estimates (in the thousands) for Italy's rural free population of:

	AD 14	AD 47
Total Roman Empire	6,200	7,500
Provinces	1,900	2,800
Italy	4,300	4,700

[798] Campbell, *Marriage and Family in the Biblical World,* 143. People from higher classes lived longer than those from the lower classes.

[799] Launaro, *Peasants and Slaves: The Rural Population of Roman Italy*. At age seventy, men were exempt from public service (493). And as mentioned in footnote 648, Pliny knew of ninety people "at least 100 years" old (186).

[800] Christian Laes, *Children in the Roman Empire: Outsiders Within* (New York: Cambridge University Press, 2011). 43 (41-43).

4. Greco-Roman Family Life

In Roman households, the father ruled over his wife, children and slaves. With slaves and servants to help run the home, Greco-Roman women were free to attend the market, recitals, festivals, and games. In each family, the oldest living male was known as the *paterfamilias* and directed the entire extended family. He ruled with a strong hand and had the power of life and death over everyone in his household. Legally the *paterfamilias* controlled ownership of property, inheritance, marriage, and divorce of his children (regardless of their age), grandchildren, and great-grandchildren. William Barclay described some of what that entailed.

> A Roman father had by law absolute power over his family. If his son should marry, the father continued to have absolute power both over him and any grandchildren there might be. It began at the beginning. A Roman father could keep or discard his newborn child as he liked. He could bind or scourge his son; he could sell him into slavery; and he even had the right to execute him. True, when a father was about to take serious steps against a member of his family, he usually called a council of all its adult male members, but he did not need to. True, later on public opinion would not permit the execution of a son by a father, but it happened as late as the time of Augustus. . . . If ever a people knew what parental discipline was the Romans did.[801]

If an infant survived birth, the decision to keep or stop his or her life was often made by the *paterfamilias*. A letter from the time, written from a traveling husband to his pregnant wife, includes instructions regarding her delivery. If the baby were a female, the mother was to expose her outside the city wall (to

---

[801] William Barclay, *The Letter to the Hebrews, revised edition* (Philadelphia, PA: Westminster Press, 1976), 176-177.

die), but if it were a male she was to raise him.[802] Augustus attempted to stop this practice through his family-focused legislation.

Several Roman leaders likewise fostered values to grow the family. The Roman philosopher Cicero (106-43 BC) praised a good family life for its positive influence on society in his book, *Republic*:

> For the sake of life and the practice of living, a prescription has been made for recognized marriages, legitimate children, and the sacred homes of the household gods . . . so that everyone should enjoy common and individual blessings. For living well is impossible without a good community and there is nothing happier than a well set-up polity.[803]

Cicero also felt "the urge to reproduce is an instinct common to all animals, society originally consists of the pair, next of the pair with their children, then one house and all things in common. This is the beginning of the city and the seedbed of the state."[804] He appreciated procreation and a unified family life. Writing at the same time that Christian disciples wrote, the stoic Socrates, or Musonius Rufus (c. AD 20-101), agreed that the purpose of marriage was to have children. "The husband and wife . . . should come together for the purpose of making a life in common and of procreating children, and furthermore of regarding all things in common between them, and nothing peculiar or private to one or the other, not even their own bodies."[805] Rufus' aspirations demonstrate an aim of egalitarianism rarely achieved in the ancient world. Roman philosophers, like their Greek predecessors, saw "human behavior as a subset of animal behavior."[806] Being "animalistic"

---

[802] Ilan, *Jewish Women in Greco-Roman Palestine.* 4, 46-48, 52.
[803] Campbell, *Marriage and Family in the Biblical World,* 132-33 quoting, *Republic* 5.7.
[804] Ibid., 145, quoting the *Republic,* 1.38.
[805] Ibid., 147.
[806] Ibid., 144-145.

was used in a positive light here, as it promoted the desire to marry and have children as the natural order of creation.

Romans based their family life on the hope of procreation. However, infertility and infant mortality made that goal difficult for many couples. The following vignette was written about a devoted couple who were unable to have children, but chose to remain married. At his wife's death, the husband wrote a eulogy in remembrance of their loyal life together.

> When you despaired of your ability to bear children and grieved over my childlessness, you became anxious lest by retaining you in marriage I might lose all hope of having children and be distressed for that reason. So you proposed a divorce outright. I must admit that I flared up so that I almost lost control of myself; so horrified was I by what you had tried to do that I found it difficult to retrieve my composure. To think that separation should be considered between us before fate had so ordained, to think that you had been able to conceive in your mind the idea that you might cease to be my wife while I was still alive, although you had been utterly faithful to me when I was exiled and practically dead![807]

Roman literature and epitaphs are full of examples of women who stood by their husbands during hardship or exile.

The archetypal Roman family relationship was lasting and committed, although in practice most couples did not choose their partners, and families were broken up by divorce repeatedly.[808] Upper-class marriages were often formed for political or financial reasons and ended in divorce. Roman plays and literature describe unfaithful husbands, affairs, multiple divorces, and broken homes.

---

[807] Ibid., 158, quoting *Laudatio Turiae* 1.31-33, 40-43.

[808] Stagg, *Woman in the World of Jesus,* 85. For example, Cicero's first marriage—with the mother of his favorite child, Terentia—lasted thirty years. However, after they divorced, Cicero married an heiress younger than his daughter, and his wife married twice again. Winer, *Life in the Ancient World,* 175.

Dramas usually describe "love" as being only for the young and nonexistent between the aged couple. In one of Plautus' plays (c. 184), the male lead Demaenetus says he'd, "rather drink bilge water" than kiss his wife. When his son asks if Demaenetus loves his wife, he responds, "Love her? I? I love her now for not being near."[809] Although it seems that many playwrights' favorite topic is love, the literature rarely describes fidelity in marriage. Some plays were so explicit that Augustus banned certain works, for example, Ovid's *The Art of Love*. Premarital and extramarital sex saturate Roman dramas.

According to Plautus, the model Roman bride was, paradoxically, a virgin. He portrayed an ideal young woman as brimming with virtue: "Personally I do not feel that my dowry is that which people call a dowry, but purity and honor and self-control, fear of God, love of parents, and affection for my family, and being a dutiful wife to you sir, lavish of loving-kindness and helpful through honest service."[810]

In yet another play, the author goes to the other extreme and portrays the shame of a husband who was "henpecked" by his wife.[811] Roman literature shows the double standard that women faced: they were expected to be chaste while living in a society that glorified explicit sexuality for men.

Arranged Roman Marriages

As mentioned above, the father or *paterfamilias* usually arranged Roman marriages, though the historical literature does include examples where the couple's feelings were taken into consideration. From the late Republic (133-27 BC) forward, Roman law allowed a woman to initiate her second marriage, but she could not refuse a proposal unless it was proven that the groom was immoral.[812] Marriage brokers also assisted in arranging upper-class Roman marriages. Roman fathers did

---

[809] Stagg, *Woman in the World of Jesus,* 81. Ovid (ca. 43 BC- AD 17) wrote much of adult love.

[810] Ibid., 94, quoting Plautus from *Amphitryon* II.839-842.

[811] Ibid., p. 79.

[812] Witherington, *Women and the Genesis of Christianity,* 21.

away with the Greek practice (from 500 to 300 BC) of selling their daughters in *a coemptio* marriages. By the time Augustus became Emperor in 27 BC, the sale of one's daughter to the highest bidder had been replaced by the powerful dowry as the motivator in arranged marriages.

Generally, youth obeyed their father's marital arrangements. The historian Stagg quoted the story of a Roman young man who already had a young lover when his father chose his wife. The young man agreed to marry his father's choice out of obedience, yet kept his sweetheart as a mistress out of love.[813] Period literature is full of stories where young couples fall in love and try to change their parents' betrothal arrangements.[814] This example comes from a school textbook on rhetoric:

> "You are to marry the wife I want you to marry," says my father. What is that to the point? Are you not aware that marriages are at our own choice? Our affections are not at your beck and call; you cannot order us to love or hate whom you want. Marriage is only eternal if it is a union brought about by mutual consent. When a wife is sought for me, the companion of my bed, the partner of my life, she must be chosen for all eternity. In any case, what is the good of compelling me against my will? If you do that, I will simply divorce her.[815]

This school passage was obviously written from the perspective of a young man. Whether the father figure's voice arranged the marriage, gave consent to the marriage, or broke up the marriage, young Greco-Roman couples were not free to make their decisions without the blessing of the head of the household.[816]

To avoid battles over the spousal choice, Roman fathers often had their daughters engaged by age ten. It is doubtful that

---

[813] Stagg, *Woman in the World of Jesus,* 83.
[814] Ibid., 80.
[815] Campbell, *Marriage and Family in the Biblical World,* 153.
[816] Ibid., 145.

young first-time brides could decline a marriage offer under any circumstance.[817] The Roman law set the minimum age to marry at twelve but most waited until their teens to share bed and board.[818] The ideal year for a Roman marriage was the year when a young woman began puberty. This assumed her chastity and amplified her childbearing potential. Young Roman men often waited to marry until they received their toga of manhood at sixteen or seventeen.[819] If a young man served in the military, he often waited until his twenties to marry. To encourage a focused full-time army, sometime between A.D 14 and 41, low-ranking soldiers were forbidden to marry. In these cases, it was not uncommon in first-time Roman marriages for a groom to be nine or ten years older than his bride.[820]

Roman Engagement and Wedding Ceremony

When a couple became engaged, the prospective groom gave the young girl a ring of gold or iron with a pair of clasped hands carved on it. The ring was worn on the middle finger of the left hand. The marriage took place as soon as the girl matured (or between ages twelve and fifteen). A civil or religious authority married them in front of their family and friends. Often, the marriage took place during the last half of

---

[817] Witherington, *Women and the Genesis of Christianity,* 20-21.

[818] Campbell, *Marriage and Family in the Biblical World,* 144. The Greek women married a little later than the Romans—fifteen and sixteen years old. The Greek men of Athens were to choose only an Athenian citizen to marry. However, the Greek men also lived with courtesans or concubines, as well as foreign women, known as "companions." This way the Athenians could limit their heirs without limiting their sex life. Witherington, *Women and the Genesis of Christianity,* 13. It appears that there was concern over the *paterfamilias* insisting on a divorce in some cases, as in AD 200, when a law was enacted that forbade the *paterfamilias* to break up a happy marriage.

[819] This toga of manhood for citizens differs from the "*toga clavata*" for officers, and even more exclusive, the "*toga picta*" for the emperor. Hugh W. Nibley, *Teachings of the Book of Mormon: Semester 3. Transcripts of lectures presented to an Honors Book of Mormon Class at Brigham Young University 1989-1990.* Provo, UT: F.A.R.M.S., 1992.

[820] Campbell, *Marriage and Family in the Biblical World,* 144.

June, as a good luck omen for marriages.[821] The bride wore a white tunic and a saffron-colored bridal veil topped by a wreath of marjoram or orange blossoms. After they signed the marriage license, the administrator read and sealed their contract as the couple clasped right hands. If it were a religious ceremony, there would be a prayer. If it were a civil ceremony, the groom asked his bride if she wanted to become "mother of the family." She answered, "yes," and she asked the groom if he wished to become "father of the family." When he answered, "yes," they were legally married. After the wedding feast, the Roman groom carried his bride over the threshold as they thought it an unlucky sign if she stumbled over the doorway.[822] After the wife had stayed with her husband's family for a full year, the marriage became final.[823] Once married, husbands and wives did not generally show affection: "Never kiss your wife unless it thunders."

Children and Servants in Roman Households

The Roman households usually included children and several slaves. The father gathered his household twice a day before the family hearth for prayers to various deities. Women, servants, and children worked spinning on their looms, preparing meals, and at various other domestic chores. This work often began at sunrise and lasted far past sunset.[824] Children assisted in the serving of meals, but did not join in the conversation.

Fathers usually taught their sons and daughters to read and write. In wealthier homes, a child's education was augmented by a Greek nurse who also served as a tutor. At age six or seven, girls and boys went to school for six hours a day. They learned to calculate math with an abacus. Most girls stopped

---

[821] Dunstan, *Ancient Rome*, 108.

[822] Winer, *Life in the Ancient World,* 175-176.

[823] Matthew Bunson, *Encyclopedia of the Roman Empire,* 352. It was a common law marriage after one year, but if the woman spent three nights away from her husband's roof, she kept her own possessions.

[824] Ruden, *Paul Among the People,* 74.

their formal education and became engaged by age ten, focusing on the domestic arts, painting, and music. Between ages twelve and fifteen, a married girl moved out of her parents' home and into her husband's family home. Young men continued their schooling by adding Greek and Latin grammar. By age fourteen, the sons of citizens added philosophy and public speaking to their education. At age seventeen, the young man could serve in the army. Slave children were not usually educated and could be separated from their families if their master sold them again.[825]

5. Greco-Roman Religious Life

The Greco-Roman world encompassed a diversity of religions—some polytheistic and others monotheistic. The more one understands about the Greco-Roman religions, the easier one understands why Jews reacted so vehemently against their Gentile neighbors and why Jesus taught a better way for both worlds. This section will first look at the state mythic religion, then the native cults, highlighting Diana and the Vestal Virgins, and finish with foreign cults, both legal and illegal.

Early Romans based their state religion on the supreme triad of Jupiter, Mars, and Quirinus. The Romans did not have a personal relationship with their gods, but rather their gods co-operated on behalf of the state. Roman worship was public, not private. People performed public ritual, not out of belief, but to entice the gods to prosper the community. Later, emperor worship or the imperial cult became the state religion. The Senate attempted to deify a few emperors posthumously, starting with Julius Caesar. Augustus capitalized on this, and used the title, "son of god," on his official nomenclature and coins throughout the empire. Augustus built temples to Julius and Romans worshiped him there. Emperor-worship unified the empire as provinces showed their loyalty to the past emperor. Worshiping past or present emperors did not replace worshiping other gods, but expanded their polytheism.

---

[825] Winer, *Life in the Ancient World,* 172-177.

State Religions: Native cults

Two basic categories divide the Greco-Roman religions at the time of the New Testament: native cults and oriental or "imported" religions. The native or Roman cults combined Latin and Greek gods. To insure that they worshiped everyone they should, they added gods to their pantheon over time.[826] State religious festivals were performed throughout the year to keep the public involved, including several women's festivals.[827] Often wealthier people played more prominent religious roles. Women who could financially support a festival

---

[826] The major Roman religious characters included:

Jupiter: master or main god.

Juno: wife of Jupiter, a goddess of women and fertility—symbolized by a peacock and pomegranate.

Mars: god of war, second-strongest god.

Venus: goddess of beauty and love.

Minerva: goddess of wisdom, learning, art, crafts, and industry—symbolized by an owl.

Neptune: god of the sea—symbolized by a trident.

Ceres: goddess of the harvest—symbolized carrying a bundle of grain.

Vulcan: god of the blacksmith and underworld. If he stoked his furnace too hard, volcanoes erupted.

Bacchus: god of wine and partying—symbolized as a young man or faun with grapes.

Mercury: messenger of the gods, the god of travelers and tradesmen—symbolized with wings on his helmet and sandals.

Vesta: goddess of the home and hearth. Almost every household worshiped Vesta, and her temple kept a flame always burning.

[827] Thurston, *Women in the New Testament,* 24-25. March 1, *Matronalia:* matrons offered flowers to Juno on the anniversary of the dedication of her temple. April 1, *Veneralia: Venus Verticordia* and *Fortuna Virilis* celebrated rites preceding the consummation of marriage at the men's baths. May 1, *Bona Dea:* honored the goddess of women by sacrificing at her temple. June 11, *Matralia: Mater Matuta* celebrated fertility rituals at her temple in the cattle market. July 6, *Fortuna Muliebris:* honored the women who marched to persuade Coriolanus to lift the siege on Rome. July 7 *Nonae Caprotinae:* celebrated women's fertility by offering sap of a wild fig tree to Juno. Early December: the highest Roman magistrate offered sacrifices at his home to the goddess of women.

served as the "festival priestess." A husband's religious or political preeminence often led to a more prominent role for his wife.

Paul's experience in Ephesus with the Roman goddess Diana (or the Greek goddess, Artemis) became famous enough to make its way into the book of Acts. Diana was the goddess of the moon, animals, forest, hunting, and women in childbirth. The growth of Christianity threatened the Roman cult. An Ephesian silversmith egged on irate cult worshipers: "Not only this our craft is in danger to be set at nought; but also that the temple of the great goddess Diana should be despised, and her magnificence should be destroyed, whom all Asia and the world worshippeth" (Acts 19:27). A town clerk stopped the riot by assuring everyone that Diana was still the dominate religion: "Men of Ephesus, what man is there that knoweth not how that the city of the Ephesians is a worshiper of the great goddess Diana, and of the [image] which fell down from Jupiter?" (Acts 19:35). In some places, her worshipers performed fertility rites, as she also represented the mother goddess. Diana was just one of many gods in the state religion, but the only one that made it into the New Testament by name.

Women's Religions. Women also belonged to private religious organizations and exercised leadership functions without their spouse's influence. Cults formed around social classes, occupations, and even stages of a woman's life.[828] Young girls worshiped the goddess *Fortuna Virginitis.* Young married women worshiped *Fortuna Primigenia* as the patroness of mothers and childbirth (who also gave virility and material success to men). Women who married only once worshiped in the cult of *Fortunata Muliebris.* The cult of Venus *Changer of Hearts* encouraged women to practice marital fidelity. Prostitutes made up part of the *Fortuna Virilis* that worshiped the god of sexual relations in men's baths.[829] Some sects specialized in training young girls and boys to be "divine

---

[828] Thurston, *Women in the New Testament,* 26.
[829] Witherington, *Women and the Genesis of Christianity*, 23.

organs of inspiration and prophecy."[830] In the Greek cult of Apollo, only women were allowed to perform the office of the divine organ. The prophetess of Apollo (called a Pythoness) was a free-born Delphian widow who faithfully tended the temple fires and acted as an oracle. Women also led the processions in the secret rituals. Women played prominent roles in orgiastic rites such as the Greek Bacchanalia and Dionysian mysteries.

Vestal Virgins. The greatest religious honor given to a woman in Rome was to be chosen as a Vestal Virgin priestess. Six virgins served at a time. They tended Vesta's state shrine in Rome's Forum. They kept her sacred flame burning continuously.[831] The fire represented male procreative power to give and sustain life, and the six virgins protected that procreative power of men. In a ceremony similar to a Roman marriage, the *pontifex maximus* chose virgins between the ages of six and ten from affluent reputable families who were free of bodily defects and had both parents living. The Vestal priestesses remained virgins for thirty years (or suffered the penalty of death). After their thirty years of service, they were free to marry, though few did.

The Vestal Virgins were among the most liberated woman in the Empire because they were not legally bound to fathers or husbands. "Their powerful position is interesting and ambiguous. They were virgins, wore the *stola* of matrons, and had the legal rights of men."[832] They were the only women in Rome who could drive in a two-wheeled chariot. When they traveled on the street a bodyguard or *lector* preceded them. They also had reserved seats on the imperial podium. Like Roman men, they could make their own wills, dispose of their own property, and testify in court. They also participated in

---

[830] Ibid., 15.

[831] Dunstan, *Ancient Rome*, 37.

[832] Thurston, *Women in the New Testament*, 25-26. A *stola* was a fabric drape that was tied at the waist and fell to the feet, worn in public by married Roman women that identified her as married.

public sacrifices. These six women received all these honors in the hopes that the tradition maintained the fertility.

State Religions: Foreign Cults

As the Empire expanded, the Romans tolerated and adopted new gods and religions (provided that the new forms of worship did not hinder the state). In addition to expanding their pantheon, Roman officials recognized ten foreign or "imported" religions, one of which was Judaism. The State promised these members the legal right to practice without persecution. Converts to Judaism received the same protection. Initially, Christianity claimed Roman legal protection by piggy-backing on Judaism's political protection.

One of the most popular (and initially illegal) cults among Greco-Roman women was the Egyptian all-powerful female goddess, Isis. Women identified with Isis as a goddess of loving mercy. The Isis cult glorified women, placing them as equal or superior to their male consorts. Either gender could join, hold office, and worship. It welcomed all classes of people and excluded no one. The Roman political leaders opposed it—even though the Isis cult approved of authority and autonomy for women, and stressed women's traditional place in Roman society. The cult grew because it met the religious and emotional needs of many individuals, especially lower-class women.

Zechariah or Zacharias was the most popular name in the Bible, possibly owing to its wonderful meaning, "who Jehovah remembers." We find thirty kings, princes, priests, prophets, servants, sons, trumpet players, and gate keepers all named Zechariah.[833]Covering a thousand years of biblical history, forty-four verses in the Old Testament and eleven in the New Testament reference men named Zechariah (also spelled Zachariah and Zacharias).

With so many of them, it is not surprising that they get confused occasionally. Even the Gospel of Matthew mixes up two of them. Complicating matters further, some early Christian writers built on the Matthean mistake and added their own apocryphal spin. The overall impact created havoc with *"Who's Who"* among the biblical Zechariahs. This is particularly poignant in the LDS community where an apocryphal account is perpetuated as prophetic. This investigation attempts to unravel the web of confusion regarding three of the most famous Zechariahs in the Bible and LDS tradition.

Biblical Confusion

The problem begins in the Gospel of Matthew where the text switches two of the most famous Zechariahs in the Hebrew Bible. One lived in the ninth century BC, the other in the sixth.

---

[833] This article published in *Religious Educator as "The Confusing Case of Zacharias"* re 14, no. 2 (2013) 107-123. The author will share the list of biblical men named Zachariah, Zechariah, or Zacharias, if requested.

306

TABLE 4:

900 BC	800 BC	700 BC	600 BC	500 BC	400 BC	300 BC	200 BC	100 BC	0

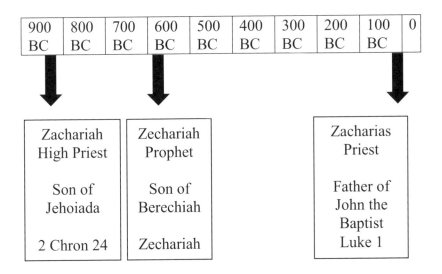

Zachariah High Priest	Zechariah Prophet		Zacharias Priest
Son of Jehoiada	Son of Berechiah		Father of John the Baptist
2 Chron 24	Zechariah		Luke 1

9th C. Zechariah son of Jehoiada.

From the ninth century, "Zechariah, son of Jehoiada," the high priest served in Solomon's Temple at Jerusalem until King Joash had him stoned to death in the courtyard of the temple (2 Chronicles 24:20-21). The irony of Zechariah's martyrdom is that a few decades earlier, Zechariah's parents saved the then infant King Joash from a political overthrow and raised him in the temple secretly for six years. Zechariah's father, the high priest Jehoiada, led an uprising and returned King Joash to the throne. But when the high priest Jehoiada died (at the ripe age of 130), King Joash forgot his allegiance to God and the family of Jehoiada, and turned to idolatry.[834] The Lord called Zechariah, son of Jehoiada, to preach repentance: "Thus God has said, 'Why do you transgress the commandments of the LORD and do not prosper? Because you have forsaken the LORD, He has also forsaken you.'" (2 Chronicles 24:20,

---

[834] During the time of Solomon's Temple, the office of high priest was hereditary, and a call for life. With this in mind, we assume that the high priest Jehoiada was followed by his son Zechariah, as the high priest.

307

NASB). King Joash did not appreciate Zechariah's call to repentance, nor did the King remember "the kindness which his father Jehoiada had shown him, but he murdered his son [Zechariah] . . . in the court of the house of the LORD" (2 Chronicles 24:22, 21, NASB).

This narrative of Joash slaying Zechariah in the temple was still popular over a thousand years later when the Jerusalem and Babylon Talmud were written. The Talmud elaborates on the murder of Zechariah in the court of the priests by appending retribution. It claims that eighty thousand priests and fourteen thousand young men were slain to atone for the blood of the high priest Zechariah.[835]

6th C. Zechariah Son of Berechiah

Our second Zechariah is from the sixth century, BC: "The word of the LORD unto Zechariah, the son of Berechiah . . . the prophet" (Zechariah 1:1). Initially, he lived in Babylon among the captives, and then left Babylon to assist Zerubbabel in the rebuilding the temple in Jerusalem. The biblical compilers named the *Book of Zechariah* after him. It includes eight visions and two prophetic sets. Zechariah prophesied of the promised Messiah in the famous foretelling: "Rejoice greatly, O daughter of Zion; shout, O daughter of Jerusalem: behold, thy King cometh unto thee: he is just, and having salvation; lowly, and riding upon an ass, and upon a colt the foal of an ass" (Zechariah 9:9). Zechariah, the son of Berechiah became the eleventh of the twelve Minor Prophets.

It appears that the Gospel of Matthew confuses these two Zechariahs by giving the ninth-century high priestly martyr the lineage of the sixth-century prophet. Ostensibly, it appears that the Matthean text got it wrong, because the parallel account found in Luke 11:51 did not mix up the Zechariahs. Both Gospels describe Jesus denouncing a group of Pharisees,

---

[835] Lightfoot, *Talmud, Hierosol, in Taannith,* fol. 69; and *Talmud, Babyl. in Sanhedr.,* fol. 96.

Scribes or Lawyers with a series of woes and followed by this prophecy (emphasis added for repetition):

Matthew 23:35	Luke 11:50-51
That upon you may come all the righteous *blood shed* upon the earth	*That* the *blood* of all the prophets, which was *shed* from the foundation of the world, may be required of this generation; *From the blood of Abel unto the blood of Zacharias,* which perished *between the altar and the temple*
from the blood of righteous *Abel unto the blood of Zacharias* son of Barachias, whom ye slew *between the temple and the altar*	

Among the textual differences within the two accounts, the Matthean text adds the parentage of Zacharias while Luke did not. Without this addition, the Lord's citation appears to refer to two Old Testament martyrs—Abel and Zechariah. I found two possible explanations for the Matthean genealogical additions:

1) Either an author or editor made the mistake by confusing two famous Old Testament Zechariahs and gave the paternity of the minor prophet, "Zechariah son of Barachias" (Zechariah 1:1) to the high priest "Zechariah son of Jehoiada" who was "stoned . . . in the court of the house of the LORD" (2 Chronicles 24:21).[836]

2) Or the Lord introduces an unknown martyr who happened to share names—both his *own name* and his *father's name*—and the same *position,* and *martyrdom* with the Old Testament prophet.

---

[836] KJV Matthew 27:9 also attributes a citation to Jeremiah but most Bibles cite Zechariah 23:35.

The former option—that someone made a mistake—is now generally accepted by biblical scholars.[837] The latter option—the Lord referred to yet another Zechariah—grew out of the theory of biblical inerrancy, that the Bible and its authors were infallible and could not write anything wrong.

Biblical Inerrancy

The theory of inerrancy fundamentally purports that the biblical writers could not make a mistake, as they functioned as tools of the Holy Spirit to produce Scripture. The theory of inerrancy developed in early Christianity. By the end of the second century, Tertullian (AD 200) hints at doctrinal infallibility.[838] This developed over two centuries later to the point that St. Augustine of Hippo (AD 354-430) clearly supported absolute inerrancy of the biblical authors and texts.[839] The Protestant reformation clung to this doctrine as they understood the inerrant text provided an encasing of divine authority. Carrying into the early nineteenth century, proponents of the reformed tradition (Puritans, Presbyterian, Congregationalists, etc.) continued to uphold the infallibility and inerrancy of the Bible to assure that the prophet-writers spoke for God in every word—whether translated or not.[840]

---

[837] Brown, *Birth*, 61.

[838] Tertullian, *Against Marcion,* IV: 2. "Never mind if there does occur some variation in the order of the [Gospel] narratives. What matters is that there is agreement in the essential doctrine of the Faith."

[839] St. Augustine's College, *Augustinian Studies* (Washington DC: Catholic University of America, 1937), 88. Augustine of Hippo wrote to St. Jerome: "On my own part I confess to your charity that it is only to those books of Scripture which are now called canonical that I have learned to pay such honor and reverence as to believe most firmly that none of their writers has fallen into any error. And if in these books I meet anything which seems contrary to truth, I shall not hesitate to conclude either that the text is faulty, or that the translator has not expressed the meaning of the passage, or that I myself do not understand."

[840] Charles Hodge, *Systematic Theology in Three Volumes* (New York: Charles Scribner's Sons, 1871), 1.152. "(1.) The Scriptures of the Old and New Testaments are the Word of God, written under the inspiration of the Holy Spirit, and are therefore infallible, and of divine authority in all things

This thinking led to conclusions that there could be no further prophecy or Scripture.[841] The Prophet Joseph Smith spoke against this theory in his eighth Article of Faith, "We believe the Bible to be the word of God, as far as it is translated correctly." He opened a possibility that some portions of the Bible were not correct.[842]

Protevangelium of James

If the confusion between Zechariahs were limited to Matthew 23:35, our problem would be minor and this explanation over. But the Matthean muddle became further entangled in the second century when more Christian literature

---

pertaining to faith and practice, and consequently free from all error whether of doctrine, fact, or precept. (2.) That they contain all the extant supernatural as of God designed to be a rule of faith and practice to his Church. (3.) That they are sufficiently perspicuous to be understood by the people, in the use of ordinary means and by the aid of the Holy Spirit, in all things necessary by faith or practice without the need of an infallible interpreter." Later, Hodge continues: "Apostles constantly refer to the Scriptures, showing beyond doubt that they believed and taught, that what sacred writers said the Holy Ghost said" (1.160; also 1.163; 1.129; 1.138-140; 1.154-155, 1.161, 1.180).

[841] Ibid., 1.140 "Modern prelates . . . claim no immediate commission; no independent knowledge derived from immediate revelation; no personal infallibility; no vision of Christ; and no gift of miracles. This is they claim the authority of the office, but not its reality. It is very plain, therefore that they are not apostles. They cannot have authority of the office without having the gifts on which that authority was founded, and from which it emanated. If a man cannot be a prophet without the gift of prophecy; or a miracle-worker without the gift of miracles; or have the gift of tongues without the ability to speak other languages than his own; no man can rightfully claim to be an apostle without possessing the gifts which made the original Apostles what they were."

842 Joseph Smith, *History of the Church,* 5:.271-27 2; ". . . and preached them quite a sermon; that error was in the Bible, or the translation of the Bible." Notes from the prophet's revision of the Bible also give evidence that he did not think it infallible: "I resumed the translation of the Scriptures. From sundry revelations which had been received, it was apparent that many important points touching the salvation of man, had been taken from the Bible, or lost before it was compiled" (1.245).

came forward to satisfy the early Christians hunger for more details about Jesus' early life, and justification for new doctrines. One of those, the *Protevangelium of James* or *"Book of James"* elaborated on the miraculous birth narratives of Mary, John the Baptist and Jesus (focusing on the perpetual virginity of Mary which developed into the immaculate conception of Mary, freeing her from original sin).[843] When it was first published in the sixteenth century, it received the name *"Protevangelium"* or *"pre-Gospel"* to imply that the events occurred prior to those recorded in the four Gospels of the New Testament.

It appears that the *Protevangelium of James* further elaborated on the misconstruction of Matthew 23:35, by claiming that the Zechariah slain near the temple altar was not the ninth-century high priest "Zechariah son of Jehoiada," nor the sixth-century prophet "Zechariah son of Barachiah," but a first-century Zacharias, the father of John the Baptist.[844] To give this confusion between Zechariahs some context, it is on the par with mistaking President Brigham Young with an Aaronic priesthood holder named Brigham who lived nearly nine hundred years later in Mexico City. The *Protevangelium of James* reads:

---

[843] Papyrus Bodmer V-VI, *Bibliotheca Bodmeriana; "Protevangil de Jacques"* (Geneve, reprint 1958). Other infancy accounts that are not canonized include *The Infancy Gospel of Thomas, The Gospel of Pseudo-Matthew* (based on the *Protevangelium of James* and on the *Infancy Gospel of Thomas*), and the so-called *Arabic Infancy Gospel,* all of which are regarded as apocryphal. The theory of Mary's perpetual virginity and her own immaculate conception were ideas added to Christian thought after the apostolic church.

[844] F. F. Bruce, *Jesus and Christian Origins Outside the New Testament* (Grand Rapids, MI: Eerdmans, 1974), 86-87. Bruce summarizes this portion of *Protevangelium of James*: "When Herod fails to find the infant, after the visit of the wise men from the east, he tries to lay hands on the child John (later the Baptist), but when he too is not to be found (having been hidden with his mother Elisabeth in a hollow mountain) Herod has his father Zechariah put to death in the temple court."

And when Herod knew that he had been mocked by the Magi, in a rage he sent murderers, saying to them: Slay the children from two years old and under. And Mary, having heard that the children were being killed, was afraid, and took the infant and swaddled Him, and put Him into an ox-stall. And Elisabeth, having heard that they were searching for John, took him and went up into the hill-country. . . And Herod searched for John . . . And Herod was enraged, and said: . . . [Zacharias'] son is destined to be king over Israel. And he sent . . . [to the temple] again, saying: Tell the truth; where is thy son? for thou knowest that thy life is in my hand. And Zacharias said: I am God's martyr, if thou sheddest my blood; for the Lord will receive my spirit, because thou sheddest innocent blood at the vestibule of the temple of the Lord. And Zacharias was murdered about daybreak . . . [his] clotted blood beside the altar . . . turned into stone. . . .The priests consulted as to whom they should put in his place; and the lot fell upon Simeon. For it was he who had been warned by the Holy Spirit that he should not see death until he should see the Christ in the flesh.[845]

The *Protevangelium* excerpt contradicts the biblical accounts in Luke's and Matthew's nativity narratives in at least five ways. First, Luke 1:5 introduces Zacharias as a priest "of the course of Abia,"[846] which was one of the twenty-four courses of Aaronic priests that David organized.[847] The course of Abia included

---

[845] Ron Cameron, ed., *The Other Gospels: Non Canonical Gospel Texts* (Louisville, KY: Westminster John Knox Press, 1982), 120-121.
[846] The same word "course" in Hebrew can also be translated, "company." Brigham Young used the same idea when he divided the early pioneers into "companies" as they paralleled the history of Israel in search for their promised land.
[847] David organized the Aaronic descendants into twenty-four courses or divisions (1 Chronicles 24:1-19), with Abijah (or Abia in Greek) as the eighth course. After the Babylonian exile, only four of the original courses returned to Palestine (Ezra 2:36-39; 10:18-22). Those four were re-divided into the traditional twenty-four and assigned the same names (Nehemiah 12:1-7).

hundreds of priests who rotated between the twenty-four Aaronic courses for their five weeks of temple service each year.[848] Jeremias estimated 18,000 priests and Levites lived in Palestine at the time of Jesus' birth.[849] Luke describes Zacharias as an Aaronic priest functioning at the temple, not the one reigning high priest.[850]

Second, Matthew records that the holy family lived in a "house" in Bethlehem by the time the magi visited "the young child" (Matthew 2:11). The biblical accounts suggest that young Jesus was somewhere between forty days and two years old when the magi visited. Matthew carefully uses the word, *"paidion,"* to describe the toddler or young child, rather than Luke's usage of *"brephos* / babe or infant" for the newborn "babe wrapped in swaddling clothes, lying in a manger" (Luke 2:12). Matthew and Luke focus on different times in Jesus' young life. Yet the *Protevangelium* disregards the passage of time before the slaughter of the innocents and describe Mary hiding the infant Jesus in "an ox stall" when Herod came to "destroy him" (Matthew 2:13).[851]

---

[848] As mentioned previously, during the Second Temple period, every six months descendants of Aaron came to the temple to fulfill their assignment for a week. Additionally, all priests were requested to return to help with the crowds at the temple during the three major pilgrimage feasts (Passover, Pentecost, and Feast of the Tabernacles or Booths).

[849] Jeremias, *Jerusalem*, 198-206. Josephus, *Against Apion,* II. 8, 108 speaks of four families of priests returning from Babylon each containing over 5,000 men, for a total of approximately 20,000 priests.

[850] F.F. Bruce, *New Testament History,* 3-4; Jeremias, *Jerusalem,* 159. By the time of the late Second Temple era, the office of high priest had deteriorated to a political appointment made for a short-term, arbitrary period. See appendix 1.

[851] Matthew uses the same word, *"apollumi* / destroy," in the passion narrative in Matthew 27:20, "but the chief priests and the elders persuaded the multitude that they should ask Barabbas and *destroy* Jesus." Even Matthew's backdrop is the same: a Jewish leader is trying to kill Jesus in both the nativity and the passion. Whether or not Matthew's double use of *"apollumi* / destroy" was intentional, Herod's attempt to murder Jesus gives the infancy narrative status as a Gospel in miniature including both a birth and death and foreshadowing that which is to come in the passion and atonement.

Third, the *Protevangelium of James* also negates Matthew's description that Joseph was forewarned and led his holy family to Egypt at night prior to the troops' arrival in Bethlehem—as in an Exodus motif (Matthew 2:13, 15). After the wise men's visit, an "angel of the Lord appeareth to Joseph in a dream" and warned him to take his family "and flee into Egypt" before Herod's guards arrived (Matthew 2:13-14).[852] The apocryphal version assumes that when Herod's troops came to Bethlehem, Mary and the infant Jesus were still in Bethlehem.

Fourth, in contrast to Matthew 2:16, the apocryphal work also claims that Herod's slaughter of the innocents extended far beyond the sparsely populated pastoral community of Bethlehem (archeologists estimate a population between 300 and 1,000 people, extending to the neighboring villages of Bethlehem) to include a broader swath across the hill country of Judea and Jerusalem.[853]

Fifth, the *Protevangelium of James* also conveniently ties the prophetic Simeon, from Luke 2:25 and 34, to Zacharias. The Lucan account suggests that, after Simeon saw "the Lord's Christ," the old man would be free to leave his mortal existence

---

[852] The Egyptian border at that time was approximately thirty-eight miles south of Bethlehem at the Rhinokolura wadi, just south of Masada. Apocryphal accounts tell fanciful tales of the family traveling hundreds of miles all the way up the Nile with miraculous happenings all the way. *Gospel of Pseudo-Matthew,* XVIII - XX, 2.

[853] The slaughter of all the male children in Bethlehem is not included in Josephus' list of atrocities ordered by King Herod (Josephus, *Antiquities,* XVII, 11:2). As a result, some assume that the massacre of the innocents is fictional. Others suggest that the slaughter in Bethlehem was a minor incident and probably unknown to Josephus amidst other many atrocities of Herod's reign filled with so much bloodshed. Moreover, Josephus is not always accurate historically, as we see in the execution of Herod's wife Mariamne. Josephus, *Antiquities* XV, 3:5-9 and *Jewish Wars,* I, 22:3, 4. Archeologists purport that Bethlehem was an insignificant village at the time, and could only have supported small number of young male children living either in or near the village. W.F. Albright and C.S. Mann, *The Anchor Bible: Matthew* (New York: Doubleday, 1971), 26.19. By examining the population of the surrounding area at the time, Raymond Brown argues that the slaughter affected a maximum of twenty boys (*Birth*, 204-205).

(Luke 2:26). Luke never includes an exchange of the two random aged temple goers and priest, but the *Protevangelium* claims that Simeon succeeded Zacharias as the high priest. Unfortunately, this conflicts with the documented reign of high priest in Jerusalem: 5 to 4 BC Matthias Simeon succeeded Zacharias Theophilus, 4 to 3 BC Eleasar ben Boethus, 3 BC Joshua ben Sie, AD 6 Joazar ben Boethus, and AD 6-15 Ananus ben Seth.[854] Regardless of the lack of historicity in the *Protevangelium of James*, it spread—in part to perpetuate Mary-worship.

Other Christian Explanations of Zacharias

Other early church leaders like the Patriarch Peter I of Alexandria (300-311) and Nestorian Bishop Solomon of Bassoria, as a spokesman for the Syrian Christians (1222), perpetuated the tale that the martyred Zacharias cited in Matthew 23:35 was actually the father of John the Baptist. At the same time, other Christians came up with different answers as they wondered what happened to John the Baptist's father, Zacharias. Origen (184–253), Gregory of Nyssa (335–395), and Cyril of Alexandria (376–444) passed on another story with a temple setting that emphasized Mary's virginity. They blamed the Jews for Zacharias's death, because, supposedly, Zacharias allowed Mary to stand in a part of the temple reserved exclusively for virgins.[855] The Jews felt that Mary's presence violated the sanctity of the temple because, from their opinion, Mary's maternity obviously disproved her virginity. The Jews blamed Zacharias for allowing it and stoned him.

Muslim Legends of Zacharias

Even Muslim legends include stories of what happened to Zacharias / Zakariya, the father of John the Baptist. They taught

---

[854] Jeremias, *Jerusalem,* 377.
[855] Origen, *Tract,* xxvi in Matthew.

that Zacharias escaped from his pursuers by hiding in a tree.[856] A tree miraculously opened to admit and enclose him. Unfortunately, the hem of his priestly cloak protruded from the base of the trunk. When the evil forces recognized it, they sawed the tree and Zacharias into pieces. Noble to the end, Zacharias did not utter even a faint cry as he died a martyr's death. Clearly, the question of what happened to John the Baptist's father, Zacharias, interested many.

19th Century American Interest

These different apocryphal tales enjoyed a resurgence of interest in antebellum America. During the Second Great Awakening a general interest in religious topics soared. Newspapers,[857] periodicals, and books perpetuated the tale from the *Protevangelium of James. The American Biblical Repository* explained that their purpose in publishing the apocryphal account was to "establish the fact of the constant tradition during the first centuries of the Christian era that purported "the father of the Baptist had been murdered." To appreciate the volume of attention this apocryphal account received, I randomly looked at one of many editions of the *Protevangelium of James* and found it published in 1820, 1821, 1824, 1825, 1832, 1835, 1847, and 1849. Thousands of copies filled the nation.[858]

Several periodicals alluded to information in the *Protevangelium of James* in the summer of 1842.[859] Including

---

[856] E.J. Brill, *First Encyclopedia of Islam: 1913-1936* (Leiden Netherlands: Brill, 1927, reprint 1933), 1202.

[857] American Periodicals: "The annunciation of the Birth and Character of John the Baptist, to Zacharias," *The Christian's Magazine: Designed to Promote Knowledge and Influence of Evangelical Truth,* Aug 1, 1811; 4, 8. Available through: "newspapers.library.cornell.edu."

858 William Hone, *The apocryphal New Testament, being all the Gospels, Epistles* (Ludgate Hill, London: 1820-1846), 36. Just for fun I checked on World Cat and found 120 copies of the1820 edition still available in libraries across the United States.

[859] Edward Robinson, *The Biblical Repositor* (and quarterly observer), Andover, Boston (1842), 129. John Holmes Agnew, *The American Biblical*

the *Biblical Repositor (and Quarterly Observer)* from Andover and Boston, and *The American Biblical Repository* in New York City and Boston. A few weeks later, on Thursday, September 1, 1842, the *Times and Seasons* (the Mormon newspaper published in Nauvoo, Illinois), ran an unsigned article entitled "Persecution of the Prophets," which included the following version of the apocryphal tale:

> When Herod's edict went forth to destroy the young children, John was about six months older than Jesus, and came under this hellish edict, and Zechariah caused his mother to take him to the mountains where he was raised on locust and wild honey. When his father refused to discover [his] hiding place, and being the officiating high priest at the temple that year, was slain by Herod's order between the porch and the alter as Jesus said [in Matthew 23:35]."

The article appears to be a recap of the apocryphal lore floating around antebellum America.

The question of authorship for this *Times and Seasons* article is important. Not only is no author listed for the article, but also it is not signed by an editor (as was the following article on baptism). Often, the man who served as editor of a newspaper did not actually write the editorials. The newspaper staff helped with the composition and printing of the newspapers in Nauvoo. With the same periodical including other articles signed by the editor or authors, it is doubtful that the prophet sanctioned the article, especially because he was not in Nauvoo at the time.

Significantly, nearly a month previous to this *Times and Season* publication, on August 8, 1842, Joseph Smith was arrested for complicity in the Governor Boggs assassination attempt and went into hiding.[860] He stayed with Edward Hunter in Nauvoo briefly and then with Carlos Granger, before retreating to an island in the Mississippi. The prophet seemed to

---

Repository. Second series. Xv-.whole no. XLVII (Boston, NYC, London: Platt and Peters, July, 1842), 139.
[860] Dean Jessee, compiled and ed., *The Personal Writings of Joseph Smith* (Salt Lake City, UT: Deseret Book, 1984), 625.

stay on top of many church issues even while in hiding.[861] But does that include endorsing every article in the daily local newspaper? Even with the obscure chance that Joseph consented to the article's printing, does that guarantee its historical accuracy?

The pertinent problem for LDS lies in the fact that, although this article has no evidence that the editor wrote, directed, or approved of its publication, it still found its way into Joseph Fielding Smith's compilation of the *Teachings of the Prophet Joseph Smith* in 1938, on page 261. Why did the compilers assume that Joseph authored the unsigned article? By attaching Joseph Smith's name to the story of Zacharias' martyrdom, some LDS have elevated this detail of the apocryphal saga to restored scriptural status.

Joseph Smith did not comment on the publication of the newspaper. He may have been occupied elsewhere, as the very day the article was published, the prophet wrote a letter that became canonized as Doctrine & Covenants 127. Just six months previous to publishing the article on Zechariah, the same periodical published the *Book of Abraham*—and a few months after, ran portions of the *Book of Moses*, both of which also became canonized Scripture. In this context, the article on Zacharias has the potential to mean more than other newspaper articles. As a result, in some LDS circles, the identity of the lowly priest from the hill country of Judea has taken on the glorified position as a martyred high priest. Stemming from this unnamed *Times and Season* article, a cascade of several LDS books including Sunday School and Institute manuals have mentioned the tale as if it were a restored truth.[862] Latter-day

---

[861] Susan Eastman Black conversation with the author. Joseph made a few appearances in Nauvoo according to lists of daily events.

[862] McConkie, *The Mortal Messiah: From Bethlehem to Calvary* (Salt Lake City, UT: Deseret Book, 1979-81), 1:304. Robert Millet and Kent Jackson, eds., *Studies in Scripture: The Doctrine and Covenants* (Sandy, UT: Randall Book, 1984), 315-316. Daniel H. Ludlow, *A Companion to Your Study of the Doctrine and Covenants* (Salt Lake City, UT: Deseret Book, 1978), 2:32. Spencer J. Condie, *Your Agency, Handle with Care* (Salt Lake City, UT: Bookcraft, 1996), 136. Larry E. Dahl and Donald Q. Cannon, *Encyclopedia of Joseph Smith's Teachings* (Salt Lake City, UT: Bookcraft, 1997).

Saint teachers perpetuate the story, not as an interesting remnant of early Christian Apocrypha, but with prophetic precision. Even though the apocryphal tale contradicts canonized Scripture in at least five areas, because of its association with the *Teachings of the Prophet Joseph Smith*, many LDS receive it as truth.

In conclusion, *The Book of James* or *Protevangelium* (22-24) combines different men named Zechariah to claim that John the Baptist's father was also a high priest and slain in the courtyard of the temple due to Herod's edict. Christian and Muslim literature responded to this confusion in a domino effect that has perpetuated different legends. I chose to write on this subject in hopes of illuminating the sources of this account in order to arrest the spread of its message as revealed revelation among Latter-day Saint authors.

Appendix 4
New Testament Women:
Named, Unnamed, and Fictional

References to Named Women[863]

1. Anna—Prophetess (Luke 2:36-38)
2. Apphia—Sister (Phil 5:2)
3. Berenice—Member of Herod's family (Acts 25:13-26:32)
4. Candace—Ethiopian queen (Acts 8:27)
5. Chloe—Head of house-church, Paul's confidant (1Cor 1:11)
6. Claudia—Female Christian (2 Tim 4:21)
7. Damaris—Christian convert from Athens (Acts 17:34)
8. Dorcas/Tabitha—Disciple from Joppa (Acts 9:36-42)
9. Drusilla—Member of Herod's family (Acts 24:24)
10. Elisabeth—Mother of John the Baptist, witness of the Messiah (Luke 1:5-80)
11. Eunice—Taught faith, Timothy's grandmother (2 Tim 1:5)
12. Euodia—Christian from Philippi (Phil 4:2-3)
13. Eve—First woman created, Adam's wife (1 Cor 11:3; 1 Tim 2:3)
14. Hagar—Servant of Sarah, second wife of Abraham (Gal 4:24-25)
15. Herodias—Granddaughter of King Herod the Great (Mark 6:17; Matt 14:1-11; Luke 3:19-20)
16. Jezebel—False prophetess (Rev 2:20-23)
17. Joanna—Healed Christian in Palestine (Luke 8:2-3; 24:10)
18. Julia—Christian from Rome (Rom 16:15)
19. Junia—Prominent among the apostles (Rom 16:7)
20. Lois—Taught faith, Timothy's mother, (Acts 16:1-3; 2 Tim 1:5)
21. Lydia—Convert from Philippi, sold purple (Acts 16:14-30, 40)

---

[863] Adapted from research published by Meyers, Craven, Kraemer, ed., *Women in Scripture*, 43-503. I organized, numbered, and systematized their work differently. I do not duplicate each scriptural citation—for example when two Gospels mentioned the widow donating her mites, I list the widow once with both scriptural references. Also I list every reference to a female in the New Testament—whether they lived during the Old Testament or are included in a fictitious story. I also added references from Strong's, *Exhaustive Concordance of the Bible*, 1539-1541.

22. Martha—Sister of Mary & Lazarus (Luke 10:38; John 11:1-6; 17-44; 12:2)
23. Mary—Mother of Jesus (Matt 1-2; 12:46-50; 13:53-58; Mark 3:31-35; 6:3-4; Luke 1-2; 3:23; 4:16-30; 8:19-21; 11:28-29; John 2:1-12; 6:42;19:25-27; Acts 1:14; Rom 1:3; Gal 4:4)
24. Mary— Disciple from Bethany, sister of Martha and Lazarus (Luke 10:38; John 11:1-6; 17-20, 28-33; 12:1-8)
25. Mary—Disciple from Magdala (Matt 27:56, 61; 28:1; Mark 15: 40-41, 47; 16:1, 9; Luke 8:2; 24:10; John 19:25-26; 20:1, 11-18)
26. Mary—Mother of James and Joses at the cross (Matthew 27:56; Mark 15:40, 47; 16:1; Luke 24:10)
27. Mary—Wife of Cleophas, woman at the cross (John 19:25)
28. Mary—Mother of John Mark (Acts 12:12)
29. Mary—Christian from Rome (Romans 16:6)
30. Nympha—Christian from Laodicea (Colossians 4:15)
31. Persis—Christian from Rome (Romans 16:12)
31. Phebe—Paul's "sister" or church member (Romans 16:1-2)
32. Priscilla/Prisca—Missionary and wife of Aquila (Acts 18:2-3, 18-19, 24-26; Romans 16:3-5)
    1 Corinthians 16:19; 2 Timothy 4:19)
33. Rachel—Mother of Joseph and Benjamin, wife of Jacob / Israel (Matthew 2:18)
34. Rahab the mother of Boaz (Matt 1:5; Hebrews 11:31; James 2:25)
35. Rebekah—Mother of Esau & Jacob, wife of Isaac (Rom 9:10-12)
36. Rhoda—Servant of Mary (John Mark's mother) in Jerusalem (Acts 12:13-15)
37. Ruth—Mother of Obed, grandmother of David (Matt 1:5)
38. Salome—Disciple at cross and tomb (Mark 15:40; 16:1)
39. Sapphira—Wife of Ananias, retained donation (Acts 5:1-11)
40. Sarah—Wife of Abraham (Rom 4:19, 9:9; Heb 11:11; 1 Peter 3:6)
41. Susanna—Healed Galilean disciple (Luke 8:3)
42. Syntyche—Co-worker with Paul (Philippians 4:2-3)
43. Tamar—Mother of Perez, daughter-in-law to Judah (Matt 1:3)
44. Tryphaena—"Worker in the Lord" (Romans 16:12)
45. Tryphosa—"Worker in the Lord" (Romans 16:12)

References to Unnamed Factual Women

1. Wife of Uriah (Matthew 1:6; named in 2 Samuel 11-12)
2. Mother-in-law of Simon Peter (Matt 8:14; Mark 1:30; Luke 4:38)

3. Woman with a twelve-year hemorrhage (Matthew 9:20-22; Mark 5:25-34; Luke 8:43-48)
4. Queen of the south (Matthew 12:42; Luke 11:31)
5. Mother of Jesus (Matthew 12:46-50; John 2:3-12; 19:25-27)
6. Sisters of Jesus (Matthew 13:56; Mark 3:32; 6:3)
7. Daughter of Herodias who danced for the head of John the Baptist (Matthew 14:6-11; Mark 6:17-28; Josephus offers her name, Salome)
8. Women fed by Jesus along with 5,000 men (Matthew 14:21)
9. Canaanite woman (Matthew 15:21-28)
10. Daughter of Canaanite woman (Matthew 15:21-28)
11. Women fed by Jesus with 4,000 men (Matthew 15:38)
12. Mother of James and John, the sons of Zebedee (Matthew 20:20; 27:56)
13. Woman of Bethany who anoints Jesus (Matthew 26:6-13; Mark 14:3-9)
14. Servant-girl of the high priest who accused Peter of being with Jesus (Matthew 26:69; Mark 14:66-69; Luke 22:56-57)
15. Another servant-girl who accused Peter of being with Jesus (Matthew 26:71)
16. Wife of Pilate (Matthew 27:19)
17. Unnamed women from Galilee at the cross (Matthew 27:55; Mark 15:40-41; Luke 23:49)
18. Daughter of Jairus (Matthew 9:18-19, 23-26; Mark 5: 22-23, 33-43; Luke 8:41-42, 49-56)
19. Wife of Jairus (Mark 5:40-43; Luke 8:51-56)
20. Syrophenician mother (Mark 7:24-30)
21. Daughter of the Syrophenician woman (Mark 7:25-30)
22. Widow with 2 mites at temple (Mark 12:41-44; Luke 21:1-4)
23. Widow of Zarephath / Sarepta fed Elijah (Luke 4:25-26)
24. Woman of the city, labeled a sinner, washed and anointed Jesus' feet (Luke 7:36-50)
25. Women healed by Jesus (Luke 8:2)
26. Women who provided for Jesus' mission (Luke 8:3)
27. Woman who praised the womb and breasts of Jesus' mother (Luke 11:27-28)
28. Woman bent over for eighteen years (Luke 13:11-16)
29. Wife of Lot (Luke 17:32)
30. Unnamed women lamenting Jesus (Luke 23:27-29)
31. Unnamed women at the tomb of Jesus (Matthew 28:5; Luke 23:55; 24:10)

32. Women who spoke with apostles (Luke 24:10, 22-24)
33. Samaritan woman at Jacob's well (John 4:7-42)
34. Woman framed for adultery (John 8:3-11)
35. Mother of a blind son (John 9:2-3,18-23)
36. Woman who guards the gate of the high priest's home (John 18:15-17)
37. Sister of Jesus' mother (John 19:25)
38. Unnamed women who stayed with the disciples after Jesus' ascension (Acts 1:14)
39. Prophesying daughters and female slaves (Acts 2:17-18)
40. Women as new believers (Acts 5:14)
41. Widows of Hellenists and Hebrews (Acts 6:1)
42. Women committed to prisoned by Saul (Acts 8:3)
43. Samaritan women baptized by Philip (Acts 8:12)
44. The Candace, or Queen of Ethiopia (Acts 8:27)
45. Women persecuted by Saul (Acts 9:2; 22:4)
46. Women of Antioch who turned against Paul and Barnabas (Acts 13:50)
47. Women at the place of prayer at Philippi (Acts 16:13)
48. Slave girl healed from spirit of divination (Acts 16:16-18)
49. Leading women converts of Thessalonica (Acts 17:4)
50. Greek women converts of high standing in Beroea (Acts 17:12)
51. Wives of the disciples at Tyre (Acts 21:5)
52. Four unmarried daughters of Philip (Acts 21:9)
53. Sister of Paul (Acts 23:16)
54. Mother of Rufus (Romans 16:13)
55. Sisters greeted by Paul (Romans16:14)
56. Sister of Nereus (Romans 16:15)
57. Woman living with her husband's son (1 Corinthians 5:1)
58. Prostitute (1 Corinthians 6:15-16)
59. Married Women (1 Corinthians 7:2-5, 11)
60. Widows (1 Corinthians 7:8-9)
61. Christian women / men married to unbelievers (1 Corin 7:12-16)
62. Unmarried women devoted to God (1 Corinthians 7:34, 38)
63. Married women devoted to family (1 Corinthians 7:35-36)
64. Sister/wife who accompanies apostles (1 Corinthians 9:5)
65. Women praying and prophesying (1 Corinthians 11:2-11)
66. Sisters to whom the risen Jesus appeared (1 Corinth 15:6)
67. Believers as daughters and sons of God (2 Corinth 6:18)
68. Chaste virgin (2 Corinthians 11:2)
69. No distinctions between male and female in Christ (Gal 3:28)

70. Born of a woman, Son of God (Galatians 4:4)
71. Free woman [Sarah], mother to Abraham's son Isaac (Gal 4:22)
72. Slave woman [Hagar], mother of Ishmael (Galatians 4:22)
73. Wives and husbands exhorted (Ephesians 5:22-33)
74. Bond women and men who serve (Ephesians 6:5-7)
75. "True yokefellow" or Paul's loyal companion (Philip 4:3)[864]
76. Wives (and husbands) exhorted (Colossians 3:18-19)
77. Nurse caring for her children (1 Thessalonians 2:7)
78. Women who profess reverence for God (1 Timothy 2:9-15)
79. Women helpers or deaconess (1 Timothy 3:11)
80. Older and younger women serve in the church (1 Timothy 5:2)
81. Widows (1 Timothy 5:3-14)
82. Younger women marry and bear children (1 Timothy 5:15)
83. Woman with dependent widows (1 Timothy 5:16)
84. "Silly" or gullible women (2 Timothy 3:6)
85. Older and younger women exhorted (Titus 2:3-5)
86. Daughter of Pharaoh (Hebrews 11:24-26)
87. Women will receive their dead at the resurrection (Heb 11:35-36)
88. Sister in need (James 2:15)
89. Women teachers (James 3:1)
90. Wives (and husbands) exhorted (1 Peter 3:1-7)
91. Holy women of the past (1 Peter 3:5)
92. Women moved by the Holy Spirit (2 Peter 1:21)
93. Elect lady (2 John v.1, 5)
94. Elect sister (2 John v. 13)

References to Fictional Women

1. Woman who hid leaven with flour (Matt 13:33; Luke 13:20-21)
2. Wife sold into slavery to pay off husband's debt (Matthew 18:25)
3. Woman married to seven brothers in succession (Matthew 22:23-30; Mark 12:18-25; Luke 20:27-36)
4. Ten bridesmaids: five foolish and five wise (Matt 25:1-13)
5. Woman who lost one of ten silver coins (Luke 15:8-9)
6. Prostitutes in a parable (Luke 15:30)
7. Widow pleading with a judge (Luke 18:2-5)
8. Goddess Diana (Acts 19:24-35)
9. Wife as church (Ephesians 5:25-27)

---

[864] The gender of Paul's yokefellow is unknown, see chapter 2, "*Yokefellow.*"

10. Sister church, "She who is in Babylon" (1 Peter 5:13)
11. Woman in labor, clothed with the sun (Rev 12:1-6, 13-17)
12. Not defiled with women (Revelation 14:4)
13. Great whore (Revelation 17:3-18:23)
14. Bride of the Lamb (Revelation 19:7-8; 21:2, 9-11; 22:17)

References to Female Gender

1. Woman looked at lustfully (Matthew 5:28)
2. Divorced wife (Matthew 5:31-32; Mark 10:11-12; Luke 16:18)
3. Daughters and daughters-in-law against mothers and mothers-in-law (Matthew 10:35; Luke 12:53)
4. Mothers, daughters, fathers and sons should not be loved More than Jesus (Matthew 10:37; Luke 14:26)
5. Those born of women (Matthew 11:11; Luke 7:28)
6. Female followers of Christ become His mother or sister (Matthew 12:50; Mark 3:34-35)
7. Divorced wife (Matthew 19:3, 7-9; Mark 10:2-12)
8. Wives become one flesh with husbands (Matt 19:5; Mark 10:7-9)
9. Honor your mother (Matthew 19:19; Mark 10:19; Luke 18:20)
10. Mothers-sisters abandoned for the Jesus' name sake (Matthew 19:29; Mark 10:29-30)
11. Daughter of Zion (Matthew 21:5)
12. Prostitutes (Matthew 21:31-32)
13. Two women grinding meal, one taken one left (Matthew 24:41; Luke 17:35)
14. Pregnant-nursing women at time of desolation (Matthew 24:19; Mark 13:17; Luke 21:23)
15. Honor mothers, do not curse them (Mark 7:10-13)
16. Among women (Luke 1:48)
17. Wife left for the kingdom of God (Luke 18:29-30)
18. Woman in labor (John 16:21)
19. Women having unnatural intercourse (Romans 1:26-27)
20. Married woman (Romans 7:2-3)
21. Question about touching a woman (1 Corinthians 7:1)
22. Woman gives birth to humans (1 Corinthians 11:12)
23. Woman with long hair (1 Corinthians 11:15)
24. Women to be silent in meetings (1 Corinthians 14:34-35)
25. Obey and honor your mother (Ephesians 6:1-2)
26. Pregnant woman in labor (1 Thessalonians 5:3)
27. Widows and orphans who need visiting (James 1:27)

Bibliography

Achtemeier, Paul J. *Harper Collins' Bible Dictionary.* San Francisco, CA: Harper Collins, 1996.

Agnew, John Holmes. *The American Biblical Repository*, *XV- XLVII.* Boston, New York, and London: Platt and Peters (July, 1842): 139.

Albright, W.S., Mann C.S. *The Anchor Bible: Matthew.* New York: Doubleday, 1971.

Allard, Robert E. "Freedom on your head (1 Corinthians 11:2-16): A Paradigm for the Structure of Paul's Ethics." *Word & World* 30/4 (Fall 2010): 399-407.

Arndt, William F. et al., *Greek-English Lexicon of the New Testament, 2nd ed.* Chicago, IL: University of Chicago Press, 1979.

Anderson, Bernhard W. *Understanding the Old Testament, 2nd Ed.* New Jersey: Prentice-Hall, 1957.

Anderson, Richard L. *Understanding Paul.* SLC, UT: Deseret Book, 1983.

Baggett, John. *Seeing Through the Eyes of Jesus: His Revolutionary View of Reality.* Grand Rapids, MI: Eerdmans, 2008.

Ballard, M. Russell. *Ensign* (May 2012).

Barclay, William. *The Letter to the Hebrews, revised edition.* Philadelphia, PA: Westminster Press, 1976.

Baskin, Judith R. and Kenneth Seeskin. *Cambridge Guide to Jewish History, Religion, and Culture.* NYC: Cambridge University Press, 2010.

Benson, Ezra Taft. "What I Hope You Will Teach Your Children about the Temple," *Ensign* (Aug 1985).

Bercot, David, ed. *A Dictionary of Early Christian Belief.* Peabody, MA: Hendrickson, 1998.

Bergant, Dianne and Robert J. Karris, ed., *The Collegeville Bible Commentary.* Collegeville, MN: Liturgical Press, 1989.

Bock, Darrell L. *Acts: Baker Exegetical Commentary on the New Testament.* Grand Rapids, MI: Baker Academic Publishing, 2007.

Borgen, Peder. *Philo of Alexandria: An Exegete for His Time.* Netherlands: Brill, 1997.

Brill, E.J. *First Encyclopedia of Islam: 1913-1936.* Leiden, Netherlands: Brill, 1927, reprint 1933, 1202.

Bromiley, Geoffrey W. ed. *The International Standard Bible Encyclopedia.* Grand Rapids, MI: Eerdmans, 1988.

Brown, Raymond E. *The Birth of the Messiah: a Commentary on the Infancy Narratives.* Garden City, NY: Image Books, 1977 and 1993.

___. *An Introduction to the New Testament.* NYC: Doubleday, 1997.

___. *Anchor Bible: John I-XII.* NYC: Doubleday, 1966.

__. *Anchor Bible: John XIII-XXI,* New York: Doubleday, 1970.

__. *The Gospel and Epistle of John: A Concise Commentary.* Collegeville, MN: The Order of St. Benedict, 1988.

__, Joseph Fitzmyer, Roland Murphy, eds. *The New Jerome Biblical*

Englewood Cliffs, NJ: Prentice Hall, 1990.

Brown, S. Kent and Richard Neitzel Holzapfel, *Between the Testaments: From Malachi to Matthew.* SLC, UT: Deseret Book, 2010.

Brownrigg, Ronald. *Who's Who in the New Testament.* NYC, NY: Routledge, 2002.

Bruce, F. F. *New Testament History.* NYC: Doubleday, 1980.

___. *1 and 2 Corinthians.* London, England: Butler & Tanner, 1971.

Buttrick, George Arthur. *The Interpreters Dictionary of the Bible,* 4 vols. New York: Abingdon Press, 1962.

Cameron, Ron ed. *The Other Gospels: Non canonical gospel texts.* Westminster: John Knox Press, 1982.

Campbell, Ken ed. *Marriage and Family in the Biblical World.* Downers Grove, IL: InterVarsity Press, 2003.

Carledge, Tony. *Vows in the Hebrew Bible and the Ancient Near East.* Sheffield, England: JSOT Press, 1992.

Charles, Robert H. ed. *The Apocrypha and Pseudepigrapha of the Old Testament.* Oxford, England: Clarendon Press, 1913.

Christian, Ed. "Prophets under God's Authority: Head coverings in 1 Corinthians 11:1-16," in *Journal of the Adventist Theological Society* 10/1-2 (1999): 291-95.

Chrysostom, *Homily XXVI*, "On the Veiling of Women," in *Nicene and Post-Nicene Fathers of the Christian Church*, ed. Philip Schaff. *Saint Chrysostom: Homilies on the Epistles of Paul to the Corinthians, 12.* Oxford: Parker, 1891.

Clanton, Dan W. *The Good, the Bold, and the Beautiful.* New York, NY: T & T Clark International, 2006.

Clark, J. Reuben, Jr. *Why the King James Version.* SLC, UT: Deseret, 1956.

Clement of Alexandria, "Miscellanies," *Stromata.* 3.6.74-76.

Cohen, Shaye. *From the Maccabees to the Mishnah.* Philadelphia, PA: Westminster Press, 1987.

Condie, Spencer. *Your Agency, Handle with Care.* SLC, UT: Bkcrft, 1996.

Connely, Douglas. *Forgiveness: Making Peace with the Past.* Madison, WI: InterVarsity, 2005.

Conzelmann, Hans. *A Commentary on the First Epistle to the Corinthians.* Philadelphia, PA: Fortress, 1988.

Coogan, Micheal D. *The Oxford History of the Biblical World.* New York: Oxford University Press, 1998.

Corbier, Mireille. "Divorce and Adoption as Roman Familial Strategies." In *Marriage, Divorce, and Children in Ancient Rome*, eds. Beryl Rawson. England: Oxford Unversity Press, 1991.

Crim, Keith ed. *The Interpreters Dictionary of the Bible.* Nashville, TN: Abingdon, 1976.

Crown, David, Pummer, Tal, eds., *A Companion to Samaritan Studies.* Tuebingen, Germany: Mohr Siebeck, 1993.

Dahl, Larry and Donald Q.Cannon. *Encyclopedia of Joseph Smith's Teachings.* SLC, UT: Bookcraft, 1997.

328

Danby, Herbert, trans., *The Mishnah.* Oxford: Oxford University, 1933.

Davies, W. D. *Paul and Rabbinic Judaism.* Philadelphia, PA: Fortress, 1980.

DeMarco, Loris. *Sweeter Than Honey.* Winston-Salem, NC: Salem Publishing Solutions, 2009.

Dunn, James, ed. *Eerdmans Commentary on the Bible.* Grand Rapids, MI: Eerdmans, 2003.

Dunn, James D. G. *Romans 1-8.* Dallas, TX: Word Books, 1988.

Dunstan, William *Ancient Rome.* Lanham, MD: Rowman and Ltlfld, 2011.

Edersheim, Alfred. *The Life and Times of Jesus the Messiah, 3rd ed.* 1838; Reprint. Mclean,VA: MacDonald. Nd.

___. *The Temple: Its Ministry and Services as they were at the time of Christ.* Reprint. Grand Rapids, MI: Wm. B. Eerdmans, 1987.

Ehat, Andrew F. and Lyndon W. Cook, eds., *The Words of Joseph Smith: The Contemporary Accounts of the Nauvoo Discourses of the Prophet Joseph.* SLC, UT: Bookcraft, 1980.

Eusebius, Pamphili. *Fathers of the Church: Ecclesiastical History—Books 1-5.* Reprint. NYC: Fathers of the Church, 1953.

Elliott, John H. *Anchor Bible: 1 Peter.* NYC, NY: Random House-Doubleday,* 1964.

Epstein, Louis M. *The Jewish Marriage Contract: A Study in the Status of the Woman in Jewish Law.* Clark, NJ: Lawbook Exchange, 2004.

Evans, Craig. *Jesus and H.is World: The Archaeological Evidence.* Louisville, KY: John Knox Press, 2012.

Farmer, William, ed. *The International Bible Commentary.* Collegeville, MN: Liturgical, 1998.

Fass, Paula S. *The Routledge History of Childhood in the Western World.* NYC, NY: Routledge, 2013.

Faust, James E. "The Prophetic Voice," *Ensign* (May, 1996).

Feldman, Louis H., Meyer Reinhold. *Jewish Life and Thought among Greeks and Romans.* Fortress Press, 1996.

Feinberg, Anat and Berenbaum, eds., *Encyclopedia Judaica, 2nd ed.* 22 vols. Detroit, NYC: Thomson Gale, 2007. "*Mishnah,*" 14. 319-330.

Finger, Reta H. *Of Widows and Meals: Communal Meals in the Book of Acts. Grand Rapids, MI: Eerdmans, 2007.*

Finney, Mark. "Honour, Head-coverings and Headship: 1 Corinthians 11.2-16 in its Social Context," in *Journal for the Study of the New Testament* 33/1 (2010).

Fitzmyer, Joseph. *Anchor Bible: The Gospel according to Luke I-IX.* NYC: Doubleday, 1981.

___. *Anchor Yale Bible: First Corinthians.* New Haven, CT: Yale, 2008.

Freedman, David Noel, *Anchor Bible Dictionary.* NYC: Doubleday, 1992.

___. *Eerdmans' Dictionary of the Bible.* Grand Rapids, MI: Eerdmans, 2000.

Fuhrmann, Christopher J. *Policing the Roman Empire: Soldiers, Administration, and Public Order.* Oxford, England: Oxford Univ, 2012.

Galinsky, Karl. *Autustan Culture: An Interpretive Introduction.* Princeton, NJ: Princeton University Press, 1996.

Garrard, Alec. *The Splendor of the Temple.* Grand Rapids, MI: Kregel, 2001.

Gaskill, Alonzo. *The Savior and the Serpent: Unlocking the Doctrine of the Fall.* SLC, UT: Deseret Book, 2002.

Gaustad, Edwin and Leigh Schmidt. *The Religious History of America.* San Francisco, CA: HarperCollins, 2004.

Glover, Alfred Kingsley. *Jewish Laws and Customs.* Well, MN: WA Hammond, 1900.

Griggs, Wilford ed., *Apocryphal Writings and the Latter-day Saints.* SLC, UT: Bookcraft, 1986.

Hafen, Bruce C. *Covenant Hearts: Why Marriage Matters and How to Make it Last.* SLC, UT: Deseret Book, 2005.

__, Marie Hafen, "Crossing Thresholds and Becoming Equal Partners," *Ensign* (Aug 2007).

Hahn, Scott. *Catholic Bible Dictionary.* NYC: Random House, 2009.

Hall, Bruce W. *Samaritan religion from John Hyrcanus to Baba Rabba: a critical examination of the relevant material in contemporary Christian literature, the writings of Josephus, and the Mishnah.* Sydney, Australia: University of Sydney, 1987.

Harding, Mark. *Early Christian Life and Thought in Social Context.* NYC, NY: T&T Clark International, 2003.

Hinckley, Gordon B. *Teachings of Gordon B. Hinckley.* SLC, UT: Deseret Book, 1997.

Hodge, Charles. *Systematic Theology in three volumes.* New York: City, NY: Chrls Scribner's Sons, 1871.

Holzapfel, Richard, Eric Huntsman, Thomas Wayment. *Jesus Christ and the World of the New Testament.* SLC, UT: Deseret, 2006.

__, and Kent Jackson eds., *To Save the Lost: An Easter Celebration.* Provo, UT: Religious Studies Center, 2009.

Hone, William. *The Apocryphal New Testament, being all the Gospels, Epistles.* Ludgate Hill, London: 1820-1846.

Hudson, Valerie and Richard Miller, "Equal Partnership in Marriage," *Ensign* (April, 2013).

Ilan, Tal. *Jewish Women in Greco-Roman Palestine.* Peabody, MA: Hendrickson, 1996.

Jackson, Kent and Robert Millet. *Studies in Scriptures vol 5.* SLC, UT: Deseret, 1986.

Jeremias, Joachim. *Jerusalem in the Time of Jesus.* Philadelphia, PA: Fortress Press, 1969.

Jessee, Dean C. compiled and ed., *The Personal Writings of Joseph Smith.* SLC, UT: Deseret Book, 1984.

Josephus*, Josephus Complete Works: Antiquities of the Jews, Against Apion, Wars, Life.* Reprint, Grand Rapids, MI: Kregel, 1978.

Kee, Howard Clark and Lynn H. Cohick. *Evolution of the Synagogue.* Harrisburg, PA: Trinity Press, 1999.

Keener, Craig. *1–2 Corinthians.* New York: Cambridge University, 2005.

Kittel, Gerhard ed. *Theological Dictionary of the New Testament.* Grand

Rapids, MI: Eerdmans Publishing, 1965.

Labovitz, Gail. Susan *Marriage and Metaphor.* Lexington, MD: Rowman and Littlefield, 2009.

Laes, Christian. *Children in the Roman Empire: Outsiders Within.* NYC, NY: Cambridge University Press, 2011.

Launaro, Alessandro. *Peasants and Slaves: The Rural Population of Roman Italy—200BC to AD 100.* NYC, NY: Cambridge University Press, 2011.

Lefkowitz, Mary R. and Maureen B. Fant. *Women's Life in Greece and Rome: A Source book in Translation,* 2nd ed. Baltimore, MD: John Hopkins University Press, 1992.

Lipman, Eugene J. *The Mishnah: Oral teachings of Judaism.* Scranton, PA: Norton, 1970.

Longman III, Tremper, Garland. *The Expositor's Bible Commentary, rev. ed 10, Luke ~Acts.* Grand Rapids, MI: Zondervan, 2009.

Ludlow, Daniel ed. *A Companion to Your Study of the Doctrine and Covenants.* SLC, UT: Deseret Book, 1978.

__. *Encyclopedia of Mormonism*, New York: Macmillan, 1992.

__, ed. *Latter-day Prophets Speak: Selections from the Sermons and Writings of Church Presidents,* John Taylor, "The Mormon." SLC, UT: Bookcraft, 1988, 1993.

Lyons, Deborah and Westbrook. *Women and Property in Ancient Near Eastern and Mediterranean Societies.* Boston, MA: Center for Hellenistic Studies, Trustees for Harvard, 2005.

Malan, S.C. *The Book of Adam and Eve.* San Diego, CA: Book Tree, 2005.

Marsman, Hennie J. *Women in Ugarit and Israel: Their Social and Religious Position in the Context of the Ancient Near East.* Boston, MA: Brill Academic Publishers, 2003.

Maxwell, Neal A. *Even As I Am.* SLC, UT: Deseret Book, 1982.

McConkie, Bruce R. *The Mortal Messiah.* SLC, UT: Deseret, 1981.

__. *Sermons and Writings of Bruce R. McConkie.* SLC,UT: Bookcraft, 1989.

McKensize, John. *The Dictionary of the Bible.* NYC: Touchstone, 1995.

Meyers, Carol. "Temple, Jerusalem," in David Noel Freedman, ed., *Anchor Bible Dictionary.* New York: Doubleday, 1992.

__, Toni Craven, Ross Shepard Kraemer, ed. *Women in Scripture: A Dictionary of Named and Unnamed Women in the Hebrew Bible, the Apocryphal/Deuterocanonical Books, and the New Testament.* Grand Rapids, MI: Eerdmans, 2001.

Millet, Robert. *Studies in Scripture: Acts to Rev.* SLC, UT: Deseret, 1987.

Milton, John. *Paradise Lost.* London: Collins, 1874.

Nelson, Russell M. "The Sacred Responsibilities of Parenthood," *Ensign* (Mar 2006).

Neufeld, Dietmar and Richard E. DeMaris, ed. *Understanding the Social World of the New Testament.* NYC: Routledge, 2010.

Neusner, Jacob, ed, *Dictionary of Judaism in the Biblical Period.* Peabody, MA: Hendrickson, 1999.

__. trans., *Sifre to Numbers: An American translation and Explanation.*

331

Atlanta, GA: Scholars Press, 1986.

__. *The Economics of the Mishnah*. Chicago, IL: Un. of Chicago, 1990.

__. *The Mishnah: A New Translation*. New Haven, CT: Yale, 1988.

Nibley, Hugh, *Approaching Zion*. Provo, UT: FARMS, 1989.

__. "The Early Christian Prayer Circle," *BYU Studies* 19 (1978).

__. *Mormonism and Early Christianity*. Provo, UT: FARMS, 1987.

__. *Old Testament and Related Studies*. Provo, UT: FARMS, 1986.

___. *Teachings of the Book of Mormon: Semester 3. Transcripts of lectures at Brigham Young University*. Provo, UT: FARMS, 1992.

__. *Temple and Cosmos: Beyond This Ignorant Present*. Provo, UT: FARMS, 1992.

Nulman, Macy. *Encyclopedia of Jewish Prayer*. Lanham, MD: Rowman and Littlefield, 1996.

Oaks, Dallin H. "The Great Plan of Happiness," *Ensign* (Nov 1993).

Orr, William and James Walther, *Anchor Yale Bible Commentaries: 1 Corinthians*. NYC: Random House-Doubleday, 1976.

Parales, Heidi Bright. *Hidden Voices: Biblical Women and Our Christian Heritage*. Macon, GA: Smyth and Helwys, 1998.

Parkin, Tim G. *Old Age in the Roman World: A Cultural and Social History*. Baltimore, MD: John Hopkins, 2003.

Parry, Donald W. ed., *Temples of the Ancient World: Ritual and Symbolism*, SLC, UT: Deseret Book and FARMS, 1994.

Perry, L. Tom. "Fatherhood an Eternal Calling," *Ensign* (May, 2004).

Peterson, David. *The Acts of the Apostles*. Grand Rapids, MI: Eerdmans, 2009.

Philo. C.D. Yonge, trans, *The Works of Philo: Complete and Unabridged*. Peabody, MA: Hendrickson Publishers, Reprint 2004.

__. *Special Laws III.,* 7 vols. (London: William Heinemann, Ltd., 1967), 3.169, 171.

Rawson, Beryl ed. *Marriage, Divorce, and Children in Ancient Rome*. New York: Oxford University Press, 1996.

___. *The Family in Ancient Rome: New Perspectives*. Ithica, NY: Cornell University Press, 1987.

Richards, Sue Poorman, Larry Richards, Angie Peters, *Every Woman in the Bible*. Nashville, TN: Thomas Nelson Publishers, 1999.

Robinson, Edward. *The Biblical Repositor and Quarterly Observer*. Andover, Boston,1842.

Rodriguez, Junius P. *The Historical Encyclopedia of World Slavery, vol 7*. Santa Barbara, CA: ABD-CLI, 1997.

Ruden, Sarah. *Paul Among the People: The Apostle Reinterpreted and Reimagined in His Own Time*. New York: Pantheon Books, 2010.

Satlow, Michael L. *Jewish Marriage in Antiquity*. Princeton, NJ: Princeton University, 2001.

Scherman, Nosson. *The Mishnah: A New Translation with a Commentary, Yad Avraham anthologized from Talmudic sources and classic commentators*. Brooklyn, NY: Mesorah, 1981.

Schmitt, John. "Gender Correctness and Biblical Metaphors: The Case of God's Revelation." *Biblical Theological Bulletin* 26, 1996.

Skinner, Andrew and Gaye Strathearn, ed., *Third Nephi: An Incomparable Scripture.* Jane Allis-Pike, "'How Oft Would I Have Gathered You': The Power of the Hen Metaphor in 3 Nephi 10:4-7." SLC, UT: Neal A. Maxwell Institute and Deseret Book, 2012.

Sebesta, Judith Lynn and Larissa Bonfante. *The World of Roman Costume.* Madison, WI: University Press, 2001.

Sedley, David. *Oxford Studies in Ancient Philosophy, XXV.* Oxford, England: Oxford University Press, winter *2003.*

Segal, Alan F. *Paul the Convert: The Apostolate and Apostasy of Saul the Pharisee.* New Haven, CT: Yale University, 1990.

Skolnik, Fred, and Michael Berenbaum, eds. *Encyclopedia Judaica, 2nd ed.* 22 vols. Detroit, NYC: Thomson Gale, 2007.

Smith, Joseph Jr. trans., *The Book of Mormon: Another Testament of Jesus Christ.* 1830. Reprint, SLC, UT: Corp. of the President, 1986.

___. *Doctrine and Covenants of the Church of Jesus Christ of Latter-day Saints.* 1835 Reprint SLC, UT: Corporation of the President, 1981.

___. *History of the Church of Jesus Christ of Latter-day Saints.* 1844. Reprint, SLC, UT: Deseret Book, Reprint 1980.

___. *Pearl of Great Price.* 1842. Reprint, SLC, UT: Corporation of the President, 1986.

Smith, Joseph Fielding. *Doctrines of Salvation.* SLC, UT: Bookcraft, 1956.

Snaith, John. *The Cambridge Commentary on the New English Bible: Ecclesiasticus or the Wisdom of Jesus Son of Sirach.* Cambridge, New York: Cambridge University Press, 1974.

Speiser, E.A. *The Anchor Bible Genesis.* New York: Doubleday, 1964.

Sperber, Daniel. *Roman Palestine 200-400, the Land: Crisis and Change in Agrarian Society.* Tel Aviv, Israel: Bar-Ilan University, 1978.

Spielvogel, Jackson J. *Western Civilization 7th ed.* Belmont, CA: Thomson & Wadsworth, 2009.

Stagg, Evelyn and Frank. *Woman in the World of Jesus.* Philadelphia: Westminster Press, 1978.

Steinberg, Avraham. *Encyclopedia of Jewish Medical Ethics.* Jerusalem, Israel: Feldheim, 2003.

Strong James, *Strong's Exhaustive Concordance of the Bible,* 1890. Reprint, New York: Abingdon Press, 1983.

Suggs, M. Jack, Sakenfeld, Mueller. *The Oxford Study Bible.* New York: Oxford University Press, 1992.

Swidler, Leonard *Jesus was a Feminist: What the Gospels Reveal about His Revolutionary Perspective.* Landham, MD: Rowman-Littlefield, 2007.

Thurston, Bonnie. *Women in the New Testament.* NYC: Crossroad Publishing, 1998.

Tertullian, *Against Marcion, IV.* Whitefish, MT: Kessinger, 2010.

VanderKam, James. *Book of Jubilees.* Sheffield England, Sheffeield Academic Press, 2001.

VanderHorst, Pieter Willem trans. *Philo's Flaccus: The First Pogrom.* Boston, MA: Brill, 2003.

Vermes, Geza, trans. *The Complete Dead Sea Scrolls in English.* New York: Penguin Press, 1997.

Wayment, Thomas A. ed. *The Complete Joseph Smith Translation of the New Testament.* SLC UT: Deseret Book, 2005.

Welch, John W. and John F. Hall, *Charting the New Testament.* Provo, UT: FARMS, 2002.

___. "The Good Samaritan: A Type and Shadow of the Plan of Salvation," *BYU Studies* 38, no. 2 (1999): 50-115.

Wenham, Gordon J. *Word Biblical Commentary.* TX: Word Bk, 1987.

Wilson, Walter T. *The Sentences of Pseudo-Phocylides.* Gottin Genesis and Berlin: Hubert & Co., 2005.

Witherington III, Ben. *Women and the Genesis of Christianity.* Cambridge: Cambridge University Press, 1984. (Ann Witherington edited a 1990 edition)

__. *Grace in Galacia.* London and NY: T&T Clark International, 2004.

__. *History, Literature, and Society in the Book of Acts.* NYC: Cambridge University Press, 1996.

Wylen, Stephen M. *The Jews in the Time of Jesus: An Introduction.* New York: Paulist Press, 1996.

Van Orden, Bruce and Brent Top. *The Lord of the Gospels: The 1990 Sperry Symposium on the New Testament.* Provo, UT: BYU, 1990.

Young, Brigham. *Journal of Discourses,* 26vols. Liverpool: F. D. Richards and Sons, 1851-1886.

Zias, Joseph. "The Cemeteries of Qumran and Celibacy: confusion Laid to Rest" *Dead Sea Discoveries: A Journal of Current Research on the Scrolls and Related Literature,* 7 (2000), 220-253.

Topical Index

336

338

Missionaries, 48, 62-5, 74, 178, 245, 322

Mosaic Law, 26, 53, 138, 146, 185, 197, 273, 284

Moses' Tabernacle, 262, 275, 283

Mother, 3, 30, 37-8, 49, 51, 59, 60, 67-8, 72, 78, 109, 115, 125, 137, 140-1, 155, 157, 184-5, 187, 198, 203, 206, 214, 217-8, 225, 250, 266, 267-8, 270, 272, 285-6, 294, 296, 300, 303, 312, 318, 322-6,

Mount Gerizim, 32, 35

Mount Moriah, 14, 35, 263

Mount Zion, 153, 261

Mourn, 45,155, 158, 207-8, 210, 229

Mourner, 45, 208

Mutuality, 111, 116, 127, 159, 161, 164, 177

Mysteries, 36, 95-6, 184, 304

Native Cults, 301-2

Nazareth, 23, 29, 133, 138, 143, 145, 258, 272

Nero, 254, 291

New Jerusalem, 153

Nibley, 96-7, 110, 115-6, 151, 186, 276, 299

Non-Believing Spouse, 182

Oral Laws, 8-9, 12, 93, 103, 193, 198, 200-1, 236, 265, 273-5

Ordinances, 88, 92-7, 103, 107, 111, 112-3, 116-7, 123, 133, 152, 163, 169, 188-9, 257, 284

Parable, 30, 50, 140-1, 149-52, 227, 228, 232-3, 325

Parenting Children, 223

Passover / Feast Of Unleavened Bread, 7-8, 149, 205, 209, 224, 262-3, 275, 279, 283, 314

Paterfamilias, 294, 297, 299

Pentecost, 7-8, 11, 224, 262, 275, 279, 283, 314

Pharisees, 9, 13, 93, 176, 182, 193-4, 194, 200, 204, 219, 221, 265, 273-4, 275, 308

Phebe, 49, 68-70, 121, 322

Philippi, 48, 61-3, 72-4, 321, 324

Philo, 1, 3-5, 9-10, 18, 22, 37, 42-4, 55, 90, 103-4, 155-6, 191, 193, 198, 212, 235, 238, 249-50

Pilgrimage Feasts, 7, 224, 279, 314

Population, 7, 16, 45, 64, 134, 145, 247, 262, 270, 275, 293, 315

Pray[er], 12, 16-7, 23-24, 42, 62, 77, 85, 88, 89, 92-3, 95, 101-2, 104, 107, 113,115, 117, 122, 123, 135, 137, 140, 170, 175, 204, 206, 214, 226, 241, 262, 280, 281, 300, 324

Pregnancy, 29, 137

Prejudices, 17, 24, 36, 56, 143, 219, 251

Priest, 9-11, 18, 27-8, 32, 35, 38, 52, 132, 152-3, 203, 205, 218, 228, 261, 264, 267, 273, 276, 278, 279-3, 285, 307-9, 312-4, 316, 318-20, 323-24

Priesthood, 6, 9, 10, 46, 82, 84-5, 111, 122, 131-3, 170, 187-8, 205, 261, 264, 273, 278, 281-3, 312

Priscilla, 59, 64-5, 121, 127, 157, 322

Prison, 22, 60, 63, 73, 185, 221, 228, 258, 292

Private, 21, 24, 103-4, 155, 174, 243, 249, 270, 289, 295, 301, 303

Procreation, 85, 111, 155, 174, 213, 295, 304 (also see sex)

Promised Messiah, 54, 210, 221, 258, 265-6, 271-2, 275, 308

Prophesy, 52, 72-3, 88, 104, 107, 115, 117-9, 122-3

Prophetess, 49, 51, 54, 72-3, 82, 266, 273, 285, 304, 321

Protevangelium of James, 311-5

Public, 2, 17, 21-2, 25-6, 37-9, 48, 66, 74, 81, 90, 103-4, 118, 120, 122, 123, 129, 139, 192, 205, 226, 249, 265, 270, 287-9, 293, 294, 301-5

Purifying, 12, 145, 262, 279 (also see washings)

339

Biblical Index

343

344

345

347

348